THE RICH GET RICHER AND THE POOR GET PRISON

For 40 years, this classic text has taken the issue of economic inequality seriously and asked: Why are our prisons filled with the poor? Why aren't the tools of the criminal justice system being used to protect Americans from predatory business practices and to punish well-off people who cause widespread harm?

This new edition continues to engage readers in important exercises of critical thinking: Why has the U.S. relied so heavily on tough crime policies despite evidence of their limited effectiveness, and how much of the decline in crime rates can be attributed to them? Why does the U.S. have such a high crime rate compared to other developed nations, and what could we do about it? Are the morally blameworthy harms of the rich and poor equally translated into criminal laws that protect the public from harms on the streets and harms from the suites? How much class bias is present in the criminal justice system – both when the rich and poor engage in the same act, and when the rich use their leadership of corporations to perpetrate mass victimization?

The Rich Get Richer and the Poor Get Prison shows readers that much of what goes on in the criminal justice system violates citizens' sense of basic fairness. It presents extensive evidence from mainstream data that the criminal justice system does not function in the way it says it does nor in the way that readers believe it should. The authors develop a theoretical perspective from which readers might understand these failures and evaluate them morally—and they do it in a short text written in plain language.

Readers who are not convinced about the larger theoretical perspective will still have engaged in extensive critical thinking to identify their own taken-for-granted assumptions about crime and criminal justice, as well as uncover the effects of power on social practices. This engagement helps readers develop their own worldview.

New to this edition:

- Presents recent data comparing the harms due to criminal activity with the harms of dangerous—but not criminal—corporate actions
- Updates statistics on crime, victimization, incarceration, wealth, and discrimination
- Increased material for thinking critically about criminal justice and criminology
- Increased discussion of the criminality of middle- and upper-class youth
- Increased coverage of role of criminal justice fines and fees in generating revenue for government, and how algorithms reproduce class bias while seeming objective
- Streamlined and condensed prose for greater clarity.

Jeffrey Reiman is the William Fraser McDowell Professor Emeritus of Philosophy at American University in Washington, DC. Dr. Reiman is the author of *In Defense of Political Philosophy* (1972), *Justice and Modern Moral Philosophy* (1990), *Critical Moral Liberalism: Theory and Practice* (1997), *The Death Penalty: For and Against* (with Louis P. Pojman, 1998), *Abortion and the Ways We Value Human Life* (1999), *As Free and as Just as Possible* (2012), and more than 60 articles in philosophy and criminal justice journals and anthologies.

Paul Leighton is a Professor in the Department of Sociology, Anthropology and Criminology at Eastern Michigan University. Dr. Leighton is the co-author of *Punishment for Sale* (with Donna Selman, 2010) and *Class, Race, Gender and Crime* (with Gregg Barak and Allison Cotton, 5th edition, 2018). He has been president of the board of his local domestic violence shelter and is currently head of the advisory board of his university's food pantry.

Twelfth Edition

THE RICH GET RICHER AND THE POOR GET PRISON

THINKING CRITICALLY ABOUT CLASS AND CRIMINAL JUSTICE

Jeffrey Reiman

and Paul Leighton

Routledge
Taylor & Francis Group

NEW YORK AND LONDON

Twelfth edition published 2020
by Routledge
52 Vanderbilt Avenue, New York, NY 10017

and by Routledge
2 Park Square, Milton Park, Abingdon, Oxon, OX14 4RN

Routledge is an imprint of the Taylor & Francis Group, an informa business

First edition published by Wiley 1979
Eleventh edition published by Routledge 2017

Library of Congress Cataloging-in-Publication Data
A catalog record has been requested for this book

ISBN: 978-0-367-23178-1 (hbk)
ISBN: 978-0-367-23179-8 (pbk)
ISBN: 978-0-429-27867-9 (ebk)

Typeset in Palatino
by codeMantra

Printed in the United Kingdom
by Henry Ling Limited

For Sue
and
For Sala and Aiko

BRIEF CONTENTS

Figure and Tables   xiii
Preface to the Twelfth Edition   xv
Acknowledgments for the First Edition   xxi

Introduction: Criminal Justice Through the Looking Glass, or Winning by Losing   1

Chapter 1   Crime Control in America: Nothing Succeeds Like Failure   11

Chapter 2   A Crime by Any Other Name ...   63

Chapter 3   ... And the Poor Get Prison   111

Chapter 4   To the Vanquished Belong the Spoils: Who Is Winning the Losing War Against Crime?   165

Conclusion: Criminal *Justice* or *Criminal* Justice   195

Appendix I   The Marxian Critique of Criminal Justice   215

Appendix II   Between Philosophy and Criminology   235

Index   249

CONTENTS

Figure and Tables   *xiii*

Preface to the Twelfth Edition   *xv*

Acknowledgments for the First Edition   *xxi*

Introduction: **Criminal Justice Through the Looking Glass, or Winning by Losing   1**

Abbreviations Used in the Notes   9

Notes   9

Chapter 1   **Crime Control in America: Nothing Succeeds Like Failure   11**

The Failure of Tough on Crime   12

Understanding the Decline in Rates of Street Crime   20

Three Excuses That Will Not Wash   26

First Excuse: We're Too Soft!   27

Second Excuse: A Cost of Modern Life   28

Third Excuse: Blame It on the Kids!   30

Known Sources of Crime, or How We Could Reduce Crime If We Wanted To   32

Poverty and Inequality   32

Prison   35

Guns   37

Drug Prohibition   38

What Works to Reduce Crime   42

Failing to Reduce Crime: Erikson, Durkheim, and Foucault   44

Erikson, Durkheim, and the Benefits of Deviance   44

A Word about Foucault   46

*Summary   48   •   Study Questions   49
•   Additional Resources   49   •   Notes   50*

Chapter 2   **A Crime by Any Other Name...   63**

What's in a Name?   64

The Carnival Mirror: Criminal Justice as Creative Art   65

The Typical Criminal and the Social
Construction of Crime 66

The Carnival Mirror and Why It Matters 68

A Crime by Any Other Name... 72

  1. Defenders' First Objection 75

  2. Defenders' Second Objection 78

  3. Defenders' Third Objection 79

  4. Defenders' Fourth Objection 80

  Work May Be Dangerous to Your Health 83

  Health Care May Be Dangerous to Your Health 88

  Waging Chemical Warfare Against America 90

  Poverty Kills 95

  Summary 98 • Study Questions 99
• Additional Resources 99 • Notes 100

Chapter 3 **...And the Poor Get Prison 111**

The Face in the Carnival Mirror 111

Weeding Out the Wealthy 116

  A Critical Review of Criminality and Class 117

  Policing and Arrest 120

  Prosecution and Charging 123

  Adjudication and Conviction 125

  Sentencing 128

Financial Frauds 134

  The Savings and Loan Scandal 134

  Enron and a Year of Corporate Financial
Scandals 136

  The Financial Meltdown of 2008 146

... And the Poor Get Prison 149

  Summary 150 • Study Questions 151
• Additional Resources 151 • Notes 152

Chapter 4 **To the Vanquished Belong the Spoils: Who Is
Winning the Losing War Against Crime? 165**

Why Is the Criminal Justice System Failing? 166

The Poverty of Criminals and the Crime
of Poverty 171

  The Implicit Ideology of Criminal Justice 172

  The Bonus of Bias 177

Ideology, or How to Fool Enough of the People
Enough of the Time   180

What Is Ideology?   180

The Need for Ideology   184

*Summary   186   •   Study Questions   186
•   Additional Resources   187   •   Notes   187*

Conclusion: **Criminal *Justice* or *Criminal* Justice   195**

The Crime of Justice   195

Rehabilitating Criminal Justice in America   198

Protecting Society   198

Promoting Justice   205

*Summary   210   •   Study Questions   210
•   Additional Resources   211   •   Notes   211*

Appendix I   **The Marxian Critique of Criminal Justice   215**

Marxism and Capitalism   217

Capitalism and Ideology   219

Ideology and Law   223

Law and Ethics   229

Notes   232

Appendix II   **Between Philosophy and Criminology   235**

Philosophical Assumptions of Social
Science Generally   236

Special Philosophical Needs of Criminology   237

The Rich Get Richer and the Poor Get Philosophy   241

Notes   247

Index   249

FIGURE AND TABLES

FIGURE

1.1   Violent Crime Rate and Incarceration Rate, 1960–2017   18

TABLES

1.1   Rates of Intentional Homicide for Countries at Different Stages
      of Economic Development   30
1.2   Crime Rates Compared with Youth Population, 1960–2010   31
1.3   Percent of Income Earned and Income Limits in the U.S.,
      by Fifths, 2017   34
2.1   Occupational Disease and Injury Compared to Crime   85
2.2   How Americans Are Murdered, 2017   89
2.3   How Americans Are *Really* Murdered, 2017   89
3.1   Federal Sentences Served for Different Classes of Crimes, 2014 132
3.2   The Savings and Loan Roster   137
3.3   Scoundrel Capitalism, 2005   139
4.1   Rate of Violent Victimization and Serious Violent
      Victimizations, by Demographic Characteristics of Victims, 2017 169
4.2   Actual, Perceived, and Ideal Distributions of Wealth in the
      United States   185

PREFACE TO THE TWELFTH EDITION

For 40 years now, *The Rich Get Richer and the Poor Get Prison* has been taking the issue of economic inequality seriously and asking: Why are our prisons filled with the poor? Why aren't the tools of the criminal justice system being used to protect Americans from predatory business practices and to punish those well-off people who cause widespread harm?

The answer offered by *The Rich Get Richer and the Poor Get Prison* is that our criminal justice system is designed to use its weapons against the poor, while ignoring or treating gently the rich who prey upon the public. *The Rich Get Richer* invites readers to look at the American criminal justice system as if it were aimed, not at protecting us against crime, but at keeping before our eyes—in our courts, prisons, news, screens, and criminology books—a large criminal population consisting primarily of poor people. This serves the interests of the rich and powerful by broadcasting the message that the real danger to most Americans comes from people below them on the economic ladder rather than from above. Looking at the criminal justice system this way makes more sense of the criminal justice policy than accepting the idea that the system is really aimed at protecting our lives and limbs and possessions. All of this is summed up by saying that *the rich get richer and the poor get prison.*

Supporting the thesis that the criminal justice system is aimed at maintaining a large visible population of poor criminals requires defending two main claims: first, that the system could reduce our high crime rates but fails to do so, and second, that the system is biased against the poor at every stage. This second claim means that *for the same crimes,* the poor are more likely than the well-off to get arrested and, if arrested, more likely to be charged and, if charged, more likely to be convicted and, if convicted, more likely to be sentenced to prison and, if sentenced to prison, more likely to receive a long sentence. But it means even more: The bias against the poor starts earlier, at the point at which legislators decide what is to be a crime in the first place. Many of the ways in which the well-off harm the public (deadly pollution, unsafe working conditions and financial predation) are not even defined as crimes, *though they do more damage to life and limb or take more money from people's pockets than the acts that* are *treated as crimes.*

But what of the first claim, namely, that the system could reduce our high crime rates but fails to do so? In the period since 1980, we have seen an enormous increase in the number of Americans behind bars and, since 1990, significant drops in our crime rates. Research shows that only a small fraction of this reduction is due to criminal justice policies. The thesis of *The Rich Get Richer* requires only that the criminal justice system fails to prevent enough crime so that there remains before our eyes a large population of poor criminals. And that is as much the case today as it was when the book was first written. Though crime is down from its peak, there is still plenty of it—much more than in developed countries similar to the United States—and our citizens are still afraid of it. And our prisons are jammed full of people who are far poorer, and far more likely to have been unemployed or underemployed before entering prison, than their counterparts in the larger population.

Moreover, the criminal justice system—by which we always mean the whole system from lawmakers to law enforcers—continues not to implement programs that could alleviate the disabilities of poverty and dramatically reduce our high crime rates. And, as this book documents in detail, little has been done to make the harmful noncriminal acts of the well-off into crimes or to reduce the bias against poor people caught up in the system. In short, though the system has had some success in reducing crime, it is still failing in the way that the thesis of *The Rich Get Richer* asserts: We are still confronted with the specter of a large and scary population of poor criminals. And the criminal justice system still fails to protect us from the well-off by *not* treating their harmful acts as crimes. For all the changes of recent years, *the rich are still getting richer, and the poor are still getting prison.*

In revising the book for the twelfth edition, we have mainly tried to show the truth of this statement by bringing statistics comparing criminal and noncriminal harms (such as those caused by preventable occupational and environmental hazards) up to date, and by incorporating the results of the relevant research that has appeared since the last edition. As always, we have tried to introduce these updates with as little violation of the original edition's style and argument as possible.

This edition reports findings of studies published as recently as 2019. However, where we compare the relative danger of criminal versus noncriminal harms, we generally use figures for 2017, the latest year for which there are adequate statistics on both types of harm. When new statistics were not available, we have, where it seemed plausible, assumed that earlier statistics reflect continuing trends and enable projections from the past into the present. In all cases, we have kept our assumptions and estimates extremely conservative in order to keep the argument on the firmest ground. In addition to new studies and data, we also continue to report some of the most striking of the older studies. This shows how deep-seated the bias in our system is, and that the findings of recent studies are not aberrations or about merely passing phenomena.

The prefaces to the last six editions noted the declining number of articles in scholarly sociology and criminology journals reporting on the relationship between economic status and arrest, conviction, and sentencing. This point bears repeating for this edition. When the first edition of *The Rich Get Richer and the Poor Get Prison* appeared in 1979, there were many such studies, largely stimulated by President Johnson's establishment in 1965 of the President's Commission on Law Enforcement and the Administration of Justice. These studies consistently showed the presence of significant bias against lower-class suspects at every stage of criminal justice processing, from arrest on. With each subsequent edition of *The Rich Get Richer*, the number of new studies on this topic has decreased and dwindled to a trickle.

The studies that do exist show the bias to be alive and well. Furthermore, this is also our twelfth effort to find a comprehensive estimate of the total amount and cost of white-collar crime in the United States. It is striking that, while we are inundated with statistics on "common" crimes, there is no public or private agency that regularly measures the full extent of white-collar crime in all its varieties and issues a regular (not to mention annual) report. Most of the statistics that do exist are collected by corporations and trade organizations only to show how they are victimized by employees, consumers, and regular people; but corporations and trade organizations do not collect statistics on their own transgressions—and exceedingly few sources document the cost of the crimes of the powerful. So insurance fraud is insured people defrauding insurers, while the wrongful denial of claims by insurers is absent; "workplace theft" means employee theft, while wage theft is not mentioned; and the same can be said for mortgage fraud, credit card fraud, and many other areas. We hope that this text can help spur more research on economic bias in criminal justice, more awareness of the crimes of the powerful, and better measurement of the full extent of white-collar crime.

From reviewers' comments, we are happy to learn that the book continues to be used both by teachers who agree with its thesis and by those who do not. This is as it should be. *The Rich Get Richer* is meant to stimulate thought. Over the years, reviewers have made numerous recommendations, many of which we have adopted and have improved the book. Some of the recommendations—to discuss epistemology and scientific method, to present evidence conflicting with our theory alongside evidence that supports it, to provide detailed proposals for solving some of the problems that the book identifies in the criminal justice system, to call for the overthrow of the capitalist system, and so on—we have resisted because following them would detract from the aim of the book. *The Rich Get Richer* is not meant to be a complete survey of the criminal justice system and certainly not a complete survey of American social problems, and it is not meant to be a complete recipe for fixing either. It is also not meant to be a balanced presentation of conservative and progressive views. The goal of *The Rich Get Richer* is more limited and more focused: *It is meant to show readers that much that goes on in the criminal justice system violates their own sense of basic fairness, to present evidence that the system does not function in the way it says it does or in the way that readers believe it should, and then to sketch a whole theoretical perspective from which they might understand these failures and evaluate them morally*—and to do it all in a short and relatively inexpensive book written in plain language.

Readers who are not convinced about the larger theoretical perspective will still have engaged in extensive critical thinking to identify their own taken-for-granted assumptions about crime and criminal justice, as well as uncover the effects of power on social practices. This engagement helps readers develop their own worldview.

Although we have resisted changing the basic structure of this text, we have added new discussions of many important events and authors, as well as many features to make the text more usable: Chapter overviews at the start of each chapter help prepare readers by highlighting the key points they will encounter. A summary at the end of the chapter helps reinforce the main points. The study questions at the end of each chapter require the student to recall what he or she has read and to think critically about it. The questions can be used by instructors for the purpose of testing and review, and by students as a way of making sure they have covered and thought about the most important issues in each chapter.

We also appreciate the need for supplementary materials. They can be found:

- In Appendixes I and II of this book
- In an anthology of readings, *The Rich Get Richer: A Reader,* edited by Jeffrey Reiman and Paul Leighton (Boston: Pearson Education, Inc., 2010)
- At the author-maintained website, www.paulsjusticepage.com/reiman.htm.

Appendix I to this book is a short essay by Jeffrey Reiman titled "The Marxian Critique of Criminal Justice." It is for those who want a larger theoretical context in which to place the thesis of *The Rich Get Richer.* The essay covers ground from a general statement of Marxian theories of capitalism, ideology, and law to a Marxian theory of criminal justice—and the ethical judgments about crime and criminals to which that theory leads. This a handy way of introducing readers to Marxian theory and its relation to criminal law and criminology. The essay addresses some of the same issues discussed in the main text of *The Rich Get Richer* and thus offers an alternative theoretical framework for understanding those issues. Although this alternative framework is compatible with that developed in the main text, the argument of *The Rich Get Richer* stands alone without it.

Appendix II, also authored by Jeffrey Reiman, is titled "Between Philosophy and Criminology." Like the first appendix, the second appendix is separate from the argument of the main text but extends it in important ways. Unlike the first appendix, however, "Between Philosophy and Criminology" is a very personal statement in that it aims to stitch together the disparate parts of Reiman's intellectual life as a professional philosopher interested in criminal justice. He argues in it that criminology has a special need for philosophical reflection that other social sciences may not have, and he goes on to spell out the philosophical framework within which *The Rich Get Richer* stands.

In addition, an author-maintained website managed by Paul Leighton can be accessed at.*www.paulsjusticepage.com/reiman.htm.* It contains chapter outlines and summaries with links to additional related resources, as well as Internet-based exercises for students. Several articles that we have written about corporate crime are available there.

Because we have revised rather than rewritten *The Rich Get Richer,* we are indebted to those who helped with the original edition. They are thanked in the section "Acknowledgments for the First Edition." Starting with the ninth edition, Paul Leighton joined Jeffrey Reiman as co-author of *The Rich Get Richer and the Poor Get Prison.* Paul has assisted with the revisions of *The Rich Get Richer* since its fourth edition.

We appreciate the dedicated work of Heather Mooney, a doctoral student at Wayne State University. As with the eleventh edition, she had the challenging task of helping update the statistics and conducting numerous literature reviews about topics in a variety of disciplines for the twelfth edition. She found helpful studies, wrote thoughtful summaries, fact checked, helped with manuscript preparation, and was a great sounding board for what appears (and does not appear) in this revision. Heather did all this efficiently, thoroughly, graciously, and with excellent judgment.

We also appreciate the thoughts of Adrienne McCarthy, a doctoral student at Kansas State University, for discussions and research that added to Chapter 4. She also did a careful read of the book and other work necessary to compile the helpful index for this edition. Elizabeth Bradshaw, of Central Michigan University, graciously reviewed several draft chapters. We are also indebted to Shigeru (Simon) Miyao, who translated the ninth edition of *The Rich Get Richer* into Japanese. Mr. Miyao's translation has been a gift to us, and the exchanges we had with him substantially improved the tenth edition— many of these improvements are carried forward into this new edition. The work of several past research assistants also still lives on in this edition, so we thank Dana Radatz, Seyed Mirmajlessi, Rachel (Songer) Stark, Carrie Buist, Donna (Killingbeck) Selman, and Bernard Demczuk. We also thank Karen Hanson, our former editor at Allyn & Bacon, for her good counsel and hard work over many editions.

Both Jeffrey and Paul thank their universities—American University and Eastern Michigan University, respectively—for providing them with the supportive and lively intellectual environments that have made this work possible and enjoyable over the years.

Jeffrey dedicates the book to his wife, friend, partner, and colleague, Sue Headlee, who continues to delight, encourage, inspire, and astonish him as she has for more than 40 years. Paul dedicates this book to his daughters Sala and Aiko, who further inspire him to work toward a less violent society.

Jeffrey Reiman
and Paul Leighton

ACKNOWLEDGMENTS FOR THE FIRST EDITION

This book is the product of seven years of teaching in the School of Justice (formerly, the Center for the Administration of Justice), a multidisciplinary criminal justice education program at American University in Washington, DC. I have had the benefit of the school's lively and diverse faculty and student body. And, although they will surely not agree with all that I have to say, I have drawn heavily on what I have learned from my colleagues over the years and stand in their debt. In addition, more than is ordinarily recognized, a teacher receives guidance from students as they test, confirm, reject, and expand what they learn in class in the light of their own experience. Here, too, I am deeply indebted. My thanks go to the hundreds of students who have shared some part of their world with me as they passed through American University, and in particular to three students whose encouragement, loyalty, and wisdom are very much a part of the development of the ideas in this book: Elizabeth Crimi, Bernard Demczuk, and Lloyd Raines.

I express my gratitude to American University for providing me with a summer research grant that enabled me to devote full time to the book in the summer of 1976, when most of the actual writing was done. I am also grateful to Bernard Demczuk, who was my research assistant during the academic year 1975 to 1976 and who gathered much of the research data. I owe thanks as well to Cathy Sacks for ably and carefully typing the final manuscript.

Drafts of the manuscript for this book were read in whole or in part by (or to) Bernard Demczuk, Sue Hollis, Richard Myren, Lloyd Raines, Phillip Scribner, I. F. Stone, and John Wildeman. I am grateful for their many comments, and I incorporate many of their recommendations in the final version. I have made my mistakes in spite of them.

Finally, for teaching me about artichokes, the meaning of history, and countless other mysteries, this book is dedicated to Sue Headlee.

J. R.
1979

Introduction
Criminal Justice Through the Looking Glass, or Winning by Losing

The inescapable conclusion is that society secretly wants crime, needs crime, and gains definite satisfactions from the present mishandling of it.

—KARL MENNINGER, *THE CRIME OF PUNISHMENT*[1]

A criminal justice system is a mirror in which a whole society can see the darker outlines of its face. Our ideas of justice and evil take on visible form in it, and thus we see ourselves in deep relief. Step through this looking glass to view the American criminal justice system—and ultimately the whole society it reflects—from a radically different angle of vision.

In particular, entertain the idea that the goal of our criminal justice system is not to eliminate crime or to achieve justice *but to project to the American public a credible image of the threat of crime as a threat from the poor.* To accomplish this, the justice system must present us with a sizable population of poor criminals. To do that, it must fail in the struggle to eliminate the crimes that poor people commit or even to reduce their number dramatically. Crime may, of course, occasionally decline as it has recently—*but largely because of factors other than criminal justice policies.*

These last two statements must be explained. The news of declines in the crime rate was quickly snatched up by leaders at all levels from the White House to the local police station as an occasion to declare the success of their "tough-on-crime" policies. But critical thinkers will rightly ask why crime did not start to decline until 20 years after the U.S. started getting tough – and why crime and incarceration have both generally fallen in the last decade. We believe criminal justice policy had a very modest effect, while there are a rich variety of factors outside the system that have contributed to the declines from the early 1990s.

In recent years, America has quadrupled its prison population and allowed the police wide discretion to stop and search people. No one can deny that if you lock up enough people and allow the police greater and greater power to interfere with the liberty and privacy of citizens you will eventually prevent some crime that might otherwise have taken place. Later, we shall point out just how costly and inefficient this means of reducing crime is—in money for new prisons, in its destructive effect on inner-city life, and in increased complaints of police brutality. To be sure, these costly means do contribute *in some small measure* to reducing crime. Thus, when we say in this book that the criminal justice system is failing, our point is that it is failing to eliminate our high crime rates. We continue to see a large population of poor criminals in our prisons and courts, while our crime-reduction strategies do not touch on the social causes of crime. Moreover, our citizens remain fearful about criminal victimization even after the recent declines, and America's crime rate is still far above those of other industrial democracies around the world. We document this failure in Chapter 1, "Crime Control in America: Nothing Succeeds like Failure."

The reader should keep in mind that when we speak of the *criminal justice system*, we mean more than the familiar institutions of police, courts, and prisons. We mean the entire system that connects the decisions of lawmakers about what acts are criminal to the decisions of police about whom to arrest, all the way to the decisions of judges, juries, and parole boards about who will be in prison to pay for these acts.

You will rightly demand to know how and why a society such as ours would tolerate a criminal justice system that fails in the fight against crime. A considerable portion of this book is devoted to answering this question. Right now, however, a short explanation of how this upside-down idea of criminal justice was born will best introduce it.

Some 45 years ago, Jeffrey Reiman taught a seminar for graduate students titled "The Philosophy of Punishment and Rehabilitation." Many of the students were law-enforcement officers or working in the field of corrections. Together the class examined the various philosophical justifications for legal punishment and then directed its attention to the actual functioning of our correctional system. For much of the semester, the class discussed the myriad inconsistencies and cruelties and the overall irrationality of the system. It discussed the arbitrariness with which offenders are sentenced to prison and the arbitrariness with which they are treated once there. It discussed the lack of privacy, the deprivation of sources of personal identity and dignity, and the ever-present physical violence, as well as the lack of meaningful counseling or job training within prison walls. It discussed the harassment of parolees, the inescapability of the "ex-con" stigma, the refusal of society to let a person finish paying his or her "debt to society," and the absence of meaningful noncriminal opportunities for the ex-prisoner. Time and again the class confronted the bald irrationality of a society that builds prisons to prevent crime, knowing full well that they do not, and that does not seriously try to rid its prisons and post-release practices of those features that guarantee a high rate of *recidivism,* the return to crime by prison alumni. How could we fail so miserably? We are neither an evil nor a stupid nor an impoverished people. How could we continue to bend our energies and spend our hard-earned tax dollars on cures we know are not working?

Toward the end of the semester, the students were asked to imagine that, instead of designing a criminal justice system to reduce and prevent crime, they were to design one that would maintain a stable and visible "class" of criminals. What would it look like? The response was electrifying. Here is a sample of the proposals that emerged in the discussion:

1. It would be helpful to have laws on the books against drug use, prostitution, and gambling—laws that prohibit acts that have no unwilling victim. This would make many people "criminals" for what they regard as normal behavior and would increase their need to engage in *secondary crime* (the drug addict's need to steal to pay for drugs, the prostitute's need for a pimp because police protection is unavailable, and so on).

2. It would be good to give police, prosecutors, and/or judges broad discretion to decide who got arrested, who got charged, and who got sentenced to prison. This would mean that almost anyone who got as far as prison would know of others who committed the same crime but were not arrested or not charged or not sentenced to prison. That would assure us that a good portion of the prison population would experience their confinement as arbitrary and unjust and thus respond with rage, which would make them more antisocial, rather than respond with remorse, which would make them feel more bound by social norms.

3. The prison experience should be not only painful but also demeaning. The pain of loss of liberty might deter future crime. But demeaning and emasculating prisoners by placing them in an enforced childhood characterized by no privacy and no control over their time and actions, as well as by the constant threat of rape or assault, is sure to overcome any deterrent effect by weakening whatever capacities a prisoner had for self-control. Indeed, by humiliating and brutalizing prisoners, we can be sure to increase their potential for aggressive violence.[2]

4. Prisoners should neither be trained in a marketable skill nor provided with a job after release. Their prison records should stand as a perpetual stigma to discourage employers from hiring them. Otherwise, they might be tempted *not* to return to crime after release.

5. Ex-offenders' sense that they will always be different from "decent citizens," that they can never finally settle their debt to society, should be reinforced by the following means: They should be deprived for the rest of their lives of rights, such as the right to vote.[3] They should be harassed by police as "likely suspects" and be subject to the whims of parole officers, who can at any time send them back to prison for things no ordinary citizens could be arrested for, such as going out of town or drinking or fraternizing with the "wrong people." And so on.

In short, *when asked to design a system that would maintain and encourage the existence of a stable and visible "class of criminals," the students "constructed" the American criminal justice system!*

What is to be made of this? First, it is, of course, only part of the truth. Some steps have been taken to reduce arbitrary exercises of discretion in arrests and sentencing. And some prison officials do try to treat their inmates with dignity and to respect their privacy and self-determination to the greatest extent possible within an institution dedicated to involuntary confinement. A few prisons do provide meaningful job training, and some parole officers not only are fair but also go out of their way to help their "clients" find jobs and make it legally. And plenty of people are arrested for doing things that no society ought to tolerate, such as rape, murder, assault, or armed robbery, and many are in prison who might be preying on their fellow citizens if they were not. *All of this is true.* Complex social practices are just that: *complex.* They are rarely either all good or all bad. Nonetheless, the "successes" of the system, the "good" prisons and the halfway houses that really help offenders make it, are still the exceptions. They are not even prevalent enough to be called the beginning of the trend of the future. *On the whole, most of the system's practices make more sense if we look at them as ingredients in an attempt to maintain rather than reduce crime!*

This statement calls for an explanation. The one we offer is that the practices of the criminal justice system keep before the public the *real* threat of crime and the *distorted* image that crime is primarily the work of the poor. The value of this *to those in positions of power* is that it deflects the discontent and potential hostility of Middle America away from the classes above them and toward the classes below them. If this explanation is hard to swallow, it should be noted in its favor that it not only explains the dismal failure of criminal justice policy to protect us against crime but also explains why the criminal justice system functions in a way that is biased against the poor at every stage from arrest to conviction. Indeed, even at an earlier stage, when crimes are defined in law, the system concentrates primarily on the predatory acts of the poor and tends to exclude or deemphasize the equally or more dangerous predatory acts of those who are well-off.

In sum, we will argue that *the criminal justice system fails in the fight against crime while making it look as if crime is the work of the poor.* This image sanctifies the status quo with its disparities of wealth, privilege, and opportunity and thus serves the interests of the rich and powerful in America—the very ones who could change criminal justice policy if they were really unhappy with it.

Therefore, we ask you to look at criminal justice "through the looking glass." On the one hand, this suggests a reversal of common expectations. Reverse your expectations about criminal justice and entertain the notion that the system's real goal is the very reverse of its announced goal. On the other hand, the figure of the looking glass suggests the prevalence of image over reality. Our argument is that the system functions the way it does *because it maintains a particular image of crime: the image that it is a threat from the poor.* Of course, for this image to be believable there must be a reality to back it up. The system must actually fight crime—or at least some crime—but only enough to keep it from getting out of hand and to keep the struggle against crime vividly and dramatically in the public's view, never enough to substantially reduce or eliminate crime.

We call this outrageous way of looking at criminal justice policy the *Pyrrhic defeat* theory. A "Pyrrhic victory" is a military victory purchased at such a cost in troops and treasure that it amounts to a defeat. The Pyrrhic defeat theory argues that the failure of the criminal justice system yields such benefits to those in positions of power that it amounts to a victory. In what follows, we will try to explain the failure of the criminal justice system to reduce crime by showing the benefits that accrue to the powerful in America from this failure. From the standpoint of those with the power to make criminal justice policy in America, *nothing succeeds like failure*. We challenge you to keep an open mind and determine for yourself whether the Pyrrhic defeat theory does not make more sense of criminal justice policy and practice than the old-fashioned idea that the goal of the system is to reduce crime substantially.

The Pyrrhic defeat theory has several components. Above all, it must provide an explanation of *how* the failure to reduce crime substantially could benefit anyone—anyone other than criminals, that is. This is the task of Chapter 4, "To the Vanquished Belong the Spoils: Who Is Winning the Losing War Against Crime?" which argues that the failure to reduce crime substantially broadcasts a potent *ideological* message to the American people, a message that benefits and protects the powerful and privileged in our society by legitimating the present social order with its disparities of wealth and privilege and by diverting public discontent and opposition away from the rich and powerful and onto the poor and powerless.

To provide this benefit, however, not just any failure will do. It is necessary that the failure of the criminal justice system take a particular shape. *It must fail in the fight against crime while making it look as if serious crime and thus the real danger to society are the work of the poor.* The system accomplishes this both by what it does and by what it refuses to do. Chapter 2, "A Crime by Any Other Name," argues that the criminal justice system refuses to label and treat as crime a large number of acts of the rich that produce as much or more damage to life and limb than the crimes of the poor. Chapter 3, "... and the Poor Get Prison," shows how, even among the acts treated as crimes, the criminal justice system is biased from start to finish in a way that guarantees that, *for the same crimes,* members of the lower classes are much more likely than members of the middle and upper classes to be arrested, convicted, and imprisoned—thus providing living "proof" that crime is a threat from the poor. (A statement of the main propositions that form the core of the Pyrrhic defeat theory is found in Chapter 2 in the section titled "The Carnival Mirror: Criminal Justice as Creative Art.")

ONE CAUTION IS IN ORDER The argument is not a conspiracy theory. It is the task of social analysis to find patterns in social behavior and then explain them. Naturally, when we find patterns, particularly patterns that serve some people's interests, we are inclined to think of these patterns as *intended* by those whose interests are served, as somehow brought into being *because* they serve those interests. This way of thinking is generally called a *conspiracy theory.* Later we will say more about the shortcomings of this way of thinking and explain in detail how the Pyrrhic defeat theory differs from it. For the present, however, note that although we speak of the criminal justice system as "not wanting" to reduce crime and of the failure to reduce crime significantly as resulting in benefits to the rich and powerful in our society, *we are not maintaining that the rich and powerful intentionally make the system fail to gather up the resulting benefits.* Our view is rather that the system has grown up piecemeal over time and usually with the best of intentions. The unplanned and unintended overall result is a system that not only fails to substantially reduce crime but also does so in a way that serves the interests of the rich and powerful. One consequence of this fact is that those who have the power to make dramatic changes to the system and society it serves feel no need to do so. And thus it keeps on rolling along.

Our criminal justice system is characterized by beliefs about what is criminal and how to deal with crime that predate industrial society. Rather than being anyone's conscious plan, the system reflects attitudes so deeply embedded in tradition as to appear natural. To understand why it persists even though it fails to protect us, it is necessary to recognize that, on the one hand, those who are the most victimized by crime are not those in positions to make and implement policy. Crime falls more frequently and more harshly on the poor than on the better-off. On the other hand, there are enough benefits to the wealthy from the identification of crime with the poor, and the system's failure to reduce crime, that those with the power to make profound changes in the system feel no compulsion or see any incentive to make them. In short, the criminal justice system came into existence in an earlier epoch and persists in the present because, even though it is failing—indeed, *because* of the way it fails—it generates no effective demand for change. When we speak of the criminal justice system as "designed to fail," we mean no more than this. We call this explanation of the existence and persistence of our failing criminal justice system the *historical inertia* explanation, which Chapter 4 spells out in greater detail.

The concluding chapter presents an argument that the conditions described in Chapters 1, 2, and 3 (whether or not one accepts our explanation for them in Chapter 4) undermine the essential moral difference between criminal justice and crime itself. This chapter, called "Criminal *Justice* or *Criminal* Justice," makes some recommendations for reform of the system. These are not offered as ways to "improve" the system, but as the minimal conditions necessary to establish the moral superiority of that system to crime itself.

The Pyrrhic defeat theory is a child of the marriage of several ideas from Western social theory. Although this is discussed at greater length in what follows, it will provide clarity to indicate from the start the parents and the grandparents of this child. The idea that crime serves important functions for a society comes from Émile Durkheim. The notion that public policy can be best understood as serving the interests of the rich and powerful in a society stems from Karl Marx. From Kai Erikson is derived the notion that the institutions designed to fight crime instead contribute to its existence. From Richard Quinney comes the concept of the "reality" of crime as *created* in the process that links the definition of some acts as "criminal" under the law to the treatment of some persons as "criminals" by the agents of the law. The Pyrrhic defeat theory combines these ideas into the view that the failure of criminal justice policy becomes intelligible when we see that it creates the "reality" of crime as the work of the poor, and thus projects an image that serves the interests of the rich and powerful in American society.

Though the Pyrrhic defeat theory draws on the ideas just mentioned, it changes them in the process. For example, the theory veers away from the traditional Marxist accounts of legal institutions insofar as those accounts generally emphasize the *repressive* function of the criminal justice system, whereas our view emphasizes its *ideological* function. Marxists tend to see the criminal justice system as serving the powerful by *successfully* repressing the poor. Our view is that the system serves the powerful by its *failure* to reduce crime, not by its success. Needless to add, insofar as the system fails in some respects and succeeds in others, these approaches are compatible. Nevertheless, in looking at the ideological rather than the repressive function of criminal justice, we will focus primarily on the image its *failure* conveys rather than on what it actually *succeeds* in repressing.[4] (A discussion of Marxian theory and its implications for ideology and criminal justice is found in Appendix I.)

Having located the Pyrrhic defeat theory in its family tree, we wish to say a word about the relationship between crime and economics. Our view is that the social order (shaped decisively by the economic system) bears responsibility for most of the crime that troubles us. This is true for all classes in society, because a competitive economy that refuses to guarantee its members a decent living places pressures on all members to enhance their economic position by whatever means available. It degrades and humiliates the poor while encouraging the greed of the well-off.[5] Nevertheless, these economic pressures work with particular harshness on the poor because their condition of extreme need and relative lack of access to opportunities for lawful economic advancement vastly intensify for them the pressures toward crime that exist at all levels of our society.

These views lead to others that, if not taken in their proper context, may strike you as paradoxical. Evidence will be presented showing that there is a considerable amount of crime in our society at all socioeconomic levels. At the same time, it will be argued that poverty is a *source* of crime. We say "source" rather than "cause" because the link between poverty and crime is not a simple relationship between cause and effect. Poverty doesn't force poor people to commit crimes. Rather it confronts them with needs that they are less able than well-off people to satisfy legally, and it offers them fewer rewards for staying straight. Thus, they face pressures and incentives that make crime more tempting, and noncriminal avenues less appealing, than they are for better-off people. Consequently, while most poor people do not commit serious crimes, evidence suggests that the particular pressures of poverty lead poor people to commit a higher proportion (in relation to their number in the population) of the crimes that people fear, such as homicide, burglary, and assault.

There is no contradiction between this and the recognition that those who are well-off commit many more crimes than is generally acknowledged, both the crimes widely feared and those not widely feared (such as white-collar crimes). There is no contradiction here because, as will be shown, the poor are arrested far more frequently than those who are well-off when they have committed the same crimes, and the well-to-do are only rarely arrested for white-collar crimes. Thus, if arrest records were brought in line with the real incidence of crime, those who are well-off would appear in the records far more than they do at present, even though the poor would still probably appear in numbers greater than their proportion of the population in arrests for the crimes people fear. In addition to this, we will argue that those who are well-off commit dangerous acts that are not defined as crimes and yet are as or more harmful than the crimes people fear. Thus, if we had an accurate picture of who is really dangerous to society, those who are well-off would receive still greater representation. On this basis, the following propositions will be put forth, which may appear contradictory if these various levels of analysis are not kept distinct.

1. Society fails to protect people from the crimes they fear by, among other things, refusing to alleviate the poverty that breeds those crimes (documented in Chapter 1).
2. The criminal justice system focuses on the crimes of the poor, and thereby fails to protect people from grave dangers by failing to treat the dangerous acts of the well-off as crimes (documented in Chapter 2), and by failing to enforce the law vigorously against the well-off when they commit acts that are defined as crimes (documented in Chapter 3).
3. By virtue of these facts, the criminal justice system succeeds in creating the image that crime is almost exclusively the work of the poor, an image that serves the interests of the powerful (argued in Chapter 4).

The view that the social order is responsible for crime does not mean that individuals are wholly blameless for their criminal acts, or that we ought not to have a criminal justice system able to protect us against them. To borrow an analogy from Ernest van den Haag, it would be foolhardy to refuse to fight a fire because its causes were suspect. The fact that society produces criminals is no reason to avoid facing the realization that many of these criminals are dangerous and must be dealt with. Also, although blaming society for crime may require that we tone down our blame of individual criminals, it does not require that we eliminate blame entirely or deny that they are responsible for their crimes. This is particularly important to remember because so many of the victims of the crimes of the poor are poor themselves. To point to the unique social pressures that lead the poor to prey on one another is to point to a mitigating, not an excusing, factor. The victims of exploitation and oppression have moral obligations not to harm those who do not exploit them or who share their oppression.

ABBREVIATIONS USED IN THE NOTES

BJS Bureau of Justice Statistics, a source of many reports cited in this book. The Bureau of Justice Statistics is an agency of the U.S. Department of Justice. Reports of the Bureau of Justice Statistics are published by the U.S. Government Printing Office in Washington, DC and can be accessed online at www.bjs.gov/.

Challenge The Challenge of Crime in a Free Society: A Report by the President's Commission on Law Enforcement and Administration of Justice (Washington, DC: U.S. Government Printing Office, February 1967).

Sourcebook University at Albany, Hindelang Criminal Justice Research Center, *Sourcebook of Criminal Justice Statistics*. References to various editions of this annual publication will be indicated by *Sourcebook*, followed by the year in the title or the table number (i.e., 6.28.2009). Earlier editions have different editors. The *Sourcebook* can be accessed at www.albany.edu/sourcebook.

Stat-Abst Statistical Abstract of the United States. References to editions of this publication will be indicated by *Stat-Abst*, followed by the year in the title. U.S. Census Bureau published editions up to 2012, which are available at www.census.gov/library/publications/time-series/statistical_abstracts. html. ProQuest has published it since 2012 and it is available through subscription via many libraries and institutions.

UCR U.S. Department of Justice, Federal Bureau of Investigation, *Crime in the United States* (the publication that contains data from the Uniform Crime Reports). References to this annual report will be indicated by *UCR*, followed by the year for which the statistics are reported. Data back to 1995 can be accessed through www.fbi.gov/about-us/cjis/ucr/ucr.

Notes

1 Karl Menninger, *The Crime of Punishment* (New York: Viking, 1968).
2 Consider the following:

> *Dr. Meredith Bombar, a social psychologist and associate professor of psychology at Elmira College, notes that it would be difficult intentionally to shape a more effective breeding ground for aggression than that which already exists in the average prison. In personal correspondence, Dr. Bombar writes, "When I teach Social Psychology class, I spend a week or so going over the social/learned causes of aggression (e.g., provocation, modeling, punishment, extreme frustration, roles and social norms calling for aggression, physical discomfort, crowding, presence of guns and other objects associated with*

aggression, etc.). After the students have digested that, I ask them to imagine a horrible fantasy world which would put together all of these known social/environmental causes of aggression. What would it be? A typical prison." (From Lee Griffith, *The Fall of the Prison: Biblical Perspectives on Prison Abolition* [Grand Rapids, MI: Eerdmans, 1993], p. 65 n.)

3 See Jeffrey Reiman, "Liberal and Republican Arguments against the Disenfranchisement of Felons," *Criminal Justice Ethics* 24, no. 1 (Winter-Spring 2005): 3–18.

4 Some Marxist theorists look specifically at the ideological functions performed by the institutions of the state: Louis Althusser, "Ideology and Ideological State Apparatuses," in his *Lenin and Philosophy and Other Essays* (London: New Left Books, 1971), pp. 121–73; and Nicos Poulantzas, *Fascism and Dictatorship* (London: New Left Books, 1974), pp. 299–309. These writers refer to the pioneering insights of Antonio Gramsci into the ideological functions of state institutions. See Quintin Hoare and Geoffrey Nowell-Smith, eds., *Selections from the Prison Notebooks of Antonio Gramsci* (London: Lawrence and Wishart, 1971); and Carl Boggs, *Gramsci's Marxism* (London: Pluto Press, 1976). For other broadly Marxian analyses of the relationship between the state and ideology, see Ralph Miliband, *The State in Capitalist Society* (New York: Basic Books, 1969), pp. 179–264; and Jürgen Habermas, *Legitimation Crisis* (Boston: Beacon Press, 1975). David Garland takes seriously the ideological message of criminal justice practices in *Punishment and Modern Society* (Chicago: University of Chicago Press, 1990), esp. Ch. 11.

5 See, for example, John Braithwaite, "Poverty, Power, and White-Collar Crime: Sutherland and the Paradoxes of Criminological Theory," in Kip Schlegel and David Weisburd (eds.) *White-Collar Crime Revisited* (Boston: Northeastern University Press, 1992), pp. 78–107.

Crime Control in America
Nothing Succeeds Like Failure

Is it crime and punishment that go hand in hand?
Or does punishment feed the crime that plagues our land?

—ROBERT JOHNSON, *A Zoo Near You**

Failure is in the eye of the beholder.

—ANONYMOUS

Chapter 1 has three main objectives: 1) to examine the exclusive focus on police and prison that characterizes America's response to its high crime rate and show the limited role that police and prisons have played in reducing street crime; 2) to review the "excuses" that are made for our high crime rates, and show how we *choose* to have the crime rates we do; and 3) to outline the Pyrrhic defeat theory that explains the continued existence of high crime rates after decades of policies that fail to reduce crime. The subtitle of Chapter 1, "Nothing Succeeds Like Failure," highlights an important aspect of the larger argument: The criminal justice system is failing even if crime rates are down from all-time highs. "Tough on crime" policies had little to do with the reduction in crime rates, and mass incarceration even had some "backfire" effects that promoted crime. Crime rates in the U.S. are still high compared to other developed countries, even though they are now down to rates not experienced since the 1960s when crime was seen as an alarming problem. Policies targeting sources of crime (inequality, guns, prison, drug policy), and evidence-based policies about what works to reduce crime, have not been seriously considered. Ultimately, American criminal justice policy makes more sense if we look at the system as wanting to have high crime rates—there are some for whom "crime pays" and for whom the system's failure is a success.

*By permission of BleakHouse Publishing.

THE FAILURE OF TOUGH ON CRIME

In the last 60 years, crime rates have mostly gone up until the 1990s, and then down substantially. Current crime rates now are similar to what they were in the early 1960s, in spite of various "tough on crime" proposals that propelled the U.S. into "the largest prison expansion the world has ever known."[1] From 1980 to 2000, the U.S. built more prisons than it had in all the rest of its history,[2] creating what has been called an incarceration binge, mass incarceration, hyperincarceration, and a *Plague of Prisons*.[3] The policies that led to the U.S. having the highest incarceration rate in the world contributed little to lowering crime rates, but it came at an enormous financial cost, heightened racial inequality and tensions–and it added to a variety of social problems, such as the breakdown of inner-city communities. The getting "tough on crime" rhetoric now has been tempered with discussions about criminal justice reform, but actual reform is infrequent and does little to undo the "four-decade mean season in Corrections."[4] The persistence and legacy of this failed policy requires examination.

In response to rising crime rates during the 1960s, President Lyndon Johnson proposed addressing the *causes* of crime with policies, such as antipoverty and economic opportunity programs, that spread the benefits of America's successful economy to more citizens. Programs that addressed social inequality were considered to be anti-crime programs because they attacked crime's "root causes." Johnson declared:

> There is something mighty wrong when a candidate for the highest office bemoans violence in the streets but votes against the war on poverty, votes against the Civil Rights Act, and votes against major educational bills that come before him.[5]

President Richard Nixon's "law and order" campaign rejected Johnson's strategy, and in his 1970 State of the Union message, Nixon stated: "We must declare and win the war against the criminal elements which increasingly threaten our cities, our homes, and our lives."[6] The four years of Jimmy Carter's presidency were an exception to the "tough on crime" agenda—for example, he proposed eliminating penalties for possession of less than one ounce of marijuana.[7] But the "get tough" pattern resumed with Ronald Reagan's election as president in 1980, including two major bills expanding mandatory minimum sentences for drug crimes. Under President Bush (I) in 1992, the Department of Justice released *The Case for More Incarceration*, with then-Attorney General William P. Barr writing that "prison works" and urging tougher sentencing.[8]

During the 20 years when crime rates were increasing, politicians never took responsibility for it. Rather than questioning whether getting tough was effective, they played to voters' fears by advocating "law and order" in many forms: more police, harsher sentences, mandatory minimums, three-strikes-and-you're-out laws (and then expanding the offenses that counted as strikes), and the increased use of capital punishment. When crime rates started to decline, however, politicians jumped to claim credit. This is "a version of 'heads I win, tails you lose,' in which decreases in crime are evidence that hard-line punishments work, whereas increases are evidence that they are needed."[9]

Bill Clinton's campaign and presidency happened as the crime rate peaked and then started to decline, so he continued the 20-year unquestioned assumption that tough on crime was necessary and started 30 years of claims that the policies worked to decrease crime. While campaigning, Clinton proposed hiring 100,000 police officers in an effort to get the endorsement of police organizations, and counter perceptions that he might be soft on crime. The Violent Crime Control and Law Enforcement Act of 1994 authorized the hiring of 100,000 officers, toughened sentences, provided $10 billion for prison construction, incentivized states to toughen sentencing laws, and created 60 new death penalty offenses. When signing the bill, Clinton called it a "great law, the toughest and smartest crime bill in our history."[10]

Although crime rates dropped noticeably for two years *before* the crime bill, President Clinton took credit for declining crime rates.[11] He claimed that putting 100,000 new police on the street "played a big role in [the] recent crime drop," but one analysis noted that "Clinton has won funding for 44,000 officers; [of whom] 20,000 are on the beat so far. Experts say that number could not have reduced crime much."[12] With officers working in shifts, taking vacations, and so on, it requires at least five officers to provide one officer on the street, around the clock, for a whole year.[13]

Further, National Academy of Sciences panels in 1978 and 1993 found there was a lack of evidence to support the assumption that harsher punishments deter crime. "Despite those nearly unanimous findings, during the 1970s, 1980s, and 1990s the U.S. Congress and every state enacted laws calling for mandatory minimum sentences."[14]

Untroubled by such facts, President Clinton again took credit for the continued decline in crime rates the next year, 1997, saying that 100,000 new officers and "tough new penalties on the books.... This approach is working." In response to crime "dropping for the fifth year in a row," Clinton said: "Now that we've finally turned crime on the run, we have to redouble our efforts"[15] with more of the same. So, in 1999 his 21st Century Crime Bill would "help to put up to 50,000 more police on the street," armed with better technology.[16]

Early in his first term, President Bush (II) noted the decline in crime, but correctly added that "the violent crime rate in the United States remains among the highest in the industrialized world."[17] This speech promoted a budget plan to spend almost one billion dollars on prisons[18] and expand the use of private for-profit prison companies.[19] And a 2005 statement shows the Bush administration's call for more of the same during its second term: "Aggressive law enforcement and tougher sentencing laws bear a good deal of the responsibility for the precipitous reduction in crime rates, especially for violent crime, over the past decade."[20]

However, a 2004 National Academy of Sciences panel, in *Fairness and Effectiveness in Policing: The Evidence*, found there was weak or no evidence to support the effectiveness of a "standard model" of policing that relied on "arrests and the threat of punishment" to reduce crime; that the effects of increasing the number of police were "ambiguous"; that rapid response "has also not been shown to reduce crime"; that "research does not provide strong support for the proposition that zero-tolerance policing reduced serious crime," and in some cities "intensive enforcement overall increased social disorder"; and community policing relying on general foot patrol and storefront offices "have not been found to reduce crime."[21] The panel noted that "a century of criminological research has documented the powerful impact of a long list of social and economic factors on crime... and they are mainly beyond the reach of the police."[22]

As a presidential candidate in 2007, Barack Obama wanted to "reduce the blind and counterproductive warehousing of nonviolent offenders."[23] But as President, Obama released a Smart on Crime program aimed at "becom[ing] both smarter and tougher on crime."[24] When his Attorney General, Eric Holder, announced that crime was down in 2011, his message was that Obama's administration would "continue to support our state, local and tribal partners and to implement the tough, smart policing policies that we know make a difference in the fight against violent crime."[25] These are the same claims made by previous presidents that are not supported by the evidence, and that ignore the social and economic factors impacting crime.

Before he ran for president, Obama said "we can't incarcerate ourselves out of the drug crisis," that the war on drugs was "an utter failure," and advocated decriminalization of marijuana.[26] He did sign into law a reduction in mandatory minimum sentences for crack cocaine and in the disparity between crack and powder cocaine sentences.[27] This change is the first reduction in drug sentences in decades, but the U.S. Sentencing Commission had been advocating for it for 15 years. More generally, though, the libertarian magazine *Reason* ran a cover story titled "Bummer: Barack Obama turns out to be just another drug warrior," which claimed that (with the exception of crack sentences) Obama's drug policies "by and large have been remarkably similar to his predecessor's."[28] And, while it exercised restraint in prosecuting marijuana businesses operating legally under state law, the Obama administration maintained marijuana as a Schedule I drug, which means it is considered among the most harmful drugs (like heroin), with a high potential for abuse and no accepted medical use.[29]

Toward the very end of his second term, Obama started discussing criminal justice reform, but his presidency oversaw increases in the Bureau of Prisons budget. The small declines in the federal prisoner population were welcome, but those statistics do not include facilities operated by Immigration and Customs Enforcement (ICE),[30] which saw its detention population grow substantially after the financial crisis of 2008.

As President Clinton was ramping up the drug war, Donald Trump called out politicians who "don't have any guts'" and said: "You have to legalize drugs to win that war. You have to take the profit away from these drug czars."[31] But as President, Trump said the U.S. has "to get really, really tough, really mean with the drug pushers and the drug dealers."[32] Aides say he privately has brought up the idea of executing drug dealers.[33]

Such statements reflect longstanding talk by Trump advocating crime policy that is tough without a pretense of also trying to be smart on crime. On the campaign trail, he said: "I'm tough on crime" and on several occasions said: "we have to get a lot tougher."[34] His first Attorney General, Jefferson Sessions, claimed that tough on crime legislation passed in the early 1980s under President Reagan lowered crime rates[35] and that "the war on crime and drugs did not fail. It was a roaring success."[36] Trump's current Attorney General is Barr, who wrote the 1992 *Case for More Incarceration* and has not voiced any regrets about that position.

In spite of this history, Trump also has claimed he is a criminal justice reformer because he signed the 2018 First Step Act. This law tasks the Bureau of Prisons with developing some rehabilitation programs, risk assessments for early release, and accomplishes minor sentencing reform.[37] As its name suggests, the First Step Act is a modest initial step—a watered-down compromise version of other modest reform bills. It's actual impact will depend on good-faith funding and implementation—neither of which should be taken for granted. Politicians of both parties who supported the bill are presenting themselves as reformers, but no legislation for second and subsequent reform steps is on the radar.

So the failed policies continue—even under those leaders who seem to understand the problems with these policies. Between 1980 and 2017, the number of persons incarcerated in state and federal prisons more than quadrupled, growing from 329,000 to just under 1.5 million. If we add those who are locked up in jails, there are now almost 2.2 million people behind bars in the United States, more people per capita than any other country.[38]

Sadly, state and local politicians have generally followed the direction set by national leaders in promoting "tough on crime" solutions, at least until the financial crisis of 2008. Substantial declines in state and local budgets precipitated what is likely to be the first sustained reduction in incarceration in decades. States are now scrambling to release nonviolent offenders and overhaul tough laws to reduce the flow of inmates into prison, testimony to how little these laws contributed to public safety. It is not yet clear if the U.S. has moved beyond "tough on crime" into a period of genuine reform or into one of "cheap on crime"[39] that trims corrections budgets without funding crime prevention or tackling the social and economic causes of crime.

Some states have taken steps to reform sentencing, but overall the *discussion* and rhetoric about reform has not translated into much *actual* reform. There were 1,505,400 inmates in American prisons at year-end 2016 down from a peak of 1,615,487 in 2009[40]—a decline of about 110,000 inmates over seven years. What Michael Tonry noted in 2014 still applies: "no statutory changes have fundamentally altered the laws and policies that created the existing American sentencing system, mass incarceration, and the human, social and economic costs they engendered."[41] He advocated for the repeal or substantial narrowing of all three-strikes, mandatory-minimum, life-without-possibility-of-parole, and truth-in-sentencing laws. Combined with the expansion of parole, these changes would eventually cut the U.S. incarceration rate in half. That rate would still be "three to four times those of other developed Western countries, [which] can hardly be considered overly ambitious."[42]

Further, the current emphasis on evidence-based policies should not obscure the plain fact that virtually no serious student of the crime problem believes we can arrest and imprison our way out of it. Yet those were the main strategies for about five decades—and they remain the ones that continue to shape our current justice system.

One troubling aspect of these policies is that the money used to fund the imprisonment boom has been taken from crime prevention, welfare, education, and public health for the poor, thereby weakening programs that reduce crime in the long run. By 2010, California spent 11 percent of its state budget on prisons and 7.5 percent on higher education, leading then Governor Arnold Schwarzenegger to propose an amendment to the state constitution requiring it to spend more on higher education than prisons.[43] The proposal died because it would have required reforms even more far-reaching than the 2011 Supreme Court order that California release 37,000 inmates to bring the system *down* to 137.5 percent of capacity, and remedy conditions that the Court found were causing "needless suffering and death."[44]

California was—and is—not alone: Between 1986 and 2013, the amount that states spent on corrections increased by 141 percent (after correcting for inflation), while higher education expenditures increased by 5.6 percent; 11 states spent as much or more on corrections than they did on higher education.[45] While some states reduce prison populations and correctional expenditures, many are also cutting aid to higher education, forcing tuition increases and cuts to student services.[46]

And what are the results? While violent crimes have declined since 1992, overall crime rates are still very high. For example, in 1992, the FBI reported a violent crime rate of 758 per 100,000 persons in the population. In 2017 the FBI reported a violent crime rate of 383 per 100,000, close to what it was in 1971 (396 per 100,000).[47] Criminologist Elliott Currie says the "declines... mainly represent a falling-off from an extraordinary peak."[48] And they have come down to rates that existed when far fewer Americans were locked up. In short, the crime reductions for which our leaders are now claiming credit are actually reductions from *very, very high* crime rates to rates that are merely *very high*.

For example, in 1999, *The Washington Post* ran a headline: "Despite Rhetoric, Violent Crime Climbs":

> Rosy assessments of the nation's declining crime rate wrongly focus on the short-term drops from crime peaks early in the decade and ignore the overall rise of violence since the 1960s, according to a new report.
>
> The 30-year update of a landmark study by the National Commission on the Causes and Prevention of Violence found that

violent crime in major cities reported to the FBI has risen by 40 percent since 1969.

The new study is intended as a counterpoint to the drumbeat of optimistic reports describing the current drop in crime, and it offers a sober reminder that the United States still suffers from a historically high level of violence.[49]

This 1999 study was conducted by the Milton S. Eisenhower Foundation, an organization devoted to continuing the work of the original 1969 National Commission on the Causes and Prevention of Violence and the 1968 National Advisory Commission on Civil Disorders (Kerner Commission). The foundation study noted the strikingly higher rates of violent crime in the United States compared to other industrialized nations. "The most optimistic view," said foundation president Lynn A. Curtis, who also worked on the 1969 violence report, "is that we are in roughly the same ballpark now in the late 1990s as we were in the late 1960s, when everyone said crime is so bad we need a national commission to study it."[50] The difference is that in 1969 the incarceration rate for state and federal prisons was 94 per 100,000 citizens but by 1999 it increased to 463, growth that has cost us billions of dollars, saddled huge numbers of nonviolent criminals with prison records, and torn up inner-city communities—but has not made much of a difference in the amount of crime we have.[51]

Figure 1.1 illustrates these concepts by comparing the violent crime rate and incarceration rate of people in prisons (jail inmates are not included). If you look at the graph from 1990 onward, you get the misleading impression that higher incarceration rates led to lower levels of crime. The longer-term view reveals a more complex reality. For most of the time, crime had an upward trend, while incarceration increased continually. Further, the graph shows that the current violent crime rate is far off its peak, but down to levels of the early 1970s. At that time, it had been increasing for more than a decade and was the subject of great concern. That same level of violent crime is now a cause for celebration and complacency.

The figure also does not fully reveal the total failure of the modern drug war, which has been a core aspect of the war on crime since President Nixon declared in 1971 that drug abuse was "public enemy number one."[52] Part of the dramatic growth in our prison population is the result of the hardening of drug enforcement policy. In 1968 there were 162,000 drug arrests nationwide, which climbed to more than 1.6 million in 2017.[53] The spread of mandatory sentences for drug possession meant that "from 1980 to 1997, the number of violent offenders doubled, the number of nonviolent offenders tripled, and the number of drug offenders increased eleven-fold."[54] The Bureau of Justice Statistics continues to report that almost half of federal inmates were serving sentences for drug violations in 2017.[55] Of state and local drug arrests, two-thirds of offenders "possess or sell a gram or less at the time of arrest. Furthermore, about 40% of arrests for hard drug are for trace amounts – a quarter of a gram or less."[56]

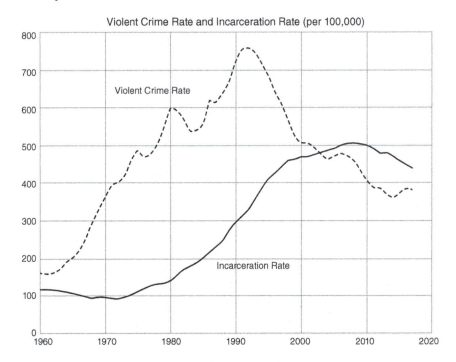

FIGURE 1.1   **Violent Crime Rate and Incarceration Rate, 1960–2017**
Source: Sourcebook, Tables 3.106.2012 and 6.28.2012; *UCR-2017,* Table 1; and BJS, *Prisoners in 2017,* Table 5.

Because numerous studies show that arrested drug dealers in inner-city neighborhoods are quickly replaced, it was apparent from the start that policing and incarceration would have little success in reducing the availability of illicit drugs.[57] What it does succeed in is leaving inner-city youths with criminal records that reduce their chances of getting a legitimate job.

In addition to arrests and incarceration, the drug war has focused on two other policies that have failed to achieve results: the U.S. has tried to have other countries eradicate crops and has used interdiction to stop illicit product from crossing into America. In spite of U.S. efforts to eradicate drug crops, drug production remains robust even as it shifts regions. The U.S. has led numerous international drug wars since 1971, but worldwide illicit opium (used to make heroin) production rose from 990 tons in 1971 to 8,800 tons in 2007.[58] A 2008 study noted that in Colombia, the "amount of land devoted to production of coca, the leaf used to make cocaine, has grown at a dramatic pace," despite an eight-year eradication program costing $5 billion.[59] And the amount of land utilized globally for opium cultivation in 2013 was "the largest area since 1998, when estimates became available."[60] This is evidence of a long history of failure to pressure foreign countries to reduce production of narcotic substances.

Likewise, attempts to use the military and Homeland Security to interdict drugs coming into the United States have failed to put a dent in the traffic. After all, America has over 88,000 miles of coastline, and policies designed to make the flow of global goods and money easy. From time to time, government officials do photo ops with large amounts of seized drugs, but the right framework for evaluating those moments is "while seizures are up, so are shipments."[61]

In summary, a report by drug policy experts gathered by the London School of Economics suggested that eradication and interdiction efforts resulted in "temporary inconvenience to the participants. The long-term consequences, in terms of availability and price to users, will be slight."[62] That's a rather generous conclusion given that a 2004 Office of National Drug Control Policy (ONDCP) report indicated that "powder cocaine prices have declined by roughly 80 percent since 1981," and "purity-adjusted prices were at or near all-time lows in 2003."[63] A National Academy of Sciences panel in 2014 concluded that "the best empirical evidence suggests that the successive iterations of the war on drugs—through a substantial public policy effort—are unlikely to have markedly or clearly reduced drug crime over the past three decades."[64]

So, 50 years into the drug war, despite expanded police powers to search citizens and increased use of military equipment, drugs are cheap, plentiful, and potent. The U.S. annually spends $48 billion on state and federal drug prohibition, including $10 billion on marijuana prohibition.[65] It spends additional money on drug prevention and treatment, yet treatment is "prohibitively expensive, overcrowded, underfunded and subject to byzantine government rules."[66] The Centers for Disease Control and Prevention reported more than 70,000 drug overdose deaths in 2017, yet another record high; the rate of drug overdose deaths has tripled from 1999 to 2017 and increased for all age groups over 15.[67] More generally, the U.S. has the highest level of drug overdose deaths in the world.[68]

None of this critique is new, and it has been made by both the political right and left.[69] We would be better off decriminalizing drugs, taxing their production and sale (almost $60 billion in estimated revenue),[70] and expanding treatment and public health initiatives. These are basic ideas of harm-reduction, which flow from the premise that drug use is inevitable and public policy should aim at reducing the negative consequences of drug use by using psychologists, social workers, and public health professions. Resources from the war on recreational drug users could be reinvested to fight child abuse and other serious harms.

President Clinton's Surgeon General, Joycelyn Elders, noted in the 1990s that "other countries had decriminalized drug use and had reduced their crime rates without increasing the use of narcotics."[71] For example, in 2001 Portugal eliminated criminal penalties for *all* drugs in amounts for personal use. Possession for personal use can still trigger a hearing before the Commission for the Dissuasion of Drug Addiction, a three-person tribunal that discourages drug use and encourages addicts to get treatment. An evaluation published in the *British Journal of Criminology* found reductions in problematic drug use and concludes that Portugal's experience

> demonstrates that—contrary to some predictions—decriminalization does not inevitably lead to rises in drug use. It can reduce the burden upon the criminal justice system. It can further contribute to social and health benefits. Moreover, such effects can be observed when decriminalizing all illicit drugs. This is important, as decriminalization is commonly restricted to cannabis alone.[72]

A more recent call for decriminalization is from the Global Commission on Drug Policy, whose members include the former presidents of Mexico, Colombia, Brazil, and Switzerland; a former Secretary General of the United Nations; a former U.S. Secretary of State; the prime minister of Greece; and a former chair of the U.S. Federal Reserve and economic advisor to President Obama. They state that "the global war on drugs has failed, with devastating consequences for individuals and societies." They suggest ending the criminalization of drugs and experimenting with models of legal regulation that "undermine the power of organized crime" and "offer health and treatment services to those in need."[73] Unfortunately, the drug czar—the head of ONDCP—is required by the legislation that created the office to "oppose any attempt to legalize the use" of a controlled substance.[74] So the highest official responsible for drug policy is legally prohibited from having an honest conversation about, and acting on, a wider range of evidence-based drug policy options.

Summarizing the war on drugs and the larger war on crime, John DiIulio, President Bush's first director of the White House Office of Faith-Based and Community Initiatives, stated:

> America in 2010 is a half-century into massive public and private anticrime investments, tougher criminal sentencing policies, and security-seeking personal life style changes; yet, for all that, nationally, crime is not demonstrably lower today than it was 50 years ago, and in many places it is worse than it was when the national alarm about crime was first sounded. Since crime climbed on to the federal policy agenda in the early 1960s, successive government wars on crime and drugs have sacrificed once-sacred civil liberties. Today, nearly 2.5 million Americans live behind prison gates while tens of millions more live in gated communities.[75]

Understanding the Decline in Rates of Street Crime

Although many Americans are confused about whether crime rates are increasing or decreasing, the overall pattern since 1992 has been one of declining crime rates. (Politicians and the media sometimes seize on the experience of specific cities or normal fluctuations in crime rates as evidence of something more when it is not.)[76] While criminologists use the term 'decline in crime rates,' no one collects systematic data on the amount of white-collar and corporate crime (see Chapters 2 and 3), so it is more accurate to say there has been

a decline in the rates of street crime. This reduction in street crime only constitutes a "success" for the criminal justice system to the extent that the system
caused the decline. A review of criminal justice literature, however, shows that
prisons and police played a quite limited role in the national crime decline,
which is better explained by non-criminal justice factors.

PRISONS Putting someone in prison means that they are no longer committing
crimes in the community, so the growth in prison populations had some
effect in reducing crime through what criminologists call "incapacitation."
This strategy has some important limitations, however, because prisons can
be schools for crime—they have a criminogenic (crime producing) effect—so
historically unprecedented levels of prison construction and incarceration
will counteract any crime reduction effect. First, criminologists find that a
small minority of offenders commit a disproportionate number of offenses.
Identifying and incarcerating them improves public safety. Further increases
in incarceration mean locking up people whose offenses and criminal histories
are less serious, so there is a diminishing benefit to public safety. American
jurisdictions have always been highly likely to imprison violent offenders, so
increases in incarceration sweep up more people with less significant criminal
propensities. Further, as offenders age, their propensity for crime declines.
Lengthening prison sentences does not improve public safety and reduce
crime rates when prison sentences in the U.S. were already long enough to
hold offenders until they have aged out of serious and violent crime.

Prison also has negative side-effects that counteract its public safety benefits (these are also reviewed below in the discussion of prison as a source of
crime). For example, prisons function as "schools for crime" by deepening
an inmate's ties with other criminals. The prison environment not only undermines personal responsibility and offers little rehabilitation, but it can be
psychologically destructive. Ex-cons have reduced job possibilities because of
their criminal record, and cynicism about the law and justice may reduce their
commitment to obey the law. Prisons also have negative effects on family formation and community well-being. For example, the children of inmates do
less well in school and are more likely to become delinquent. Under conditions of mass incarceration, moving offenders back and forth between prison
and home leads to community disorganization and the erosion of informal
social controls that prevent crime.[77]

One evaluation of the effect of incarceration on the decline in street crime
noted: "The crucial issue is not whether some negative effects [from incarcera-
tion] occur in communities; they most certainly do. Rather it is whether those
effects overwhelm the crime reducing mechanisms of prison, deterrence and
incarceration, which also most certainly occurs."[78] The relative weight of the
positive and negative effects changes over time depending on the number of
people incarcerated.

An extensive review of the research on the decline in street crime by the
Brennan Center for Justice combined the strengths of the highest quality studies with data on additional variables that could influence the crime rate. The

Brennan Center concluded that during the 1990s, incarceration had no effect (0 percent) on violent crime and reduced property crime by 6 percent; from 2000 to 2013, incarceration had no effect (0 percent) on violent crime and reduced property crime by 0.2 percent.[79] The models from seven high-quality studies, when updated with new data for subsequent years, showed that between 2000 and 2013 incarceration caused between a 4 percent decline to a 1 percent increase in violent crime.

This is consistent with the views of Mark Holden, who has led the conservative Koch brothers' initiatives on criminal justice reform: "we put a lot of people in prison, but there's no evidence that made us any safer."[80] It's also consistent with the findings of the 2014 National Academy of Sciences panel on incarceration, which found that "mandatory minimum sentence and three-strike laws have little or no effect on crime rates," and with respect to the effect of the overall increase in incarceration, "the evidence suggests it was unlikely to have been large."[81]

This conclusion is also supported by an analysis showing that between 2007 and 2017, 34 states had declining rates of incarceration and declining rates of street crime.[82] Further, a rigorous study of California after enactment of sweeping reform that reduced the prison and jail population found "no evidence" of an impact on rates of homicide, rape, aggravated assault, robbery, and burglary.[83] In reviewing the research on crime reduction and the social, economic and human costs of incarceration, the 2014 National Academy of Sciences panel on incarceration concluded: "The evidence reviewed in this report reveals that the costs of today's unprecedented rate of incarceration, particularly the long prison sentences imposed under recent sentencing laws, outweigh the observable benefits."[84]

POLICE   Another popular theory is that police actions contributed substantially to the decline in crime rates. However, we have already seen the effect of police arresting people and getting them off the street in the review of the effect of the imprisonment binge, just discussed. The claim to be evaluated now is that the reduction in street crime happened because of 1) increases in the number of police or 2) changes in their strategies—such as community policing or aggressive stop and frisk tactics.

The National Academy of Sciences (2004) panel on policing (quoted earlier) found weak or no evidence that standard (reactive) policing contributed much to declining street crime rates. Within certain levels, adding more police to investigate and respond to service calls is not likely to impact crime rates significantly. Indeed, a 2005 report by the Government Accountability Office found that between 1993 and 2000, President Clinton's COPS plan for 100,000 officers "amounted to about 5 percent of the overall decline."[85]

The Brennan Center analysis of the crime decline suggests that the increasing number of —from sources in addition to COPS—had a "downward effect on crime in the 1990s, likely between 0 and 10 percent." But the effect did not continue into the 2000s because the number of police per 1,000 population leveled off and then declined.[86] While the police played some role in the decline of street crime as public guardians, scholars note the "crucial part" played by community groups and "residents, mobilized in new organizations specifically formed to build community life and control violence."[87]

The second claim involves assessing a variety of tactics that a recent National Academy of Sciences (2018) panel categorized as proactive policing,[88] some of which could have a modest impact. But to be responsible for a long-term, geographically widespread crime decline, strategies must be widely implemented, and do more than temporarily suppress crime at a hot spot or displace it elsewhere in a jurisdiction—but both of these points are largely lacking from the knowledge base, according to the panel.[89] Community policing has been widely implemented, but the panel found its impact "on crime prevention and control remains questionable."[90] More promising strategies like problem-solving policing that tries to change underlying conditions[91] have not been implemented widely enough to have contributed to a substantial decline in the crime rate.[92]

The war on crime led to a variety of aggressive forms of policing. According to the 2004 National Academy of Sciences panel on policing: "There is a widespread perception among police, policy makers, and the public that enforcement strategies (primarily arrest) applied broadly against offenders committing minor offenses lead to reductions in serious crime. Research does not provide strong support for this proposition."[93] The 2018 policing panel found "mixed outcomes" for city-wide Stop, Question, and Frisk programs, with better outcomes for deployment in geographically smaller areas and focused on guns or high-risk repeat offenders.[94]

Consider that police in New York City went from 685,000 "reasonable suspicion" stops in 2011 to 46,000 three years later[95] (after a judge declared them unconstitutional), and both the crime and murder rate continued to fall. Similarly, "broken windows" policing often meant zero tolerance policies for minor wrongdoing, but the 2018 panel found that "aggressive practices based solely on increasing the misdemeanor arrest rate to control disorder generate small to null impacts on crime."[96] And aggressive policing can have criminogenic impacts, at least among minority youth, who experience stops as "physically invasive and abusive" in ways that "increased [their] engagement in delinquent behavior."[97]

NONCRIMINAL JUSTICE FACTORS   A variety of studies attribute the decline in crime rates to factors other than criminal justice policies. Alfred Blumstein argues that the extreme growth in violence during the late 1980s and early 1990s was driven by a "homicide epidemic" made up primarily of murders committed by young men using guns. This was the period in which crack cocaine was introduced into inner cities. Older drug dealers were being incarcerated, so juveniles were recruited into the drug business because they were "less vulnerable to the punishments imposed by the increasingly punitive adult criminal justice system."[98] At the same time there was a large influx of handguns into inner cities, often with higher power and more bullets than traditional handguns. The mixture of young men and powerful guns was highly volatile, and conflicts that previously would have been resolved by fists or knives were increasingly solved with guns, indeed, often with extremely lethal semiautomatic pistols. Blumstein observed,

> It is somewhat ironic that the growth in violence with handguns was at least partly a consequence of the drug war's incarceration of many of the older drug sellers.... As older sellers were taken off the street, the drug market turned to younger individuals, particularly inner-city African Americans. The reduction in age of the workers in the crack trade entailed a predictable increase in violence, as the inclination to deliberate before acting is simply less developed in the young.[99]

By 1993, murders started to decline and so too did homicide arrests of young men. Blumstein acknowledged that the imprisonment binge played a small role in this decline, but crime was still rising in the 1980s, when the prison population had already been growing for a decade.[100] Also, the growth in violent crime was driven by turf wars between inner-city drug gangs that were not disrupted by incarceration. After enough fighting, more or less stable informal distribution agreements arise and the rate of violence subsides—not because the police have succeeded but because the (surviving) drug dealers create a more stable inner-city business. The late James Fyfe, distinguished criminologist and former New York City police captain, commented, "When a new illegal and profitable substance comes along, there is fighting and scratching for control. Then dealers kill each other off, and the market stabilizes and the amount of violence decreases."[101] The turf wars among drug gangs that were a "staple of the late 1980s and early 1990s" gave way to the "routinization of the drug trade."[102] The increased use of cell phones also disrupted the pattern of drug dealing where gangs controlled dealing on street corners: "as the turf lost its value, so did the turf war."[103]

Further crime reductions occurred as the popularity of crack cocaine declined, which reduced the profitability of drug markets and the associated violence. Blumstein noted: "As recognition of its deleterious effects became widespread, word spread through the streets that crack was an undesirable drug... diminishing the number of new users." He also pointed to the reduction in the use of handguns by juveniles, credited to a combination of police pressure and action by community groups trying to clean up their neighborhoods, and the robust economy at the time that "provided legitimate job opportunities for [many young people], which has created incentives to avoid illegal activities."[104] Following the recession of 2008, Congress extended unemployment benefits several times, thus providing people with resources that prevented or delayed criminal activities. In previous economic downturns, inflation was high (meaning consumer prices increased dramatically) and created strong "underground markets, specifically markets for stolen goods."[105] Indeed, criminologist Richard Rosenfeld found that homicide rates would have been 24 percent higher if inflation had been as high as it was in the 1970s and 1980s.[106]

The final non-criminal justice factor to consider is the reduction in lead in the environment starting in the 1970s. Lead is a neurotoxin, which means it is a poison that kills brain cells and the nerves connecting them; it "can muck up brain cell communication and growth."[107] Children exposed to lead can have permanent problems like lowered IQ and attention deficits, which can create problems in school, and an increased likelihood of dropping out or being expelled and then becoming delinquent. Lead also affects "the executive functions—judgment, impulse control, anticipation of consequences"—making aggressive and anti-social behavior more likely as children grow up into teenagers and young adults with decreased self-command.[108] Indeed, after an extensive review of the literature on the sources, uses, and effects of lead, criminologist Kimberly Barrett concludes that "empirical assessments of lead and crime have demonstrated associations between lead exposure and homicide rates, delinquency, and violent crime" as well as a variety of other conduct disorders.[109]

The accumulated data linking lead to permanent neurobehavioral disorders (especially through the exposure of preschool children) was so strong that in 1974 the Environmental Protection Agency (EPA) began shifting the country to using unleaded gasoline, thus preventing tons of lead in car exhaust from entering the air. They also removed lead from paint, which reduced the likelihood of poor and hungry children ingesting lead by eating chipped or peeling paint. Both of these actions greatly reduced the amount of lead in the blood of children, which would reduce crime as those children grew up.

Environmental and health economist Jessica Reyes argues that "between 1992 and 2002, the phase-out of lead from gasoline was responsible for approximately a 56% decline in violent crime"—and "may cause further declines in the future."[110] At a National Academy of Sciences roundtable, "most experts seem to believe that lead played some role, but maybe not as high as the finding presented by Reyes."[111] Criminologist Mark Kleiman, author of a book on "how to have less crime and less punishment," says that the EPA regulations "were a major driver of the crime decline that started in the mid-1990s."[112]

A number of other theories of the crime decline have also been suggested, including that the legalization of abortion in the 1970s decreased crime decades later because "women who have abortions are most at risk to give birth to children who would engage in criminal activity."[113] Other researchers link lower crime rates to increased obesity,[114] increased immigration (they stay out of trouble to avoid being deported),[115] increased time playing video games,[116] and the increased number of local nonprofit organizations that delivered community services.[117] The increased use of electronic benefit transfer (EBT "Bridge") cards reduces cash for robberies and burglaries.[118]

Whatever the relative merits of these theories, none involves the success of the criminal justice system. A recent review of 24 theories of the crime decline found eight that were "promising explanations," but only one of those—offender reentry programs—involved the criminal justice system.[119] Indeed, Tonry argues that the crime decline is a global phenomenon, so U.S. criminal justice policy was "pretty much besides the point in terms of crime rates and patterns."[120]

So while politicians claim credit for the recent declines in crime, the real story appears to be that the enormous growth in our prison population over the last decades, coupled with questionable police tactics, has contributed only slightly to the decline. Non-criminal justice system factors were the main cause of reducing our extremely high crime rates to rates that are lower *but high nonetheless*. In short, crime is still rampant and, for all their crowing and claiming credit, politicians and criminal justice policy makers are still losing the war against crime.

In sum, when we look behind the politicians' claims to have turned the tide against violence, the fact remains that criminal justice policy is failing to make our lives substantially safer. It appears that our government is neglecting to fulfill the most fundamental task of governance: keeping our streets and homes safe, assuring us of what the Founding Fathers called "domestic tranquility," and providing us with the minimum requirement of civilized society.

One way to come to terms with this failure is to look at the *excuses* that are offered for it. This we will do—but mainly to show that they do not hold up! We shall look at these excuses in detail and show that they do not explain our failure to reduce crime, and we will present evidence to support the claim that we could reduce crime and the harm it causes if we wanted to. What has to be explained is not why we *cannot* reduce crime but why we *will not!*

Oddly enough, this paradoxical result points us in the direction of an answer to our question. Failure is, after all, in the eye of the beholder. Here lies the key to understanding our failing criminal justice system: The failure of policies and institutions can serve vested interests and thus amount to success for them! If we look at the system as "wanting" to reduce crime, it is an abysmal failure that we cannot understand. If we look at it as *not* wanting to reduce crime, it's a howling success, and all we need to understand is *why* the goal of the criminal justice system is to fail to reduce crime. If we can understand this, then the system's "failure," as well as its obstinate refusal to implement the policies that could remedy that "failure," becomes perfectly understandable. In other words, we can make more sense out of criminal justice policy by assuming that its goal is to maintain crime than by assuming that its goal is to reduce crime!

The remainder of this chapter explores the excuses for the failure to reduce crime and offers evidence to back up our assertion that there are policies that could reduce crime that we refuse to implement. We then briefly outline the relationship between the Pyrrhic defeat theory and the criminological theory of Kai Erikson and Émile Durkheim, to which it is akin. The chapter closes with a word on the work of Michel Foucault, whose views run parallel for a while to those defended in this book before heading off in a different direction.

THREE EXCUSES THAT WILL NOT WASH

Because the crime rate is down substantially, many Americans may not feel the rates of crime and violence are high. But rates are higher than in 1965, when crime was a big enough problem that President Johnson established the President's Commission on Law Enforcement and Administration of Justice to investigate the causes and nature of crime, to collect existing knowledge about our criminal justice system, and to make recommendations about how that system might better meet "the challenge of crime in a free society." A few years later, the 1968 Safe Streets Act was, according to the *Congressional Quarterly Almanac*, "the most extensive anticrime legislation in the nation's history" to that point in time.[121]

When the Commission started its work and interest in the Safe Streets Act began to take shape, the violent crime rate was 200 per 100,000 in the population (in 1965) and climbed to 383 in 2017.[122] Even now, with crime rates down, the rate of intentional homicide for the U.S. – at 5.4 per 100,000 – is closer to the rate of 7.7 for countries listed by the World Bank as "fragile and conflict affected" than the rate of 1 per 100,000 for the European Union.[123]

This high rate of crime and violence exists in spite of ongoing wars on crime and drugs. When the commission met, about $4 billion was being spent annually at the national, state, and local levels to pay for police, courts, and correctional facilities.[124] That would be about $30 billion in current dollars[125], yet in 2015 justice expenditures were more than $284 billion.[126] And this doesn't even count the more than $100 billion spent each year on private security,[127] the extra money people spend to live in gated communities, and all the personal safety products people buy.

Those who recognize the U.S. has a high rate of crime and violence make excuses for our failure to reduce crime significantly in the face of increased expenditure, personnel, research, and knowledge. Three excuses have sufficient currency to make them worthy of consideration.

First Excuse: We're Too Soft!

One excuse is that we are too soft on crime.[128] From the 1970s to mid-1990s, "85 to 90 percent of the public consistently expressed the opinion that criminal sentencing was 'not harsh enough'," and in 2016 more than 45 percent still supported that view.[129] Conservative critics of criminal justice policy have long maintained the view that "non-punishment is the major 'social' cause of crime."[130] This view is hard to disprove because, no matter how harsh we are, one can always say we should have been harsher – although the evidence presented above demonstrates that getting tougher had only modest effects in reducing crime and may have some criminogenic effects.

Comparisons with other countries do not suggest that the U.S. is soft or lenient in any major respect: not in the range of acts covered by law (especially drug use and prostitution); not in the likelihood of being arrested, charged, convicted, or sentenced to prison; not in the actual time served in prison; and not in the likelihood of having parole or probation revoked (especially for technical reasons rather than because of a new crime).[131]

The U.S. is not unique in criminalizing drug possession and sales but is more likely to use incarceration—in some "67 percent of drug cases, followed distantly by the Netherlands at 46 percent and Switzerland (38 percent)." Prison sentences were an average of 23 months, twice as long as the countries with the next longest sentences (England and Wales).[132]

The U.S. drug war especially stands in contrast to Portugal, which in 2001 decriminalized "the possession of *all* drugs, when deemed for personal use."[133] In 2003, Canada decriminalized possession of small amounts of marijuana and started embracing "safe injection centers" for users of harder drugs.[134] In response to a government challenge, Canada's Supreme Court ruled unanimously that one of these projects, Insite, should remain open: "Insite has saved lives and improved health without increasing the incidence of drug use and crime in the surrounding area. It is supported by the Vancouver police."[135]

At year-end 2016, the U.S. rate of incarceration (in jails and prisons) was 655 per 100,000 in the national population. For the United Kingdom, it was 139, for Germany 77, and for Canada (a society much like our own), it was 107 prisoners for every 100,000 persons in the national population.[136] Before and after the recent declines in crime, we had *far* greater percentages of our population under lock and key than comparably advanced European nations, as well as our neighbor to the north.

Nor should it be forgotten that we are the only Western industrialized nation that still has the death penalty, let alone (until 2005) the only such nation that executed people who had committed crimes while under the age of 18. At the close of 2016, the state and federal prison systems held 2,814 prisoners under sentence of death and executed 20 individuals that year.[137] Also, the United States makes much more extensive use of the sentence of *life without the possibility of parole* than other Western nations,[138] and is the only developed nation to impose them on juveniles.[139] We also use solitary confinement more frequently, allow it for more consecutive days, and for more total days per month and year – even for juveniles – and often without a mental health screening.[140]

Finally, our incarceration rate doesn't include those who are currently on probation and parole. When these are added to those in jail or prison, the number of *adults* under some form of correctional supervision at yearend 2016 was 6.6 million; that is, one of every 38 American adults—2.6 percent of the U.S. adult population—was incarcerated or on probation or parole.[141] The U.S. is also exceptional in its imposition of criminal justice fines and fees, as well as imposing collateral consequences (civil penalties that can effect housing, government benefits, employment, and many other areas).[142]

Our high rate of crime and lethal violence has persisted in the face of decades of getting tougher, leading one criminologist to characterize the get-tough approach to crime as a social experiment that has been tested and found to fail.[143]

Second Excuse: A Cost of Modern Life

Another excuse is that crime is an inescapable companion of any complex, populous, technologically advanced society. As the population grows and society becomes more complex, and particularly more *urbanized*, we will have more crime as inevitably as we will have more ulcers and more traffic. These are costs of modern life, the benefits of which abound and clearly outweigh the costs. Crime, then, takes its place alongside death and taxes. We can fight, but we cannot win, and we shouldn't tear our hair out about it.

This is less an explanation than a recipe for resignation. Furthermore, it does not account for the fact that other complex, populous, highly industrialized and technologically advanced nations such as Japan have crime rates that are considerably lower than ours. Japan has slightly less than half the U.S. population crowded onto a landmass about the size of California and Oregon. In 2016, Japan had a homicide rate of less than 1 per 100,000 (895 homicides) and about 23 violent offenses for every 100,000 inhabitants. That same year, the United States had a homicide rate of 5.3 per 100,000 (17,250 homicides) and a violent crime rate of 386 for every 100,000 inhabitants.[144] In 2016, Tokyo, with a population of 13.7 million densely packed people, recorded 81 homicides;[145] that same year, the entire state of Illinois, with almost the same population (12.8 million), had 1,054 homicides—and the 1.8 million residents of West Virginia committed the same number of homicides as the 13.7 million who live in Tokyo.[146]

Table 1.1 lists rates of intentional homicide for the U.S. and a sampling of countries in different stages of development. Our rate is an outlier among the industrialized democratic nations, and closer to the rate for countries the United Nations classifies as least developed. Currie's review of international homicide data, which he believes provides the most reliable comparisons, leads him to conclude:

> The risks of dying by violence in the United States are more than double those of the next closest advanced industrial country—Canada—and roughly six times the average for the European Union. In the mid-2000s, they were 10 times higher than those in Germany or Austria, and 12 times those in the United Kingdom.... The chances of dying by intentional violence among youth aged 15–29 years in the United States are 10 times those of the Netherlands and Denmark, 16 times those in Norway, and more than 25 times those in Germany. Indeed, the violent death rate for young Americans more closely resembles that of youth in Russia, or some Latin American nations, than it does the rest of the affluent industrial world.[147]

The "costs of modern life," or urbanization, excuse also fails to account for the striking differences in the crime rates *within* our own modern, complex, populous, and urbanized nation. Within the United States in 2017, the violent crime rate ranged from a high of 829 per 100,000 in Alaska to 121 in Maine, and homicide rates ranged from 12.4 in Louisiana to 1.0 in New Hampshire.[148] According to FBI data, there is some correlation between city size and crime rate. But the rate of violent crime is higher in cities with populations of between 250,000 and 999,999 than in cities of more than one million people.[149] Official data suggests most rural areas have less crime than urban areas. However, the emerging area of rural criminology challenges the stereotype of idyllic safe rural communities and finds that the FBI data for violent and property crime does not include rural crimes like labor trafficking, environmental harm (especially from resource extraction), and drug production and abuse.[150]

TABLE 1.1   Rates of Intentional Homicide for Countries at Different Stages of Economic Development

Country	Intentional Homicide Rate (per 100,000 people)
Japan, Indonesia, Norway, Switzerland, Netherlands, Spain, Portugal, Greece, Ireland, Australia	Less than 1
New Zealand, Sweden, Germany, United Kingdom, Bosnia and Herzegovina, Canada	1–1.9
Hungary, Bangladesh, Rwanda	2–2.9
India, Chile	3–3.9
Somalia, Pakistan, Kazakhstan, Kenya	4–4.9
United States	5.4
Least developed countries: UN classification	6.2

Source: UN Office on Drugs and Crime's International Homicide Statistics database. Rates for 2014–2016.

Even if death and taxes are inevitable (unfortunately not in that order), some die prematurely and some die suspiciously, and some pay too much in taxes and some pay none at all. None of these variations is inevitable or unimportant, and so too with crime. Even if crime is inevitable in modern societies, its rates and types vary extensively, and this is neither inevitable nor unimportant. Indeed, the variations in crime rates between modern cities and nations are proof that the *extent* of crime is not a simple consequence of urbanization or modernization. Other factors must explain the differences. These differences suggest that although some crimes may be an unavoidable consequence of urbanization, this in no way excuses our failure to reduce crime at least to the lowest rates reported in modern cities and nations.

Third Excuse: Blame It on the Kids!

A third excuse attributes crime to young people, particularly young men between the ages of 14 and 25: Young people in our society, especially males, find themselves emerging from the security of childhood into the frightening chaos of adult responsibility. Little is or can be done by the adult society to ease the transition by providing meaningful outlets for the newly bursting youthful energy aroused in still immature and irresponsible youngsters. Hence, these youngsters both mimic the power of manhood, and attack the society that frightens and ignores them by resorting to violent crime. The media sensationalizes these crimes for ratings and spread fear, and the troubled teen industry profits by stoking concern about deviant youth.[151] We have another explanation that amounts to a recipe for resignation (and increased repression) because we can no more expect to reduce crime than we can hope to eradicate adolescence.

TABLE 1.2   Crime Rates Compared with Youth Population, 1960–2010

14–24 Year Olds (% of Population)	Violent Crime Rate (Per 100,000 Persons)	Property Crime Rate (Per 100,000 Persons)	Year
14	404	2,942	2010
15.1	161	1,726	1960
15.4	507	3,618	2000
16.2	730	5,073	1990
19.9	364	3,621	1970
20.4	597	5,353	1980

Sources: Sourcebook 2003, Table 3.106, pp. 278–279; *UCR—2005*, Table 1; *UCR—2010*, Table 1; *StatAbst—2011*, Table 8, p. 12; *StatAbst—2008*, Table 7, p. 10; *StatAbst—2001*, Table 11, p. 13; *StatAbst—1995*, p. 17; *StatAbst—1992*, pp. 14–15; and *StatAbst—1987*, p. 14.

Youngsters do show up disproportionately in crime statistics. In 2017, persons between the ages of 15 and 24 constituted 13.5 percent of the nation's population, but they represented 28.5 percent of those arrested for all crimes.[152] However, there are problems with attributing crime to youth. The most important is that crime rates have grown faster than either the absolute number of young people or their percentage of the population.

Table 1.2 compares national crime rates over the past 40 years with the percentage of the population represented by people aged 14 to 24. A strong correlation between the youth population and crime would mean that as the percentage of young people in the population increased (column 1 in Table 1.2), violent and property crime rates (columns 2 and 3) would also rise. While there is some correlation between them, there are also important divergences: The percentage of young people in the population was about the same in 2000 and 1960, yet the crime rate in 2000 was almost *four times higher* than that of 1960. Obviously, this growth in crime cannot be attributed to youth. And between 1980 and 1990 the youth percentage dropped more than 4 points while the violent crime rate grew significantly. In that same period, the number of 14 to 24 year olds decreased absolutely by 5,660,000, while the absolute number of Index crimes rose by over 1 million.[153] Even when crime rates went down recently, they never returned to the levels of the 1940s, when the percentage of young people aged 16 to 24 was about 14, roughly comparable to what it is now.[154] Similar discrepancies show up when the National Crime Victimization Survey (NCVS) is used.

We do not deny that a large number of crimes are committed by young people. The facts suggest, however, that although the number of youngsters in the populace has an important effect on crime rates, it cannot fully explain them. That young people have higher rates of crime than older folks does not mean that young people always have the same rate of crime. When the number of youngsters declined, crime went down but not in proportion to the decline in the youth population. When this group was growing, the crime rates were growing faster. If the crime rate of 15–24 year olds changes, then this certainly is not explained by their youth. Something other than their youth or their numbers must explain why they are committing more crimes than people their age did in other periods.[155]

In any case, the greater likelihood of young people committing crime provides no excuse for failing to reduce the growth of crime at least to the rate at which the number of young people is growing (or shrinking). So another excuse for our failure fails to excuse. To get an idea of what criminal justice policy truly aimed at reducing crime might look like, let's examine the known sources of crime and some promising crime-prevention programs.

KNOWN SOURCES OF CRIME, OR HOW WE COULD REDUCE CRIME IF WE WANTED TO

Currie notes that the amount of crime and violence in a country is "strongly influenced by social policy and can be substantially mitigated, or exacerbated, by it." The level of crime in a society

> represents a social and political choice—not simply an individual one, or even a reflection of abstract, impersonal forces operating pristinely above deliberate human intervention. In short, to a significant extent, we make the world of violence that surrounds us.[156]

We agree and argue that if the United States were serious about crime reduction, much more support would be given to policies that address the known sources of crime. Note that we say *sources* rather than *causes* because pathways to crime are less direct and more complicated than simple cause and effect. We know that poverty, unemployment, and concentrated disadvantage are *sources* of street crime. But, we know as well that most poor, unemployed inner-city residents do not engage in street crime. So we say that poverty and inequality, prison, guns, and drug prohibition are sources because they increase the likelihood of crime and violence.

Poverty and Inequality

Understanding crime requires examining individual choices, and those who commit crimes often say they got involved with crime because it was what was going on in their neighborhood.[157] Understanding neighborhood crime requires examining economic policies about employment, public assistance benefits, education, and taxes. Factors such as the distribution of income, wealth, and economic power shape these policies and the context within which individuals make choices.

The U.S. has higher levels of inequality[158] than other developed democracies, and it also has higher rates of crime, especially violent crime. The *Oxford Handbook of Criminological Theory* states, "the idea that structural inequality contributes to community-level variations in crime is uncontroversial."[159] What is in dispute are the exact mechanisms: Is it strain (limited legitimate opportunities and high cultural value placed on economic success), relative or absolute deprivation, concentrated disadvantage, poverty, reduced loyalty to an unfair society, social disorganization or reduced collective efficacy (the ability of people to come together to solve community problems), and/or subcultural values?[160] One of the most in-depth reviews of the research, covering 214 studies, concluded that "resource/economic deprivation theory" was "well supported": "The relatively strong effects for indicators of resource/economic deprivation on crime remain stable across various methodological conditions."[161]

The hundreds of studies supporting the importance of inequality were based on studies of street crime, but we also maintain (in the next two chapters) that there is a high level of white-collar and corporate crime. Crimes of the powerful cannot be explained by poverty, but they are also related to strain theory and inequality. For example, rich people also desire more—and not all of them are faced with legitimate means to add millions (or billions) to their income. (Because criminology generally ignores class, this point is seldom made.)

Further, Braithwaite synthesizes a number of theoretical connections supported by research when he argues that "Inequality worsens both crimes of poverty motivated by need and crimes of wealth motivated by greed." He believes that "need" applies in an absolute sense to those lacking basic subsistence needs. It also leads to crime based on "the need for a decent standard of living," which includes what people see others having, what whites generally but not as many blacks might enjoy, and what people were led to expect to enjoy by the "advertising and dramatization of bourgeois lifestyles."[162] Violence can be generated by the structural humiliation of the poor, who are surrounded by visions of the "American Dream" and messages implying that they are personal failures because success is attainable for all.

The wealthy continue to pursue additional wealth because money still has value for them. With increasing inequality, wealth is concentrated in the hands of those who can access financial institutions and create "new forms of illegitimate opportunity" involving fraud—"and the more capital, the bigger the opportunities."[163] Some of these novel illegitimate strategies include the savings and loan frauds, the Enron-era financial misstatements, and the financial hijinks that led to the 2008–2009 financial crisis (see Chapter 3).

Crime is also more likely if inequality means that the wealthy are unaccountable for their harmful actions—as in the 2008–9 financial crisis, in which financial firms that were "too big to fail" were not held criminally accountable. Braithwaite also argues that increasing inequality makes crime more likely because the wealthy come to have less respect for those who are poorer. The wealthy develop an ideology, a system of beliefs that justifies inequality and their exploitation of others as natural, inevitable, and ultimately fair. (Chapter 4 elaborates on issues of ideology.)

While some level of inequality may be inevitable, that does not make the extent of U.S. inequality inevitable or fair. Nobel Prize winning economist Joseph Stiglitz notes that "inequality is the result of political factors as much as of economic ones."[164] The U.S. has chosen, through political processes heavily influenced by the wealthy, to have extreme inequality. Table 1.3 shows

TABLE 1.3 Percent of Income Earned and Income Limits in the U.S., by Fifths, 2017

Population Share	Share of Total Income	Highest Income in Group (Limit)
Lowest 20% (poorest)	3.1%	$24,638
Second	8.2%	$47,110
Third	14.3%	$77,552
Fourth	23%	$126, 855
Top 20% (richest)	51.5%	$2,000,000,000

Sources: U.S. Census Bureau, Current Population Survey, Annual Social and Economic Supplements, Historical Income Tables: Households, Table H-1. Kayla Fontenot, Jessica Semega, and Melissa Kollar, U.S. Census Bureau, *Current Population Reports,* P60–263, *Income and Poverty in the United States: 2017* (Washington, DC: U.S. Government Printing Office, 2018), Table 2. Nathan Vardi, "The 25 Highest-Earning Hedge Fund Managers and Traders" *Forbes,* April 17, 2018.

that 80 percent of Americans have an income of less than $126,855. The top 5 percent of income earners starts at $237,034, but goes up to $2 billion in 2017. (That's down from the nearly $4 billion hedge fund manager John Paulson made in 2007 by creating situations where the worse the mortgage crisis became the more profit he made.)[165]

Wealth—the lifetime accumulation of assets minus debt—is even more unequally distributed than income. This is of concern because wealth affects social, political, and economic power. In 2018, the poorest 50 percent collectively owned 1 percent of all the wealth, and the top 1 percent owned 32 percent. The richest 1 percent own more wealth than the bottom 90 percent, and the distribution of wealth has become more unequal over the last 40 years.[166]

Those at the bottom, whom Braithwaite believes are motivated to crime by "the need for a decent standard of living," are primarily impoverished inner-city youth with a very limited likelihood of entering college or amassing sufficient capital (legally) to start a business or to get into the high-wage, skilled job markets. In 2018, among those in the crime-prone ages of 16 to 19, 11.3 percent of white youngsters and 21.9 percent of black youngsters were jobless. (This pattern of black unemployment rates being twice the white rate has characterized adult unemployment rates for 50 years; currently 3.5 percent of white workers are unemployed compared to 6.5 percent of blacks.)[167]

Many of these young people have been brought up in poverty. In 2017, 17.1 percent of American children were living in families below the poverty level, including about 28.8 percent of black children and 24.7 percent of Latino children, compared with 10.5 percent of white children.[168] While some people can and do escape poverty and rise in the class structure, this is rarer than Americans believe.[169] And, "despite less discrimination" than in previous decades, "the odds of escaping the station of one's birth are no higher today than they were decades ago."[170]

We know that poverty and inequality are *sources* of crime, yet we do little to improve the life chances of the vast majority of the inner-city poor. Many experts agree that "policies aimed at ameliorating the effects of economic deprivation and family disruption" are "likely to have a significant impact on crime reduction."[171] Criminologist Todd Clear suggested the same in 1993: "Let's start investing in things that really reduce crime: good schools, jobs and a future for young parents and their children."[172] Why don't we?

Prison

We know that prison produces more criminals than it cures. As far back as 1973, the National Advisory Commission on Criminal Justice Standards and Goals recommended building no new adult prisons because "the prison, the reformatory and jail have achieved only a shocking record of failure. There is overwhelming evidence that these institutions create crime rather than prevent it."[173] Contrary to the Commission's recommendation, the U.S. built a record number of "warehouse" prisons,[174] called that because they make no attempt at rehabilitation.

In 2014, the National Academy of Science panel on incarceration reviewed literature that "concludes that there is little evidence of a specific deterrent or rehabilitative effect of incarceration, and that all the evidence on the effect of imprisonment on reoffending points to either no effect or a criminogenic effect."[175] A joint publication by Havard's Kennedy School and the National Institute of Justice stated that juvenile facilities

> are damaging the very people they are supposed to help and have been for generations. It is difficult to find an area of U.S. policy where the benefits and costs are more out of balance, where the evidence of failure is clearer, or where we know with more clarity what we should be doing differently.[176]

A Bureau of Justice Statistics (BJS) study found that 67.5 percent of inmates released in 1994 were rearrested within three years "almost exclusively for a felony or serious misdemeanor," and almost 52 percent were back in prison.[177] A newer BJS study using data from inmates released in 2005 finds that 68 percent were rearrested within three years, and 83 percent within nine years.[178]

Prisons seem to do everything but give inmates the skills they will need to make it on the outside. The bipartisan Commission on Safety and Abuse in America's Prisons found that:

> there is still too much violence in America's prisons and jails, too many facilities that are crowded to the breaking point, too little medical and mental health care, unnecessary uses of solitary confinement and other forms of segregation, a desperate need for the kinds of productive activities that discourage violence and make rehabilitation possible, and a culture in many prisons and jails that pits staff against prisoners and management against staff.[179]

Prison inmates are denied autonomy and privacy and are subjected to indignities and acts of violence as regular features of their confinement, all of which is worsened by overcrowding. Prisoners are not offered training on how to handle daily problems in competent and socially constructive ways, inside or outside of prison. The predictable result "is that the prison's survivors become tougher, more pugnacious, and less able to feel for themselves and others, while its nonsurvivors become weaker, more susceptible, and less able to control their lives."[180]

Prison rapes are common, and provoke more violence. The organization Just Detention International reports on the consequences of prison rapes: "Feelings of rage can be suppressed until release, when survivors may engage in violent, antisocial behavior."[181] According to a Human Rights Watch report, "the only way to avoid the repetition of sexual abuse, many prisoners assert, is to strike back violently." The report quotes a victim of prison rape saying, "People start to treat you right, once you become deadly."[182]

Further, according to the National Center on Addiction and Substance Abuse (NCASA) at Columbia University, 65 percent of prison and jail inmates met medical criteria for substance abuse and addiction, but only 11 percent received treatment for this disorder.[183] Among jail inmates, 60 percent reported having symptoms of a mental health disorder in the prior year. But the Vera Institute found that 83 percent of them "did not receive mental health care after admission"; when combined with the lights, noise, and threats of violence, "jail is likely to mean further deterioration in their illness."[184]

Once on the outside, burdened with the stigma of a prison record and rarely trained in a marketable skill, inmates generally find "their lives often continue to be characterized by violence, joblessness, substance abuse, family breakdown, and neighborhood disadvantage."[185] Nor does this affect all groups in America alike. According to Tonry in his presidential address to the American Society of Criminology:

> If its aims were to reduce black men's chances of earning a decent living, or being successfully married and a good father, or being socialized into prosocial values, it is hard to know how the criminal justice system could do those things better.[186]

In addition, a study by the Sentencing Project indicates that the large number of African American men who have been convicted of felonies and, therefore, deprived of their right to vote, is "having a profound [negative!] impact on the black community's ability to participate in the political process."[187]

Much of the recent increase in imprisonment has been of inner-city black men who were involved in families and who had at least part-time legitimate employment at the time of their arrest and incarceration. The result is that massive imprisonment undermines the family and other community institutions, weakens the stigma of incarceration and thus the deterrent value of imprisonment, and strengthens ties between prison gangs and offenders on the street.[188]

Can we honestly act as if we do not know that our prison system (including our failure to ensure a meaningful post-release noncriminal alternative for the ex-con) is a *source* of crime? Should we really pretend, then, that we do not *know* why ex-cons turn to crime? Recidivism does not happen because ex-cons miss their alma mater:

> a tough veneer that precludes seeking help for personal problems, the generalized mistrust that comes from the fear of exploitation, and the tendency to strike out in response to minimal provocations are highly functional in many prison contexts and problematic virtually everywhere else.[189]

Guns

Most people know the expression "Guns don't kill people, people kill people," but guns make it much easier for people to kill people, so the huge stock of civilian guns (especially handguns) is a source of violence.[190] It is not a coincidence that Americans are heavily armed and have a firearm homicide rate that is "extraordinarily high by the standards of other industrialized countries" according to Oxford's *Crime and Public Policy*.[191] A recent survey found that 44 percent of American adults knew someone who had been shot.[192]

We have about four times the number of guns per capita than countries such as Canada, New Zealand, Germany, France, and Sweden.[193] As a result, the U.S. has a death rate from firearm homicides 20 times higher than a sample of 23 other developed nations.[194] In addition, "children ages 5 to 14 in America are 13 times as likely to be murdered with guns as children in other industrialized countries," according to David Hemenway, a public health specialist at Harvard.[195] And, because the fatality rate for robberies using a gun is three times higher than for robberies with knives and ten times higher than for robberies with other weapons, countries like Italy and Australia that have both effective gun control and robbery rates comparable to the U.S., have far fewer robberies that end up as homicides.[196]

The President's Crime Commission concluded in 1965 that "as long as there is no effective gun-control legislation, violent crimes and the injuries they inflict will be harder to reduce than they might otherwise be."[197] But there has been virtually no gun control, even as guns have been designed to hold more bullets and fire more quickly, leading to more and deadlier mass shootings. Gun violence takes its toll especially among the young in minority communities. A medical journal article about "alarming trends" said, "It is sobering to reflect that in 2017 there were 144 US police officers who died in the line of duty, fewer than 1000 deaths among active duty military, and 2462 school-age children killed with firearms."[198]

In the face of facts like these, Congress regularly directs the Bureau of Alcohol, Tobacco, Firearms, and Explosives (ATF) not to put gun sales records into a computer database, with the result that police officers tracing guns used in crimes must pore over boxes of paper files. "It can take people at the tracing center 70 phone calls on one trace alone" to find the right box, "and there is no effort afoot to make it work any better."[199]

Congress passed a law prohibiting ATF from "making more than one unannounced inspection a year on a gun dealer, a rule that serves no purpose other than protecting unscrupulous dealers."[200] And when inspections turn up serious problems, even among gun sellers with a history of not complying with the law, senior ATF officials allow the stores to keep their licenses.[201] Congress has prohibited federal agencies from promoting gun control—but because that term is not defined, agencies shy away from research on gun injuries.[202]

The Brady Law is America's main piece of gun-control legislation. It requires a criminal record check for gun buyers. While this law prohibits sales of guns to individuals with prior felony convictions, it applies only to dealers and not private sellers, such as at gun shows and sales through websites.

Can we believe that our leaders sincerely want to cut down on violent crime and the injuries it produces when they oppose even as much as *registering* guns or *licensing* gun owners, much less actually restricting the sale and movement of guns as a matter of national policy? (Many people wrongly believe that universal registration and licensing of guns exists, when in fact only a few states require this.) Or when so many guns sales do not require a background check?

Can we really believe that if guns were less readily available, violent criminals would simply switch to other weapons to commit the same number of crimes and do the same amount of damage? Is there a weapon other than the handgun that works as quickly, that allows its user so safe a distance, or that makes the criminal's physical strength (or courage, for that matter) irrelevant? Could a bank robber hold a row of tellers at bay with a switchblade? Studies indicate that, if gun users switched to the next deadliest weapon—the knife—and attempted the same number of crimes, we could still expect *two-thirds fewer fatalities* because the fatality rate of the knife is roughly one-third that of the gun. In other words, if guns were eliminated and the number of crimes held steady, we could expect to save as many as two out of every three persons who are now the victims of firearm homicide.

Drug Prohibition

The United States has an enormous drug abuse and addiction problem. There is considerable evidence, however, that our attempts to cure it are worse than the disease itself. Most people associate drugs with crime because addicts often steal to support their habits. However, the cost of street drugs is high because of their illegality. Everyone in the distribution chain needs to profit enough to compensate for the risk of being caught and locked up. Much of the violence surrounding the drug trade is also related to drugs being illegal because then the drug trade is in the hands of gangs and organized crime, and their disputes are not resolved through free markets or the legal system. In response, the U.S. has engaged in a war on drugs that has cost billions, incarcerated millions, and has brought about little change in drug usage. Moreover, the criminalization of drugs undercuts public health efforts to deal with drug addiction. Paul Goldstein provides a useful categorization of the relationship between drugs and crime:

- *Pharmacological/psychological consequences:* Criminal activity is caused by the chemical properties of the drug acting on the person's brain.
- *Economic/compulsive crimes:* Criminal activity is caused by drug users committing crimes to get money to support their habit.
- *Systemic crime:* Criminal activity like violence and corruption are a regular part of doing business in the illicit drug trade because there is no regulation and formal dispute-resolution mechanisms are unavailable.[203]

About the pharmacological consequences of drugs, according to Blumstein, the drug

> that has the strongest pharmacological effect is alcohol.... Heroin is a downer, so heroin doesn't do much. And there hasn't been shown to be much pharmacological effect of the other serious drugs on crime, not anything comparable to that of alcohol, which has been shown to be a strong stimulator of violence.[204]

James Q. Wilson, a defender of the prohibition of heroin and other drugs, admits that "there are apparently no specific pathologies—serious illnesses or physiological deterioration—that are known to result from heroin use per se."[205] Prior to 1914, when anyone could go into a drugstore and purchase heroin and other opiates the way we buy aspirin today, hundreds of thousands of upstanding, law-abiding citizens were hooked.[206] On the basis of available scientific evidence, there is every reason to suspect that we do our bodies more *irreversible* damage by smoking cigarettes and drinking liquor than by using heroin. The physical damage associated with heroin use is attributable to the trauma of withdrawal, a product not so much of heroin as of its occasional unobtainability.

Even though many states have legalized marijuana, the FBI reported almost 600,000 arrests for marijuana possession in 2017.[207] This is so even though the active ingredient in marijuana "is a very safe drug," according to *The Science of Marijuana.*[208] A 2007 study of Florida autopsies found that "cocaine, heroin and all methamphetamines caused 989 deaths, while legal opioids—strong painkillers in brand name drugs like Vicodin and OxyContin—caused 2,328." No deaths were attributed to marijuana.[209] And a Police Foundation review in 2000 concluded that: "By any of the major criteria of harm—mortality, morbidity, toxicity, addictiveness and relationship with crime—cannabis is less harmful than any of the other major illicit drugs, or than alcohol or tobacco."[210]

Some argue that the evil of drugs (especially heroin and crack) is that they are *addicting,* because this is a bad thing even if the addicting substance is not itself harmful. It is hard to deny that the image of a person enslaved to a chemical is ugly and repugnant to our sense that the dignity of human beings lies in their capacity to control their destinies. More questionable, however, is whether this is, in the case of adults, anybody's business but their own. Even so, suppose we agree that addiction is an evil worthy of prevention. Isn't imprisoning someone as punishment for using drugs an irrational way to express concern about the enslavement of addiction—especially when we could offer treatment instead? And, doesn't that make us hypocrites given our inconsistent policies regarding all our other addictions? What about cigarette smoking, which unlike heroin, contributes to cancer and heart disease? Nicotine's addictiveness is similar to that of heroin and *more addicting than cocaine,* more likely to addict the new user, and more difficult to quit once addicted.[211] What about the millions of alcoholics in the nation working their way through their livers and into their graves?

Former Washington, DC, Police Chief Maurice Turner helps explain the economic crimes associated with drugs:

> If you see an addict going through withdrawal, he's in some kind of damn pain.... When they get pretty well strung out, they have about a $100- to $120-a-day habit. When they get that type of habit, they're going to have to steal approximately six times that much [because fences don't pay list price].[212]

Professor Blumstein agrees that "you need money to buy drugs, so the higher the price of the drug, the greater the incentive to commit the crime."[213] The high price of drugs is partly due to them being illegal; there is nothing about heroin itself, for example, that makes it extremely costly. However, once sale or possession of heroin is made a serious criminal offense, a number of consequences follow. First, the prices go up because those who supply it face grave penalties, while those who want it, want it bad. Second, because the supply (and the quality) of the drug fluctuates depending on how vigorously the agents of the law try to prevent it, addicts live in constant uncertainty about the next fix and must devote much of their wit and energy to getting it and to getting enough money to pay for it. They do not, then, fit easily into the routines of a nine-to-five job, even if they could get one that would pay enough to support their habits.

If we add to this the fact that overall drug use has remained widespread and possibly even increased in spite of all our law enforcement efforts, can we doubt that the cure is a *source* of crime? The result is a recipe for large-scale and continual robbery and burglary, which would not exist if the drugs were available legally. There is "strong evidence that there is a strong causal relationship, at least in the United States, between addiction to narcotics and property crime levels."[214] Many addicts were criminals before they were addicts, but "while involvement in property crime activities generally precedes the addiction career, after addiction occurs the highly elevated property crime levels demonstrated by addicts appear to be regulated by similarly high narcotics use levels."[215] Thus, even for addicts who already were criminals, addiction increases the amount they need to steal and works to make them virtually immune to attempts to wean them from a life of crime or prostitution. Consequently, even if all addicts were criminals before they were addicts, the illegality of drugs would still be a source of crime because of the increased pressure it places on the addict to steal a lot and to steal often.

Do a little arithmetic: Making some very conservative assumptions, suppose that there are half-a-million addicts with $100-a-day habits. Suppose that they fill their habits only 250 days a year (sometimes they're in jail or in hospital). Suppose that they have to steal for half their drug needs and that they must steal three times the dollar value of what they need because they must convert their booty into cash through a fence. This means the half-million addicts need to steal almost $19 billion a year to support their habits. This is more than the $15.3 billion that the FBI estimates as the loss due to property crimes during 2017,[216] and it doesn't even take into consideration theft by those addicted to other drugs.

The Bureau of Justice Statistics reports that in 2004 nearly 20 percent of state and federal inmates said that they had committed their current offense in order to get money for drugs, and according to jailed inmates, "around a quarter of property and drug offenders said they committed their offense to get money for drugs."[217] One addiction specialist suggests that 85 percent of inmates meet the medical criteria for substance abuse or addiction, have a history of substance abuse, were under the influence when they engaged in the crime, committed crime to get drug money, and/or were incarcerated for a drug or alcohol violation.[218] Generally, it isn't the pharmacological effects producing crime and recidivism. *It is our steadfast refusal to experiment with alternative, noncriminal forms of drug control, and to de-escalate the drug war in favor of increased treatment, that translates a physical need for a drug into a physical need to steal billions of dollars worth of property a year.*

Finally, much of the violence associated with drugs falls under Goldstein's third category: systemic crime. Harvard's Danielle Allen, noting how much Americans spend on illegall drugs, explains: "You just can't move $100 billion worth of illegal [drug] product without a lot of assault and homicide."[219] We have already seen the link between the crack trade and the murder epidemic of the late 1980s and early 1990s.[220]

The large quantities of cash generated by drug dealers and the relatively low salaries of police officers also create temptations for corruption. A *New York Times* report during the height of crack cocaine's popularity noted that "researchers say there are now more than 100 cases each year in state and Federal courts in which law enforcement officials are charged or implicated in drug corruption."[221] Says William Green, assistant commissioner for internal affairs at the U.S. Customs Service, "The money that's being offered by the drug dealers is so big it is just hard to visualize."[222] The Mollen Commission report on police corruption in New York City found "willful blindness" to corruption throughout the police department, resulting in networks of rogue officers who dealt in drugs and preyed on black and Hispanic neighborhoods.[223]

A Government Accountability Office review found that drug-related corruption was more likely to involve multiple officers rather than a lone offender. The review of

> drug-related police corruption found on-duty officers engaged in serious criminal activities, such as (1) conducting unconstitutional searches and seizures; (2) stealing money and/or drugs from drug dealers; (3) selling stolen drugs; (4) protecting drug operations; (5) providing false testimony; and (6) submitting false crime reports.[224]

Add to this the corruption of border control agents and some military officials involved in interdiction campaigns.

In sum, we have an anti-drug policy that is failing at its own goals and succeeding only in adding to crime. First, there are the heroin and crack addicts, who must steal to support their habits. Then there are the drug merchants who—due to the illegality of drugs—have financial incentives to provide illicit substances to a willing body of consumers. This in turn contributes to the high rate of inner-city murders and other violence as drug gangs battle for the enormous sums of money available. Next, there are the law enforcement officials who, after risking their lives for low salaries, are corrupted by irresistible amounts of money. Finally, there are the otherwise law-abiding citizens who are made into criminals because they use cocaine, a drug less harmful than tobacco, and those who are made into criminals because they use marijuana, a drug that is safer than alcohol and less deadly than aspirin.

WHAT WORKS TO REDUCE CRIME

The previous sections have argued that the rate of crime and violence in the United States is high for a developed country, and that a different set of policies could substantially reduce our crime problem. Poverty and inequality, warehouse prisons, drug policy emphasizing criminalization, and lack of gun control are areas where our policies make crime more likely because of how they shape families, communities, and individual choices. Many options exist to intervene in communities, families, and individual decision-making to help prevent crime as well. There are many evidence-based and promising ideas—often outside of the criminal justice system or on its margins—but a substantial investment in crime prevention seems to be lost in efforts to reform criminal sentencing.

Effective crime prevention not only reduces violence and the losses from theft, but it is a good return on investment in other ways. As Professor Blumstein observed, "If you intervene early, you not only save the costs of incarceration, you also save the costs of crime and gain the benefits of an individual who is a taxpaying contributor to the economy."[225] In his survey of crime prevention, Currie concludes that "four priorities seem especially critical: preventing child abuse and neglect, enhancing children's intellectual and social development, providing support and guidance to vulnerable adolescents, and working extensively with juvenile offenders." About these programs, he observes that "the best of them work, and they work remarkably well given how limited and underfunded they usually are."[226]

A report from the Rand Corporation titled *Investing in Our Children: What We Know and Don't Know about the Costs and Benefits of Early Childhood Interventions*, evaluated nine programs in which early interventions were targeted at disadvantaged children. The study concluded that such programs lead to decreased criminal activity and save taxpayer dollars at the same time.[227]

A review of more than 500 crime-prevention program evaluations yielded a list of what works. Among the programs that appear effective in reducing crime, the report lists family therapy and parent training for delinquent and at-risk adolescents, teaching of social competency skills in schools and coaching high-risk youth in "thinking skills," vocational training for older male ex-offenders, rehabilitation programs with risk-focused treatments for convicted offenders, and therapeutic community treatment for drug-using offenders in prisons.[228] Criminologists David Farrington and Brandon Welsh have scoured this literature on crime prevention in their book *Saving Children from a Life of Crime: Early Risk Factors and Effective Interventions*.[229] It includes not just programs to reduce risk factors but also strategies to strengthen protective factors that reduce crime. Irvin Waller's *Science and Secrets of Ending Violent Crime* also effectively explores the research basis for violence prevention, as well as programs and strategies for building support for them.[230]

In 2007, the journal *Criminology and Public Policy* devoted an entire issue to "taking stock" of the field, as a way "not to offer innovative or new policies," but rather as "a complete issue devoted to noted scholars taking the position that we now have enough knowledge about some aspect of crime and justice that a policy is advised." The titles of some of the published papers included "Build the Capacity of Communities to Address Crime," "Restore Rationality to Sentencing Policy," "Make Rehabilitation Corrections' Guiding Paradigm," "Target Juvenile Needs to Reduce Delinquency," "Save Children from a Life of Crime," and "Protect Individual Punishment Decisions from Mandatory Penalties."[231]

Finally, commenting on a plan to spend $20 billion a year for 20 years on removing lead from people's homes and communities, Kleiman holds that it would result in a *permanent crime reduction* of "at least 10 percent. All the other cognitive and health benefits would be gravy. It's hard to imagine any other crime-control expenditure with anything like that much bang for the buck."[232]

In short, there is a growing body of knowledge showing that early childhood intervention, drug treatment, and numerous other programs can work to reduce crime. But, as Peter Greenwood, author of the Rand Corporation Study, *Diverting Children from a Life of Crime*, says, "The big policy question is, who will act on this?"[233]

* * *

In the face of all this, it is hard not to share the frustration expressed by Norval Morris, former dean of the University of Chicago Law School:

> It is trite but it remains true that the main causes of crime are social and economic. The question arises whether people really care. The solutions are so obvious. *It's almost as if America wished for a high crime rate.*[234]

The remainder of this chapter explores that idea. We do not believe all Americans consciously wish for a high crime rate. Nonetheless, it serves the interests of those with power to change the system to have a high crime rate among the poor. If this is so, then *the system's failure is only in the eyes of its victims: For those in control, it is a roaring success!*

FAILING TO REDUCE CRIME: ERIKSON, DURKHEIM, AND FOUCAULT

As the Introduction noted, we contend that the criminal justice system does actually fight crime—or at least some crime—enough to keep commerce and business functioning, and to keep the struggle against crime vividly and dramatically in the public's view. But the system fails to implement the policies that could significantly reduce crime, and this serves the interests of the those with the power to change the system. We call this way of looking at criminal justice policy the Pyrrhic defeat theory. A "Pyrrhic victory" is a military victory purchased at such a cost in troops and treasure that it amounts to a defeat. The Pyrrhic defeat theory argues that the failure of the criminal justice system yields such benefits to those in positions of power that it amounts to a victory (see Chapter 4 for a full explanation of those benefits).

Erikson, Durkheim, and the Benefits of Deviance

The Pyrrhic defeat theory draws heavily upon Kai T. Erikson's claim in his book *Wayward Puritans* that societies derive benefit from the existence of crime, and thus that social institutions work to maintain rather than to eliminate crime. It will serve to clarify our view if we compare it with Erikson's.

Professor Erikson's theory is based on the view of crime set forth in one of the classic works of sociological theory, *The Division of Labor in Society* by Émile Durkheim. Writing toward the end of the nineteenth century, Durkheim

> suggested that crime (and by extension other forms of deviation) may actually perform a needed service to society by drawing people together in a common posture of anger and indignation. The deviant individual violates rules of conduct which the rest of the community holds in high respect; and when these people come together to express their outrage over the offense and to bear witness against the offender, they develop a tighter bond of solidarity than existed earlier.[235]

The solidarity that holds a community together, in this view, is a function of the intensity with which the members of the community share a sense of the group's cultural identity. The boundary between acceptable and unacceptable behavior gives the group its distinctive character. It is necessary, then, for the existence of a community as a *community* that its members learn and constantly relearn the location of its "boundaries." Erikson writes that these boundaries are learned in dramatic confrontations with policing agents whose special business it is to guard the cultural integrity of the community. Whether these confrontations take the form of criminal trials, excommunication hearings, courts-martial, or even case conferences, they act as boundary-maintaining devices in the sense that they demonstrate to whatever audience is concerned where the line is drawn between behavior that belongs in the special universe of the group and behavior that does not.[236]

In brief, this means that a community *positively needs unacceptable behavior*. Not only does unacceptable behavior cast in relief the terrain of behavior acceptable to the community, it also reinforces the intensity with which the members of the community identify that terrain as their shared territory. On this view, *deviant behavior is an ingredient in the glue that holds a community together.* "This," Erikson continues,

> raises a delicate theoretical issue. If we grant that human groups often derive benefit from deviant behavior, can we then assume that they are organized in such a way as to promote this resource? Can we assume, in other words, *that forces operate in the social structure to recruit offenders and to commit them to long periods of service in the deviant ranks?...*
>
> Looking at the matter from a long-range historical perspective, it is fair to conclude that prisons have done a conspicuously poor job of reforming the convicts placed in their custody; but the very consistency of this failure may have a peculiar logic of its own. Perhaps we find it difficult to change the worst of our penal practices because we expect the prison to harden the inmate's commitment to deviant forms of behavior and draw him more deeply into the deviant ranks.[237]

Drawing on Durkheim's recognition that societies benefit from the existence of deviants, Erikson entertains the view that societies have institutions whose unannounced function is to recruit and maintain a reliable supply of deviants. Modified for our purposes, Erikson's view would become the hypothesis that the American criminal justice system fails to reduce crime because a visible criminal population is essential to maintaining the "boundaries" that mark the cultural identity of American society and to maintaining the solidarity among those who share that identity. In other words, in its failure, the criminal justice system succeeds in providing some of the cement necessary to hold American society together as a society by pointing out the bad and the deviant.

As we said in the Introduction, this idea is one of several that contribute to the Pyrrhic defeat theory, but the idea is also transformed in the process. Here, then, we aim to acknowledge the debt to the Durkheim-Erikson thesis and to state the difference between it and the view that we will defend. The debt is to the insight that societies may promote behavior that they seem to desire to stamp out, and that failure to eliminate deviance may be a success of some sort.

The difference, on the other hand, is this: Both Durkheim and Erikson jump from the *general* proposition that the failure to eliminate deviance promotes social solidarity to the *specific* conclusion that the form in which this failure occurs in a particular society can be explained by the contribution the failure makes to promoting consensus on shared beliefs and thus feelings of social solidarity. This is a "jump" because it leaves out the important question of how a social group forms its particular consensus around one set of shared beliefs rather than another; that is, Durkheim and Erikson implicitly assume that a consensus already exists (at least virtually) and that deviance is promoted to manifest and reinforce it. This leads to the view that social institutions reflect beliefs already in people's heads, largely and spontaneously shared by all of them.

In our view, even if it is granted that societies work to strengthen feelings of social solidarity, the set of beliefs about the world around which those feelings will crystallize is by no means already in people's heads and spontaneously shared. A consensus is made not born, although, again, we do not mean that it is made in a conspiratorial way. It is created, not just reflected, by social institutions. Thus, the failure to stamp out deviance does not simply reinforce a consensus that already exists; it is part of the process by which a very particular consensus is created and reinforced.[238]

In developing the Pyrrhic defeat theory, we try to show how the failure of criminal justice works to create and reinforce a very particular set of beliefs about the world, about what is dangerous and what is not, who is a threat and who is not, and where the crime problem lies and where it does not. This does not merely shore up general feelings of social solidarity; it allows those feelings to be attached to a social order characterized by striking disparities of wealth, power, and privilege, and by considerable injustice.

A Word about Foucault

Michel Foucault is another thinker who has suggested that the failure of the criminal justice system—prisons in particular—serves a function for society. His view of this failure and its function is, at points, close to the one for which we argue here, but there are differences as well. In his book, *Discipline and Punish,* Foucault notes that complaints about the failure of prisons to curb crime, indeed their tendency to increase crime by promoting recidivism, have accompanied the prison throughout its history—so much so that Foucault asks, "Is not the supposed failure part of the functioning of the prison?"[239] In response, Foucault writes that the prison "has succeeded extremely well in producing delinquents, in an apparently marginal, but in fact centrally supervised milieu; in producing the delinquent as a pathologized subject."[240] That is, the prison regime transforms the offender from a lawbreaker into a *delinquent in need of correction,* an abnormal individual in need of treatment, and this development licenses a permanent policing of the potentially troublesome classes.

Foucault suggests that the new prison regime that emerged in France in the nineteenth century was a response to a "new threat" posed by peasants and workers against the "new system of the legal exploitation of labor,"[241] by which he means capitalism. This is a class-based explanation of the new prison regime in which criminality gets identified "almost exclusively [with] a certain social class... the bottom rank of the social order."[242] Among the advantages produced by this prison regime and the policing that accompanies it are the maintenance of crime at a sufficiently low level so that it does not pose a general threat to the social order—all the while maintaining a high enough level of crime to weaken the poorer classes—from whom both the delinquents and their victims tend to come—by dividing the poor against themselves. Moreover, says Foucault, "[d]elinquency, controlled illegality, is an agent for the illegality of the dominant groups."[243] Here he has in mind the profits to be made from drugs and prostitution, alongside a general toleration of the "delinquency of wealth."[244] This much is generally in accord with the thesis of *The Rich Get Richer,* which argues that the failure of the criminal justice system to significantly reduce crime, as well as the identification of crime with the harmful acts of poor people, serves the interests of the rich and powerful by creating the general belief that the greatest threat to the well-being of ordinary folks comes from the poor rather than from the rich.[245]

But Foucault goes further. He contends that delinquency, "with the generalized policing that it authorizes, constitutes a means of perpetual surveillance of the population: an apparatus that makes it possible to supervise, through the delinquents themselves, the whole social field."[246] For Foucault, then, the prison is part of a "general tactics of subjection" that amount to a system of permanent social surveillance. Stretching from the "Panopticon" model of a prison, in which a single guard can watch a large number of inmates without himself being seen, to the emergence of a "scientific" criminological establishment that observes and studies delinquents, and from there to the modern medical-psychological establishment that keeps records on just about everyone, ubiquitous surveillance works to make people feel observed and thus makes them into the agents of their own normalizing discipline. In this way, the prison spreads out into a "carceral archipelago," a whole system of institutions and practices, including the disciplines such as psychology and medicine, aimed at "normalization."[247] In sum, writes Foucault,

> the normalizing power has spread. Borne along by the omni-
> presence of the mechanisms of discipline, basing itself on all the
> carceral apparatuses, it has become one of the major functions of
> our society. The judges of normality are everywhere. We are in the
> society of the teacher-judge, the doctor-judge, the educator-judge,
> the "social-worker"-judge; it is on them that the universal reign of
> the normative is based; and each individual, wherever he may find
> himself, subjects to it his body, his gestures, his behavior, his apti-
> tudes, his achievements.[248]

With this, Foucault has left criminal justice behind and presented a theory of the nature of modern society generally. Also left behind is the class structure of the exercise of power that was present in the origins of the prison system as Foucault described it. Now power is everywhere, exercised by everyone on him or herself and on everyone else.[249] No doubt, this captures something of the flavor of modern life in which people at all levels of society are subjected to myriad pressures to be "normal," from the tsk-tsks of teachers and doctors to the self-help books and advice columns that offer to make us better earners and better lovers and better parents. The judges of normality are, indeed, everywhere.

But this account also mystifies the exercise of power. Rather than operating along a class axis that might be eliminated and serving interests that might be identified and critiqued, for Foucault power now seems to be its own goal, a universal fact of modern life, driven by no particular interest beyond that of discipline—"the policing of normality" as an end in itself.[250] The enemy is everywhere and nowhere in particular, so there is no clear target for resistance. Not only is the class structure of the exercise of power—particularly criminal justice power—flattened out here, the moral status of the exercise is obscured as well. Absent from Foucault's analysis is attention to the difference between those forms of discipline that are necessary for the freedom of each to coexist peacefully with the freedom of the rest, and those forms of discipline that simply serve the interests of the rich and powerful. In this way there is no clear guidance about what should be resisted. The analysis in *The Rich Get Richer* strives to keep the class nature of the criminal justice system in view while recognizing the importance of distinguishing between those exercises of power that are necessary for the protection of freedom and those that simply serve the interests of the wealthy.

Summary

This chapter has tried to establish the first part of the Pyrrhic defeat theory, namely that the war on crime is a failure and an avoidable one: The American criminal justice system—the entire process from lawmaking to law enforcing—has failed to eliminate the high rates of crime that characterize our society and threaten our citizens. Over the last several decades crime has generally risen, although in recent decades it has declined. Numerous causes—economic and social—have contributed to this, such that serious observers agree that criminal justice policy and practice cannot be credited with more than a fraction of the recent declines. At the same time, however, neither should it be thought on this basis that public policy cannot reduce the crime we have. Crime is not a simple and unavoidable consequence of either the number of youngsters in our populace or the degree of urbanization of our society. Moreover, there are a number of policies that, there is good reason to believe, would succeed in reducing crime—effective gun control, decriminalization of illicit drugs, amelioration of poverty, prevention of child abuse and neglect, and early intervention with at-risk youngsters—but we refuse to implement them on any significant scale. The Pyrrhic defeat theory shares the Durkheim-Erikson view of the functional nature of crime, as well as the idea that societies may in fact promote behavior that they seem to want to eliminate. However, it differs from their view in insisting that the failure to stamp out crime doesn't simply reflect an existing consensus but contributes to creating one, one that is functional for only a certain part of our society. This chapter concluded by discussing Foucault's claim that the failure of the prison is part of a larger structure of disciplinary surveillance that pervades modern society. His account of the beginnings of this regime parallels the class analysis for which we shall argue. However, as he develops his theory, Foucault leaves class structure behind and thus mystifies the nature of the power exercised in the criminal justice system.

Study Questions

1. What is meant by the comparison of crime policy to "a version of 'heads I win, tails you lose'"? What evidence do the authors present to support this view?
2. What are some of the criminal justice factors involved in the declining crime rate, and how much impact have they had?
3. What non-criminal justice factors are involved in the declining crime rate and how does each contribute?
4. What excuses have been given for our inability to reduce the amount of crime we have? How do you evaluate these excuses?
5. What causes crime? How, and why, do the authors distinguish a "cause" from a "source" of crime? What do the authors say are sources of crime? Be sure to explain how they link each source with higher crime rates.
6. Do you think that we "make the world of violence that surrounds us" as Currie says? If so, what could we do to reduce the amount of crime? To what extent are these solutions within the criminal justice system, or do non-criminal justice policies have a greater impact on crime?
7. What does it mean to say that "the criminal justice system is 'designed to fail'" and that "crime is functional for a society"? How does the Pyrrhic defeat theory differ on this from the Durkheim-Erikson theory?
8. List the costs and benefits of our current war on drugs. Is it worth it? Do you think that legalizing all or some illicit drugs would reduce crime? If so, would you agree to legalization?

Additional Resources

Jeffrey Reiman and Paul Leighton, eds., *The Rich Get Richer and the Poor Get Prison: A Reader* (New York: Routledge, 2016). This volume is a collection of accessible articles that is divided into sections that parallel the chapters of *The Rich Get Richer*, and each section of the reader opens with a substantial introduction, written by the editors, that provides article summaries, context, and linkages to *The Rich Get Richer*.

The authors also maintain a companion website to the text at http://www.paulsjustice page. *com/reiman.htm*

Notes

1. Joel Dyer, *The Perpetual Prisoner Machine* (Boulder, CO: Westview Press, 2000), p. 2.
2. Lynne Vieraitis, Tomislav Kovandzic, and Thomas Marvell, "The Criminogenic Effects of Imprisonment," *Criminology and Public Policy* 6, no. 3 (2007): 590.
3. John Irwin and James Austin, *It's About Time: America's Imprisonment Binge,* 3rd ed. (Belmont, CA: Wadsworth Publishing, 2001); Loïc Wacquant, "Class, Race & Hyperincarceration in Revanchist America," *Daedalus* 139, no. 3 (2010): 74–90; Ernest Drucker, *A Plague of Prisons* (New York: The New Press, 2011).
4. Francis Cullen, "Rehabilitation: Beyond Nothing Works," *Crime and Justice* 42, no. 1 (2013): 307.
5. Katherine Beckett and Theodore Sasson, *The Politics of Injustice: Crime and Punishment in America* (Thousand Oaks, CA: Pine Forge Press, 2000), p. 52.
6. Richard Nixon, State of the Union Address, 1970, www.presidency.ucsb. edu/ ws/index.php?pid=2921.
7. Jimmy Carter, Drug Abuse Message to Congress, 1977, www.presidency. ucsb. edu/ws/index.php?pid=7908.
8. William Barr, *The Case for More Incarceration,* NCJ 139583, October 28, 1992.
9. Franklin Zimring, "The New Politics of Criminal Justice," *Perspectives on Crime and Justice: 1999–2000 Lecture Series,* NCJ 184245, March 2001, p. 3.
10. See President Bill Clinton, "Remarks on Signing the Violent Crime Control and Law Enforcement Act of 1994," September 13, 1994, www.govinfo.gov/content/ pkg/PPP-1994-book2/pdf/PPP-1994-book2-doc-pg1539.pdf.
11. Fox Butterfield, "A Large Drop in Violent Crime Is Reported," *New York Times,* September 18, 1996, p. A14.
12. Ted Gest, "Popgun Politics," *U.S. News & World Report,* September 30, 1996, p. 41. In 2016 Clinton claimed that "because of that bill we had a 25-year low in crime, a 33-year low in the murder rate." Robert Farley, "Bill Clinton and the 1994 Crime Bill," April 12, 2016, www.factcheck.org/2016/04/ bill-clinton-and-the-1994-crime-bill/.
13. David H. Bayley, "The Cop Fallacy," *New York Times,* August 13, 1993, p. A17.
14. National Research Council Committee on Causes and Consequences of High Rates of Incarceration, Jeremy Travis, Bruce Western, and Steve Redburn (eds.), *The Growth of Incarceration in the United States: Exploring Causes and Consequences* (Washington, DC: The National Academies Press, 2014), p. 90.
15. The White House, Office of the Press Secretary, "Radio Address of the President to the Nation," January 11, 1997.
16. William Jefferson Clinton, State of the Union Address. January 20, 1999, www. washingtonpost.com/wp-srv/politics/special/states/docs/sou99.htm.
17. President George W. Bush, "Remarks by the President on Project Safe Neighborhoods," May 14, 2001, www.presidency.ucsb.edu/ws/index.php?pid=45608.
18. "Combat Crime and Drug Abuse," Ch. 9, *A Blueprint for New Beginnings: A Responsible Budget for America's Priorities* (Washington, DC: U.S. Government Printing Office, 2001), www.gpoaccess.gov/usbudget/fy02/pdf/blueprnt.pdf.
19. Private prisons are for-profit companies that build and/or manage prisons. They are part of a larger criminal justice-industrial complex that has a vested interest in crime and is discussed more in Chapter 4.
20. Executive Office of the President, "Statement of Administration Policy: H.R. 1279: Gang Deterrence and Community Protection Act of 2005," May 11, 2005, www.presidency.ucsb.edu/ws/index.php?pid=24850.

21. National Research Council Committee to Review Research on Police Policy and Practices, Wesley Skogan and Kathleen Frydl (eds.), *Fairness and Effectiveness in Policing: The Evidence* (Washington, DC: The National Academies Press, 2004), pp. 4, 223, 225, 226, 229, and 233.

22. Ibid., p. 247.

23. See Senator Barack Obama, "Remarks at Howard University Convocation," September 28, 2007, www.howard.edu/newsroom/news/2007/071001Remarks of SenatorBarackObama.htm.

24. Office of the Attorney General, *The Attorney General's Smart on Crime Initiative*, December 1, 2015, www.justice.gov/ag/attorney-generals-smart-crime-initiative.

25. Eric Holder, "Statement of Attorney General Eric Holder on the 2011 Preliminary Uniform Crime Report, 2011," December 11, 2011, www.justice.gov/opa/pr/2011/December/11-ag-1666.html.

26. Jacob Sullum, "Bummer: Barack Obama Turns Out to Be Just Another Drug Warrior," *Reason*, September 12, 2011, http://reason.com/archives/2011/09/12/bummer.

27. Federal laws required a mandatory five-year sentence for crimes involving 500 grams (about a pound) of powder cocaine or 5 grams (about one-sixth of an ounce) of crack cocaine. See Chapter 3 for more discussion.

28. Sullum, "Bummer: Barack Obama Turns Out to Be Just Another Drug Warrior."

29. Michelle Ye Hee Lee, "Can Eric Holder Change the Federal Drug Classification of Marijuana?" *The Washington Post*, February 26, 2015, www.washingtonpost.com/blogs/fact-checker/wp/2015/02/26/can-eric-holder-change-the-federal-drug-classification-of-marijuana/.

30. BJS, *Correctional Populations in the United States, 2016*, NCJ251211, April 26, 2018, Appendix Table 2.

31. Knight-Ridder Newspapers, "Trump Backs Legalizing Drugs," *Chicago Tribune*, April 15, 1990, www.chicagotribune.com/news/ct-xpm-1990-04-15-9001310473-story.html.

32. Ronald Bailey, "Trump Wants Us 'To Get Really, Really Tough, Really Mean with the Drug Pushers,'" *Reason*, February 6, 2018, https://reason.com/2018/02/06/trump-have-to-get-really-really-tough-re.

33. Jonathan Swan, "Exclusive: Trump Privately Talks Up Executing All Big Drug Dealers," *Axios*, February 25, 2018, www.axios.com/exclusive-trump-privately-talks-up-executing-all-big-drug-dealers-1519595170-402cc386-8729-4684-a7ef-a5bf31876afa.html.

34. German Lopez, "Donald Trump Wants to Bring Back the 'Tough on Crime' Policies that Helped Cause Mass Incarceration," *Vox*, September 21, 2016, www.vox.com/2016/5/25/11737264/donald-trump-criminal-justice-republican-president.

35. See Attorney General Jeff Sessions, "Remarks to the National Sheriffs' Association Annual Conference," June 18, 2018, www.justice.gov/opa/speech/attorney-general-sessions-delivers-remarks-national-sheriffs-association-annual.

36. See Attorney General Jeff Sessions, "Remarks to the Gatlinburg Law Enforcement Training Conference," May 8, 2018, www.justice.gov/opa/speech/attorney-general-sessions-delivers-remarks-gatlinburg-law-enforcement-training-conference. See also, Molly Ball, "Jeff Sessions is Winning for Donald Trump. If Only He Can Keep His Job," *Time*, March 29, 2018, https://time.com/5220086/jeff-sessions-is-winning-for-donald-trump-if-only-he-can-keep-his-job/.

37. Julie Samuels, Nancy La Vigne, and Chelsea Thomson, "Next Steps in Federal Corrections Reform," *Urban Institute*, May 2019, www.urban.org/sites/default/files/publication/100230/next_steps_in_federal_corrections_reform_1.pdf.

38. Elliot Currie, *Crime and Punishment in America* (New York: Metropolitan Books, Henry Holt, 1998), p. 12; BJS, *Correctional Populations in the United States, 2016*, NCJ 251211, April 2018, Table 1, p. 2.

39. Hadar Aviram, *Cheap on Crime: Recession-Era Politics and the Transformation of American Punishment* (Oakland: University of California Press, 2015). See also Jeremy Travis, "Assessing the Sate of Mass Incarceration," *Criminology and Public Policy* 13, no. 4 (2014): 567–577.

40. BJS, *Prisoners in 2017*, NCJ 252156, April 2019, Table 1.

41. Michael Tonry, "Remodeling American Sentencing," *Criminology and Public Policy* 13, no. 4 (2014): 510.

42. Ibid., p. 527.

43. Josh Keller, "Calif. Governor Proposes Amending Constitution to Bolster Higher Education," *Chronicle of Higher Education*, January 6, 2010, http://chronicle.com/article/Calif-Governor-Proposes/63440/.43. *Brown v. Plata*, No. 09–1233.

44. *Brown v. Plata*, No. 09–1233, www.supremecourt.gov/opinions/10pdf/09-1233.pdf, p. 3.

45. Danielle Douglas-Gabriel, "These States Spend More on Prisons than Colleges," *The Washington Post*, October 5, 2015, www.washingtonpost.com/news/grade-point/wp/2015/10/05/these-states-spend-more-on-prisons-than-colleges/.

46. Michael Mitchell et al., "Unkept Promises: State Cuts to Higher Education Threaten Access and Equity," Center on Budget and Policy Priorities, October 4, 2018, www.cbpp.org/research/state-budget-and-tax/unkept-promises-state-cuts-to-higher-education-threaten-access-and.

47. *UCR-2017*, Table 1 and *Sourcebook*, Table 3.106.2009.

48. Elliott Currie, "Reflections on Crime and Criminology at the Millennium," *Western Criminology Review* 2, no. 1 (1999), www.westerncriminology.org/documents/WCR/v02n1/currie/currie.html.

49. David Vise and Lorraine Adams, "Despite Rhetoric, Violent Crime Climbs," *The Washington Post*, December 5, 1999, p. A3.

50. Quoted in ibid.

51. *Sourcebook 2012*, Table 6.28; *Prisoners in 2004*, p. 1.

52. Richard Nixon, "Remarks about an Intensified Program for Drug Abuse Prevention and Control," June 17, 1971, www.presidency.ucsb.edu/ws/?pid=3047.

53. Doug Bandow, "War on Drugs or War on America?" *Stanford Law and Policy Review*, 242, no. 3 (Fall 1991): 243; Alfred W. McCoy and Alan Block, "U.S. Narcotics Policy: An Anatomy of Failure," in Alfred W. McCoy and Alan A. Block (eds.), *War on Drugs: Studies in the Failure of U.S. Narcotics Policy* (Boulder, CO: Westview Press, 1992), p. 6; *UCR-2017*, Table 29.

54. Vincent Schiraldi, "Spend More Money on Education, Not Prisons," *Newsday*, August 29, 2002, p. A39.

55. BJS, *Prisoners in 2017*, Table 14.

56. Joseph E. Kennedy, "Most US Drug Arrests Involve a Gram or Less," *The Conversation*, June 17, 2019, https://theconversation.com/most-us-drug-arrests-involve-a-gram-or-less-118440.

57. Michael Tonry, "Racial Politics, Racial Disparities, and the War on Crime," *Crime & Delinquency* 40, no. 4 (1994): 487.

58. United Nations Office on Drugs and Crime, *Afghanistan Opium Survey 2007 Executive Summary*, p. 8, *http://www.unodc.org/pdf/research/AFG07_ExSum_web.pdf*.

59. Juan Forero, "Coca Cultivation Rises in Columbia, U.N. Says," *Washington Post*, June 19, 2008, p. A10.

60. United Nations Office on Drugs and Crime, *World Drug Report*, 2014, p. x, www.unodc.org/wdr2014/press/World_Drug_Report_2014_exsum_ embargoed.pdf.

61. *New York Times* editorial board, "Not Winning the War on Drugs," *New York Times*, July 2, 2008, www.nytimes.com/2008/07/02/opinion/02wed1.html.

62. Peter Reuter, "The Mobility of Drug Trafficking," in John Collins (ed.), *Ending the Drug Wars: Report of the LSE Expert Group on the Economics of Drug Policy* (London: London School of Economics and Political Science, May 2014), p. 33, www.lse.ac.uk/IDEAS/publications/reports/pdf/LSE-IDEAS-DRUGS-REPORT-FINAL-WEB.pdf.

63. Office of National Drug Control Policy (ONDCP), *The Price and Purity of Illicit Drugs: 1981 through the Second Quarter of 2003*, NCJ 207768, November 2004, pp. v–vi.

64. Jeremy Travis and Bruce Western, *The Growth of Incarceration in the United States: Exploring Causes and Consequences* (Washington: The National Academies Press, 2014), p. 154.

65. Jeffrey Miron, "The Budgetary Effects of Ending Drug Prohibition," *Tax & Budget Bulletin, Cato Institute*, July 23, 2018, https://object.cato.org/sites/cato.org/files/pubs/pdf/tbb-83.pdf.

66. Marc Fisher and Katie Zezima, "This Is Where Heroin Almost Killed Her," *The Washington Post*, October 3, 2015, www.washingtonpost.com/sf/national/2015/10/03/this-is-where-heroin-almost-killed-her/.

67. Holly Hedegaard, Arialdi Minino, and Margaret Warner, "Drug Overdose Deaths in the United States, 1999–2017," NCHS Data Brief #329, November 2018, www.cdc.gov/nchs/data/databriefs/db329-h.pdf.

68. United Nations Office on Drugs and Crime, *World Drug Report 2014* (United Nations publication, Sales No. E.14.XI.7), p. 4. See also Maps and Tables, Drug Related Mortality, www.unodc.org/wdr2014/en/maps-and-graphs.html.

69. David Boyum and Peter Reuter, *An Analytic Assessment of U.S. Drug Policy* (Washington, DC: AEI Press, 2005). "Yet despite the incarceration of hundreds of thousands of drug dealers and steadfast attempts to stop overseas cultivations and trafficking, drugs have become substantially cheaper, casting doubt on the effectiveness of this strategy" (p. 2).

70. Jeffrey Miron, "The Budgetary Effects of Ending Drug Prohibition."

71. Surgeon General Joycelyn Elders reiterated the suggestion after "reviewing many studies" and after President Clinton's opposition to the idea: "Elders Reiterates Her Support for Study of Drug Legalization," *The Washington Post*, January 15, 1994, p. A8.

72. Caitlin E. Hughes and Alex Steven, "What Can We Learn from the Portuguese Decriminalization of Illicit Drugs?" *British Journal of Criminology* 50, no. 6 (2010): 1016.

73. Global Commission on Drug Policy, *War on Drugs*, 2011, p. 2, www.globalcommissionondrugs.org/.

74. 21 USC 1703(b)12.

75. John DiIulio, "Rethinking Crime-Again," *Democracy* 16 (Spring 2010): 46–57. www.democracyjournal.org/16/6739.php.

76. Andrew Wheeler and Tomislav Kovandzic, "Monitoring Volatile Homicide Trends Across U.S. Cities," *Homicide Studies* 22, no. 2 (2018): 119–144, https://doi.org/10.1177/1088767917740171.

77. Joan Petersilia, "Community Corrections: Probation, Parole, and Prisoner Reentry," in James Q. Wilson and Joan Petersilia (eds.), *Crime and Public Policy,* 2nd ed. (Oxford: Oxford University Press, 2011), pp. 499–531.

78. Bert Useem and Anne Morrison Piehl, *Prison State: The Challenge of Mass Incarceration* (Cambridge: Cambridge University Press, 2008), p. 52.

79. Oliver Roeder, Lauren-Brooke Eisen, and Julia Bowling, *What Caused the Crime Decline?* (New York: The Brennan Center for Justice, 2015), p. 22.

80. Ball, "Jeff Sessions is Winning for Donald Trump. If Only He Can Keep His Job."

81. National Research Council, Travis, Western, and Redburn (eds.), *The Growth of Incarceration in the United States,* pp. 83 and 155.

82. Cameron Kimble and Ames Grawert, "Between 2007 and 2017, 34 States Reduced Crime and Incarceration in Tandem," The Bennan Center for Justice, August 6, 2019, www.brennancenter.org/blog/between-2007-and-2017-34-states-reduced-crime-and-incarceration-tandem.

83. Bradley J. Bartos and Charis E. Kubrin, "Can We Downsize Our Prisons and Jails Without Compromising Public Safety?" *Criminology & Public Policy* 17, no. 3 (2018): 703.

84. National Research Council, Travis, Western, and Redburn (eds.), *The Growth of Incarceration in the United States,* p. 31.

85. Government Accountability Office, *Community Policing Grants: COPS Grants Were a Modest Contributor to Declines in Crime in the 1990s* (Washington DC: Government Accountability Office GAO-06 104, October 2005), p. 1, www.gao.gov/new.items/d06104.pdf.

86. Roeder et al., *What Caused the Crime Decline?* p. 41. See also John A. Eterno and Eli B. Silverman, *The Crime Numbers Game: Management by Manipulation* (Boca Raton, FL: CRC Press, 2012).

87. P. Sharkey, *Uneasy Peace: The Great Crime Decline, the Renewal of City Life, and the Next War on Violence,* 1st ed. (New York: W.W. Norton & Company, 2018), p. 55. See also p. 171.

88. National Academies of Sciences, Engineering, and Medicine, *Proactive Policing: Effects on Crime and Communities* (Washington, DC: The National Academies Press, 2018), https://doi.org/10.17226/24928.

89. *Proactive Policing,* p. 169.

90. *Proactive Policing,* p. 152.

91. *Proactive Policing,* p. 135. See also National Research Council, Skogan and Frydl (eds.), *Fairness and Effectiveness in Policing,* pp. 238 and 244. Anthony A. Braga, Brandon C. Welsh, and Cory Schnell, "Can Policing Disorder Reduce Crime? A Systematic Review and Meta-Analysis," *Journal of Research in Crime and Delinquency* 52, no. 4 (2015): 567–588.

92. Philip Cook, Anthony Braga, and Mark Moore, "Gun Control," in James Q. Wilson and Joan Petersilia (eds.), *Crime and Public Policy,* 2nd ed. (Oxford: Oxford University Press, 2011), pp. 257–292; Robert Apel and Daniel Nagin, "General Deterrence: A Review of Recent Evidence," ibid., pp. 411–436; Richard Rosenfeld, "Changing Crime Rates," ibid., pp. 559–588.

93. National Research Council, Skogan and Frydl (eds.), *Fairness and Effectiveness in Policing,* p. 229.

94. *Proactive Policing,* p. 150.

95. Joe Sexton, "In New York, Crime Falls Along with Police Stops," *ProPublica*, January 16, 2018, www.propublica.org/article/in-new-york-crime-falls-along-with-police-stops.

96. *Proactive Policing*, pp. 167–168.

97. Juan Del Toro, Tracey Lloyd, Kim S. Buchanan, Summer Joi Robins, Lucy Zhang Bencharit, Meredith Gamson Smiedt, Kavita S. Reddy, Enrique Rodriguez Pouget, Erin M. Kerrison, and Phillip Atiba Goff, "The Criminogenic and Psychological Effects of Police Stops on Adolescent Black and Latino Boys," *Proceedings of the National Academy of Sciences* 116, no. 17 (April 2019): 8261–8268, doi: 10.1073/pnas.1808976116.

98. Alfred Blumstein, "Why Is Crime Falling—or Is It?" in National Institute of Justice, *Perspectives on Crime and Justice: 2000–2001 Lecture Series*, vol. 5 (Rockville, MD; U.S. Department of Justice, NCJ 187100, March 2002), p. 16.

99. Alfred Blumstein, "The Recent Rise and Fall of American Violence," in Alfred Blumstein and Joel Wallman (eds.), *The Crime Drop in America*, 2nd ed. (New York: Cambridge University Press, 2006), pp. 4–5.

100. Blumstein, "Why Is Crime Falling—or Is It?" pp. 19–21.

101. Quoted in Pierre Thomas, "In a Reversal, U.S. Homicide Numbers Fall," *The Washington Post*, December 31, 1995, p. A8.

102. Gest, "Popgun Politics," p. 33.

103. Lena Edlund and Cecilia Machado, "It's the Phone, Stupid: Mobiles and Murder," *NBER Working Paper Series*, #25883, May 2019, National Bureau of Economic Research, www.dropbox.com/s/as1uiy26zqi215g/w25883.pdf?dl=0.

104. Blumstein, "Why Is Crime Falling—or Is It?" pp. 12, 17–18, and 24. An improving economy helped reduce crime rates, but the financial crisis and recession did not cause crime rates to increase because people who are unemployed or have reduced income shift gradually to crime as their economic resources become depleted. Congress extended unemployment benefits and people have savings that they draw down before turning to crime. Further, unemployed people "find themselves in routine activities that are more home-based," thus reducing their time spent in public places where they are at higher risk of victimization. The unemployed become "guardians for their residences," which lowers property-based crime victimization. See also Shawn D. Bushway, "Labor Markets and Crime," in Wilson and Petersilia (eds.), *Crime and Public Policy*, p. 191.

105. Richard Rosenfeld, "Crime and Inflation in Cross-National Perspective," in Michael Tonry (ed.), *Why Crime Rates Fall and Why They Don't* (Chicago: University of Chicago Press, 2014), p. 360.

106. Ibid., p. 359.

107. Lauren Wolf, "The Crimes of Lead," *Chemical and Engineering News* 92, no. 5 (2014): 27–29, http://cen.acs.org/articles/92/i5/Crimes-Lead.html.

108. Ibid.

109. Kimberly L. Barrett, "Lead and Crime," in Beth Huebner (ed-in-chief), Oxford Bibliographies Online: Criminology, updated November 27, 2013, www.oxford bibliographies.com/view/document/obo-9780195396607/obo-9780195396607-0096.xml. See also David Marcus, Jessica Fulton, and Erin Clarke, "Lead and Conduct Problems: A Meta-Analysis," *Journal of Clinical Child & Adolescent Psychology* 39, no. 2 (2010): 234–241.

110. Jessica Wolpaw Reyes, "Environmental Policy as Social Policy? The Impact of Childhood Lead Exposure on Crime," *The B.E. Journal of Economic Analysis & Policy* 7, no. 1 (2007): 1–43, www.bepress.com/bejeap/vol7/iss1/art51.

111. As reported by Roeder et al., *What Caused the Crime Decline?*, p. 63.

112. Mark Kleiman, *When Brute Force Fails: How to Have Less Crime and Less Punishment* (Princeton, NJ: Princeton University Press, 2011). The quote is from Mark Kleiman, "Smart on Crime," *Democracy* 28 (Spring 2013), p. 16, http://democracyjournal.org/magazine/28/smart-on-crime/.

113. John T. Donohue and Steven D. Levitt, "The Impact of Legalized Abortion on Crime," *The Quarterly Journal of Economics* 116, no. 2 (2001), p. 381.

114. David E. Kalist and Freddy Siahaan, "The Association of Obesity with the Likelihood of Arrest for Young Adults," *Economics and Human Biology* 11, no. 1 (2013): 8–17.

115. Tim Wadsworth, "Is Immigration Responsible for the Crime Drop? An Assessment of the Influence of Immigration on Changes in Violent Crime Between 1990 and 2000," *Social Science Quarterly* 91, no. 2 (2010): 531–553; Robert J. Sampson, "Rethinking Crime and Immigration," *Contexts* 7, no. 1 (2008): 28–33.

116. A. Scott Cunningham, Benjamin Engelstätter, and Michael R. Ward, "Understanding the Effects of Violent Video Games on Violent Crime," ZEW Centre for European Economic Research, *Discussion Paper No. 11–042*, 2014, http://ftp.zew.de/pub/zew-docs/dp/dp11042.pdf.

117. Patrick Sharkey, Gerard Torrats-Espinosa, and Delaram Takyar, "Community and the Crime Decline: The Causal Effect of Local Nonprofits on Violent Crime," *American Sociological Review* 82, no. 6 (2017): 1214–1240, https://doi.org/10.1177/0003122417736289.

118. Richard Wright et al., "Less Cash, Less Crime: Evidence from the Electronic Benefit Transfer Program," *National Bureau of Economic Research Working Paper 19996*, March 2014, www.nber.org/papers/w19996.

119. M. Tcherni-Buzzeo, "The 'Great American Crime Decline': Possible Explanations," in M. D. Krohn et al. (eds.), *Handbook on Crime and Deviance*, 2nd ed. (New York, NY: Springer, 2019).

120. Michael Tonry, "Why Crime Rates Are Falling Throughout the Eastern World," in Tonry (ed.), *Why Crime Rates Fall and Why They Don't*, p. 3.

121. "1968 Safe Streets Act," in J. Austin (ed.), *Congressional Quarterly Almanac 2010*, 66th ed. (Washington, DC: CQ-Roll Call Group, 2011), http://library.cqpress.com/cqalmanac/document.php?id=cqal68-1283625.

122. *Sourcebook 2003*, Table 3.106; *UCR-2017*, Table 1.

123. UN Office on Drugs and Crime's International Homicide Statistics database, "Intentional Homicides (per 100,000 people)" 2016, https://data.worldbank.org/indicator/VC.IHR.PSRC.P5.

124. *Challenge*, p. 35.

125. CPI Inflation Calculator, https://data.bls.gov/cgi-bin/cpicalc.pl.

126. BJS, *Justice Expenditures and Employment Extracts, 2015 – Preliminary*, NCJ251780, June 2018, Tables 1 and 2.

127. Randall Shelden, *Controlling the Dangerous Classes* (Boston: Allyn and Bacon, 2001), p. 280.

128. On this issue, we have made ample use of the discussion and references in Victor Kappeler, Mark Blumberg, and Gary Potter, *The Mythology of Crime and Criminal Justice*, 3rd ed. (Prospect Heights, IL: Waveland, 2000), pp. 257–272.

129. Justin McCarthy, "Americans' Views Shift on Toughness of Justice System," October 20, 2016, Gallup Social & Policy Issues, https://news.gallup.com/poll/196568/americans-views-shift-toughness-justice-system.aspx.

130. Ernest van den Haag, "When Felons Go Free: Worse Than a Crime," *National Review*, January 20, 1992, p. 50.

131. James Lynch and William Alex Pridemore, "Crime in International Perspective," in James Q. Wilson and Joan Petersilia (eds.), *Crime and Public-Policy*, 2nd ed. (Oxford: Oxford University Press, 2011), pp. 5–52.

132. Ibid.

133. Caitlin E. Hughes and Alex Steven, "What Can We Learn from the Portuguese Decriminalization of Illicit Drugs?" *British Journal of Criminology* 50, no. 6 (2010): 1001.

134. David Montgomery, "Whoa! Canada! Legal Marijuana. Gay Marriage. Peace. What the Heck's Going on Up North, Eh?" *The Washington Post*, July 1, 2003, p. C01; DeNeen L. Brown, "A Tolerance for IV Drug Users: Vancouver Seeks to Protect Addicts, Not Punish Them," *The Washington Post*, August 21, 2001, p. A01.

135. *Canada (Attorney General) v. PHS Community Services Society*, SCC 44. Supreme Court of Canada ruling available via CBC News online, "Vancouver's Insite Drug Injection Clinic Will Stay Open," September 30, 2011, www.cbc.ca/news/canada/montreal/story/2011/09/29/bc-insite-supreme-court-ruling-advancer. html.

136. International Centre for Prison Studies, www.prisonstudies.org/highest-to-lowest/prison_population_rate?field_region_taxonomy_tid=All#tabletop (accessed July 9, 2019). Figures for the UK are from 2015 and do not include juveniles or those held in immigration detention centers; Germany and Canada figures are from 2014.

137. BJS, *Capital Punishment 2016 – Statistical Brief*, NCJ251430, April 2018, p. 2.

138. Michael Tonry, "Crime and Human Rights—How Political Paranoia, Protestant Fundamentalism, and Constitutional Obsolescence Combined to Devastate Black America," *Criminology* 46, no. 1 (2008): 6–7. In Europe, the longest sentence for a single offense, even murder, is 14 years. A German court struck down life sentences without parole, and Tonry explains their reasoning as being that "hope for the future and belief in the possibility of a better life is a basic human right" so there must be meaningful review of the need for continued incarceration after the passage of not more than 14 years.

139. Cara Drinan "The War on Kids Post #1," August 3, 2018. Sentencing Law and Policy blog, https://sentencing.typepad.com/sentencing_law_and_policy/2018/08/the-war-on-kids-post-1.html.

140. A. B. Clark, "Juvenile Solitary Confinement as a Form of Child Abuse," *The Journal of the American Academy of Psychiatry and the Law*, 45, no. 3 (2017): 350–357; C. Haney, "Restricting the Use of Solitary Confinement," *Annual Review of Criminology* 1 (2018): 285–310; Tamar R. Birckhead, "Children in Isolation: The Solitary Confinement of Youth," *Wake Forest Law Review* 50, no. 1 (2015): 1.

141. BJS, *Probation and Parole in the United States, 2016*, NCJ251148, April 2018, p. 1; *Prisoners in 2016*, p. 1.

142. Kevin R. Reitz (ed.), *American Exceptionalism in Crime and Punishment* (Oxford: Oxford University Press, 2017).

143. Elliott Currie, *Confronting Crime: An American Challenge* (New York: Pantheon, 1985), p. 12.

144. See "Crime Cases Known to The Police, Cases Cleared Up and Arrestees by Type of Crime," *Japan Statistical Yearbook 2019*, edited by the Statistical Research and Training Institute, and published by the Statistics Bureau, both under the Ministry of Internal Affairs and Communications, Chart 28–1, www.stat.go.jp/english/data/nenkan/index.htm. Crime totals were based on the sum for homicide, robbery, rape, and "bodily injury" (which translates to aggravated assault) to make them comparable with *UCR* categories for violent crime. Population

used for calculation was 127 million from Chart 2.1 B of the yearbook. (Thanks to Satoko Motohara for help clarifying the meanings of the categories.) *UCR-2016,* Table 1.

145. Tokyo Metropolitan Police Department statistics, www.keishicho.metro.tokyo. jp/about_mpd/jokyo_tokei/tokei/k_tokei28.html. Thanks to Satoko Motohara for finding this statistic.

146. *Japan Statistical Yearbook 2016,* Table 28–1 and Table 2–1 B; *UCR-2016,* Table 3.

147. Elliott Currie, "Violence and Social Policy," in Walter DeKeseredy and Molly Dragiewicz (eds.), *Routledge Handbook on Critical Criminology* (New York: Routledge, 2012), p. 466.

148. *UCR-2017,* Table 5.

149. *UCR-2016,* Table 16.

150. Joseph F. Donnermeyer and Walter DeKeseredy, *Rural Criminology* (New York: Routledge, 2013), p. 11.

151. M. Szalavitz, *Help at Any Cost: How the Troubled-Teen Industry Cons Parents and Hurts Kids* (New York: Penguin, 2006); Heather Mooney and Paul Leighton, "Troubled Affluent Youth's Experiences in a Therapeutic Boarding School: The Elite Arm of the Youth Control Complex and Its Implications for Youth Justice," *Critical Criminology* 27, no. 4 (2019), doi: 10.1007/s10612-019-09466-4.

152. *Stat-Abst-2018,* Table 6; *UCR-2017,* Table 38.

153. *UCR-1990,* p. 50, Table 1; *UCR-1985,* p. 41, Table 1; and *Stat-Abst-1992,* p. 14, Table 12.

154. George James, "Serious Crime Rises Again in New York," *New York Times,* March 23, 1988, pp. B1 and B6, www.nytimes.com/1988/03/23/nyregion/serious-crime-rises-again-in-new-york.html.

155. Research reviewed by Conklin also notes that in Japan and Scotland, there was no correlation between the proportion of young males and homicide rates between 1901 and 1970. Conklin, *Why Crime Rates Fell* (Boston: Allyn & Bacon, 2003), p. 155.

156. Currie, "Violence and Social Policy," p. 466.

157. William S. Tregea, *Prisoners on Criminology: Convict Life Stories and Crime Prevention* (Lanham, MD: Lexington Books, 2014).

158. Drew Desilver, "Global Inequality: How the U.S. Compares," Pew Research Center, December 19, 2013, www.pewresearch.org/fact-tank/2013/12/19/global-inequality-how-the-u-s-compares/. We are referring to the data about inequality after taxes and transfers.

159. Graham C. Ousey and Matthew R. Lee, "Community, Inequality, and Crime," in Francis T. Cullen and Pamela Wilcox (eds.), *The Oxford Handbook of Criminological Theory* (New York: Oxford University Press, 2013), p. 363.

160. Ching-Chi Hsieh and M. D. Pugh, "Poverty, Inequality and Violent Crime," *Criminal Justice Review* 18, no. 2 (1993): 192.

161. Travis C. Pratt and Francis T. Cullen, "Assessing Macro-Level Predictors and Theories of Crime: A Meta-Analysis," *Crime and Justice* 32 (2005): 412–413.

162. John Braithwaite, "Poverty, Power, and White-Collar Crime," in Kip Schlegel and David Weisburd (eds.), *White-Collar Crime Reconsidered* (Boston: Northeastern University Press, 1992), pp. 81 and 83.

163. Ibid., pp. 85 and 87.

164. Joseph Stiglitz, *The Price of Inequality* (New York: W.W. Norton, 2012), p. 30.

165. Devin Leonard, "Economy's Loss was One Man's Gain," *New York Times,* December 5, 2009, www.nytimes.com/2009/12/06/business/economy/06shelf.html.

166. Michael Batty et al., "Introducing the Distributional Financial Accounts of the United States," *Finance and Economics Discussion Series 2019-017* (Washington: Board of Governors of the Federal Reserve System, 2019), https://doi.org/10.17016/FEDS.2019.017, p. 26; Board of Governors of the Federal Reserve System, *Distribution of Household Wealth in the U.S. Since 1989*, Table 2019Q1 for top 1 percent and bottom 90 percent, www.federalreserve.gov/releases/z1/dataviz/dfa/distribute/chart/.

167. BLS, "Employment Status of the Civilian Noninstitutional Population by Race, Sex, and Age," www.bls.gov/cps/cpsaat05.pdf. See also, "Racial Gulf: Blacks' Hopes, Raised by '68 Kerner Report, Are Mainly Unfulfilled," *The Wall Street Journal,* February 26, 1988, pp. 1 and 9; and Jacob V. Lamar Jr., "Today's Native Sons," *Time,* 128, no. 22 (December 1, 1986): 26–29.

168. *Stat-Abst-2004-5,* Table 672, p. 447; *Stat-Abst-1972,* Table 528, p. 324; Kayla Fontenot, Jessica Semega, and Melissa Kollar, U.S. Census Bureau, *Current Population Reports,* pp. 260–263, *Income and Poverty in the United States: 2017* (Washington, DC: U.S. Government Printing Office, 2018), Tables 2 and B2.

169. Janny Scott and David Leonhardt, "Class in America: Shadowy Lines That Still Divide," *New York Times,* May 15, 2005, p. A1, www.nytimes. com/2005/05/15/us/class/shadowy-lines-that-still-divide.html.

170. David Leonhardt, "Upward Mobility Has Not Declined, Study Says," *New York Times,* January 23, 2014, p. B1, www.nytimes.com/2014/01/23/business/upward-mobility-has-not-declined-study-says.html.

171. Pratt and Cullen, "Assessing Macro-Level Predictors and Theories of Crime," p. 438.

172. Todd R. Clear, "'Tougher' Is Dumber," *New York Times,* December 4, 1993, p. 21.

173. Quoted in Michelle Alexander, *The New Jim Crow* (New York: The New Press, 2011), p. 8.

174. National Research Council, Travis, Western, and Redburn (eds.), *The Growth of Incarceration in the United States,* p. 150.

175. Ibid.

176. Patrick McCarthy, Vincent Schiraldi, and Miriam Shark, *The Future of Youth Justice: A Community-Based Alternative to the Youth Prison Model,* New Thinking in Community Corrections Bulletin (Washington, DC: U.S. Department of Justice, National Institute of Justice, 2016), NCJ 250142. p. 2.

177. BJS, *Recidivism of Prisoners Released in 1994,* NCJ 193427, June 2002, p. 1.

178. BJS, *Recidivism of Prisoners Released in 30 States in 2005,* NCJ 244205, April 2014, p. 1. Mariel Alper, Matthew R. Durose, and Joshua Markman, "2018 Update on Prisoner Recidivism: A 9-Year Follow-up Period (2005–2014)" NCJ 250975, Bureau of Justice Statistics, May 2018, www.bjs.gov/content/pub/pdf/18upr9yfup0514.pdf.

179. Quoted in National Research Council, Travis, Western, and Redburn (eds.), *The Growth of Incarceration in the United States,* p. 170.

180. Robert Johnson and Hans Toch, "Introduction," in Robert Johnson and Hans Toch (eds.), *The Pains of Imprisonment* (Beverly Hills, CA: Sage, 1982), pp. 19–20.

181. Just Detention International, *Prisoner Rape Factsheet,* http://justdetention.org/en/fact_sheets.aspx.

182. Human Rights Watch, "No Escape: Male Rape in U.S. Prisons," www.hrw.org/reports/2001/prison (no longer available).

183. David Sack, "We Can't Afford to Ignore Drug Addiction in Prison," *The Washington Post,* August 14, 2014, www.washingtonpost.com/news/to-your-health/wp/2014/08/14/we-cant-afford-to-ignore-drug-addiction-in-prison/.

184. Vera Institute of Justice, *Incarceration's Front Door,* February 2015, www. vera.org/ sites/default/files/resources/downloads/incarcerations-front-door-report.pdf.
185. National Research Council, Travis, Western, and Redburn (eds.), *The Growth of Incarceration in the United States,* p. 6.
186. Tonry, "Crime and Human Rights," p. 24.
187. Pierre Thomas, "Study Suggests Black Male Prison Rate Impinges on Political Process," *The Washington Post,* January 30, 1997, p. A3. See also Jeffery Reiman, "Liberal and Republican Arguments against the Disenfranchisement of Felons," *Criminal Justice Ethics* 24, no. 1 (2005): 3–18.
188. Conklin, *Why Crime Rates Fell,* pp. 83–84; Todd Clear, *Imprisoning Communities: How Mass Incarceration Makes Disadvantaged Neighborhoods Worse* (New York: Oxford University Press, 2009).
189. National Research Council, Travis, Western, and Redburn (eds.), *The Growth of Incarceration in the United States,* p. 178.
190. Philip J. Cook and Harold A. Pollack, "Reducing Access to Guns by Violent Offenders," *The Russell Sage Foundation Journal of the Social Sciences* 3, no. 5 (October 2017): 2–36. 178.
191. Cook, Braga, and Moore, "Gun Control," pp. 260–261.
192. John Gramlich, "7 Facts about Guns in the U.S.," Pew Research Center, December 27, 2018, www.pewresearch.org/fact-tank/2018/12/27/facts-about-guns-in-united-states/.
193. *UCR-1995,* p. 36.
194. Sabrina Tavernise, "For Americans Under 50, Stark Findings on Health," *New York Times,* January 9, 2013, www.nytimes.com/2013/01/10/health/americans-under-50-fare-poorly-on-health-measures-new-report-says.html.
195. Nicholas Kristof, "Do We Have the Courage to Stop This?" *New York Times,* December 15, 2012, www.nytimes.com/2012/12/16/opinion/sunday/kristof-do-we-have-the-courage-to-stop-this.html.
196. Philip J. Cook and Jens Ludwig, *Gun Violence: The Real Costs* (New York: Oxford University Press, 2000), pp. 15, 34, and 35.
197. *Challenge,* p. 239.
198. A. Rubenstein et al., "Alarming Trends in Mortality from Firearms among United States Schoolchildren," *The American Journal of Medicine,* 132, Issue 8: 992–994, doi: doi.org/10.1016/j.amjmed.2019.02.012, p. 994.
199. Jeanne Marie Laskas, "Inside the Federal Bureau of Way Too Many Guns," *GQ,* August 30, 2016, www.gq.com/story/inside-federal-bureau-of-way-too-many-guns.
200. New York Times Editorial Board, "A Broken System for Tracking Guns," *New York Times,* December 30, 2012, www.nytimes.com/2012/12/31/opinion/a-broken-system-for-tracking-guns.html.
201. Ali Watkins, "When Guns Are Sold Illegally, A.T.F. Is Lenient on Punishment," *New York Times,* June 3, 2018, www.nytimes.com/2018/06/03/us/atf-gun-store-violations.html.
202. Allen Rostron. "The Dickey Amendment on Federal Funding for Research on Gun Violence: A Legal Discussion," *American Journal of Public Health* 108, no. (7 (2018): 865–867, doi: 10.2105/AJPH.2018.304450.
203. Cited in Blumstein, "Why Is Crime Falling—or Is It?" p. 13.
204. "A LEN Interview with Professor Alfred Blumstein of Carnegie Mellon University," *Law Enforcement News,* 21, no. 422 (April 30, 1995): 11.
205. Quoted in Bandow, "War on Drugs or War on America?" p. 246.

206. Troy Duster, *The Legislation of Morality: Law, Drugs, and Moral Judgment* (New York: Free Press, 1970), pp. 3, 7, inter alia.
207. *UCR-2017*, Table 29, https://ucr.fbi.gov/crime-in-the-u.s/2017/crime-in-the-u.s.-2017/tables/arrest-table.
208. Leslie Iverson, *The Science of Marijuana*, 2nd ed. (Oxford: Oxford University Press, 2008), p. 58. Further, "although there have been many rumors that the longterm use of marijuana leads to irreversible damage to higher brain functions, the results of numerous scientific studies have failed to confirm this," p. 167.
209. Damien Cave, "Legal Drugs Kill Far More than Illegal, Florida Says," *New York Times*, June 14, 2008, www.nytimes.com/2008/06/14/us/14florida.html.
210. Iverson, *Science of Marijuana*, p. 186.
211. Surgeon General C. Everett Koop quoted in Bandow, "War on Drugs or War on America?" p. 249.
212. Quoted in Bandow, "War on Drugs or War on America?" p. 250.
213. "A LEN Interview with Professor Alfred Blumstein," p. 11.
214. M. Douglas Anglin and George Speckart, "Narcotics Use and Crime: A Multi-sample, Multimethod Analysis," *Criminology* 26, no. 2 (1988): 226.
215. Ibid., p. 197.
216. *UCR-2017*, Property Crime, https://ucr.fbi.gov/crime-in-the-u.s/2017/crime-in-the-u.s.-2017/topic-pages/property-crime.
217. BJS, *Drug Use and Dependence, State and Federal Prisoners 2004*, NCJ 213530, October 2006, p. 1; BJS, *Substance Dependence, Abuse, and Treatment of Jail Inmates, 2002*, NCJ 209588, July 2005, p. 7.
218. Sack, "We Can't Afford to Ignore Drug Addiction in Prison."
219. Danielle Allen, "How the War on Drugs Creates Violence," *The Washington Post*, October 16, 2015, www.washingtonpost.com/opinions/how-the-war-on-drugs-creates-violence/2015/10/16/6de57a76-72b7-11e5-9cbb-790369643cf9_story.html.
220. Sari Horwitz and Nancy Lewis, "Drug Wars Push D.C. to Brink of Homicide Record," *The Washington Post*, October 26, 1988, p. A1, www.washingtonpost.com/archive/politics/1988/10/26/drug-wars-push-dc-to-brink-of-homicide-record/b900558c-f98b-4e7f-ba99-7ac34ab7407d/.
221. Philip Shenon, "Enemy Within: Drug Money Is Corrupting the Enforcers," April 11, 1988, pp. A1 and A12, www.nytimes.com/1988/04/11/us/enemy-within-drug-money-is-corrupting-the-enforcers.html.
222. Ibid.
223. Clifford Krauss, "2-Year Corruption Inquiry Finds a 'Willful Blindness' in New York's Police Dept," *New York Times*, July 7, 1994, p. A1.
224. Government Accountability Office, *Law Enforcement: Information on Drug-Related Police Corruption* (GAO/GGD-98–111) (Washington, DC: Government Accountability Office, 1998), p. 8.
225. Quoted in Butterfield, "Intervening Early Costs Less than '3-Strikes' Laws," *New York Times*, June 23, 1996, p. A24.
226. Currie, *Crime and Punishment in America*, pp. 81 and 98.
227. Peter W. Greenwood, "Costs and Benefits of Early Childhood Intervention," *OJJDP Fact Sheet no. 94* (Washington, DC: U.S. Department of Justice, Office of Juvenile Justice and Delinquency Prevention, February 1999).
228. Lawrence Sherman et al., "Preventing Crime: What Works, What Doesn't, What's Promising," *NIJ Research in Brief*, NIJ171676 (Washington, DC: National Institute of Justice, July 1998), www.ncjrs.gov/pdffiles/171676.PDF. See also David

Farrington and Brandon Welsh, *Saving Children from a Life of Crime: Early Risk Factors and Effective Interventions* (Oxford: Oxford University Press, 2007).

229. Farrington and Welsh, *Saving Children from a Life of Crime.*
230. Irvin Waller, *Science and Secrets of Ending Violent Crime* (Lanham, MD: Rowman & Littlefield, 2019.
231. *Criminology and Public Policy* 6, no. 4 (2007).
232. Kleiman, "Smart on Crime," pp. 16–17.
233. Quoted in Butterfield, Intervening early Costs Less Than '3-Strikes' Laws," p. A24.
234. "Crime Wave," *Time* 105, no. 27 (June 30, 1975): 17 (emphasis added).
235. Kai T. Erikson, *Wayward Puritans* (New York: Wiley, 1966), p. 4. Reprinted by permission of John Wiley & Sons, Inc.
236. Ibid., p. 11.
237. Ibid., pp. 13–15 (emphasis added).
238. David Garland suggests that this is true of Erikson's study even if Erikson does not highlight this aspect. Garland writes that Erikson's study:

    is a description of the deep social and religious tensions within [a Puritan] community …. In this context, it becomes clear that the exercise of criminal punishments … was also the forceful imposition of a particular framework of politico-religious authority on a society riven by factions and deep tensions (Garland, *Punishment and Modern Society: A Study in Social Theory* [Chicago: University of Chicago Press, 1990], p. 79).

239. Michel Foucault, *Discipline and Punish: The Birth of the Prison,* trans. Alan Sheridan (London: Allen Lane, 1977), p. 271.
240. Ibid., p. 277.
241. Ibid., p. 274.
242. Ibid., p. 275.
243. Ibid., p. 279.
244. Ibid., p. 288.
245. Foucault writes that the system includes an attempt to shape "the common perception of delinquents: to present them as close by, everywhere present and everywhere to be feared" (ibid., p. 286).
246. Ibid., p. 281.
247. Ibid., pp. 296–297.
248. Ibid., p. 304.
249. "Foucault's description of Western liberal democracy as a society of surveillance, disciplined from end to end, is deliberately reminiscent of … totalitarianism" (Garland, *Punishment and Modern Society,* p. 151).
250. According to Nicos Poulantzas,

    Now, for Foucault, the power relation never has any other basis than itself: it becomes a pure "situation" in which power is always immanent; and the question what power and power to do what appears as a mere obstacle. This leads Foucault into a particular logical impasse from which there is no possible escape …. For if power is always already there, if every power situation is immanent in itself, why should there ever be resistance? From where would resistance come, and how would it be even possible?" (Nicos Poulantzas, *State, Power, Socialism,* trans. P. Camiller [London: NLB, 1978], p. 149).

CHAPTER **2**

A Crime by Any Other Name ...

If one individual inflicts a bodily injury upon another which leads to the death of the person attacked we call it manslaughter; on the other hand, if the attacker knows beforehand that the blow will be fatal we call it murder. Murder has also been committed if society places hundreds of workers in such a position that they inevitably come to premature and unnatural ends. Their death is as violent as if they had been stabbed or shot.... Murder has been committed if society knows perfectly well that thousands of workers cannot avoid being sacrificed so long as these conditions are allowed to continue. Murder of this sort is just as culpable as the murder committed by an individual.

—FREDERICK ENGELS, *THE CONDITION OF THE WORKING CLASS IN ENGLAND*

Based on an examination of the various ways that Americans are harmed, this chapter shows that some of the greatest dangers that we face come from acts that are not labeled crimes. Readers are asked to compare the harms produced by crimes with the harms of noncriminal behavior as a step toward determining if the harsh treatment of those who impose criminal harms, and the gentle treatment of those who impose noncriminal harms, represent intelligent policy. As the response to the Defenders of the Present Legal Order shows, the acts that lead to these noncriminal harms share many elements of criminal conduct—they are harmful acts done knowingly or recklessly. However, they tend to be ignored or minimized by the criminal justice system. The inclusion of certain harmful acts within the criminal law, and the exclusion of other comparably harmful acts, mean that the criminal law does not reflect an objective reality of "dangerous crime." The criminal justice system acts as a carnival mirror that distorts reality by magnifying the threat of street crime while minimizing the threat from the dangerous acts of the rich?

WHAT'S IN A NAME?

If you read this book for 30 minutes, by the time you're done, one of your fellow citizens will have been murdered. *During that same time, more than four Americans will die as a result of unhealthy or unsafe conditions in the workplace!* Although these work-related deaths were due to human actions, they are not called murders. Why not? Doesn't a crime by any other name still cause misery and suffering? What's in a name?

The label "crime" is not used in America to name all or the worst of the morally blameworthy actions that cause misery and suffering to Americans. It is reserved primarily for the dangerous actions of the poor.

The *New York Times* ran a story in 2005 with the headline "14 Die in Blast at BP Oil Refinery in Texas."[1] Ultimately, 15 people died and another 170 were injured. A sergeant in the fire department noted, "It looked like a small war zone of bodies being loaded up" onto medical helicopters running evacuation missions. A report by the U.S. Chemical Safety and Hazard Investigation Board found that "BP management did not implement adequate safety oversight, provide needed human and economic resources, or consistently model adherence to safety rules and procedures."[2] The night before the explosion, important operational records had not been filled out. So day shift workers "had no precise information of what steps the night crew had completed and [thus] what the day shift was to do"[3] with hundreds of thousands of gallons of oil heating up, according to the report.

As BP was settling the fines, an article appeared in the *Chicago Tribune* with the headline: "Massacre at Mall in Omaha: 8 Killed."[4] Robert Hawkins had fired several dozen rounds from "an AK-47-style semi-automatic weapon" at shoppers before killing himself.[5] Hawkins was surely a murderer and may have committed a massacre. Our question is: Why wasn't the death of BP's refinery workers also murder? Why weren't 14 dead and 170 injured refinery workers regarded as a massacre?

"Massacre" suggests a murderer, whereas "blast" and "explosion" suggest the work of impersonal forces. However, a 2002 safety audit found "serious concerns about the potential for a major site incident" and "mechanical integrity" issues because the site was "in complete decline."[6] Safety audits in 2003 and 2004 found similar concerns. A survey of 1,000 employees by an auditor hired by BP found they had an "exceptional degree of fear."[7] Yet during this time, BP was increasing its profits by cutting safety inspectors and maintenance workers.[8] The result was a lax safety culture. Someone was responsible for the conditions that led to the 14 deaths. Is that person not a murderer, perhaps even responsible for a massacre?

BP, which reported a profit of $22.6 billion that year, paid a fine to the Occupational Safety and Health Administration (OSHA) of $21 million for the Texas City explosion. A Department of Labor spokesman said, "This citation and penalty—nearly double the next largest fine in OSHA history—sends a strong message to all employers about the need to protect workers and to make health and safety a core value."[9] They also pleaded guilty to a single criminal felony violation of the Clean Air Act and were fined $60 million—the "Largest Criminal Fine Ever for Air Violations" noted the Environmental Protection Agency (EPA)'s press release.[10]

So BP was criminally fined—for pollution—but no one was tried for *murder*. No one was even thought of as a murderer. *Why not?*

This question is at this point rhetorical. Our aim is not to discuss this case but rather to point to the blinders we wear when we look at such an "accident." While the question is rhetorical, the answer matters greatly for justice and the lives of hard-working Americans. Another investigation report found "material deficiencies" in safety at five of BP's U.S. refineries.[11] The *Houston Chronicle* notes that the same number of refinery workers died in the decade after the explosion as in the decade before it.[12] And, of course, in 2010, BP's Deepwater Horizon exploded, killing 11 and causing the largest oil spill in the history of offshore oil drilling.[13]

Wouldn't many industrial workers be safer if the people at BP responsible for the explosion were treated as murderers? Might the workers on the Deepwater Horizon still be alive if executives were being charged as criminals for acts like what happened at the Texas City refinery? Didn't those workers have a right to be protected by the criminal justice system against the violence that took their lives? *And if not, why not?*

Will a president of the United States address the Yale Law School and recommend mandatory prison sentences for such people? Will he mean these people when he says, "These relatively few, persistent criminals who cause so much misery and fear are really the core of the problem. The rest of the American people have a right to protection from their violence."[14]

Once we are ready to ask this question seriously, we are in a position to see that the reality of crime—the acts we label crime and the actors and actions we treat as criminal—is *created*: It is a reality shaped by decisions as to *what* will be called crime and *who* will be treated as a criminal.

THE CARNIVAL MIRROR: CRIMINAL JUSTICE AS CREATIVE ART

The Pyrrhic defeat explanation for the "failure" of criminal justice in America holds that criminal justice *fails* (that is, it does little to reduce our high crime rates) in order to project a particular *image* of crime. Chapter 1 described the failure to adopt policies that could eliminate our high crime rates. It is the task of this chapter and the next to prove that the reality of crime is *created* and that it is created in a way that promotes a particular *image* of crime: *The image that serious crime—and, therefore, the greatest danger to society—is the work of the poor.*

In this chapter, we start by acknowledging that the BP executives do not seem like typical criminals, nor do countless other executives who endanger workers, consumers, and communities. We use this observation as an opportunity to examine the collective image Americans have of the typical criminal. This leads to a discussion of the social construction of crime, whereby morally blameworthy harmful behaviors become what we know as crime. Out of this process emerges the typical criminal, as well as the common understanding of what the "crime problem" means and which groups should be the target of crime control. This construction should mirror the greatest threats to our well-being. But we argue that the criminal justice system shows a distorted image— like a carnival mirror—that magnifies the threat of street crime and diminishes the threat from corporate misbehavior and the harms of the powerful.

The Typical Criminal and the Social Construction of Crime

What do we see when we look in the criminal justice mirror? Look more closely at the face in today's criminal justice mirror and we shall see the Typical Criminal.

The person is, first of all, a *he*. Of 8.2 million persons arrested for crimes in 2017, 73 percent were males. Of persons arrested for violent crimes, 80 percent were men. Second, he is predominantly *urban*.[15] Third, he is disproportionately *black*: In 2017, with blacks representing 13 percent of the nation's population, they made up 38 percent of violent crime arrests and 27 percent of all crime arrests.[16] Finally, he is *poor*. According to a Brookings Institution analysis, "two years prior to the year they entered prison, 56 percent of individuals have essentially no annual earnings (less than $500)."[17] As the President's Commission on Law Enforcement and Administration of Justice reported in 1967, "The offender at the end of the road in prison is likely to be a member of the lowest social and economic groups in the country."[18]

This is the Typical Criminal feared by law-abiding Americans. Poor, young, urban, (disproportionately) black males make up the core of the enemy forces in the crime war. They are seen as a menace, threatening the lives, limbs, and possessions of the law-abiding members of society, necessitating recourse to the ultimate weapons of force and detention in our common defense. This picture is widely shared. A 1995 survey asked respondents to "close your eyes for a second, envision a drug user, and describe that person. Ninety-five percent (95%!) pictured someone black."[19] In *The Color of Crime*, Kathryn Russell speaks of the "criminalblackman" to highlight the close connection between these words in popular culture.[20]

Where do we get this picture? How do we know who the criminals are who so seriously endanger us that we must stop them with force and lock them in prisons? "From the arrest records, probation reports, and prison statistics," the President's Commission on Law Enforcement and Administration of Justice, authors of *The Challenge of Crime in a Free Society*, tells us, the "'portrait' of the offender emerges."[21] But note, *these sources are not merely objective readings taken at different stages in the criminal justice process: Each of them represents human decisions.* "Prison statistics" and "probation reports" reflect *decisions* of juries on who gets convicted and *decisions* of judges on who gets probation or prison and for how long. "Arrest records" reflect police *decisions* about which crimes to investigate and which suspects to take into custody. All these decisions rest on the most fundamental of all decisions: The *decisions* of legislators as to which acts shall be labeled "crimes" in the first place.

In short, our picture of crime reflects a reality—criminal acts, arrests, convictions, imprisonment, and so on—but this reality of crime is not a simple objective threat to which the criminal justice system reacts: *It is a reality that takes shape as it is filtered through a series of human decisions running the full gamut of the criminal justice system*—from the lawmakers who determine what behavior shall be in the province of criminal justice to the law enforcers who decide which individuals will be brought within that province.

And it doesn't end with the criminal justice system as such because the media—through news and TV crime dramas—contribute to the image that people have of crime in our society.[22] Here, too, human decisions are fundamental. The news media do not simply report the facts. There are too many facts out there. A selection must be made. People working in the news media must choose which facts are *news*; they must choose how to represent or "frame" those facts—like "crime waves" or "violent youth"—and do so in a way that attracts viewers and makes a profit. Criminology too, generally presents street crime as if it is all crime, with only 5.7 percent of the pages from best-selling introductory textbooks and 3.4 percent of the articles in the most prestigious journals about white collar crime.[23]

Note that by emphasizing the role of "human decisions," we do not mean to suggest that police officers intentionally ignore corporate crime and go after the poor, in order to create the idea for the public that street crime is the biggest threat. Rather, police decisions are themselves shaped by the social system, much as a child's decision to become an engineer rather than a samurai warrior is shaped by the social system in which he or she grows up. Thus, to have a full explanation of how the reality of crime is created, we have to understand how our society is structured in a way that leads people to make the decisions they do. In other words, *the decisions of people in the criminal justice system are part of the social phenomena that need to be explained.*

The present discussion, however, emphasizes the role of the decisions themselves for the following reasons: First, they are conspicuous points in the social process, relatively easy to spot and verify empirically. Second, because they are decisions aimed at protecting us from the dangers in our midst, we can compare the decisions with the real dangers and determine whether they are accurately responding to the real dangers. Third, because the reality of crime—the real actions labeled crimes, the real individuals identified as criminals, and the real faces we watch in the news as they travel from arrest to court to prison—results from these decisions, we can determine whether that reality corresponds to the real dangers in our society. Where that reality does correspond to the real dangers, we can say that the reality of crime simply reflects the real dangers in society. Where the reality of crime does not correspond to the real dangers, we can say that it is a reality *created* by those decisions. Then we can investigate the role played by the social system in encouraging, reinforcing, and otherwise shaping those decisions.

The Carnival Mirror and Why It Matters

The notion that the reality of crime is created is derived from Richard Quinney, who maintained that crime has a "social reality" rather than an objective reality.[24] He meant that the reality of a crime as *a crime* does not lie simply in the objective characteristics of an action, such as taking people's money or harming their bodies. It lies in the "social" meaning attached to that action and the pattern of "social" behavior—particularly the behavior of criminal justice officials–in response to it. In other words, the reality of crime means more than physical actions, such as poisoning or wounding, and includes the reality that a society gives those physical actions by labeling them and treating them as criminal. Thus, this reality of crime is *created* and is a definition of behavior conferred by "agents of the law (legislators, police, prosecutors, and judges)."[25]

One implication of the idea that crime is created is that eliminating criminal laws eliminates crime and criminals. This is true, but it does not take us very far. Even without criminal law and a criminal justice system, there would still be dangerous acts. The criminal law *labels* some harmful and dangerous acts as "crimes." In doing this, it identifies those acts as so dangerous, blameworthy, and preventable that we must use the extreme coercion of criminal justice to protect ourselves against them. This does not mean that criminal law *creates* crime—what it calls "crime" "mirrors" real dangers that threaten us. What is true of the criminal law is true of the whole justice system. Police, prosecutors, judges, and juries *react* to real dangers in society. The criminal justice system—from lawmakers to law enforcers—is just a mirror of the real dangers that lurk in our midst. *Or so we are told.*

Here critical questions arise. Recognizing the social reality of crime prompts us to ask whether the label of crime is applied appropriately to harmful behavior. This question often does not arise in criminology because its focus is on street crime where there is a high degree of consensus that acts like murder, rape, and robbery are rightfully labeled crimes. Because of this, many people (including criminologists) assume that all intentional harmful acts are defined as crimes. They do not critically examine the political process that determines what crime is, and thus they don't reflect for themselves on what criminology should study. In contrast, we contend that there should be critical reflection on whether the criminal law mirrors the harms that *should* be defined as crimes—and what types of behavior criminology should study. (Appendix II elaborates on this concept.)

Technically, the definition of "crime" is "an act prohibited by a criminal law." But the point of prohibiting an act by the criminal law is to protect society from injurious or dangerous actions. Indeed, as Agnew explains, the more general definition of crime means "unjustifiable and inexcusable" harms that involve "voluntary and intentional behavior with intention broadly defined" as involving "purposeful, knowledgeable, reckless, and negligent behavior."[26] While this definition includes acts that should be crimes, it also includes morally blameworthy harms that are not criminalized—"unrecognized blameworthy harms." And, "much state and corporate harm falls into this category, since the power of state and corporate actors makes it easier for them to justify and excuse harm, hide blameworthiness, and prevent state sanction."[27]

The label of crime is applied appropriately when it is used to identify all, or at least the worst, voluntary, preventable, and unjustifiable acts that are harmful to society. The label is applied inappropriately when it is attached to harmless acts or when it is not attached to seriously harmful acts. When we argue that the reality of crime is created, we point to the ways in which the label "crime" has not been applied appropriately. It is, of course, appropriate to label muggings and rapes as crimes. What is inappropriate is to fail to label equally or even more harmful intentional acts as crimes.

To capture this way of looking at the relation between the reality of crime and the real dangers "out there" in society, we refer to the criminal justice system as a "mirror." We need to investigate how accurate the mirror is in order to know whether or how well the criminal justice system is protecting us against the complete range of real threats to our well-being. The more accurate a mirror is, the more the image it shows is created by the reality it reflects. The more misshapen a mirror is, the more distorted the image shown is, created by the mirror itself not by the reality reflected in it. It is in this sense that we will argue that the image of crime is *created*: The American criminal justice system is a mirror that shows a *distorted image* of the dangers that threaten us—an image created more by the shape of the mirror than by the reality reflected.

We believe that the mugger, the rapist, the murderer, the burglar, and the robber all pose a definite threat to our well-being—and they ought to be dealt with in ways that promote public safety without making the criminal justice system itself a threat to our lives and liberties. Our concern is that the threats posed by the Typical Criminal are not the only threats that we face; the Typical Crimes are not the only acts that endanger us nor are they the acts that endanger us the most. As this chapter will demonstrate, we have as great, and sometimes even a greater, a chance of being killed or disabled by an occupational injury or disease, by unnecessary surgery, or by shoddy medical services, than by aggravated assault or even homicide! Yet even though these threats to our well-being are graver than that posed by our poor young criminals, they do not show up in the FBI's *UCR* as serious crimes. The individuals responsible for them do not turn up in arrest records or prison statistics. *They don't become part of the reality reflected in the criminal justice mirror, although the danger they pose is at least as great as, and often greater than, the danger posed by those who do!*

Similarly, the general public loses more money *by far* (as shown in Chapter 3) from tax cheating, wage theft by employers, fraud, and consumer deception than from all the property crimes reported by the FBI. Yet these far more costly acts are either not criminal, or if technically criminal, not prosecuted, or if prosecuted, not punished, or if punished, only mildly. The individuals responsible for these acts take more money out of the ordinary citizen's pocket than our Typical Criminal, but they rarely show up in arrest statistics and almost never in prison populations. *Their faces rarely appear in the criminal justice mirror, although the danger they pose is at least as great as, and often greater than, that of those who do.*

The criminal justice system is like a mirror in which society can see the face of the evil in its midst. Because the system deals with some evils and not with others, because it treats some minor evils as grave and treats some of the gravest evils as minor, the image it throws back is distorted, like the image in a carnival mirror. Thus, the image cast back is false, not because it is invented out of thin air, but because the proportions of the real are distorted: Large becomes small, and small, large; grave becomes minor, and minor, grave. Like a carnival mirror, although nothing is reflected that does not already exist in the world, the image is more a creation of the mirror than a picture of the world.

The inescapable conclusion is that the criminal justice system does not simply *reflect* the reality of crime; it has a hand in *creating* the reality we see. It magnifies the real threat of street crime while minimizing the real harms of corporate misbehavior.

If criminal justice really gives us a carnival-mirror image of "crime," we are doubly deceived. First, we are led to believe that the criminal justice system is protecting us against the gravest threats to our well-being when, in fact, the system is protecting us against only some threats and not necessarily the gravest ones. We are deceived about how much protection we are receiving and thus are left vulnerable to serious harms. The second deception is just the other side of this one. If people believe that the carnival mirror is a true mirror—that is, if they believe the criminal justice system simply reacts to the gravest threats to their well-being—they come to believe that whatever is the target of the criminal justice system must be the greatest threat to their well-being. In other words, if people believe that the most drastic of society's weapons are wielded by the criminal justice system *in reaction to* the gravest dangers to society, they will believe the reverse as well: that those actions that call forth the most drastic of society's weapons *must be* those that pose the gravest dangers to society.

A strange alchemy takes place when people accept uncritically the legitimacy of their institutions: What *needs* justification becomes *proof* of justification. People come to believe that prisoners must be dangerous criminals *because* they are in prison and that the inmates of insane asylums must be *crazy* because they are in insane asylums.[28] The criminal justice system's use of extreme measures—such as force and imprisonment—is thought to be justified by the extreme gravity of the dangers it combats. By this alchemy, however, these extreme measures become *proof* of the extreme gravity of those dangers, and the first deception, which merely misleads the public about how much protection the criminal justice system is actually providing, is transformed into the second, which deceives the public into believing that the acts and actors that are the targets of the criminal justice system pose the gravest threats to its well-being. Thus, the system not only fails to protect us from dangers as great as or greater than those listed in the FBI's

UCR, it does still greater damage by creating the false security of the belief that only the acts treated as serious in the FBI's *UCR* really threaten us and require control.

* * *

The carnival mirror distortions exist because of the way the reality of crime is created by human actors—from lawmakers to police to judges—who define it and respond to it. By calling crime created, we want to emphasize the *fact that decisions as to what to label and treat as crime are not compelled by objective dangers, and thus that, to understand the reality of crime, we must look to the social processes that shape those decisions.* This picture of crime—the portrait that emerges from lawmakers, arrest statistics, prison populations, politicians' speeches, criminology, news media, and fictionalized presentations—is a piece of creative art. It is a picture in which some dangers are distorted, some magnified, some minimized. Because it cannot be explained as a straight reflection of real dangers, we must look elsewhere to understand the shape it takes.

This argument, which will occupy us in this chapter and the next, leads to *five hypotheses* about the way in which the public's image of crime is created. To demonstrate that the reality of crime is created, and that the criminal justice system is a carnival mirror that shows us a distorted image of the dangers that threaten us, we will try to prove that, at each of the crucial decision-making points in criminal justice, the decisions arrived at do not appropriately reflect the real and most serious dangers we face. The five hypotheses are as follows.

1. *Of the decisions of legislators:* The definitions of crime in the criminal law do not reflect the only or the most dangerous of antisocial behaviors.
2. *Of the decisions of police and prosecutors:* The decisions on whom to arrest or charge do not reflect the only or the most dangerous behaviors legally defined as "criminal."
3. *Of the decisions of juries and judges:* Criminal convictions do not reflect the only or the most dangerous individuals among those arrested and charged.
4. *Of the decisions of sentencing judges:* Sentencing decisions do not reflect the goal of protecting society from the most dangerous of those convicted by meting out punishments proportionate to the harmfulness of the crimes committed.
5. *Of all these decisions taken together:* What criminal justice policy decisions (in hypotheses 1 through 4) do reflect is the identification of crime with the dangerous acts of the poor, an identification amplified by media representations of crime and criminology's focus on street crime.

The Pyrrhic defeat theory comprises these five hypotheses *plus* the proposition that the criminal justice system is failing in avoidable ways to eliminate our high crime rates (argued in Chapter 1) *plus* the *historical inertia* explanation of how this failure is generated and left uncorrected because of the ideological benefits it produces (argued in Chapter 4). Note that the fifth hypothesis goes beyond the criminal justice system to point to the role of the media and the study of crime. That is, while criminal justice practice creates an image of crime as the work of the poor, the media serve as the conveyor of that image to the wider public, and criminology books authoritatively reinforce key points to an audience of future experts. Moreover, this conveyor adds a twist of its own: it magnifies the biases of the criminal justice system. So, we shall see that the media portray crime—in reality and in fiction—in ways that overrepresent the *types* of crimes committed by poor people (even when committed by rich folks on TV), and that obscure the social factors that lead to crime in reality (argued in this chapter and in Chapter 4). Finally, we defend the *historical inertia* explanation of why the criminal justice system functions the way it does. We will try to show how the biased image of crime persists because the particular distribution of costs and benefits to which those decisions give rise serves to make the system self-reinforcing.

A CRIME BY ANY OTHER NAME...

Think of a crime, any crime. Picture the first crime that comes into your mind. What do you see? The odds are you are not imagining an oil company executive sitting at his desk, calculating the costs of proper safety precautions and deciding not to invest in them. Probably what you do see with your mind's eye is one person assaulting another physically or robbing something from another via the threat of physical attack. Look more closely. What does the attacker look like? It's a safe bet he (and it is a *he*, of course) is not wearing a suit and tie. In fact, you—like us, like almost anyone else in America—picture a young, tough, lower-class male when the thought of crime first pops into your head. You (we) picture someone like the Typical Criminal described earlier. The crime itself is one in which the Typical Criminal sets out to attack or rob some specific person.

This last point is important. It indicates that we have a mental image not only of the Typical Criminal but also of the *Typical Crime*. If the Typical Criminal is a young, lower-class male, the Typical Crime is *one-on-one* or *interpersonal harm*—where "harm" means physical injury, loss of something valuable, or both. Certainly this is the Typical Crime portrayed on any random sample of police or private-eye shows on television.

Moreover, the media portray violent crime way out of proportion to its occurrence in the real world. One in-depth study of local and cable news found that 30 percent of all stories on news programs were about crime, and half of those were about murder.[29] In contrast, murder makes up about 17,284 of the 8.9 million violent and property crimes reported to the police—that's about one-fifth of 1 percent.[30] Those who watch TV news in general, and local TV news in particular, seem more likely to believe that crime is rising, as do viewers of crime investigation dramas.[31] Further, popular police TV programs do not show the policing of consumer fraud, environmental pollution, financial crimes, or unsafe workplaces. When *Law &*

Order detectives track down a well-heeled criminal, it is for a one-on-one harm, usually murder.

Notice, then, that TV crime shows focus on the crimes typically committed by poor people, but they do not present these as only committed by poor people. Rather than contradict the Pyrrhic defeat theory, this combination confirms it in a powerful way. The result of this combination is that TV crime shows broadcast a double-edged message: (1) that the one-on-one crimes of the poor are the typical crimes that rich and poor criminals alike commit—thus, they are not caused uniquely by the pressures of poverty; *and* (2) that the criminal justice system pursues both rich and poor criminals—thus, when the criminal justice system happens mainly to pounce on the poor in real life, it is not from any class bias. By overrepresenting violent, one-on-one crimes, television creates and confirms the commonsense view that these are the crimes that threaten us. Since, in the real world those crimes are disproportionately committed by poor people, the image that it is the poor who pose the greatest danger to law-abiding Americans is projected for all to see.

It is important to identify this model of the Typical Crime because it functions like a set of blinders. It keeps us from calling an industrial "disaster" a massacre even if 14 men were killed and 170 were injured—even if someone was responsible for the unsafe conditions in which they worked. One study of newspaper reporting of a food-processing plant fire, in which 25 workers were killed and criminal charges were ultimately brought, concludes that "the newspapers showed little consciousness that corporate violence might be seen as a crime."[32] More recently, the *Washington Post* reported that the Peanut Corporation of America "knowingly shipped out contaminated peanut butter 12 times in the past two years." The company's salmonella-tainted peanuts were linked to 9 deaths and over 700 cases of illness, many requiring hospitalization.[33] Media covered the recall of more than 4,000 peanut-based products but made no mention of "mass murder" or even "crime," though federal law makes it a felony to intentionally place adulterated food into commerce. A press conference, at which the victims called for criminal charges, received no attention from mainstream media.[34]

This is due to our fixation on the model of the Typical Crime. This particular piece of mental furniture so blocks our view that it keeps us from using the criminal justice system to protect ourselves from the greatest threats to our bodies and possessions.

What keeps an industrial "disaster" from being a mass murder in our eyes is that it is not a one-on-one harm where the *desire of someone (or someones) is to harm someone (or someones) else.* An attack by a gang on one or more persons or an attack by one individual on several still fits the one-on-one harm model of interpersonal violence. Once he selects his victim, the rapist, the mugger, or the murderer all want that person to suffer. An executive, on the other hand, does not want his employees to be harmed. He would truly prefer that there be no accident and no injured or dead workers. What he does want is something legitimate. It is what he has been hired to get: maximum profits at minimum costs. If he cuts corners to save a buck, he is just doing his job.

If ten men die because he cut corners on safety, we may think him crude or callous but not a murderer. He is, at most, responsible for *indirect harm* not one-on-one harm. For this, he may even be criminally indictable for violating safety regulations but not for murder. The men are dead as an unwanted consequence of his (perhaps overzealous or under-cautious) pursuit of a legitimate goal. So, unlike the Typical Criminal, he has not committed the Typical Crime and therefore should not be a target of the criminal justice system—or so we generally believe. As a result, men are dead who might be alive now if cutting corners of the kind that leads to loss of life, whether specifically aimed at or not, were treated as murder.

This is our point. Because we accept the belief—encouraged by our politicians' statements about crime and by the (corporate-owned) media's portrayal of crime—that the model for crime is one person specifically and directly trying to harm another, we accept a legal system that leaves us unprotected against much greater dangers to our lives and well-being than those threatened by the Typical Criminal. Before developing this point further, let us anticipate and deal with some likely objections. Defenders of the present legal order are likely to respond to our argument at this point with irritation. Because this will surely turn to outrage in a few pages, let's talk to them now, while the possibility of rational communication still exists.

The "Defenders of the Present Legal Order" (we'll call them "the Defenders" for short) are neither foolish nor evil people. They are not racists nor are they oblivious to the need for reform in the criminal justice system to make it more even-handed and for reform in the larger society to make equal opportunity more of a reality for all Americans. Their response to our argument at this point is that the criminal justice system *should* occupy itself with one-on-one harm. Harms of the sort exemplified in the refinery explosion are really *not* murders, and are better dealt with through stricter government enforcement of safety regulations. The Defenders might admit that this enforcement has been rather lax and could be improved. Basically, though, they think this division of labor is right because it fits our ordinary moral sensibilities.

The Defenders maintain that, according to our common moral notions, someone who tries to do another harm is really more evil than someone who jeopardizes others while pursuing legitimate goals but doesn't aim to harm anyone. The one who jeopardizes others in this way doesn't want to hurt them. He or she doesn't have the goal of hurting someone in the way that a mugger or a rapist does. Moreover, being directly and purposely harmed by another person, the Defenders believe, is terrifying in a way that being harmed indirectly and impersonally, say, by a safety hazard, is not, even if the resultant injury is the same in both cases. And we should be tolerant of the one responsible for lax safety measures because he or she is pursuing a legitimate goal—his or her dangerous action occurs as part of a productive activity, something that ultimately adds to social wealth and thus benefits everyone—whereas doers of one-on-one harm benefit no one but themselves. Thus, the latter are rightfully in the province of the criminal justice system with its drastic weapons, and the former are appropriately dealt with by the milder forms of regulation (or, perhaps, treated legally as responsible for civil *torts* rather than for crimes).[35] Further, the Defenders insist, the crimes targeted by the criminal justice system are imposed on their victims totally against their will, whereas the victims of occupational hazards chose to accept their risky jobs and thus have, in some degree, consented to subject themselves to the dangers. Where dangers are consented to, the appropriate response is not blame but improved safety, and this is most efficiently done by regulation rather than with the guilt-seeking methods of criminal justice.

In sum, the Defenders make four objections: (1) Someone who purposely tries to harm another is really more evil than someone who harms another without aiming to, even if the degree of harm is the same; (2) being harmed directly by another person is more terrifying than being harmed indirectly and impersonally, as by a safety hazard, even if the degree of harm is the same; (3) someone who harms another in the course of an illegitimate and purely self-interested action is more evil than someone who harms another as a consequence of a legitimate and socially productive endeavor; and (4) the harms of typical crimes are imposed on their victims against their wills, whereas harms such as those due to occupational hazards are consented to by workers when they agree to a job.

All four of these objections are said to reflect our common moral beliefs, which are a fair standard for a legal system to match. Some or all of these objections may have already occurred to the reader. Thus, it is important to respond to the Defenders. In doing so, we will show that neither our common moral beliefs nor our traditional legal notions justify treating indirect harms as regulatory matters rather than serious crimes.

1. Defenders' First Objection

Someone who purposely tries to harm another is really more evil than someone who harms another without aiming to, even if the degree of harm is the same. Thus, the Typical Criminal is rightly subject to criminal justice, while the cost-cutting executive who endangers workers, consumers, or the public is rightly subject to noncriminal safety regulations.

RESPONSE The Defenders' first objection confuses intention with aim or purpose, and it is intention that brings us properly within the reach of the criminal law. It is true that a mugger aims to harm his victim in a way that a corporate executive who maintains an unsafe workplace does not, but the corporate executive acts knowingly, recklessly, or negligently nonetheless. These are all states of awareness and volition that make his actions appropriately subject to criminal law. What we intend is not just what we want to make happen.[36] Whether the actor *wants* his conduct to harm someone is a different matter, which is relevant to the actor's *degree* of culpability (not to whether he or she is culpable at all).

Here's an example (adapted from one given by criminal law theorist Hyman Gross) to help understand the legally recognized degrees of culpability: Suppose a construction worker digs a trench in a neighborhood where children regularly play and leaves the trench uncovered. One rainy day, children are killed while playing in the trench when its walls cave in on them. If the construction worker dug the trench and left it uncovered in order to kill the children, then their deaths were caused *purposely*. But suppose that the trench was dug and left uncovered not in order to harm the children but merely with the knowledge that children played in the area. Then, their deaths were brought about *knowingly*. If digging the ditch and leaving it uncovered were done both without knowing that children played in the area and without making sure that they did not, then their deaths were brought about *recklessly*. Finally, if the trench was dug and left uncovered without knowledge that children played in the area and some, but inadequate, precautions were taken to make sure no children were there, then their deaths were brought about *negligently*.[37]

What's important here is that all these ways of causing death count as criminally culpable. The difference between purposely, knowingly, recklessly, or negligently causing death is a difference within the range of intentional action. Second, culpability decreases as we go from purposely to knowingly to recklessly to negligently killing because, according to Gross, the outcome is increasingly due to chance and not to the actor. The one who kills on purpose leaves less to chance that death will occur than the one who kills knowingly (the one who kills on purpose will take precautions against the failure of his killing, which the one who kills knowingly won't do). The one who kills recklessly leaves wholly to chance whether there is a victim at all. The one who kills negligently reduces this chance, but insufficiently.

The kernel of truth in the Defenders' first objection is that the common street mugger harms on purpose, while the executive harms only knowingly or recklessly or negligently. However, both act intentionally. Nancy Frank concludes from a review of state homicide statutes that "a large number of states recognize unintended deaths caused by extreme recklessness as murder."[38] We also have criminal laws against reckless or negligent harming. But when "there is a substantial probability that death or serious physical harm could result and the employer knew, or should have known, of the hazard" the Occupational Safety and Health Administration (OSHA) issues a citation for a "serious" violation.[39] Thus, refusal to treat those responsible for occupational hazards (and the like) as criminals is not justified by our ordinary moral sensibilities, as the Defenders claim.

Further, Great Britain has its Corporate Manslaughter Act, under which corporations can be found guilty of manslaughter when gross negligence in supervision leads to a death. These deaths are reported in crime statistics. An Australian territory also has a corporate manslaughter law that can apply to senior executives where their gross negligence in supervision causes a death, and a Canadian bill (C-45) helps clarify how the regular criminal law applies to organizations, which has been applied in cases of occupational deaths.[40]

Moreover, don't be confused into thinking that, because all workplaces have some safety measures, all workplace deaths are at most due to negligence.

To the extent that precautions are not taken against particular known dangers (like faulty equipment) deaths due to those dangers are—by Gross's standard—caused recklessly or even knowingly (because the executive knows that potential victims are in harm's way from the danger he fails to reduce).

There is more to be said. Remember that Gross attributes the difference in degrees of culpability to the greater role left to chance as we descend from purposely to knowingly to recklessly to negligently harming. In this light, it is important to note that the executive (say, the refinery owner) imposes danger on a larger number of individuals than the Typical Criminal typically does. So while the Typical Criminal purposely harms a particular individual, the executive knowingly subjects a large number of workers or consumers to a risk of harm. As the risk becomes greater and the number of workers or consumers increases, it becomes increasingly likely that the executive will harm one particular individual (or more). This means that the gap between the executive and the Typical Criminal shrinks toward nothing.

By not harming workers purposely, the executive leaves more to chance, but by subjecting large numbers to risk, he leaves it less and less to chance that *someone* will be harmed. Thus, he rolls back his moral advantage over the Typical Criminal. The executive at the Peanut Corporation of America knew that salmonella makes people sick and that it can kill the young, the old, and those with compromised immune systems. When he received test results showing unacceptable levels of salmonella in batches of his product, he still shipped them to school lunch programs, to companies he knew resold to nursing homes, and to mass food distributors like Kellogg.[41] With more and more peanuts that tested positive for salmonella shipped out, we start to approach 100 percent likelihood that at least someone will die. That means that the culpability of the executive approaches that of the Typical Criminal.

A different way to make the Defenders' first objection is to say that the executive has failed to protect his workers while the Typical Criminal has acted positively to harm his victim. In general, people think it is worse to harm someone than to fail to prevent them being harmed. (Perhaps you should feed starving people on the other side of town or of the world, but few people will think you are a murderer if you don't and the starving die.) But people are normally held responsible for the effects of inaction when they have a special obligation to aid people. This applies to the parent who causes his child's death by failing to feed her and the doctor who causes her patient's death by failing to care for him. It also applies to the managers of workplaces who cause employee deaths by failing to take legally mandated safety precautions. This is another way in which the moral difference between the safety-cutting executive and the Typical Criminal shrinks away.

Further, the Defenders overestimate the importance of specifically trying to do evil in our moral estimate of people. The mugger who aims to hurt someone is no doubt an ugly character but so too is the well-heeled executive who calmly and callously chooses to put others at risk. Most murders, we know, are committed in the heat of some passion, such as rage or jealousy, and/or under the influence of drugs or alcohol. Two neighbors or relatives or bar patrons find themselves in a heated argument. One (often it is a matter of chance *which* one) picks up a weapon and strikes the other a fatal blow. Such a person is clearly a murderer and rightly subject to punishment by the criminal justice system. Is this person more evil than the executive who, knowing the risks, calmly makes a calculation that profits for owners are more important than safety equipment for workers?

The one who kills in a heated argument kills from passion. What he does he probably would not do in a moment of calm. He is likely to feel "he was not himself." We do not suggest that this is true of all killers, although there is reason to believe that it is true of many, nor do we suggest that such a state of mind justifies murder. What it does do, however, is suggest that the killer's action, arising out of anger at a particular individual, does not show general disdain for the lives of others. Here is where he is different from our executive. The executive wanted to harm no one in particular, but *he knew his acts were likely to harm someone.* Once someone is harmed, the victim is someone in particular. Our executive cannot claim that "he was not himself." His act wasn't done out of passion but out of cool reckoning. It is here that his evil shows. In order to make a few bucks, he willingly jeopardizes the lives of unspecified others (workers, consumers, neighboring communities) who pose him no threat. In this way he shows his general disdain for all his fellow human beings. Can it really be said that he is less evil than one who kills from passion? The Model Penal Code includes within the definition of murder any death caused by "extreme indifference to human life."[42] Is our executive not a murderer by this definition?

It's worth noting that, in answering the Defenders here, we have portrayed harms from occupational hazards in their best light. They are not, however, all just matters of well-intentioned but excessive risk-taking. Consider, for example, the Manville (formerly Johns Manville) asbestos case. It is predicted that 240,000 Americans who worked with asbestos will die from asbestos-related cancer over a period of 30 years, with many more dying from other diseases. Documents made public during congressional hearings in 1979 show "that Manville and other companies within the asbestos industry covered up and failed to warn millions of Americans of the dangers associated with the fireproof, indestructible insulating fiber."[43] An article in the *American Journal of Public Health* attributes thousands of deaths to the cover-up.[44] Later in this chapter we document similar intentional cover-ups, such as the falsification of reports on coal-dust levels in mines, which leads to crippling and often fatal black lung disease. Surely someone who knowingly subjects others to risks and tries to hide those risks from them is culpable in a high degree.

2. Defenders' Second Objection

Being harmed directly by another person is more terrifying than being harmed indirectly and impersonally, as by a safety hazard, even if the degree of harm is the same.

RESPONSE The Defenders are largely right in believing that direct personal assault is terrifying in a way that indirect impersonal harm is not. We say "largely right" here because deaths from some occupational hazards—slowly suffocating to death in a collapsed mine or living in fear of an occupational cancer spreading and becoming fatal—may well be as terrifying as some direct personal assaults. Nonetheless, even granting the Defenders their point that direct assault is usually more terrifying than indirect harm, it does not follow that indirect harms should be treated as noncriminal regulatory matters. This difference in degree of terror is no stranger to the criminal justice system. Prosecutors, judges, and juries constantly have to consider how terrifying an attack is in determining what to charge and what to convict offenders for. In short, the difference the Defenders are pointing to here might justify treating a one-on-one murder as graver than murder due to lax safety measures, but it doesn't justify treating one as a grave crime and the other as a mere regulatory (or very minor criminal) matter. After all, although it is worse to be injured with terror than without, it is still the injury that constitutes the worst part of violent crime. If that is so, then the worst part of violent crime is shared by the indirect harms that the Defenders would relegate to regulation.

As with the first objection, we should keep in mind that indirect harms can have a large number of victims. Pollution, unsafe work places, hazardous products, and tainted food can have a widespread impact. The financial fraud of Enron and other companies, and the financial crisis of 2008 (discussed in Chapter 3), affected tens of thousands of people, who lost more money than they would have in a mugging–and led to about 2,500 excess suicides in 2009 alone because of the financial crisis.[45] Judge Miles Lord noted this issue in a speech from the bench to executives of the A.H. Robbins Company, which made a birth control device called the Dalkon Shield. The device was not just ineffective, but its design caused many women to get pelvic infections, which led to 18 deaths and 350,000 claims of injury. Judge Lord said, "If one poor young man were, by some act of his—without authority or consent—to inflict such damage upon one woman, he would be jailed for a good portion of the rest of his life. And yet your company without warning to women invaded their bodies by the millions and caused them injuries by the thousands."[46]

3. Defenders' Third Objection

Someone who harms another in the course of an illegitimate and purely self-interested action is more evil than someone who harms another as a consequence of a legitimate and socially productive endeavor.

RESPONSE There is also something to the Defenders' claim that indirect harms, such as ones that result from lax safety measures, are part of legitimate productive activities, whereas one-on-one crimes generally are not. No doubt, we must tolerate the risks that are necessary ingredients of productive activity (unless those risks are so great as to outweigh the gains of the productive activity), but this doesn't imply we shouldn't identify the risks that are excessive and use the law to protect innocent people from them. If those risks are great enough, the fact that they may further a productive or otherwise legitimate activity is no reason against making them crimes if that's what's necessary to protect workers, consumers, and communities.

A person can commit a crime to further an otherwise legitimate endeavor and it is still a crime. If a manager threatens to assault his workers if they don't work faster, the fact that getting them to work faster is a legitimate goal for a manager doesn't make the manager's act any less criminal. Using child labor may help legitimate businesses reap higher profits, but the law wisely prohibits this exploitation. By the same logic, cutting safety and maintenance expenditures in an aging refinery may serve the legitimate purpose of cutting costs, but it is no reason against treating such dangerous acts as crimes. If acts that endanger others ought to be crimes, then the fact that the acts are means to legitimate aims doesn't change the fact that they ought to be illegal.

4. Defenders' Fourth Objection

The harms of typical crimes are imposed on their victims against their wills, whereas harms such as those due to occupational hazards are consented to by workers when they agree to a job.

RESPONSE The Defender exaggerates the "free consent" with which consumers buy products and with which workers take on the risks of their jobs. You can consent to a risk only if you know about it, and often the risks are deliberately minimized or concealed outright. Consumers of peanut-based products had no way of knowing that they were produced by Peanut Corporation of America in a former sausage factory that had sat empty for 30 years with a leaking roof, dead animals in the ventilation system, and no inspections by the Texas Department of Health.[47] Many people who take jobs – even in hazardous occupations—do not get full disclosure of the severity of workplace hazards or the toxicity of the chemicals to which they are exposed.

Moreover, the Defenders overestimate generally the degree to which workers freely consent to the conditions of their jobs. More generally, although no one is forced at gunpoint to accept a particular job, virtually everyone is forced by the requirements of necessity to take some job. Moreover, workers can choose jobs only where there are openings, which means they cannot simply pick their place of employment at will. At best, workers can choose among the dangers present at various worksites, but rarely can they choose to face no danger at all.

For nonwhites and women, the choices are further narrowed by discriminatory hiring and long-standing occupational segregation (funneling women into nursing or food-processing jobs and blacks into janitorial and other menial occupations), not to mention subtle and not-so-subtle practices that keep nonwhites and women from advancing within their occupations.

Remember that, while here we have been focusing on harms due to occupational hazards, much of the indirect harm that we shall document in what follows is done not to workers but, for example, to hospital patients (subjected to careless medical care) or neighbors of industrial sites (breathing dangerous concentrations of pollutants). And these victims surely don't consent to those risks.

Finally, recall that the basis of all of the Defenders' objections is that the idea that one-on-one harms are more evil than indirect harms is part of our common moral beliefs. Though it is fair to judge criminal justice practices in light of ordinary moral beliefs, it is also important not to overlook the role of legal institutions in shaping our ordinary moral beliefs about right and wrong. The great historian of English law, Sir James Fitzjames Stephens, held that a

> great part of the general detestation of crime which happily prevails amongst the decent part of the community in all civilized countries arises from the fact that the commission of offences is associated in all such communities with the solemn and deliberate infliction of punishment wherever crime is proved.[48]

One cannot simply appeal to ordinary moral beliefs to defend the criminal law because the criminal law has already had a hand in shaping ordinary moral beliefs. At least one observer has argued that making narcotics use a crime at the beginning of the twentieth century *caused* a change in the public's ordinary moral notions about drug addiction, which prior to that time had been viewed as a medical problem.[49] It is probably safe to say that, in our own time, antidiscrimination legislation has sharpened the public's moral condemnation of racial and gender discrimination. Hence, we might speculate that if the criminal justice system began to prosecute—and if the media began to portray—those who inflict *indirect harm* as serious criminals, our ordinary moral notions would change on this point as well.

We are left with the conclusion that there is no moral basis for treating *one-on-one harm* as criminal and *indirect harm* as merely a regulatory affair (or as only a civil tort). What matters, then, is whether the purpose of the criminal justice system will be served by including, in the category of serious crime, actions that are predictably likely to produce serious harm yet that are done in pursuit of otherwise legitimate goals and without the desire to harm anyone.

What is the purpose of the criminal justice system? No esoteric answer is required. Norval Morris and Gordon Hawkins write that "the prime function of the criminal law is to protect our persons and our property."[50] *The Challenge of Crime in a Free Society*, the report of the President's Commission on Law Enforcement and Administration of Justice, tells us that "any criminal justice system is an apparatus society uses to enforce the standards of conduct necessary to protect individuals and the community."[51] Whatever else we think a criminal justice system should accomplish, no one would deny that its central purpose is to protect us against the most serious threats to our well-being. *This purpose is seriously undermined by taking one-on-one harm as the model of crime.* It prevents the criminal justice system from protecting our persons and our property from dangers at least as great as those posed by one-on-one harm. This is so because, as we will show, a large number of actions that are not labeled *criminal* lead to loss of life, limb, and possessions on a scale comparable to those actions that are represented in the FBI Crime Index. A crime by any other name still causes misery, suffering, and death.

* * *

The remainder of this chapter identifies some acts that are *crimes by other names:* acts that cause harm and suffering comparable to that caused by acts called crimes. Our purpose is to confirm the first of our five hypotheses: That the definitions of crime in the criminal law do not reflect the only or the most dangerous behaviors in our society. To do this, we will need some measure of the harm and suffering caused by crimes with which we can compare the harm and suffering caused by noncrimes. Our measure need not be too refined because the point can be made by showing that some acts that we do not treat as crimes cause harm *roughly comparable* to that caused by acts we do treat as crimes. Because the harms caused by noncriminal acts fall into the categories of death, bodily injury (including the disabling effects of disease), and property loss, we will compare the harms done by noncriminal acts with the injuries caused by the crimes of murder, aggravated assault, and theft. In order to compare the harms produced by both criminal and noncriminal acts, we will generally use the most recent year for which there are ample statistics from both categories.

According to the FBI's *UCR,* in 2017 there were 17,284 murders and non-negligent manslaughters and 810,825 aggravated assaults. "Murder and non-negligent manslaughter" includes all "willful (non-negligent) killing of one human being by another." "Aggravated assault" is defined as an "attack by one person on another for the purpose of inflicting severe or aggravated bodily injury."[52] Thus, as measures of the harm done by crimes in 2017, we can say that serious crimes led to roughly 17,000 deaths and 800,000 instances of serious bodily injury short of death that year. As a measure of monetary loss due to property crime, we can use $15.3 billion, the figure the FBI estimates to be the total loss due to property crime in 2017.[53] Whatever the shortcomings of these reported crime statistics, they are the statistics on which public policy has traditionally been based.[54] Thus, we will consider any actions that lead to loss of life, physical harm, and property loss, comparable to these figures, as actions that pose grave dangers to the community comparable to the threats posed by crimes. They are precisely the kinds of harmful actions from which a criminal justice system whose purpose is to protect our persons and property ought to protect us. *They are crimes by other names.*

In making this case, the following sections review a number of research reports, both historical and contemporary. The continued inclusion of older reports—sometimes seen as "outdated"—is meant to underscore that these harms are neither new nor recently discovered. High levels of harm are ongoing, and the inclusion of findings reported over several decades should bolster confidence in the validity of sometimes scarce contemporary research.

Work May Be Dangerous to Your Health

Numerous studies have documented the alarmingly high incidence of disease, injury, and death due to hazards in the workplace *and* the fact that much or most of this carnage is the consequence of the refusal of management to pay for safety measures, of government to enforce safety standards, and sometimes of management's willful defiance of existing law.[55]

For 2017, the U.S. Department of Labor's Bureau of Labor Statistics (BLS) reports 2.8 million non-fatal workplace injuries and illnesses, of which 1.1 million were serious enough to result in lost workdays. BLS also reports 169,900 cases of nonfatal occupational illness.[56] BLS notes that "some conditions (for example, long-term latent illnesses caused by exposure to carcinogens) often are difficult to relate to the workplace and are not adequately recognized and reported. These long-term latent illnesses are believed to be understated in the survey's illness measures."

The data for the survey come from OSHA logs that some employers are required to keep, but millions of workers are employed in establishments not required to keep safety records. Companies covered by OSHA laws are on their honor to keep an accurate tally of "recordable events" and report that information honestly to OSHA. But a Government Accountability Office (GAO) report notes that disincentives discourage workers from reporting and employers from recording illnesses and injuries:

> [W]orkers may not report a work-related injury or illness because they fear job loss or other disciplinary action, or fear jeopardizing rewards based on having low injury and illness rates. In addition, employers may not record injuries or illnesses because they are afraid of increasing their workers' compensation costs or jeopardizing their chances of winning contract bids for new work.[57]

In hearings on the topic "Hidden Tragedy: Underreporting of Workplace Injuries and Illnesses," the House Committee on Education and Labor heard testimony addressing all of these problems. Witnesses reported employers and insurance companies pressuring doctors to write up results and recommendations so that the injury would not be a recordable event. Testimony further cited a number of studies finding that the BLS data misses 30 to 60 percent of injuries and illnesses, including 30 percent of work-related amputations.[58]

OSHA—which in 2002 changed the record keeping standard so "fewer injuries and illnesses were required to be recorded"[59]—used the low and declining numbers of injuries to demonstrate its own effectiveness. Still, they admit: "Numerous studies provide documentation that many, and perhaps the majority, of work-related injuries are not recorded by employers, and that the actual number of workers injured each year is likely to be far higher than the BLS estimate."

For these reasons, we must look elsewhere for accurate figures. Authoritative sources in the late 1980s and early 1990s pointed to between 50,000 and 95,000 deaths each year from occupational disease.[60] A 1997 article in the

American Medical Association (AMA) journal aggregated many national and large regional data sets and came up with an estimate of 60,300 deaths from occupational illness.[61] Dr. Samuel Epstein, Professor Emeritus of Environmental and Occupational Medicine and then-chairman of the Cancer Prevention Coalition, states, "Over 10 percent of adult cancer deaths result from occupational exposures, which are also a recognized cause of cancer in children: parents exposed to carcinogens on the job often expose their unborn children to the same cancer-causing chemicals."[62] With estimates of annual cancer deaths running above 570,000 at that time, approximately 57,000 adult deaths a year would be from occupationally caused cancer alone. A report using 2007 data estimates 53,000 annual deaths from occupational disease.[63]

In 2019 Congressional testimony, a Clinical Professor of Environmental Health Sciences who had been in leadership positions at OSHA and EPA, stated: "All of the independent biostatistical studies of the problem agree that roughly 50,000 U.S. workers each year die prematurely (primarily from cancer, lung diseases, and cardiovascular disease) from toxic exposures on the job." He also noted that while de-industrialization has removed some occupational exposures from manufacturing jobs, "the overall problem is not decreasing significantly, as other exposures stay high and new substances replace older ones, sometimes with equal or greater toxicity."[64]

In light of these estimates, we will assume that occupational disease causes 50,000 deaths a year. In 2015, OSHA itself stated that "studies have estimated that approximately 50,000 annual U.S. deaths are attributable to past workplace exposure to hazardous agents." They also note: "Many chronic illnesses occur long after exposure has ended and are generally not identified as work-related."[65]

That estimate is *only* for occupational deaths from *diseases* and does not include death and disability from work-related injuries. Here, too, the statistics are gruesome. BLS's *National Census of Fatal Occupational Injuries* reports 4,689 workplace fatalities in 2017 (not counting work-related homicides).[66] Added to the previous figure of 50,000 fatalities from occupational disease, this brings the number of occupation-related deaths to 54,689 a year.

The BLS reported that, in 2017, there were 2.8 million recordable cases of nonfatal injuries and illnesses. A recordable case involves days away from work, medical treatment other than first aid, loss of consciousness, restriction of work or motion, transfer to another job, or "cancer, chronic irreversible disease, a fracture or cracked bone, or a punctured eardrum."[67] Even though these are fairly serious, to make sure that we are counting only more serious harms, we will use the measure of cases requiring days away from work. Research shows that these lost work day incidents cause substantial lost earnings, medical costs, depression and anxiety, and a decline in workers' lifespan.[68] According to BLS, there were 1.1 million cases involving lost work days, a figure that includes physical harms from both disease and injury.

This is an especially conservative estimate given that another national database of occupational injuries and illnesses that result in treatment in an *emergency* department of a hospital recorded 3.4 million visits for 2003, a level fairly constant since 1982.[69] Note also that these figures don't include the effects of workers' exposure to occupational illnesses on the health of their families.[70] But "science is increasingly finding that children born to workers – both women and men– who are exposed to chemicals on the job are at increased risk of a variety of health problems" and "families of workers can be exposed to unreasonable risks from the smaller quantities workers bring home on their clothes, hair, and skin."[71]

Before jumping to any conclusions about how this compares to the threat of crime, note that the official risk of occupational disease and death falls only on members of the labor force, whereas the risk of crime falls on the whole population, from infants to the elderly. Because the civilian labor force is about half of the total population (160 million in 2017 out of a total civilian population of 325 million),[72] to get a true picture of the *relative* threat posed by occupational diseases compared with that posed by crimes, we should multiply the crime statistics (17,000 deaths and 800,000 instances of serious bodily injury) by half (0.5) when comparing them with the figures for occupational disease and death. Using the crime figures for 2017 (cited earlier in this chapter), we note that the *comparable* figures would look like Table 2.1.

Those who believe that this paints an inaccurate picture because so many crimes go unreported should consider that homicides are by far the most completely reported of crimes. It is easier to avoid reporting a rape or a mugging than a corpse. Second, although not the best, aggravated assaults are among the better-reported crimes. Estimates from the Justice Department's National Crime Victimization Survey indicate that 57 percent of aggravated assaults were reported to the police in 2017.[73] On the other hand, we should expect more, not less, underreporting of industrial than criminal victims because diseases and deaths are likely to cost firms money in increased insurance premiums and the possibility of increased inspections. Many occupationally caused diseases do not show symptoms or lead to death until after the employee has left the job, and there is no BLS surveillance system to capture slower-onset illnesses.

In sum, both occupational and criminal harms are underreported, though there is reason to believe that the underreporting is worse for occupational than for criminal harms. Bear in mind, also, that we have accepted the statistics on criminal harms as reported, while we have reduced substantially the reported estimates for occupational harms. However one may quibble with the figures presented here, if anything, they understate the extent of occupational harm compared with criminal harm.

TABLE 2.1   Occupational Disease and Injury Compared to Crime

	Occupational Disease and Injury	Crime (× 0.5)
Death	54,689	8,500
Other physical harm	1,100,000	400,000

Can there be any doubt that workers are more likely to stay alive and healthy in the face of the danger from the underworld than from the work world? Former Secretary of Labor Hilda Solis noted that the thousands of deaths and millions of injuries "are preventable tragedies that disable our workers, devastate our families, and damage our economy."[74]

To say that some of these workers died from accidents due to their own carelessness is about as helpful as saying that some of those who died at the hands of murderers deserved it. It overlooks the fact that when workers are careless, it is largely because they have production quotas to meet, quotas that they themselves do not set. If quotas were set with an eye to keeping work at a safe pace rather than keeping profitability as high as possible, it might be more reasonable to expect workers to take the time to be careful. Beyond this, we should bear in mind that the vast majority of occupational deaths result from disease, not accident, and disease is generally a function of conditions outside a worker's control. Examples of such conditions are:

- *The level of coal dust in the air:* In February of 2018, "federal investigators this month identified the largest cluster of *advanced* black lung cases ever officially recorded." It "adds to a growing body of evidence that a new black lung epidemic." An epidemiologist for the National Institute for Occupational Safety and Health noted "there's an unacceptably large number of younger miners who have end-stage disease and the only choice is to get a lung transplant or wait it out and die."[75]
- *Textile dust:* Some 100,000 American cotton textile workers suffer breathing impairments caused by acute byssinosis, or brown lung; another 35,000 former mill workers are totally disabled with chronic brown lung.[76]
- *Asbestos fibers:* It has been estimated that, under the lenient asbestos standard promulgated by OSHA in 1972, anywhere from 18,400 to 598,000 deaths from lung cancer would result from exposure to asbestos.[77]
- *Coal tars:* "Workers who had been employed five or more years in the coke ovens died of lung cancer at a rate three and a half times that for all steelworkers"; coke oven workers develop cancer of the scrotum at a rate five times that of the general population.[78]
- *Repetitive motion:* According to the National Academy of Sciences, there are more than one million repetitive motion injuries annually.[79] Repetitive strain disease reportedly afflicts "keyboard operators, assembly-line workers, meat processors, grocery check-out clerks, secretaries and other employees everyday.... OSHA officials argue that... carpal tunnel problems lead the list in average time lost from work (at a median of 30 days per case), well above amputations (24 days) and fractures (20)."[80]

To blame the workers for occupational disabilities and deaths is to ignore the history of governmental attempts to compel industrial firms to meet safety standards that would keep dangers (such as chemicals or fibers or dust particles in the air) that are outside the worker's control down to a safe level.

This has been a continual struggle, with firms using everything from their own "independent" research institutes to more direct (and often questionable) forms of political pressure to influence government in the direction of loose standards and lax enforcement. So far industry has been winning because OSHA has been given neither the personnel nor the mandate to fulfill its purpose. Between 1990 and 2018, the number of OSHA inspectors declined from 1,300 to less than 1,000.[81] OSHA's website proudly proclaims that "with our state partners we have approximately 2,100 inspectors responsible for the health and safety of 130 million workers, employed at more than 8 million worksites around the nation—which translates to about one compliance officer for every 59,000 workers."[82]

The problem does not lie with OSHA alone. It starts with the legislators who decided in 1970 that causing the death of an employee by willfully violating safety laws was a misdemeanor. As noted by a *New York Times* investigation: "The maximum sentence, six months in jail, is half the maximum for harassing a wild burro on federal lands." Although Congress rarely voted down tougher sentences for street crime, it has rejected every attempt to get tougher with those who willfully (and sometimes repeatedly) violate safety laws, in spite of evidence that stricter laws could save lives. On top of lax laws, OSHA discourages prosecutions and criminal referrals to such an extent that a 1988 congressional report noted, "A company official who willfully and recklessly violates federal OSHA laws stands a greater chance of winning a state lottery than being criminally charged."[83] Despite thousands of worker deaths every year, less than 100 cases have been criminally prosecuted under the Occupational Safety and Health Act since 1970.[84]

After OSHA fines were initially set in 1970, they did not increase until 1990. They increased again in 2016, when fines were finally allowed to increase with inflation. The maximum fine for a serious violation ("those that pose a substantial probability of death or serious physical harm to workers") was raised to $13,260 in 2019, and the penalty for "willful or repeated" violations increased to $132,598.[85] In spite of these paltry fines for endangering life, employers do not pay nearly that much in reality: In 2018, the average penalty for a serious violation was $3,580 for federal OSHA (less for state OSHA) enforcement, and the median penalty for killing a worker was $7,761 for federal OSHA (less for state OSHA) enforcement.[86]

Is a person who kills another in a bar brawl a greater threat to society than a business executive who refuses to cut into his profits to make his plant a safe place to work for dozens, hundreds, or thousands of employees? By any measure of death and suffering, the latter is a far greater danger than the former. However, because he wishes his workers no harm and because he is only indirectly responsible for death and disability while pursuing legitimate economic goals, his acts are not labeled "crimes." Once we free our imagination from the blinders of the one-on-one model of crime, can there be any doubt that the criminal justice system does *not* protect us from the gravest threats to life and limb? It seeks to protect us when danger comes from a young, lower-class male in the inner city. When a threat comes from an upper-class business executive in an office, the criminal justice system looks the other way. This is in the face of growing evidence that for every American citizen murdered by thugs, more than three American workers are killed by the recklessness of their bosses and the indifference of their government.

Health Care May Be Dangerous to Your Health

An article in the *Journal of the American Medical Association (JAMA)* in 2000 estimated that there were 225,000 deaths a year *due to medical treatment*, making it "the third leading cause of death in the United States, after deaths from heart disease and cancer."[87] A more recent 2013 estimate based on a review of studies about patient adverse events concluded that the lower bound was "210,000 preventable adverse events per year that contribute to the death of hospitalized patients"[88] and an upper bound of 440,000, with two to four million serious but non-lethal patient adverse events. Doctors from Johns Hopkins in 2016 concluded that 251,454 deaths resulted from medical errors, and advocated that the Centers for Disease Control and Prevention (CDC) revise the way it lists causes of death to recognize medical error as the third leading cause of death in the U.S.[89] Even using the conservative lower limit of 210,000 preventable deaths, medical errors cause more than 12 times the number of deaths due to homicides, and these are all deaths that could have been prevented. And this is only the beginning.

In 1976, the AMA claimed that "2.4 million unnecessary operations were performed on Americans at a cost of $3.9 billion and that 11,900 patients had died from unneeded operations."[90] This is lower than other expert opinions at the time, which ranged up to 16,000 deaths from unnecessary surgery.[91] The number of surgical operations performed in the United States rose from 16.7 million in 1975 to 27.2 million in 2016,[92] so there is reason to believe that at least somewhere between (the AMA's) 11,900 and (other authoritative estimates of) 16,000 people a year still die from unnecessary surgery. A 2017 medical journal article stated that "unnecessary surgery remains a daunting reality."[93]

In 2017, the FBI reported that 1,591 murders (in which the weapon is known) were committed with a "cutting or stabbing instrument."[94] Obviously, the FBI does not include the scalpel as a cutting or stabbing instrument. If it did, it would have had to report that between 13,491 and 17,591 persons were killed by "cutting or stabbing" in 2017, depending on which estimate you take (11,900 or 16,000). No matter how you slice it, the scalpel is more dangerous than the switchblade.

The FBI also should add the hypodermic needle and the prescription drug to the list of potential murder weapons. The Harvard Medical Practice Study found that, of the 1.3 million medical injuries (which they estimated on the basis of hospital records for 1984), 19 percent (247,000) were related to medications, and 14 percent of these (34,580) resulted in permanent injury or death.[95] Further, "experts have estimated that more than one million serious drug errors occur annually in hospitals alone."[96] (This serves as a conservative estimate since it does not include the irresponsible marketing and other behavior by the pharmaceutical industry that caused the latest opiate crisis, "a for-profit slaughter" that was "predictable and tremendously lucrative."[97])

If someone had the temerity to publish a *UCR* that really portrayed the way Americans are murdered, the FBI's statistics on the *type* of weapon used in murder would have to be changed from those shown in Table 2.2 to something like those shown in Table 2.3. The figures shown in Table 2.3 would give American citizens a much more honest picture of what threatens them. Nonetheless, we are not likely to see such a table published by the criminal justice system, perhaps because it would also give American citizens a more honest picture of *who* threatens them.

The problem is not just the large amount of harm, but also the little progress that has been made in eliminating this preventable harm. The initial awareness of the extent of medical errors came from a report issued in 1999 by the National Academy of Sciences' Institute of Medicine (IOM) stating that up to "98,000 hospitalized Americans die every year and 1 million more are

TABLE 2.2   How Americans Are Murdered, 2017

Total Murders Where Weapon Is Known	Firearms	Knife or Other Cutting Instrument	Other Weapon: Blunt Objects, Arson, Strangulation, Poison, etc.	Personal Weapons: Hands, Fists, etc.
15,129*	10,982	1,591	1,860	696

*This figure is lower than the number of murders and non-negligent manslaughters mentioned earlier because the FBI lacks data on the weapons used in some of the homicides. "Other Weapon" represents all the other categories that are not reported separately here, including the category "Other Weapon/Not Stated."

Source: UCR-2017, Expanded Homicide Data Table 8.

TABLE 2.3 How Americans Are *Really* Murdered, 2017

Total Murders Where Weapon Is Known	Occupational Hazard or Disease	Firearms	Knife or Other Cutting Instrument, Including Scalpel	Other Weapon: Blunt Objects, Poison, Strangulation, Prescription Drug, Other Medical Treatment, etc.	Personal Weapons: Hands, Fists, etc.
174,818*	54,689	10,982	13,491	94,960	696

*The figures in this row represent the relevant figures in Table 2.2 plus the most conservative figures for the relevant categories discussed in the text. Under "Knife ... Including Scalpel" we have used the AMA's old estimate of 11,900 deaths not adjusted to reflect more overall surgeries. Under "Other Weapon," we have assumed 210,000 preventable deaths from medical errors, but taken only the one-half that the IOM says could be prevented by creating a centralized database of errors, and subtracted out 11,900 deaths due to unnecessary surgery.

injured as a result of preventable medical errors."[98] (Subsequent research has shown the figure to be much higher—recall the 210,000 to 400,000 figure cited in the opening paragraphs of this section.)

The results of large-scale research published in 2010 by the *New England Journal of Medicine* confirm that little progress has occurred. A review of the research appeared in the *New York Times* under the headline, "Study Finds No Progress in Safety at Hospitals." It quoted the chief of hospital medicine at the University of California, San Francisco as saying: "We need to do more, and to do it more quickly."[99] In 2014, Senators heard testimony in hearings titled, "More Than 1,000 Preventable Deaths a Day Is Too Many." Witnesses pointed to some areas of limited progress but also cited research (discussed in the opening paragraph of this section) that preventable health care errors were between 200,000 and 400,000 a year. One witness commented: "Despite all the focus on patient safety, it seems we have not made much progress at all."[100]

The original IOM report suggested that if a "centralized system for keeping tabs on medical errors" were put in place, "the number of deaths from medical mistakes could be cut in half within five years."[101] That still has not happened, and the lack of transparency by hospitals about their errors is an issue noted whenever there is another major study on the number of medical errors.[102] Electronic medical records that were supposed to prevent errors "were originally optimized for billing rather than for patient care." Doctors "complain about clumsy, unintuitive systems" that mean "death by 1,000 clicks."[103] A poll of nearly 6,600 clinic and hospital physicians found that 54 percent reported symptoms of burnout, 33 percent reported excessive fatigue, and 6.5 percent reported recent suicidal ideation, all of which increase the likelihood of error.[104] Also contributing to the problem, according to the author of the 2013 study claiming 210,000 to 440,000 deaths from medical errors, are "the movement of the medical industry toward higher productivity and expensive technology, which encourages rapid patient flow and overuse of risky, invasive, revenue-generating procedures."[105]

Recall the example of digging a trench: "Suppose that the trench was dug and left uncovered, knowing that children played in the area. Then, their deaths were brought about *knowingly*." *Knowingly* was the second degree of culpability, right below *purposely*—and is more culpable than *recklessly* or *negligently*. Didn't the doctors and hospital officials who resisted correcting previously identified dangerous practices bring about 210,000 preventable deaths *knowingly or recklessly*—and aren't many others negligent in continuing to practice without adequate regard for patient safety?

Waging Chemical Warfare Against America

The American Cancer Society (ACS) estimates that in 2019 about 606,880 Americans are expected to die from cancer, and doctors will diagnose more than 1.7 million new cases.[106] In spite of advances in medicine, cancer rates – especially among children–are increasing.[107] A 2010 report from the President's

Cancer Panel stated that "approximately 41 percent of people in the U.S. will be diagnosed with cancer at some point in their lives, and about 21 percent of Americans will die from cancer."[108] An editorial in the *New England Journal of Medicine* in 2000 notes a "widely accepted estimate that 80 to 90 percent of human cancer is due to environmental factors."[109] And, "a long list of diseases, including diabetes, hypospadias (male reproductive disorders), infertility, Alzheimer's, autoimmune disease, obesity, and cancers, can all be associated or exacerbated by environmental exposures to man-made chemicals."[110]

This means that a concerted national effort could result in saving 450,000 or more lives a year and reducing each individual's chances of getting cancer in his or her lifetime from nearly 1 in 2 to 1 in 12, or less. If you think this would require a massive effort in terms of money and personnel, you are right. How much of an effort, though, would the nation make to stop foreign terrorists who were killing 1,500 people a day and bent on slaughtering one-fifth of the present population? Unfortunately, the "cancer establishment"—the publicly funded National Cancer Institute (NCI) and the private ACS—has not made the needed effort. Less than 14 percent of NCI's budget went to occupational and environmental cancer issues, and ACS spent less than $4 million on environmental cancer.[111] NCI spent 2.5 percent of its budget on prevention and ACS spent 0.1 percent of revenue on environmental research. A 2002 review of U.S. and international cancer policies noted, "The cancer establishment's funding for primary prevention is trivial," adding that there is "minimal research on avoidable exposures to a wide range of occupational and environmental industrial carcinogens."[112]

Not only are we losing the chemical war on all fronts, but it also looks as if we do not even have the will to fight. Over the 40 years this book has been in print, there has been ample material to support the contention that under Democrats and Republicans, environmental policy has been more industry-friendly than dedicated to public health. However, President Trump represents perhaps the strongest pro-industry, anti-environment, and climate change denial stances. For agencies protecting people against threats from chemicals, Trump has cut budgets, reduced staff, cut enforcement, cut regulations, and reduced the role of science in policymaking.[113]

The enduring problem, however, is noted by the President's Cancer Panel: "With nearly 80,000 chemicals on the market in the United States, many of which are used by millions of Americans in their daily lives and are un- or understudied and largely unregulated, exposure to potential environmental carcinogens is widespread."[114] The main legislation in this area for four decades was the 1976 Toxic Substances Control Act (TSCA), which did not require industry or government to confirm the safety of new chemicals, unlike regulatory systems in Europe.[115] In fact, because chemical companies were required to report information about known health hazards caused by their products, they generally did not conduct tests that might reveal such problems.[116] Of the 80,000 chemicals in use, only 200 have been subject to testing and less than ten banned under the TSCA, indicating how little accountability there is with chemicals. Indeed, the National Academy of Sciences, the U.S. General

Accounting Office, the Congressional Office of Technology Assessment, the University of California, and others "concluded that TSCA has fallen short of its objectives and has not served as an effective vehicle for the public, industry, or government to assess the hazards of chemicals in commerce or control those of greatest concern."[117]

In 2016, the Frank R. Lautenberg Chemical Safety for the 21st Century Act became law with great hype about reform, but public health advocates say it only "slightly strengthens the existing law."[118] The law does allow for a safety review before new chemicals are brought to market. Also, it mandates that the EPA assess only 20 chemicals at a time, with each chemical permitted to be under review for seven years. Writing, finalizing, and implementing regulations about one chemical will take additional years, so simply studying the first 90 chemicals of concern will take decades and "the children of today's children will have been exposed to them—probably for years."[119]

Under Trump administration guidelines, these safety assessments are limited to direct uses and not to reasonably foreseeable exposures related to production, improper disposal, and accidents–all of which are essential to understanding risk in the real world. So, a chemical used as a dry-cleaning solvent and degreaser has an assessment based only on those uses, "but the agency will not focus on exposures that occur from traces of the chemical found in drinking water in 44 states as a result of improper disposal over decades, the E.P.A. documents say."[120] Nicholas Ashford, Director of the Technology and Law Program at Massachusetts Institute of Technology, says: "They're basically subverting the purpose of the act, which is protection."[121]

Chemical warfare is being waged against us on three fronts:

- pollution
- cigarette smoking
- food additives.

Pollution includes air pollution, water contamination, toxic waste, and other environmental pollution from chemicals. A commission on pollution and health assembled by the prestigious medical journal *The Lancet* states that "pollution endangers the stability of the Earth's support systems and threatens the continuing survival of human societies."[122] Further, "pollution is the largest environmental cause of disease and premature death in the world today."[123] The World Health Organization (WHO) estimates suggest that in the U.S., 13 percent of preventable deaths and years of life lost due to premature death were caused by these forms of pollution.[124]

Americans have a great deal of exposure to industrial chemicals because the U.S. manufactures and imports 9.5 trillion pounds of them per year– about 30,000 pounds per person.[125] The *Lancet* noted that of the chemicals synthesized since 1950, about 5,000 are widespread and have achieved "nearly universal human exposure." But "fewer than half of these high-production volume chemicals have undergone any testing for safety or toxicity," and even less is known about their combined effects. So, "chemicals and pesticides whose effects on human health and the environment were never examined have repeatedly been responsible for episodes of disease, death, and environ-mental degradation."[126]

While hazardous waste is an obvious reminder of the problem, chemicals that are not considered toxic waste can still assault people's bodies after being delivered through consumer products. Many are endocrine disruptors, which interfere with the natural hormone systems in our body. "These chemicals are manufactured in volumes of millions of kilograms per year and are used widely in consumer products such as soaps, shampoos, perfumes, plastics, and food containers," notes the *Lancet* commission. Even "extremely low doses of endocrine-disrupting chemicals during early development can lead to perma-nent impairments in organ function and increased risk of disease."[127] The ef-fects overall include cancer, lowered fertility, early puberty, diabetes, changes in immune function, obesity, and neurodevelopmental delays in children.[128]

Pesticides target the nervous systems of animals that feed on crops, but they are also toxic to humans. The U.S. uses 1.1 billion pounds of pesticides a year.[129] They "are found in nearly every stream in the United States, over 90 per-cent of wells," and, as might be expected, "every human tested is found to have pesticides in his or her body fat."[130] After reviewing the literature on pesticides and health, the American Academy of Pediatrics concludes: "the evidence base is most robust for associations to pediatric cancer and adverse neurodevelop-ment." Studies link early-life exposure to reductions in IQ and development of attention-deficit/hyperactivity disorder (ADHD) and autism.[131] With certain classes of pesticide in "extensive use," the *Lancet* Commission found "very lit-tle information is available on the possible human health effects" even though "they are water-soluble and can persist for years in soils, dust, wetlands, and groundwater and are detected in commonly consumed foods."[132]

In addition to outdoor air pollution–chemical releases, small particles, and the release of greenhouses gasses that contribute to climate change–indoor air pollution from building materials and consumer products harms people. With outdoor air pollution, less than 200 of thousands of chemicals are regulated by the EPA under the Clean Air Act.[133] In addition to diseases from chemical exposure to polluting industries, soot and particles cause lung disease, heart attacks, and strokes. Some small-particle air pollution is a car-rier for other toxic chemicals in the air, which are breathed deeply into the lungs, enter the bloodstream, and can cause heart disease, cancer, dementia, and cognitive deterioration to cerebral functions like memory and attention span.[134] Research estimates that deaths due to small particles from coal-fired power plants were 13,200 to 34,000 a year, and that was not counting a number of relevant power plants.[135] Overall, small particle pollution alone is linked to 107,000 premature deaths, and an economic cost of $886 billion.[136]

In spite of the ubiquity of chemicals of dubious safety, the Trump admin-istration has proposed substantial cuts to EPA. In 2018, the number of cases EPA referred to the Department of Justice for criminal prosecution was at a 30-year low, following a downward trend since 2012. Noticeable declines also occurred in criminal fines along with "civil settlement amounts, cases filed against polluters, compliance orders and criminal enforcement."[137]

So the chemical war goes on. No one can deny that we know the enemy. No one can deny that we know the toll it is taking. Indeed, we can compute the number of deaths that result for each day that we refuse to mount an offensive, yet we still refuse.

The same reasoning applies to *cigarette smoking*, which overwhelming evidence links to many types of cancer and other chronic illnesses. A recent report by the Surgeon General includes a statement that tobacco smoke "is deadly" and cigarettes are "not just dangerous but *unreasonably* dangerous, killing half their long-term users. And addictive by design."[138] The report reviews evidence that "smoking affects nearly every organ of the body."[139] These include cancers of the lung, liver, colon, prostate, and breasts; adverse reproductive effects; diseases of the eyes, bowels, immune system, and mouth, as well as diabetes and arthritis. The CDC simply notes, "Tobacco use is the leading preventable cause of death in the United States"[140] Cigarettes are widely estimated to cause 40 percent of all cancer deaths, and annual costs attributed to smoking are $300 billion.[141]

This is enough to expose the hypocrisy of keeping marijuana as a controlled substance under federal law while allowing cigarette sales and advertising to flourish. Once again, there are threats to our lives much greater than criminal homicide. Our government fails to protect us against these threats. The U.S. Congress has turned down more than 1,000 proposed tobacco control bills since 1964, the year of the first Surgeon General's Report on the dangers of tobacco. If you think that tobacco harms only people who knowingly decide to take the risk, consider the following. In 1995, *JAMA* devoted a special issue to several thousand pages of internal documents from the Brown and Williamson Tobacco Corporation and BAT Industries (formerly British American Tobacco Company). Brown and Williamson (B&W) is the third-largest cigarette maker in the United States and a wholly owned subsidiary of BAT, the world's second-largest private producer of cigarettes. An editorial in this issue states that

> [t]he documents show... that executives at B&W knew early on that tobacco use was harmful and that nicotine was addictive, that the industry decided to conceal the truth from the public, that despite their knowledge to the contrary, the industry's public position was (and continues to be) that the link between smoking and ill health was not proven, and that nicotine was not addictive.

The editorial concludes that "the evidence is unequivocal: the U.S. public has been duped by the tobacco industry."[142]

Research has documented the dangers of secondhand ("environmental") tobacco smoke that nonsmokers breathe when smoking is going on around them. As the Surgeon General explains, secondhand smoke results "in a lower dose of tobacco smoke, compared with active smoking, but to the same toxic mixture from a health perspective."[143] The death toll from lung cancer and heart disease due only to secondhand smoke is 42,000 annually. Those are only two of many fatal diseases linked to tobacco smoke, which also causes respiratory infections and asthma.[144]

Let's be clear: We do not advocate making cigarette smoking illegal on the model of our country's failed drug war. We would like to see continued restrictions on advertising aimed at youngsters, more substantial and pointed warnings on tobacco packaging, easier access to cessation programs, and measures to protect nonsmokers from secondhand smoke.

Another long-standing harm comes from chemical *food additives*, of which the average American consumes *one pound* per year.[145] In 1982, Beatrice Hunter wrote *The Mirage of Safety*, putting people on notice about the dangers in our foods. It also described how the Food and Drug Administration (FDA), through a combination of lax enforcement and uncritical acceptance of the results of the food industry's own "scientific" research, had allowed the American public to be a guinea pig for food additives. As a result, we were—and are—subjected to chemicals strongly suspected of producing cancer, gallbladder ailments, ADHD in children; and still others are suspected of causing birth defects.[146]

Today, the problem is the same and worse: there are an estimated 10,000 chemicals added to food or used in food packaging, but the exact number is unknown because the FDA program for registering food additives and submitting safety information is voluntary. According to the American Academy of Pediatrics (AAP), of 4,000 chemicals added directly to food, 64 percent had not been studied for toxicology.[147] The FDA lacks the authority to reassess the safety of additives on the market, an issue "of great importance and concern for chemicals approved decades ago on the basis of limited and sometimes antiquated testing methods"—and even when such chemicals are now reasonably considered to be carcinogens.

A manufacturer that has developed a food additive can have a panel of its own experts deem it as "generally recognized as safe" and put it in food without FDA notification or approval. Approximately 1,000 ingredients have been added to our food supply without FDA review. The AAP notes simply that "the FDA is not able to ensure the safety of existing or new additives through this approval mechanism."[148]

Further, Americans consume more than 15 million pounds of artificial food dyes. The European Union requires foods and beverages containing any of six dyes to carry "a warning on the label that the colour 'may have effects on activity and attention in children.'"[149] Because of this warning, many multinational corporations reformulate food to be dye-free for Europe while leaving dyes in for U.S. consumers.

Based on the knowledge we have, there can be no doubt that air pollution, tobacco, and food additives amount to a chemical war that makes the crime wave look like a football scrimmage. Even with the most conservative estimates, it is clear that *the death toll in this war is far higher than the number of people killed by criminal homicide!*

Poverty Kills

Poverty is "caused" by lack of money, which means that once a society reaches a level of prosperity at which many enjoy a relatively high standard of living, then poverty can be eliminated or at least reduced significantly by transferring some of what the "haves" have to the "have-nots." Regardless of what caused poverty in the past, what causes it to continue in the present is the refusal of those who have more to share with those who have less. Now you may think of these remarks as trite or naïve. They are not offered as an argument for redistribution of income, although we believe that such redistribution is long overdue. These remarks are presented to make a much simpler point, namely, that poverty exists in a wealthy society like ours *because we allow it to exist.* Therefore, we[150] share responsibility for poverty and for its consequences.

The poverty for which we are responsible "remains," in the words of *BusinessWeek* in 1991, "stubbornly high."[151] The problem has persisted, and the economic recovery has simply returned poverty levels to their pre-financial crisis rates. But the poverty has particularly nasty features. For example, it affects blacks and children at a rate higher than the national average. In 2017, 10.7 percent of white (non-Hispanic) Americans and 21.2 percent of black Americans were below the poverty level.[152] Among children, in 2016, about 15 percent of white children and 31 percent of black children lived in poverty[153]—a rate that has increased over the last decade[154] as the wealth of the *Forbes* 400 wealthiest individuals has grown considerably. A National Academy of Sciences panel on childhood poverty found that "by most measures, poverty among U.S. children is higher than in peer English-speaking countries such as Canada and Australia, and it is much higher than in most other industrialized countries."[155]

We are prone to thinking that the consequences of poverty are fairly straightforward: Less money means fewer things, so poor people have fewer clothes or cars or appliances, go to the movies less often, and live in smaller homes with less or cheaper furniture. This is true and sad but perhaps not intolerable. In addition, however, one of the things poor people have less of is *good health.* Less money means less food, less heat in winter, worse air quality in summer, less distance from other sick people or from unhealthy work or toxic waste dumping sites, fewer doctor visits and childhood immunizations, fewer dental visits, less preventive health care, and less first-quality medical attention when all these other deprivations take their toll and a poor person finds him- or herself seriously ill. And a National Academy of Sciences panel noted, "economic hardship can increase psychological distress in parents and decrease their emotional well-being."[156] Children living in deep poverty – family incomes less than half the poverty line – have "the worst outcomes among all children on important health and development indicators, such as blood lead levels, obesity, and a composite indicator of flourishing."[157] Poverty robs the poor of their "well-being and full participation in society"[158] while they are alive, and kills them before their time. A prosperous society that allows poverty in its midst is a party to murder.

A review of more than 30 studies undertaken in the 1970s on the relationship between economic class and life expectancy affirms the conclusion that "class influences one's chances of staying alive. Almost without exception, the evidence shows that classes differ on mortality rates."[159] An article in

JAMA in 1993 confirms this cost of poverty: "People who are poor have higher mortality rates for heart disease, diabetes mellitus, high blood pressure, lung cancer, neural tube defects, injuries, and low birth weight, as well as lower survival rates from breast cancer and heart attacks."[160] A 1998 news release from the U.S. Department of Health and Human Services confirms the continued "strong relationship between socioeconomic status and health in the United States for every race and ethnic group studied."[161] A 2000 report from the Pew Environmental Health Commission says that "the burden of asthma falls most heavily on those below the poverty line" and "this gap has been constant for at least 20 years."[162] A 2016 article in *JAMA* found that the gap in life expectancy between the richest 1 percent and poorest 1 percent of individuals was almost 15 years for men and 10 years for women.[163] This difference increased from 2001 to 2014, a time when economic inequality also increased.

A comparison of the health and mortality of blacks and whites in America yields further insight into the relationship of health and mortality to economic class. In 2017, one of every four blacks lived below the poverty line, as compared with one of every ten whites. In 2014, black infant mortality (during the first year of life) was 11.1 per 1,000 live births, compared with 4.9 per 1,000 for whites.[164] In short, black mothers lost their babies within the first year of life more than twice as often as white mothers did. The racial gap in health care, and thus in health and life expectancy, is not new. A 2005 *Washington Post* article headlined "Race Gap Persists in Health Care, Three Studies Say" reports on a study by a Harvard School of Public Health researcher published in the *New England Journal of Medicine*. The researcher is quoted as commenting,

> We have known for 20 years that we have a problem in our health care system: blacks and whites do not receive equal care. We hoped all the attention paid to this topic would result in some improvement. What we found is that we have not made much progress.[165]

For example, one study found that almost 900,000 deaths could have been prevented during the decade of the 1990s if African Americans had received the same care as whites did.[166]

Cancer survival statistics show a similar picture. Between 2005 and 2011, 62.2 percent of blacks diagnosed with cancer were still alive five years after the diagnosis, compared with 69.7 percent of whites.[167] This disparity has been noted since at least the early 1970s. One important cause of this difference is that "white patients tended to have higher percentages of cancers diagnosed while localized,"[168] that is, earlier in their development. Some of this is due to better access to medical care, higher levels of education about the early-warning signs of cancer, and so on, all of which correlate strongly with higher income levels. Data reported in the journal *Science* suggest that "blacks get more cancer not because they're black, but because they're poor."[169] A study of the stage at which women had breast cancer diagnosed found that white and black women living in areas characterized by lower average income and educational attainment were diagnosed later than those in areas marked by higher income and educational attainment. Within the same areas, black women were diagnosed later than whites, except in the areas of highest income and education, where the black disadvantage disappeared.[170] "And while black women show a lower incidence of breast cancer than white women, they nevertheless die from it more often," according to the article in *Science*.[171] For 2016, life expectancy among blacks born that year was 74.8 years, whereas among whites it was 78.5 years.[172] That this difference cannot be attributed wholly to genetic factors is borne out by research in the *American Journal of Preventive Medicine*, which says,

> ethnic differences in health are more likely to reflect profound differences in people's experiences from birth on, based on the relatively advantaged or disadvantaged position in society of the race or ethnic group of the families into which they are born.[173]

In short, *poverty hurts, injures, and kills—just like crime.* A society that could remedy its poverty but does not is an accomplice in crime.

Summary

The criminal justice system does not protect us against the gravest threats to life, limb, or possessions. Its definitions of crime are not simply a reflection of the objective dangers that threaten us. The workplace, the medical profession, the air we breathe, and the poverty we refuse to rectify lead to far more human suffering, far more death and disability, and far more dollars taken from our pockets than the murders, aggravated assaults, and thefts reported annually by the FBI. What is more, this human suffering is preventable. The government could treat many of these harmful behaviors as criminal and turn the massive powers of the state against their perpetrators in the way that they are turned against the perpetrators of the so-called common crimes. But it does not. A government really intent on protecting us would strengthen and enforce work safety regulations, police the medical profession, require that clean-air standards be met, be more attentive to the massive chemical exposure faced by the public, and devote sufficient resources to the poor to alleviate the major disabilities of poverty. But it does not. Instead we hear a lot of cant about law and order and a lot of rant about crime in the streets. It is as if our leaders were not only refusing to protect us from the major threats to our well-being but also trying to cover up this refusal by diverting our attention to crime, as if it were the only real threat.

As we have seen, the criminal justice system is a carnival mirror that presents a distorted image of what threatens us. The distortions do not end with the definitions of crime. As we will examine in the following chapter, the criminal justice system is biased against the poor at its every level, so that, in the end, when we look in our prisons to see who really threatens us, virtually all we see are poor people. By that time, most of the well-to-do people who endanger us have been discreetly weeded out of the system. As we watch this process unfold in the next chapter, bear in mind the conclusion of the present chapter: All the mechanisms by which the criminal justice system comes down more frequently and more harshly on the poor criminal than on the well-off criminal take place *after most of the dangerous acts of the well-to-do have been excluded from the definition of crime itself.* Demonstrating this has been the purpose of the present chapter.

Note that the question of what should be defined as crimes is a philosophical question that requires us to reflect on the proper aims of a criminal justice system. In this chapter, we have pointed out the important consequences for criminal justice and public well-being of how "crime" is defined. In Appendix II, Jeffrey Reiman argues that the social science of criminology needs a similar philosophical reflection on the proper definition of crime "in order to establish its intellectual independence of the state, which ... is equivalent to declaring its status as a social science rather than an agency of social control, as critical rather than servile, as illumination rather than propaganda."

Study Questions

1. What should be our definition of the term "crime"? Why does it matter what we call things? Should there be an overlap between the acts we label crimes and the acts we think are morally wrong?
2. Quickly—without thinking about it too much—picture a criminal. Describe what you see. Where did this picture come from? Are there people in our society who pose a greater danger to you than the individual you pictured? Why or why not?
3. What is meant by likening the criminal justice system to a "carnival mirror"?
4. Do you believe the criminal law as it stands is correct in what it labels as a crime? In answering, be sure to review the objections made by the Defenders of the Present Legal Order and the authors' responses.
5. Do you think a business executive who refuses to invest in safety precautions with the result that several workers die is morally better than, equal to, or worse than a mugger who kills his victim after robbing him? What if the executive knowingly violated a safety regulation? What if the mugger was high on drugs? Explain your response.
6. What is meant by speaking of criminal justice as "creative art"? How does the view presented here differ from that of Quinney?
7. Give examples of social practices that are more dangerous to your well-being than common crime. How should these practices be dealt with?

Additional Resources

Jeffrey Reiman and Paul Leighton, *The Rich Get Richer and Poor Get Prison: A Reader* (Boston: Pearson, 2010). This volume is a collection of accessible articles that were either used as reference material for *The Rich Get Richer* or provide lively complementary examples or analysis. The reader is divided into sections that parallel the chapters of *The Rich Get Richer,* and each section of the reader opens with a substantial introduction, written by the editors, that provides article summaries, context, and linkages to *The Rich Get Richer.*

The authors also maintain a companion website to the text at www.paulsjustice-page. com/reiman.htm.

Notes

1. Ralph Blumenthal, "14 Die in Blast at BP Oil Refinery in Texas," *New York Times*, March 24, 2005, www.nytimes.com/2005/03/24/us/14-die-in-blast-at-bp-oil-refinery-in-texas.html.
2. U.S. Chemical Safety and Hazard Investigation Board, Investigation Report, *Investigation Report: Refinery Explosion and Fire*, 2005–04-I-TX, March 2007, p. 179, www.csb.gov/assets/1/19/csbfinalreportbp.pdf.
3. Ibid, p 52.
4. Henry J. Cordes, "Massacre at Mall in Omaha," *Chicago Tribune*, December 6, 2007, http://articles.chicagotribune.com/2007–12–06/news/0712060183_1_westroads-mall-wound-hawkins. ABC and NBC also ran headlines containing the word "massacre."
5. Jeff Zeleny and Maria Newman, "Details of Omaha Shooting Emerge," *New York Times*, December 6, 2007, www.nytimes.com/2007/12/06/us/06cnd-shoot.html.
6. U.S. Chemical Safety and Hazard Investigation Board, *Final Investigation Report: Refinery Explosion and Fire (15 Killed, 180 Injured) BP Texas City, Texas*, Report No. 2005–04-I-TX, March 2007, pp. 155–156, www.csb.gov/bp-america-refinery-explosion/.
7. Ryan Knutson, "Blast at BP Texas Refinery in '05 Foreshadowed Gulf Disaster," *ProPublica*, July 2, 2010, www.propublica.org/article/blast-at-bp-texas-refinery-in-05-foreshadowed-gulf-disaster.
8. Knutson, "Blast at BP Texas Refinery in '05 Foreshadowed Gulf Disaster."
9. Department of Labor, "OSHA Fines BP Products North America more than $21 Million Following Texas City Explosion," national news release USDL 05–1740, September 22, 2005, www.osha.gov/pls/oshaweb/owadisp.show_document?p_table=NEWS_RELEASES&p_id=11589.
10. Environmental Protection Agency, "BP to Pay Largest Criminal Fine Ever for Air Violations," news release, October 25, 2007, https://archive.epa.gov/epapages/newsroom_archive/newsreleases/1af659cf4ce8a7b88525737f005979be.html.
11. U.S. Chemical Safety and Hazard Investigation Board, *Final Investigation Report: Refinery Explosion and Fire*, p. 27 (quoting an investigation lead by former Secretary of State James Baker).
12. Mark Collette, Lise Olsen, and Jim Malewitz, "Ten Years after a Texas City Refinery Blast Killed 15 and Rattled a Community, Workers Keep Dying," *Houston Chronicle*, March 21, 2015, www.houstonchronicle.com/texascity/.
13. Environmental Protection Agency, "Deepwater Horizon – BP Gulf of Mexico Oil Spill," January 6, 2016, www.epa.gov/enforcement/deepwater-horizon-bp-gulf-mexico-oil-spill.
14. Gerald R. Ford, "To Insure Domestic Tranquility: Mandatory Sentence for Convicted Felons," speech delivered at the Yale Law School Convocation, New Haven, CT, April 25, 1975, in *Vital Speeches of the Day* 41, no. 15 (May 15, 1975): 451.
15. *UCR-2017*, Tables 41 and 42.
16. *UCR-2017*, Table 43; and calculations from *Stat-Abst-2018*, Table 9, p. 12. New census procedures allow for counting of multiple races, so those who identify as black only are 13.3 percent (43,001,000 out of a total population of 323,128,000); those who identify as two or more races are 2.6 percent (8,480,000).

17. Adam Looney and Nicholas Turner, "Work and Opportunity Before and After Incarceration," Brookings Institution, 2018, www.brookings.edu/wp-content/uploads/2018/03/es_20180314_looneyincarceration_final.pdf.
18. *Challenge*, p. 44; see also p. 160.
19. Michelle Alexander, *The New Jim Crow* (New York: The New Press, 2012), p. 160.
20. Kathryn Russell, *The Color of Crime* (New York: New York University Press, 1998), p. 3.
21. *Challenge*, p 44; see also p. 160.
22. "Mass news representations in the 'information age' have become the most significant communication by which the average person comes to know the world outside his or her immediate experience"; Gregg Barak, *Media, Process and the Social Construction of Crime* (New York: Garland, 1994), p. 3.
23. Danielle McGurrin et al., "White Collar Crime Representation in the Criminological Literature Revisited, 2001–2010," *Western Criminology Review* 14, no. 2: 3–19, www.westerncriminology.org/documents/WCR/v14n2/McGurrin.pdf, p. 10.
24. Richard Quinney, *The Social Reality of Crime* (Boston: Little, Brown, 1970). In *Critique of Legal Order* (Boston: Little, Brown, 1973) and *Class, State & Crime* (New York: McKay, 1977), Quinney moves into a Marxist problematic and his conclusions dovetail with many in this book. However, Quinney has not yet accomplished a satisfactory synthesis between the "social reality" theory and his later Marxism. See Jeffrey H. Reiman, "Doing Justice to Criminology: Reflections on the Implications for Criminology of Recent Developments in the Philosophy of Justice," in Marc Riedel and Duncan Chappell (eds.), *Issues in Criminal Justice: Planning and Evaluation* (New York: Praeger, 1976), pp. 134–142.
25. Quinney, *The Social Reality of Crime*, p. 15.
26. Robert Agnew, *Toward a Unified Criminology: Integrating Assumptions about Crime, People and Society* (New York, NY : NYU Press, 2011). p. 35.
27. Ibid., p. 38.
28. This transformation has been noted by Erving Goffman in his sensitive description of total institutions:

    The interpretative scheme of the total institution automatically begins to operate as soon as the inmate enters, the staff having the notion that entrance is prima facie evidence that one must be the kind of person the institution was set up to handle. A man in a political prison must be traitorous; a man in a prison must be a lawbreaker; a man in a mental hospital must be sick. If not traitorous, criminal, or sick, why else would he be here? (Asylums [Garden City, NY: Doubleday, 1961], p. 84).

    So, too, a person who calls forth the society's most drastic weapons of defense must pose the gravest danger to its well-being. Why else the reaction? The point is put well and tersely by D. Chapman: "There is a circular pattern in thinking: we are hostile to wicked people, wicked people are punished, punished people are wicked, we are hostile to punished people because they are wicked" ("The Stereotype of the Criminal and the Social Consequences," *International Journal of Criminology and Penology* 1 [1973]: 16).
29. Travis Dixon, "Good Guys Are Still Always in White?" *Communication Research*, April 2015, doi: 10.1177/0093650215579223.
30. *UCR-2017*, Table 1.

31. Andrew J. Baranauskas and Kevin M. Drakulich, "Media Construction of Crime Revisited: Media Types, Consumer Contexts, and Frames of Crime and Justice," *Criminology* 56, no. 4 (2018): 679–714.

32. John P. Wright, Francis T. Cullen, and Michael B. Blankenship, "The Social Construction of Corporate Violence: Media Coverage of the Imperial Food Products Fire," *Crime & Delinquency* 41, no. 1 (1995): 32. We discuss this case in Chapter 3.

33. Lyndsey Layton, "Peanut Processor Ignored Salmonella Tests, Knowingly Sold Tainted Products," *The Washington Post,* January 28, 2009, www.washington post.com/wp-dyn/content/article/2009/01/27/AR2009012702992. html?hpid=topnews.

34. Paul Leighton, "Mass Salmonella Poisoning by the Peanut Corporation of America: State-Corporate Crime Involving Food Safety," *Critical Criminology* 24, no. 1 (2016): 75–91.

35. Another way to put the Defenders' claim here is that one-on-one harms are appropriately "crimes," while indirect harms are appropriately "torts." *Torts* are noncriminal harms that justify civil suits for damages but not criminal prosecution and punishment. Since our dispute with the Defenders is about whether indirect harms *should* be crimes, these legal labels cannot resolve our dispute. They may, however, give readers familiar with legal terminology a different way of understanding what is at stake: The Defenders think that indirect harms are rightly treated as torts, while we think that many of them should count as crimes, and serious ones at that.

36. Hyman Gross, *A Theory of Criminal Justice* (New York: Oxford University Press, 1979), p. 78. See generally Chapter 3, "Culpability, Intention, Motive," which we have drawn on in making the argument of this and the following two paragraphs.

37. We owe this example, modeled on one by Hyman Gross, to Andrew W. Austin of the University of Wisconsin-Green Bay.

38. Nancy Frank, "Unintended Murder and Corporate Risk-Taking: Defining the Concept of Justifiability," *Journal of Criminal Justice* 16, no. 1 (1988): 18.

39. Occupational Safety and Health Administration (OSHA), "Enforcement," n.d., www.osha.gov/dep/2014_enforcement_summary.html. For 2014, there were 49,616 serious violations out of 67,941 total violations (73 percent serious).

40. Paul Leighton and Jeffrey Reiman, "A Suitable Amount of Street Crime and a Suitable Amount of White Collar Crime: Inconvenient Truths about Inequality, Crime and Criminal Justice," in Bruce Arrigo and Heather Bersot (eds.), *The Routledge Handbook of International Crime and Justice Studies* (New York: Routledge, 2014).

41. Paul Leighton, "Mass Salmonella Poisoning by the Peanut Corporation of America: State-Corporate Crime Involving Food Safety," *Critical Criminology* 24, no. 1 (2016): 75–91.

42. *Model Penal Code,* final draft (Philadelphia: American Law Institute, 1962).

43. Russell Mokhiber, *Corporate Crime and Violence: Big Business Power and the Abuse of Public Trust* (San Francisco: Sierra Club, 1988), pp. 278 and 285.

44. David E. Lilienfeld, "The Silence: The Asbestos Industry and Early Occupational Cancer Research—A Case Study," *American Journal of Public Health* 81, no. 6 (1991): 791. This article shows how early the industry knew of the link between asbestos and cancer and how hard they tried to suppress this information. See also Paul Brodeur, *Outrageous Misconduct: The Asbestos Industry on Trial* (New York: Pantheon, 1985).

45. Chang, Shu-Sen et al. "Impact of 2008 Global Economic Crisis on Suicide: Time Trend Study in 54 Countries," *BMJ* (Clinical research ed.) 347 (Sept. 17, 2013): 5239, doi:10.1136/bmj.f5239. www.ncbi.nlm.nih.gov/pmc/articles/PMC3776046/.

46. Morton Mintz, "A Crime Against Women: A. H. Robins and the Dalkon Shield," *Multinational Monitor* 7, no. 1 (January 15, 1986), multinationalmonitor.org/hyper/issues/1986/0115/index.html.

47. Leighton, "Mass Salmonella Poisoning by the Peanut Corporation of America."

48. Sir James Fitzjames Stephen, *History of the Criminal Law of England 2* (1883), excerpted in Abraham S. Goldstein and Joseph Goldstein (eds.), *Crime, Law and Society* (New York: Free Press, 1971), p. 21.

49. Troy Duster, *The Legislation of Morality: Law, Drugs and Moral Judgment* (New York: Free Press, 1970), pp. 3–76.

50. Norval Morris and Gordon Hawkins, *The Honest Politician's Guide to Crime Control* (Chicago: University of Chicago Press, 1970), p. 2.

51. *Challenge,* p. 7.

52. *UCR-2017,* Table 12; definitions available at https://ucr.fbi.gov/crime-in-the-u.s/2017/crime-in-the.u.s.-2017/topic-pages/murder and https://ucr.fbi.gov/crime-in-the-u.s/2017/crime-in-the-u.s.-2017/topic-pages/aggravated-assault.

53. *UCR-2017,* Property Crime Overview.

54. See Willard Oliver, "The Power to Persuade: Presidential Influence over Congress on Crime Control Policy," *Criminal Justice Review* 28, no. 1 (2003). The author finds *UCR*-reported crime "to have the most impact on congressional committees and subcommittees initiating hearings on crime and drugs" (p. 125), and this factor remains significant across several variations in model specifications.

55. White House, *President's Report on Occupational Safety and Health* (Washington, DC: U.S. Government Printing Office, 1972).
    James Messerschmidt, in a comprehensive review of research studies on job-related accidents, determined that somewhere between 35 and 57 percent of those accidents occurred because of direct safety violations by the employer. Laura Shill Schraeger and James Short Jr. found 30 percent of industrial accidents resulted from safety violations and another 20 percent resulted from unsafe working conditions. (Victor E. Kappeler and Gary W. Potter, *The Mythology of Crime and Criminal Justice*, 3rd ed., p. 104).

    See James Messerschmidt, *Capitalism, Patriarchy, and Crime: Toward a Socialist Feminist Criminology* (Totowa, NJ: Rowman & Littlefield, 1986); Laura Shill Schraeger and James Short, "Toward a Sociology of Organizational Crime," *Social Problems* 25 (April 1978): 407–419. See also Joseph A. Page and Mary-Win O'Brien, *Bitter Wages: Ralph Nader's Study Group Report on Disease and Injury on the Job* (New York: Grossman, 1973); Rachel Scott, *Muscle and Blood* (New York: Dutton, 1974); Jeanne M. Stellman and Susan M. Daum, *Work is Dangerous to Your Health* (New York: Vintage, 1973); Joel Swartz, "Silent Killers at Work," *Crime and Social Justice* 3 (Summer 1975): 15–20.

56. BLS, "Employer-Reported Workplace Injury and Illness-2017," November 8, 2018, Chart 1 and SNR07, www.bls.gov/news.release/pdf/osh.pdf. Note that this survey "excludes farms with fewer than 11 employees." "2017 Survey of Occupational Injuries & Illnesses Charts Package," November 8, 2018, Slide 9, www.bls.gov/iif/osch0062.pdf.

57. Government Accountability Office, "Enhancing OSHA's Records Audit Process Could Improve the Accuracy of Worker Injury and Illness Data," GAO-10-10, 2009, p. 1, www.gao.gov/new.items/d1010.pdf.

58. House Committee on Education and Labor, "Hidden Tragedy: Underreporting of Workplace Injuries and Illnesses," 110th Congress, Second session, June 19, 2008, www.gpo.gov/fdsys/pkg/CHRG-110hhrg42881/html/CHRG-110hhrg42881.htm.

59. Lee Friedman and Linda Forst, "The Impact of OSHA Recordkeeping Regulation Changes on Occupational Injury and Illness Trends in the US," *Occupational and Environmental Medicine* 64, no. 7 (2007): 459.

60. Philip Landrigan, testimony before the Senate Committee on Labor and Human Resources, April 18, 1988, p. 2. For cancer deaths, see *Stat-Abst-1988*, Table 117, p. 77 and Table 120, p. 80. "Safety Group Cites Fatalities Linked to Work," *The Wall Street Journal*, August 31, 1990, p. B8; Sally Squires, "Study Traces More Deaths to Working than Driving," *The Washington Post*, August 31, 1990, p. A7.

61. J. Paul Leigh et al., "Occupational Injury and Illness in the United States: Estimates of Costs, and Morbidity, and Mortality," *Archives of Internal Medicine* 157, no. 14 (1997): 1557–1568.

62. Cancer Prevention Coalition, "U.S. National Cancer Institute," www. preventcancer. com/losing/nci/why_prevent.htm.

63. J. Paul Leigh, "Economic Burden of Occupational Injury and Illness in the United States," *The Milbank Quarterly* 89, no. 4 (2011): 728–772.

64. Adam M. Finkel, "Hearing on 'Mismanaging Chemical Risks: EPA's Failure to Protect Workers,'" Testimony before U.S. House of Representatives, Committee on Energy and Commerce, Environment and Climate Change Subcommittee, March 13, 2019, https://docs.house.gov/meetings/IF/IF18/20190313/109117/HHRG-116-IF18-Wstate-FinkelA-20190313.pdf, p. 3.

65. David Michaels, "Adding Inequality to Injury," OSHA, 2015, www.osha.gov/Publications/inequality_michaels_june2015.pdf

66. BLS, "Census of Fatal Occupational Injuries Summary, 2017, www.bls.gov/news.release/cfoi.nr0.htm. (BLS reports a total of 5,147 workplace fatalities, of which 458 are homicides in Table 2.)

67. BJS, "Occupational Health and Safety Definitions," www.bls.gov/iif/oshdef.htm.

68. L. I. Boden et al., "The Impact of Non-Fatal Workplace Injuries and Illnesses on Mortality," *American Journal of Industrial Medicine* 59 (2016): 1061–1069, doi:10.1002/ajim.22632.

69. Friedman and Forst, "The Impact of OSHA Recordkeeping Regulation Changes on Occupational Injury and Illness Trends in the US," p. 459, citing the National Electronic Injury Surveillance System.

70. National Institute for Occupational Safety and Health (NIOSH), *Worker Health Chartbook, 2000: Nonfatal Illness* (Atlanta, GA: U.S. Department of Health and Human Services Centers for Disease Control and Prevention [HHS/CDC], April 2002). See also NIOSH, "Protecting Workers' Families: A Research Agenda," (Atlanta, GA: HHS/CDC, May 2002); Finkel, "Hearing on 'Mismanaging Chemical Risks,'" p. 15.71;

71. Adam M. Finkel. "Hearing on 'Mismanaging Chemical Risks'" p. 15.

72. *Stat-Abst-2018*, Tables 2 and 609.

73. BJS "Criminal Victimization, 2017," December 2018, Table 6, p. 7.

74. Hilda Solis, "One is Too Many," 2011, http://social.dol.gov/blog/one-is-too-many/.

75. Nadja Popovich, "Black Lung Disease Comes Storming Back in Coal Country," *New York Times*, February 22, 2018, www.nytimes.com/interactive/2018/02/22/climate/black-lung-resurgence.html (emphasis in original).

76. Joan Claybrook and the Staff of Public Citizen, *Retreat from Safety: Reagan's Attack on America's Health* (New York: Pantheon, 1984), p. 83. Chronic brown lung is a severely disabling occupational respiratory disease. See also Page and O'Brien, *Bitter Wages*, p. 18.

77. Claybrook, *Retreat from Safety*, p. 97. See also Page and O'Brien, *Bitter Wages*, p. 23; and Scott, *Muscle and Blood*, p. 196.

78. Scott, *Muscle and Blood*, pp. 45–46; cf. Page and O'Brien, *Bitter Wages*, p. 25.

79. Cindy Skrzycki, "Alarm over a Sheepish Non-rule," *The Washington Post*, October 29, 2002, p. E1.

80. Curt Suplee, "House to Consider 'Ergo Rider' Restraints on OSHA," *The Washington Post*, July 11, 1996, p. A4. In 2014, carpal tunnel required a median of 32 days to recuperate. BLS, "Nonfatal Occupational Injuries and Illnesses Requiring Days Away from Work," 2014, Table 5, www.bls.gov/news.release/osh2.pdf.

81. Friedman and Forst, "The Impact of OSHA Recordkeeping Regulation Changes on Occupational Injury and Illness Trends in the US," p. 459. Suzy Khimm. "Number of OSHA Workplace Safety Inspectors Declines under Trump," *NBC News*, January 8, 2018, https://www.nbcnews.com/politics/whitehouse/exclusive-number-osha-workplace-safety-inspectors-declines-under-trump-n834806.

82. U.S. Department of Labor, Occupational Safety and Health Administration, "Commonly Used Statistics," www.osha.gov/oshstats/commonstats.html.

83. David Barstow, "When Workers Die: U.S. Rarely Seeks Charges for Deaths in Workplace," *New York Times*, December 22, 2003, p. A1, www.nytimes.com/2003/12/22/national/22OSHA.html. Barstow found 1,242 cases of deaths related to willful violations between 1982 and 2002, but OSHA declined prosecution in 93 percent of the cases. Recently "OSHA began to accede to employer demands that it replace the word 'willful' with 'unclassified' in citations involving workplace deaths."

84. AFL-CIO, *Death on the Job: The Toll of Neglect*, 28th Edition, April 2019. https://aflcio.org/sites/default/files/2019-05/DOTJ2019Fnb_1.pdf.

85. David Michaels, Testimony before the Subcommittee on Workforce Protections, Committee on Education and Labor, U.S. House of Representatives, March 16, 2010, www.osha.gov/pls/oshaweb/owadisp.show_document?p_table= TESTIMONIES&p_id=1062; AFL-CIO, *Death on the Job*, 2011, www.aflcio.org/issues/safety/memorial/upload/dotj_2011.pdf, p. 21 (citing an April 2008 report on OSHA enforcement in fatality cases prepared by the majority staff of the Senate Committee on Health, Education, Labor and Pensions). Protecting America's Workers Act (PAWA) proposed to increase penalties for cases involving willful or repeat violations that result in a fatality to $250,000—"the level where they will have the same value, accounting for inflation, as they had in 1990." PAWA died in Congress and has not even been reintroduced. U.S. Department of Labor, Occupational Safety and Health Administration, "OSHA Penalties," www.osha.gov/penalties.

86. AFL-CIO, *Death on the Job*.

87. Barbara Starfield, "Is US Health Really the Best in the World?" *Journal of the American Medical Association (JAMA)* 284, no. 4 (July 26, 2000): 483, http://jama.jamanetwork.com/article.aspx?articleid=192908.

88. J. T. James, "A New, Evidence-based Estimate of Patient Harms Associated with Hospital Care," *Journal of Patient Safety*, 9, no. 3: 122–128, doi: 10.1097/PTS.0b013e3182948a69, pp. 125, 127 and 126.

89. Steve Sternberg, "Medical Errors are Third Leading Cause of Death in the U.S.," *U.S. News*, May 3, 2016, www.usnews.com/news/articles/2016-05-03/medical-errors-are-third-leading-cause-of-death-in-the-us.

90. P. F. Stahel, T. F. VanderHeiden, and F. J. Kim, "Why Do Surgeons Continue to Perform Unnecessary Surgery?" *Patient Safety in Surgery* 11, no. 1 (2017), doi:10.1186/s13037-016-0117-6.

91. *The Washington Post*, July 16, 1975, p. A3 (16,000 deaths); George A. Silver, "The Medical Insurance Disease," *Nation* 222, no. 12 (March 27, 1976): 369 (15,000 deaths).

92. *Stat-Abst-2019*, Table 190.

93. Stahel et al., "Why Do Surgeons Continue to Perform Unnecessary Surgery?"

94. *UCR-2017* Expanded Homicide Data Table 8.

95. Paul Weiler et al., *A Measure of Malpractice: Medical Injury, Malpractice Litigation and Patient Compensation* (Cambridge, MA: Harvard University Press, 1993), p. 54. The data given here come from the Harvard Medical Practice Study. See also Christine Russell, "Human Error: Avoidable Mistakes Kill 100,000 Patients a Year," *The Washington Post Health*, February 18, 1992, p. 7.

96. Sandra G. Boodman, "No End to Errors," *The Washington Post*, December 3, 2002, p. F1. The original report was Linda T. Kohn, Janet M. Corrigan, and Molla S. Donaldson (eds.), *To Err is Human: Building a Safer Health System* (Washington, DC: National Academy Press, 1999).

97. Jessica Bruder. "The Worst Drug Crisis in American History," *New York Times*, July 31, 2018, www.nytimes.com/2018/07/31/books/review/beth-macy-dopesick.html.

98. Sandra G. Boodman, "No End to Errors," The Washington Post Health, December 3, 2002, p. F1.

99. Denise Grady. "Study Finds No Progress in Safety at Hospitals," *New York Times*, November 24, 2010, www.nytimes.com/2010/11/25/health/research/25patient.html.

100. U.S. Senate Committee on Health, Education, Labor and Pensions, Subcommittee on Primary Health and Aging, Testimony of Ashish K. Jha, July 17, 2014, www.help.senate.gov/hearings/more-than-1-000-preventable-deaths-a-day-is-too-many-the-need-to-improve-patient-safety.

101. Rick Weiss, "Medical Errors Blamed for Many Deaths: As Many as 98,000 a Year in U.S. Linked to Mistakes," *The Washington Post*, November 30, 1999, p. A1.

102. Sternberg, "Medical Errors are Third Leading Cause of Death in the U.S."

103. Fred Schulte and Erika Fry, "Death by 1,000 Clicks: Where Electronic Health Records Went Wrong," *Kaiser Health News*, March 18, 2019, https://khn.org/news/death-by-a-thousand-clicks/.

104. Daniel Tawfik et al., "Physician Burnout, Well-Being, and Work Unit Safety Grades in Relationship to Reported Medical Errors," *Mayo Clinic Proceedings* 93, no. 11 (2018): 1571–1580.

105. James, "A New, Evidence-Based Estimate of Patient Harms Associated with Hospital Care."

106. American Cancer Society, "Cancer Facts & Figures 2019," p. 1, www.cancer.org/content/dam/cancer-org/research/cancer-facts-and-statistics/annual-cancer-facts-and-figures/2019/cancer-facts-and-figures-2019.pdf.

107. Valerie Watnick, "The Lautenberg Chemical Safety Act of 2016: Cancer, Industry Pressure, and a Proactive Approach," *Harvard Environmental Law Review*, 43, no. 2 (2019): 373–414.

108. President's Cancer Panel, *Reducing Environmental Cancer* (2008–2009 Annual Report) (Washington, DC: U.S. Department of Health and Human Services, 2010), p. 1, http://deainfo.nci.nih.gov/advisory/pcp/annualReports/index.htm.

109. Editorial, "Cancer—Nature, Nurture, or Both," *New England Journal of Medicine* 343, no. 2 (July 13, 2000): 135.
110. Watnick, "The Lautenberg Chemical Safety Act of 2016: Cancer, Industry Pressure, and a Proactive Approach."
111. President's Cancer Panel, *Reducing Environmental Cancer*, pp. 5–6.
112. Samuel S. Epstein et al., "The Crisis in U.S. and International Cancer Policy," *International Journal of Health Services* 32, no. 4 (2002): 693.
113. Lindsey Dillon et al. "The Environmental Protection Agency in the Early Trump Administration: Prelude to Regulatory Capture," *American Journal of Public Health*, 108, no. S2 (April 1, 2018): S89–S94, doi:10.2105/AJPH. 2018.304360; State Energy & Environmental Impact Center – NYU School of Law, "Climate and Health Showdown in the Courts: State Attorneys General Prepare to Fight," March 2019, www.law.nyu.edu/sites/default/files/climate-and-health-showdown-in-the-courts.pdf; Warren Cornwall, "Critics Allege EPA's New Transparency Rule has Hidden Pro-industry Agenda," *Science*, May 1, 2018, www.sciencemag.org/news/2018/05/critics-allege-epa-s-new-transparency-rule-has-hidden-pro-industry-agenda.
114. President's Cancer Panel, *Reducing Environmental Cancer*, transmittal letter (page not numbered).
115. Watnick, "The Lautenberg Chemical Safety Act of 2016: Cancer, Industry Pressure, and a Proactive Approach."
116. President's Cancer Panel, *Reducing Environmental Cancer*, p. 19. See also IOM (Institute of Medicine) Roundtable on Environmental Health Sciences, Research, and Medicine, Robert Pool and Erin Rusch (rapporteurs), *Identifying and Reducing Environmental Health Risks of Chemicals in Our Society: Workshop Summary* (Washington, DC: The National Academies Press, 2014), chapter 3.
117. American Public Health Association, "Calling on the US Congress to Restructure the Toxic Substances Control Act of 1976," 2017, www. apha.org/policies-and-advocacy/public-health-policy-statements/policy-database/2014/07/08/13/04/calling-on-the-us-congress-to-restructure-the-toxic-substances-control-act-of-1976. Citations and links are available from the URL above.
118. Coral Davenport, "Senate Approves Update of Toxic-Chemical Regulations," *New York Times,* June 7, 2016, www.nytimes.com/2016/06/08/us/politics/senate-approves-update-of-toxic-chemical-regulations.html.
119. Catherine Traywick and Jack Kaskey, "EPA Wins Clout to Fight Toxic Chemicals, but It May Take a While," *Bloomberg*, June 8, 2016, www.bloomberg.com/politics/articles/2016–06–08/with-chemical-safety-law-congress-hands-epa-herculean-task.
120. Eric Lipton, "The Chemical Industry Scores a Big Win at the E.P.A.," *New York Times,* June 7, 2018, www.nytimes.com/2018/06/07/us/politics/epa-toxic-chemicals.html; Watnick, "The Lautenberg Chemical Safety Act of 2016: Cancer, Industry Pressure, and a Proactive Approach."
121. Annie Sneed, "Trumps's EPA May be Weakening Chemical Safety Law," *Scientific American*, August 16, 2017, www.scientificamerican.com/article/trump-rsquo-s-epa-may-be-weakening-chemical-safety-law/.
122. Philip Landrigan et al. (2018). "The Lancet Commission on Pollution and Health," *The Lancet Commissions*, 391, Issue 10119: 462–512, www.thelancet.com/journals/lancet/article/PIIS0140-6736(17)32345-0/fulltext.
123. Ibid., p. 1.

124. Bob Weinhold, "Assessing the Global Composite Impact of Chemicals on Health," *Environmental Health Perspectives* 119 (2011): a162–a163.

125. Program on Reproductive Health and the Environment, University of California, San Francisco, "What the Science Says: How EPA Matters to Children's Health," December 18, 2017, https://prheucsf.blog/2017/12/18/what-the-science-says-how-epa-matters-to-childrens-health/.

126. Landrigan et al., "The Lancet Commission on Pollution and Health," p. 1.

127. Ibid., p. 20.

128. Linda S. Birnbaum, "When Environmental Chemicals Act Like Uncontrolled Medicine," *Trends in Endocrinology and Metabolism* 24, no. 7 (2013): 321–323. A. C. Gore et al., "Executive Summary to EDC-2: The Endocrine Society's Second Scientific Statement on Endocrine-Disrupting Chemicals," *Endocrine Reviews* 36, no. 6 (2015): 593–602, https://doi.org/10.1210/er.2015-1093.

129. Landrigan et al., "The Lancet Commission on Pollution and Health," p. 20.

130. Mark Bittman, "Pesticides: Now More Than Ever," *New York Times,* December 11, 2012, http://opinionator.blogs.nytimes.com/2012/12/11/pesticides-now-more-than-ever/.

131. American Academy of Pediatrics, "Pesticide Exposure in Children (Policy Statement)," 130, no. 6 (2013): 2012–2757.

132. Landrigan et al., "The Lancet Commission on Pollution and Health," p. 20.

133. Watnick, "The Lautenberg Chemical Safety Act of 2016: Cancer, Industry Pressure, and a Proactive Approach."

134. Anahad O'Connor, "Air Pollution Linked to Heart and Brain Risks," *New York Times,* February 15, 2012, http://well.blogs.nytimes.com/2012/02/15/air-pollution-tied-to-heart-and-brain-risks/; Deborah Blum, "Air Pollution as a Heart Threat," *New York Times,* November 15, 2013, http://well.blogs.nytimes.com/2013/11/15/an-airborne-heart-threat/.

135. Michael Lynch and Kimberly Barrett, "Death Matters: Victimization by Particle Matter from Coal Fired Power Plants in the US, a Green Criminological View," *Critical Criminology* 23, no. 3 (2015): 219–234.

136. Andrew L. Goodkind et al. (2019)."Fine-scale Damage Estimates of Particulate Matter Air Pollution Reveal Opportunities for Location-specific Mitigation of Emissions," *Proceedings of the National Academy of Sciences of the U.S.A* 116, no. 8: 8775–8780, https://doi.org/10.1073/pnas.1816102116.

137. Miranda Green, "GAO Investigating EPA's Low Enforcement Numbers," *The Hill,* January 15, 2019, https://thehill.com/policy/energy-environment/425485-gao-investigating-epas-low-enforcement-numbers.

138. U.S. Department of Health and Human Services, *The Health Consequences of Smoking—50 Years of Progress: A Report of the Surgeon General Executive Summary* (Atlanta, GA: U.S. Department of Health and Human Services, Centers for Disease Control and Prevention, 2014), p. 15.

139. Ibid., p. iii.

140. Centers for Disease Control and Prevention, "Tobacco-Related Mortality," January 17, 2108, www.cdc.gov/tobacco/data_statistics/fact_sheets/health_effects/tobacco_related_mortality/index.htm.

141. U.S. Department of Health and Human Services. *The Health Consequences of Smoking Executive Summary,* p. 11, www.cdc.gov/tobacco/data_statistics/fact_sheets/economics/econ_facts/index.htm.

142. James S. Todd et al., "The Brown and Williamson Documents: Where Do We Go from Here?" *JAMA* 274, no. 3 (1995): 256, 258.

143. U.S. Department of Health and Human Services, *The Health Consequences of Smoking*, p. 28.

144. Wendy Max, Hai-Yen Sung, and Yanling Shi, "Deaths from Secondhand Smoke Exposure in the United States: Economic Implications," *American Journal of Public Health* 102, no. 11 (2012): 1273–2180.

145. Beatrice Hunter, *The Mirage of Safety* (New York: Penguin, 1982), p. 4.

146. Hunter, *The Mirage of Safety*.

147. Leonardo Trasande, Rachel M. Shafer, and Sheela Sathyanarayana, "Food Additives and Child Health," *Pediatrics* 142, no. 2 (2018), https://pediatrics.aappublications.org/content/142/2/e20181408.

148. Ibid. Erin Quinn, "Why the FDA Doesn't Really Know What's in Your Food," *Public Integrity*, April 14, 2015, www.publicintegrity.org/2015/04/13/17112/why-fda-doesnt-really-know-whats-your-food.

149. Sarah Kobylewski and Michael F. Jacobson, *Food Dyes: A Rainbow of Risks* (Washington, DC: Center for Science in the Public Interest, 2010), p. 4, http://cspinet.org/new/pdf/food-dyes-rainbow-of-risks.pdf; Food Standards Agency (UK), "Compulsory Warnings on Colours in Food and Drink," www.food.gov.uk/news/newsarchive/2010/jul/eucolourswarn.

150. At the very least, "we" includes all the households that earn considerably above the median income for the nation (around $57,652 for a household in 2017) and who resist, or who vote for candidates who resist, moves to redistribute income significantly.

151. Karen Pennar, "The Rich Are Richer—and America May Be the Poorer," *Business-Week*, November 18, 1991, pp. 85–88.

152. Kayla Fontenot, Jessica Semega, and Melissa Kollar. *U.S. Census Bureau, Income and Poverty in the United States: 2017, Current Population Reports*, pp. 60–263 (Washington, DC: U.S. Government Printing Office, 2018), Table 3.

153. *Stat-Abst-2018*, Table 736, 145. The Urban Institute, *A New Look at Homelessness in America*, February 1, 2000, www.urban.org/url.cfm?ID=900302.

154. Linda Giannarelli et al. (2015) "Reducing Child Poverty in the US: Costs and Impacts of Policies Proposed by the Children's Defense Fund", Urban Institute, www.urban.org/sites/default/files/publication/39141/2000086-Reducing-Child-Poverty-in-the-US.pdf.

155. National Academies of Sciences, Engineering, and Medicine, 2019. A Roadmap to Reducing Child Poverty (Washington, DC: The National Academies Press, 2019), https://doi.org/10.17226/25246, p. 1-1 (Uncorrected proofs).

156. Ibid.

157. Ibid.

158. Paula A. Braveman, Susan A. Egerter, and Robin E. Mockenhaupt, "Broadening the Focus," *American Journal of Preventive Medicine* 40, no. 1S1 (2011): p. S4.

159. Aaron Antonovsky, "Class and the Chance for Life," in Lee Rainwater (ed.), *Inequality and Justice* (Chicago: Aldine, 1974), p. 177.

160. McGinnis and Foege, "Actual Causes of Death in the United States," *JAMA* 270, no. 18 (Nov 10, 1993): 2207–2212.

161. *HHS News*, "Health in America Tied to Income and Education," July 30, 1998, www.cdc.gov/nchs/pressroom/98news/huspr98.htm. See also R. Wilkinson, *Unhealthy Societies: The Afflictions of Inequality* (London: Routledge, 1996).

162. Pew Environmental Health Commission. *Attack Asthma: Why America Needs a Public Health Defense System to Battle Environmental Threats* (Baltimore, MD: Johns Hopkins University of Public Health, 2000), p. 10.

163. R. Chetty et al., "The Association Between Income and Life Expectancy in the United States, 2001–2014," JAMA 315, no. 16 (2016): 1750–1766, doi:10.1001/jama.2016.4226.

164. *Income and Poverty in the United States: 2017*, p. 13; and *Stat-Abst-2018*, Table 121.

165. Rob Stein, "Race Gap Persists in Health Care, Three Studies Say," *The Washington Post*, August 18, 2005, p. A1.

166. January Payne, "Dying for Basic Care," *The Washington Post*, December 21, 2004, p. HE1. The report itself notes that "socioeconomic conditions represent a more pertinent cause of disparities than race."

167. *StatAbst-2016*, Table 200, p. 133.

168. National Institutes of Health, *Cancer Patient Survival Experience*, June 1980, pp. 4–5.

169. Ann Gibbons, "Does War on Cancer Equal War on Poverty?" *Science* 253, no. 5017 (1991): 260.

170. Barbara L. Wells and John W. Horm, "Stage at Diagnosis in Breast Cancer: Race and Socioeconomic Factors," *American Journal of Public Health* 82, no. 10 (1992): 1383.

171. Gibbons, "Does War on Cancer Equal War on Poverty?" p. 260.

172. *Stat-Abst-2018*, Table 111; Richard Allen Williams reports that "there is no reason why the life span of the White should differ from that of the Black," in his *Textbook of Black-Related Diseases* (New York: McGraw-Hill, 1975), p. 2.

173. Braveman, Egerter, Mockenhaupt, "Broadening the Focus," pp. S7–S8.

CHAPTER 3

... And the Poor Get Prison

When we come to make an intelligent study of the prison at first hand... we are bound to conclude that after all it is not so much crime in its general sense that is penalized, but that it is poverty which is punished.

Take a census of the average prison and you will find that a large majority of people are there not so much because of the particular crime they are alleged to have committed, but for the reason that they are poor and lacked the money to engage the services of first class and influential lawyers.

—EUGENE V. DEBS, *WALLS AND BARS*

Laws are like spiders' webs: they catch the weak and the small, but the strong and the powerful break through them.

—SCYTHIAN, *ONE OF THE SEVEN WISE MEN OF ANCIENT GREECE*

Chapter 3 of *The Rich Get Richer* continues our examination of the processes by which our prisons and jails come to be occupied predominately by those from the lowest social and economic classes. Having argued in Chapter 2 that the criminal law does not treat as crimes many serious harmful acts done by the well-off, Chapter 3 now argues that, among the acts that are treated as crimes, the criminal justice system "weeds out the wealthy." For similar crimes, the poor are more likely to be arrested, more likely to be charged, more likely to be convicted, and more likely to be sentenced to longer prison sentences than members of middle and upper classes.

THE FACE IN THE CARNIVAL MIRROR

The offender at the end of the road in prison is likely to be a member of the lowest social and economic groups in the country.[1]

This statement in the *Report of the President's Commission on Law Enforcement and Administration of Justice* is as true today as it was when it was written five decades ago. Our prisons are indeed, the "national poorhouse."[2] To most citizens, this comes as no surprise—recall the Typical Criminal and the Typical Crime. Dangerous crimes, they think, are committed mainly by poor people. Seeing that prison populations are made up primarily of the poor only makes them surer of this. They think, in other words, that the criminal justice system gives a true reflection of the dangers that threaten them.

In our view, it also comes as no surprise that our prisons and jails predominantly confine the poor. This is not because these are the individuals who most threaten us. It is because the criminal justice system effectively weeds out the well-to-do, so that *at the end of the road in prison,* the vast majority of those we find there come from the lower classes. This weeding-out process starts before the agents of law enforcement go into action. Chapter 2 argued that our very definition of crime *excludes* a wide variety of actions at least as dangerous as those included and often worse. Even before we mobilize our troops in the war on crime, we have already guaranteed that large numbers of upper-class individuals will never come within their sights.

This process does not stop at the definition of crime. It continues throughout each level of the criminal justice system. At each step, from arresting to sentencing, the likelihood of being ignored or released or treated lightly by the system is greater the better off one is economically. As the late U.S. Senator Philip Hart wrote,

> Justice has two transmission belts, one for the rich and one for the poor. The low-income transmission belt is easier to ride without falling off and it gets to prison in shorter order. The transmission belt for the affluent is a little slower and it passes innumerable stations where exits are temptingly convenient.[3]

This means that the criminal justice system functions from start to finish in a way that makes certain that "the offender at the end of the road in prison is likely to be a member of the lowest social and economic groups in the country." *For the same criminal behavior,* the poor are more likely to be arrested; if arrested, they are more likely to be charged; if charged, more likely to be convicted; if convicted, more likely to be sentenced to prison; and if sentenced, more likely to be given longer prison terms than members of the middle and upper classes.[4] In other words, the image of the criminal population one sees in our nation's jails and prisons is distorted by the shape of the criminal justice system itself. It is the face of evil reflected in a carnival mirror, but it is no laughing matter.

The face in the criminal justice carnival mirror is also, as we have already noted, very frequently a black face. Although blacks do not make up the majority of the inmates in our jails and prisons, they make up a proportion that far outstrips their percentage of the population. Here, too, the image we see is distorted by the processes of the criminal justice system itself—a distortion that has been going on for decades. Edwin Sutherland and Donald Cressey wrote, in the 1974 edition of their widely used textbook *Criminology*, that

> numerous studies have shown that African-Americans are more likely to be arrested, indicted, convicted, and committed to an institution than are whites who commit the same offenses, and many other studies have shown that blacks have a poorer chance than whites to receive probation, a suspended sentence, parole, commutation of a death sentence, or pardon.[5]

The latest edition of this classic says much the same, adding only that blacks are not arrested or convicted more in those cases where a black victimizes a black—suggesting that bias against black victims works together with bias against black offenders.[6]

Many still believe that blacks are overrepresented in prison *only* because they commit more than their share of crimes, but extensive research about disproportionate minority contact (DMC) in three different cities concluded that "the often stated reason for DMC—that it simply reflects the difference in offending rates among different racial/ethnic groups—cannot be supported by the information provided by these three studies, and we suspect that it is simply incorrect in general."[7] Cassia Spohn concludes her extensive review of the literature saying that "whether because of conscious bias, unconscious stereotypes linking race with crime, or colorblind application of racially tinged policies, judges' and prosecutors' decisions regarding bail, prosecution, and sentencing are not racially neutral."[8] The National Academy of Sciences panel on incarceration has the same conclusion, and highlighting the importance of *cumulative disadvantage*, notes that "the cumulative effect of small differences at each stage was substantial."[9]

Interestingly, statistics on differential treatment of races are available in abundance while statistics on differential treatment of economic classes are rare. (The Department of Justice includes questions about income in its surveys of prison inmates, but does not release the data—another case of missing information on class and criminal justice.)[10] Although the FBI tabulates arrest rates by race (as well as by sex, age, and geographic area), it omits class or income. The *Sourcebook of Criminal Justice Statistics* shows household income categories only for crime victims.

Both independent and government data gatherers are more willing to own up to America's racism than to its class bias. Writes Majorie Zatz, "Class is one of the paramount sociological variables, yet our measures of it in criminal justice data are abysmal." She continues, "There is general recognition among scholars that some of the race effects that have been found [in research on sentencing] may be due in part to class effects."[11] Indeed, research looking at whether young men had ever been jailed, and for how long, found that "class explains at least half of racial disparities for each outcome."[12]

Although racism is a distinct form of bias in our system, and it often targets well-off blacks, class bias and race bias overlap sufficiently for us to use race as a rough proxy for class. We recognize that racism is resilient and powerful, with a long, inglorious history in American society. Many observers consider the recent massive imprisonment of young black men as but the latest in a series of policies controlling and isolating blacks that spans slavery, Jim Crow,[13] and northern ghettoization.[14] In emphasizing class, we do not wish to minimize the importance of race. Our goal is to provide much-needed discussion about the reality of economic discrimination. As sociologist William Julius Wilson wrote in *The Declining Significance of Race,* the point is not to deny the reality of racism but to highlight the importance of class structure, even for blacks.[15]

Research on discrimination tends to focus on race or gender, and sometimes the intersection of those two, but class is less often examined.[16] To help illustrate the importance of class for blacks, consider the story of Doug Glanville, a retired professional baseball player and ESPN commentator. When Glanville (who is black) was shoveling snow on his driveway, a police officer from the next town passed by several whites shoveling their driveways and approached him. The town the officer was from had an ordinance prohibiting door to door solicitations, like asking people to shovel their driveways for money. Although the officer was out of his jurisdiction and the ordinance did not apply, the office questioned Glanville "without respect."[17] Glanville felt like "a suspect offering a defense" when explaining he owned the home. The officer left without an apology. Glanville's wife, an attorney, emailed a state senator who lived in the neighborhood about "shoveling while black." Glanville subsequently had a meeting at the town hall with city officials. While race is clearly a factor here, the trajectory of the encounter was very different from those of poor blacks, highlighting the importance of class.

More generally, Michelle Alexander's *The New Jim Crow* argues that illegal discrimination against blacks has been replaced by legal discrimination against black criminals.[18] But calling this phenomenon a "new Jim Crow" suggests that class is not important because the old Jim Crow treated rich and poor blacks similarly—neither could use the "whites only" drinking fountains, for example. Today's mass incarceration, by contrast, is reserved for poor blacks (and whites). We focus, then, on class bias because our criminal justice system now weeds out wealthy blacks as well as wealthy whites, even if wealthy blacks continue to have encounters with police because of their race.

Though we use data on economic class where it is available, we will supplement this by using evidence of differential treatment of blacks and Hispanics as evidence for differential treatment of members of the lower classes. Here are the reasons that support this strategy:

1. First and foremost, black Americans are disproportionately poor. In 2017, 8.7 percent of white non-Hispanic Americans lived below the poverty line compared to 21.2 percent of black Americans.[19] The picture is even worse when we shift from income to wealth (property such as a home, stocks, and savings). On average, the wealth of white non-Hispanic households in America is 10 times that of black households (in 2016).[20] Further, in 2018, 3.5 percent of white workers and 6.5 percent of black

workers were unemployed. Among those in the crime-prone ages of 16 to 19, about 11.3 percent of white youngsters and 21.9 percent of black youngsters were jobless.[21]

2. The factors most likely to keep one out of trouble with the law and out of prison—such as a suburban living room instead of a tenement alley to take drugs in, or legal counsel able to devote time to one's case instead of an overburdened public defender—are the kinds of things that money can buy regardless of one's race, creed, or national origin. Zatz states, "Some of the racial differences found in processing and sanctioning decisions may be attributable to class differences in access to resources."[22] Moreover, as we shall see, arrests of blacks for illicit drug possession or dealing are way out of proportion to drug arrests for whites, though research shows no greater drug use among blacks than among whites. Drug arrests are most easily made in "disorganized innercity" areas, where drug sales are more likely to take place out-of-doors and dealers are more willing to sell to strangers, and where unemployed, poor Blacks and Hispanics are more likely than whites to live.[23] What might at first look like a straightforward racial disparity turns out to reflect lower economic status as well.

3. Some studies suggest that race works to heighten the effects of economic conditions on criminal justice outcomes so that "being unemployed *and* black substantially increase[s] the chances of incarceration over those associated with being either unemployed or black."[24] The National Academy of Sciences panel on incarceration found that 70 percent of the African Americans "who dropped out of school served time in state or federal prison," and it is the combination of race and dropping out of school that has "produced extraordinarily high incarceration rates."[25] This means that racism will produce a kind of selective economic bias, making a certain segment of the uneducated and unemployed even more likely to end up behind bars.

4. Finally, in light of the relatively high incidence of poverty and/or unemployment among blacks and Hispanics, both racially biased criminal justice policies and economically biased criminal justice policies will result in poor people being disproportionately arrested and imprisoned. We are more concerned with this consequence than with the intention behind it.

For all these reasons, while racism is a distinct and powerful phenomenon in America, we will treat it here as a kind of economic bias or a tool that achieves the same end. It *weeds out the wealthy*, starting at the very entrance to the criminal justice system: The decision about whom to investigate, arrest, or charge is not made simply on the basis of the offense committed or the danger posed. It is a decision distorted by a systematic economic bias that works to the disadvantage of the poor.

Further, economic bias is a two-edged sword. First, the poor are arrested and charged out of proportion to their numbers for the kinds of crimes that tend to be committed by poor people—burglary, robbery, assault, and so forth. Second, when we reach the kinds of crimes poor people almost never have the opportunity to commit, such as antitrust violations, industrial safety violations, embezzlement, and large-scale tax evasion, the criminal justice system shows an increasingly benign and merciful face. When it comes to crime in the streets, where the perpetrator is apt to be poor, he or she is even more likely to be arrested and formally charged. When it comes to crime in the suites, where the offender is apt to be affluent, the system is more likely to deal with the crime noncriminally, that is, by civil litigation or informal settlement. When it does choose to proceed criminally, as we will see in the section on sentencing, it rarely goes beyond a slap on the wrist. Not only is the main entry to the road to prison held wide open to the poor, but the access routes for the wealthy are largely sealed off. Once again, we should not be surprised at whom we find in our prisons.

When thinking about economic bias, keep in mind that this chapter argues both that (1) for the same crime, the wealthy fare better than the poor, and (2) that frauds and economic harms of the rich, while taking more more money from people than street crimes, are treated more leniently than are the crimes that are typical of the poor. The second point relates to white-collar crime, a term Sutherland coined to refer to a range of crimes committed by professionals in the course of their occupations. In contrast to media depictions, like the series *White Collar* (where white-collar criminals are high-end professional thieves),[26] Sutherland lists typical white-collar crimes:

> White-collar criminality in business is expressed most frequently in the form of misrepresentation in financial statements of corporations, manipulation of the stock exchange, commercial bribery, bribery of public officials directly or indirectly in order to secure favorable contracts and legislation, misrepresentation in advertising and salesmanship, embezzlement and misapplication of funds, short weights and measures and misgrading of commodities, tax frauds, misapplication of funds in receiverships and bankruptcies.[27]

Like the property crimes on the street, white-collar crimes inflict financial losses and psychological harm while eroding public confidence. They often result in mass financial victimization.

WEEDING OUT THE WEALTHY

The remainder of this chapter shows how the criminal justice system functions to *weed out the wealthy* (meaning both middle- and upper-class offenders) at each stage of the process and, thus, produces a distorted image of the crime problem. Before entering into this discussion, however, three points are worth noting.

First, it is not our view that the poor are all innocent victims persecuted by the evil rich. The poor do commit crimes, and the vast majority of the poor who are confined in our prisons are guilty of some crime. In addition, there is good evidence that the poor do commit a greater portion of the crimes against persons and property listed in the FBI Index than the middle and upper classes do, relative to their numbers in the national population. What we have already tried to prove is that the crimes in the FBI Index are not the only acts that threaten us nor are they the acts that threaten us the most. Many harmful acts of the well-off are not crimes. What this chapter shows is that when we consider acts that are crimes, the poor are arrested and punished by the criminal justice system much more frequently and more harshly than better-off folks who commit the same crimes.

Second, the following discussion has been divided into three sections that correspond to the major criminal justice decision points and that also correspond to hypotheses 2, 3, and 4 stated in Chapter 2. But, bear in mind that many of the distorting processes operate at all criminal justice decision points, leading to cumulative disadvantage for the poor and cumulative advantage for the rich.

Third, the movement from arrest to sentencing is a funneling process so that discrimination that occurs at any early stage shapes the population that reaches later stages. Thus, for example, the population that reaches the point of sentencing has already been subject to whatever discrimination exists at earlier stages. If, for example, among people with similar offenses and records, poor people are more likely to be charged and more likely to be convicted, then, even if the sentencing of convicted criminals is evenhanded, it will reproduce the discrimination that occurred before.

A Critical Review of Criminality and Class

Most official records of who commits crime are really statistics on who gets arrested and convicted. If the police are more likely to arrest some people than others, these official statistics tell us as much about police behavior as they do about criminal behavior. In any event, they give us little reliable data about those who commit crimes and do not get caught.

The President's Crime Commission conducted a survey of 10,000 households and discovered that "91 percent of all Americans have violated laws that could have subjected them to a term of imprisonment at one time in their lives."[28] A number of other studies, some dating back to the 1940s, support the conclusion that serious criminal behavior is widespread among middle- and upper-class individuals, although these individuals are rarely, if ever, arrested.[29] The authors of a 1990 review of literature on class and delinquency conclude, "Research published since 1978, using both official and self-reported data suggests... that there is no pervasive relationship between SES [socioeconomic status] and delinquency."[30] Other studies suggest that some forms of serious crime—forms usually associated with lower-class youth—show up *more frequently* among higher-class persons than among lower-class ones.[31]

Currie, in his underappreciated book *The Road to Whatever*, notes that the "long tradition of research on juvenile delinquency has shown us again and again that the problems of drugs and violence among middle-class youth were both widespread and surprisingly severe, though mostly absent from our official statistics."[32] For example, Chambliss' classic article, "The Saints and the Roughnecks," is an early report on bad behavior among upper-class youth and the biases of police. Chambliss called the upper-class group the Saints ironically, because they "were constantly occupied with truancy, drinking, wild driving, petty theft and vandalism. Yet not one was officially arrested for any misdeed during the two years I observed them."[33]

Chambliss noted that the lower-class Roughnecks also committed crimes, but "in the sheer number of illegal acts, the Saints were more delinquent." Nevertheless, the police saw the Roughnecks as more delinquent, watched them more carefully and enforced the lawmore vigorously against them. Chambliss argues that this is because of the "class structure of U.S. society":

> If the police treat middle- and upper-class delinquents (or cocaine-snorting college students) the same way they treat lower-class delinquents (or black, ghetto crack users), they are asking for trouble from people in power. If, on the other hand, they focus their law enforcement efforts on the lower classes, they are praised and supported by "the community," that is, by the middle- and upper-class white community.[34]

The same class bias Chambliss observed is still present, and also blinds criminology to the delinquency of middle- and upper-class youth. Yet researching delinquent non-poor youth can shed light on the criminogenic dynamics of the middle- and upper-classes, revealing that higher economic class is not a protective factor against delinquent behavior; it is just protective against official labeling. For example, Luthar researched peer support for substance abuse among affluent (white) suburban youth. She found delinquency rates were "comparable" and "substance use levels among affluent, suburban teenagers were significantly higher than among their inner-city counterparts," as was peer support for it.[35] Her subsequent research found criminogenic pressures in the "overemphasis on status and wealth"; "scheduled hyperactivity" that lead to a "work hard-party hard" environment; an emphasis on accomplishment over the development of moral character; emotional and physical parental absence; and easy access to alcohol, fake forms of identification, pharmaceuticals, and other illegal drugs.[36]

Currie's research reveals middle-class youth having substantial problems with drug addiction, anger, desperation, and delinquency because of a culture that "breeds adolescent disasters with frustrating predictability."[37] He sees where individualism can produce a "high demand, low support environment"[38] that is "quick to punish and slow to help."[39] When youth had problems, psychotropic drugs were "systematically over-prescribed,"[40] and youth were dealt with through exclusion and "the withdrawal of support."[41] All of these strategies make the problems of middle-class youth worse. That's not to say non-poor youth have it worse than poor youth, but to say that the troubles of middle-class youth mirror the troubles of society, which is to say that they experience widespread delinquency even if society and the police turn a blind eye to it.

Further, because criminologists tend to study the deviance of those below them rather than "studying up" and examining the more powerful, the prevalence of criminality among executives and corporations is neglected. Indeed, "the most important things done for good or ill . . . [are] done by corporate rather than individual actors,"[42] so criminologists should study corporate misbehavior and the criminal justice response to it. Sutherland, in a classic 1949 study, analyzed the behavior of 70 of the 200 largest U.S. corporations over a period of some 40 years:

> The records reveal that every one of the seventy corporations had violated one or more of the laws, with an average of about thirteen adverse decisions per corporation and a range of from one to fifty adverse decisions per corporation.... Thus, generally, the official records reveal that these corporations violated the trade regulations with great frequency. The "habitual criminal" laws of some states impose severe penalties on criminals convicted the third or fourth time. If this criterion were used here, about 90 percent of the large corporations studied would be considered habitual white-collar criminals.[43]

The author of a 2019 article in the *Harvard Business Review* notes that for "three innovative Fortune 100 companies—none of which has faced a recent civil or criminal charge—I found that on average, each firm had experienced a violation that could lead to regulatory sanctions (such as a bribe or financial fraud) once every three days." And these 120 violations a year are at companies that "have some of the most robust and effective controls I've seen."[44] The number of violations and their seriousness will be higher at other firms, especially where "a culture of making the [revenue and profit] numbers at all costs trumped any concerns about how the targets were being met."[45]

We accounted for some of the harm of these crimes in Chapter 2, which focused on death, injury, and disease. Supplementing that is an estimate of financial losses from both white-collar and corporate crime. These direct financial losses are difficult to quantify, both because of the lack of a clear definition and limited data. But an earlier (2013) edition of *The Rich Get Richer and the Poor Get Prison* calculated a conservative and incomplete direct economic loss figure of $610.3 billion.[46] An estimate in the *Oxford Handbook of White Collar Crime* claimed that "total victimization costs exceed $1.6 trillion and many costly crimes are not included in these estimates."[47] While these data are sparse, they suggest that the most conservative estimates of the cost of white-collar and corporate crime dwarf the $15.3 billion that the FBI calculates is the total amount stolen in all reported property crimes for 2017.

In light of the avalanche of statistics on street crimes, it's worth wondering why there is no public or private agency that regularly measures the full extent of white-collar crime and issues a regular report. (The FBI's *Crime in the United States* should include street crime and white-collar crime given its title.) The statistics that do exist are collected by corporations and trade organizations to show how they are victimized by employees, consumers, and regular people; but corporations and trade organizations do not collect statistics on their own transgressions—and exceedingly few sources document the cost of the crimes of the powerful. So statistics about the cost of white-collar crime reflect an understanding that insurance fraud is insured people defrauding insurers, while the wrongful denial of claims by insurers is absent; 'workplace theft' means employee theft, while wage theft is not mentioned; and the same can be said for mortgage fraud, credit card fraud, and many other areas.

While this is a problem with government data that reflect economic power and accountability, it is also a problem within criminology. Just as few criminologists recognized the importance of Sutherland's call to study white-collar crime, even fewer took up the call to study corporate crime. Indeed, at a time when corporations have grown in size to have revenues larger than the GDPs of many countries, Snider published an obituary for research on corporate crime.[48] The trickle of scholarship of crimes of the powerful demonstrates corporate misbehavior is widespread and deeply harmful to people's lives, health, finances, and the environment.[49]

Policing and Arrest

For the same offense, poor people are more likely than better-off people to come to the attention of the police. Once that happens, *a poor person is more likely to be arrested and, if arrested, more likely to be charged than a middle- or upper-class person.*[50] As far back as 1966, Gold observed that

> at each stage in the legal process from charging a boy with an offense to some sort of disposition in court, boys from different socioeconomic backgrounds are treated differently, so that those eventually incarcerated in public institutions, that site of most of the research on delinquency, are selectively poorer boys.[51]

When individuals were apprehended, "if the offender came from a higher status family, police were more likely to handle the matter themselves without referring it to the court."[52]

Terence Thornberry reached a similar conclusion in his study of 3,475 delinquent boys in Philadelphia. He found that among boys arrested *for equally serious offenses* and who had *similar prior offense records*, police were more likely to refer the lower-class youths than the more affluent ones to juvenile court, and the poorer youngsters were more likely to be institutionalized than were the affluent ones. The police generally dealt with the wealthier youngsters informally, for example, by holding them in the station house until their parents came rather than instituting formal procedures. Wealthier youths who ended up in court were more likely to receive probation than the poorer ones. As might be expected, Thornberry found the same relationships when comparing the treatment of black and white youths apprehended for equally serious offenses.[53]

Later studies continue to show similar effects. For example, Sampson found that, for the same crimes, juveniles in lower-class neighborhoods were more likely to have some police record than those in better-off neighborhoods.[54] In some studies,

> court officials acknowledge that they consciously and affirmatively take steps to direct low-income families into the juvenile justice system, because they believe that the court will 'help' the youth and 'facilitate the services, accountability, and discipline' needed to become a productive adult.[55]

Unfortunately, "such hopes all too often fail to be realized" and leave the youth with the stigma and burdens of contact with the criminal justice system.[56]

If you think these differences are not so important because they are true only of young offenders, remember that this group accounts for much of the crime problem. Moreover, other studies not limited to the young tend to show the same economic bias.[57]

As indicated earlier, we take racial bias as a proxy for bias against the poor, and blacks are more likely to be suspected or arrested than whites. A 1988 *Harvard Law Review* overview of studies on race and the criminal process concludes that "most studies... reveal what many police officers freely admit: that police use race as an independently significant, if not determinative, factor in deciding whom to follow, detain, search, or arrest."[58] Furthermore, according to Jerome Miller, a 1994 study of juvenile detention decisions found that "[n]ot only were there direct effects of race, but indirectly, socioeconomic status was related to detention, thus putting youth of color again at risk for differential treatment."[59]

In a 2007 research report, criminologists reviewed high-quality research on disproportionate minority contact with the juvenile justice system. They concluded that: "Minority youth are more likely to have contact with the system and to penetrate further into it than non-minority youth." The same researchers then analyzed their own data from three U.S. cities and found that "African Americans have somewhat higher rates of delinquent behavior than Whites, but their contact/referral rates far exceed those of Whites."[60] For example, Pittsburgh showed the smallest difference, where 38.1 percent of whites who committed an offense were apprehended and referred to court, but 66.3 percent of African-American offenders were apprehended and referred to court.[61]

This analysis is based on the number of offenders and thus already controls for the higher amount of crime committed by blacks. Further, 32 of 44 states that have studied disproportionate minority contact found "evidence of ethnic or racial differences in juvenile justice system decision-making that was unaccounted for by differential criminal activity."[62] The National Academy of Sciences panel on incarceration indicates an "increasing disjunction between racial patterns in crime and imprisonment."[63]

Evidence from 4.4 million stops in a federal civil rights case challenging New York City's extensive use of stop-and-frisk showed that "officers were much *more likely to stop and frisk African-Americans and Latinos than whites, but they were more likely to find weapons or contraband on whites than either African-Americans or Latinos.*"[64] Most recently, Stanford University did an analysis of 100 million traffic stops by geographically diverse state and municipal police. Compared to whites, blacks and Hispanics were more likely to be stopped and searched, but the "hit rate" for finding contraband was highest for white drivers.[65]

In contrast to the poor and members of minorities getting stopped on the street even when they are not doing anything illegal, the authors of *Dorm Room Dealers* report on the "anti-targets" of the drug war—a network of affluent, mostly white, college students in Southern California bringing in $80,000 to $160,000 a month in drug sales. Almost all these dealers were from "middle/upper class to affluent/upper class" families and "had parents of considerable economic standing"—mayors, businesspeople, and doctors.[66] Because of their class status, they operated with relative impunity despite "the near absent or, perhaps more accurately, pathetic risk-minimization strategies."[67] The authors, while fully aware of class biases in the criminal justice system, "were still taken aback by the lack of criminal justice and university administration attention paid these dealers, despite the brazenness, incompetence, and general dearth of street smarts that tended to characterize the dealers' daily practices."[68]

In contrast, based on research in Oakland, California, Victor Rios describes a "youth control complex" in which a range of criminal justice, community, media, and business institutions "treat young people's everyday behaviors as criminal activity."[69] Rios points to a citation for "not wearing a properly fitted bicycle helmet" and describes how "talking back" or "looking at them crazy" can lead to a citation for disorderly conduct.[70] This "hypercriminalization" is not confined to Oakland: An analysis of 10,000 tickets issued to bicyclists by Tampa, Florida police found that "even though blacks make up about a quarter of the city's population, they received 79 percent of the bike tickets." The investigation "found that Tampa police are targeting poor, black neighborhoods with obscure subsections of a Florida statute that outlaws things most people have tried on a bike, like riding with no light or carrying a friend on the handlebars."[71]

The pattern observed by Rios and in the biking-while-black analysis fits a pattern of policing focused on low-level misdemeanors or sub-misdemeanor citations, targeted against poor and minority communities, and often done for revenue from fines and fees rather than order maintenance ("cash register justice").[72] The problem is that citations for trivial infractions drew the boys deeper into the criminal justice system. Because they could not pay the fine, they skipped the court date, which led to more fines and an arrest warrant–and an inability to pay those fines led to probation, which entailed more intense police scrutiny.[73]

One conclusion is inescapable: One of the reasons the offender "at the end of the road in prison is likely to be a member of the lowest social and economic groups in the country" is that the police officers who guard the access to the road to prison make sure that a lot more poor people make the trip than well-to-do people.

This pattern is reinforced by the fact that regulatory agencies, whose job is to police white-collar and corporate crime, are not given the same tools and resources as those given to police fighting less sophisticated crime. For example, "under federal law, the SEC [Securities and Exchange Commission] isn't permitted to listen to live wiretaps"—only recordings delivered somewhat after the fact. Notes one SEC employee: "The U.S. Fish and Wildlife Service has access to wiretaps, but the SEC doesn't? And somehow you expect us to oversee Wall Street?"[74]

Further, both the federal and state governments are supposed to police for wage theft, which occurs when employers do not pay their employees all the money they have earned under the laws covering minimum wage, overtime pay, and breaks. Although the workforce and number of workplaces has increased, the number of federal Wage and Hour Division investigators is less than in the 1970s under President Carter. In response to political pressures, several states totally or partially defunded those divisions for one or more years. Idaho had three employees to police employer compliance with wage laws, and other states relied partly on senior citizen volunteers. Further, "agencies in Michigan, Oklahoma and Texas lacked authority to initiate investigations, so all their activity was in response to worker claims,"[75] which is like only giving the police power to respond to 911 calls. Agencies policing wage theft should be able to investigate businesses that are typically at the highest risk of wage theft.[76]

Prosecution and Charging

When prosecutors select cases in which they will bring charges, they add to the cumulative advantage and disadvantage. The *Harvard Law Review* overview of studies on race and the criminal process asserts, "Prosecutors are more likely to pursue full prosecution, file more severe charges, and seek more stringent penalties in cases involving minority defendants than in cases involving nonminority defendants."[77] A more recent review similarly states: "Race plays a role in charging decisions, bail determinations, plea bargaining, convictions, and sentencing."[78] So too with wealth. In contrast to all of the people prosecuted for small amounts of drug possession (see Chapter 1), tech billionaire Henry Nicholas smoked large amounts of marijuana on a private jet, "causing marijuana smoke and fumes to enter the cockpit and requiring the pilot flying the plane to put on an oxygen mask." The charges against him were dropped, unlike with many poor people who posed no hazard to a pilot and air travel safety.[79]

We shall see later that a large number of potential criminal cases arising out of the savings and loan scandals were dismissed by federal law enforcement agencies because they lacked the personnel to pursue them, even
as thousands of new police officers were being hired to fight street crime. And
nothing has changed: a former chief of the frauds bureau in New York City
commented that "the number of people benefiting from large-scale, economic
crime is immense, the number of victims is immense, but the number of prosecutions is limited by small and declining budgets."[80] Systematic data from
the Department of Justice bears out this observation, showing that in January 2019, prosecutions for white-collar and corporate crime hit "an historic
low since monthly tracking began in October 1998."[81] The trend under President Trump continued a decline started under Obama, who filed no criminal
charges against the financial institutions or executives whose criminal acts
caused the 2008 financial crisis.

Prosecutors have also shown a kinder face to the pharmaceutical industry, which contributed to the opiate crisis and 200,000 opiate overdose
deaths, than they have to drug addicts whose friends have overdosed. Laws
that were designed to hold drug dealers accountable for overdose deaths of
clients have been used to go after "friends, partners and siblings."[82] A *New
York Times* investigation found "more than 1,000 prosecutions or arrests in accidental overdose deaths since 2015," in "36 states, with charges ranging from
involuntary manslaughter to first-degree murder." In contrast, executives of
Purdue Pharma, makers of OxyContin, had knowledge in the first years of the
drug's release in 1996 that it was being abused but denied that knowledge,
and continued to market the drug aggressively, saying falsely it was less likely
to result in addiction and abuse than other prescription opioids.[83] The company and three executives were charged with "misbranding," a misdemeanor
related to false information on labels. The indictment "did not accuse them
of wrongdoing," and the executives paid fines and were required to perform
community service.

More generally, prosecutors take collateral consequences and economic
impact into account when charging corporations but not people. Collateral
consequences are civil penalties that are consequences of a criminal conviction; they are not considered part of the criminal sentence, even though they
can include losing the right to vote, hold certain professional licenses, and
receive benefits such as access to public housing, unemployment benefits,
food stamps, and student loans. A review of the American Bar Association
database found "roughly 46,000 collateral consequences existed in federal and
state laws and regulations." Just at the federal level, "there are 641 collateral
consequences that can be triggered by nonviolent drug convictions," and 78
percent of those could potentially last a life-time.[84] Prosecutors are more likely
to consider the economic impact of criminal charges on a corporation's licenses, contracts, and its "innocent shareholders," than they are the impact of
incarceration, fines, fees, and collateral consequences on an offender's family–
including innocent children.[85]

To a greater extent than with individual offenders, offending corporations can join "Club Fed Deferred" by getting a non-prosecution agreement (NPA) or deferred prosecution agreement (DPA), which provides that the Department of Justice will not prosecute if the company agrees to implement certain reforms.[86] According to the Government Accountability Office,

> DOJ intends for these agreements to promote corporate reform; however, DOJ does not have performance measures in place to assess whether this goal has been met. Therefore, it could be difficult for DOJ to justify its increasing use of these tools. [87]

Nevertheless, DOJ has expanded their use, even though one judge argues that "the future deterrent value of successfully prosecuting individuals far outweighs the prophylactic benefits of imposing internal compliance measures that are often little more than window-dressing."[88] Even where a negotiated settlement is preferable to a trial, plea bargains can achieve the same reforms in a way that is reviewed and recorded by the court in a public record rather than being a private contract between the government and a wrong-doer.[89]

With upper-class criminals, the authorities prefer to sue in civil court than treat the wealthy as common criminals. Judges have, on occasion, stated in open court that they would not make criminals of reputable businessmen. One would think it would be up to the businessmen to make criminals of themselves by their actions, but alas, that privilege is reserved for the lower classes. And white-collar criminals often try to point to their lack of a criminal record and say prosecutors are picking on them, but both of these excuses are related to the "federal government's decades of underperformance" in prosecuting white-collar crime.[90]

The clientele of the criminal justice system forms an exclusive club, most of whose members are poor. The crimes they commit are the crimes that qualify one for admission, and they are admitted in greater proportion than their share of those crimes. Curiously enough, the crimes the affluent commit are not the kind that easily qualify one for membership in the club.

Adjudication and Conviction

Between arrest and imprisonment lies the crucial process that determines guilt or innocence. Studies of individuals accused of similar offenses, and with similar prior records, show that the poor defendant is more likely to be adjudicated guilty than is the wealthier defendant.[91] In the adjudication process the only thing that *should* count is whether the accused is guilty and whether the prosecution can prove it beyond a reasonable doubt. Unfortunately, at least two other factors that are irrelevant to guilt or innocence significantly affect the outcome: One is the ability of the accused to be free on bail prior to trial, and the second is access to legal counsel able to devote adequate time and energy to the case. Because both bail and high-quality legal counsel cost money, it should come as no surprise that here, as elsewhere, the poor do poorly.

Being released on bail is important in several respects. First and foremost is that those who are not released on bail are kept in jail like individuals who have been found guilty. They are thus punished while they are still legally innocent. The Bureau of Justice Statistics reported that local jails held 745,200 inmates in 2017, and 64.7 percent of inmates had not been convicted, up from 56 percent in 2000.[92] Indeed, since 1998 the jail population has grown by 45 percent, and virtually all that growth has been people not convicted of a crime.[93] While some detainees may be dangerous or a flight risk, "seventy-five percent of pretrial detainees are charged with relatively minor property crimes, drug offenses or other non-violent acts, and remain in jail simply because the money bond was set at an amount they cannot afford to pay."[94]

Beyond the obvious ugliness of punishing people before they are found guilty, confined defendants cannot actively aid in their own defense by seeking out witnesses and evidence, and they are more likely to be convicted than those who are released.[95] But,

> nearly every study on the impact of race in bail determinations has concluded that African Americans are subjected to pretrial detention at a higher rate and are subjected to higher bail amounts than are white arrestees with similar charges and similar criminal histories.[96]

In an effort to reduce bias, many jurisdictions are turning to computerized risk assessments to supplement or even replace a judge's decision. The algorithms behind the assessments have been trained on criminal justice data such as patterns of rearrest. But if the data represent patterns laden with bias–as all criminal justice data do–then the algorithm "learns" these patterns, and bases its so-called "objective" recommendation on biased data.[97] Even if patterns of arrest and conviction were not based on conscious bias, the class- and race-based differences become the input for systems aimed at reducing bias, and "the[ir] predictions appear impartial."[98] Not only is bias hidden, but the data and the weighting for each factor are often commercial secrets that cannot be disclosed to defendants, and are thus beyond legal challenge.[99]

Contrary to the image conveyed by dramatic courtroom arguments in televised crime dramas, about 95 percent of convictions are the result of a negotiated plea.[100] There's no trial, just a bargain in which the accused agrees to plead guilty (usually to a lesser offense than he or she is charged with, or to one offense out of many he or she is charged with) in return for a promise of leniency from the prosecutor with the consent of the judge.

Furthermore, because the time spent in jail prior to adjudication of guilt may count as part of the sentence, the accused are placed under situational coercion. Suppose you are innocent and have been in the slammer for several months awaiting trial. The prosecutor offers a deal: If you plead guilty to such-and-such (usually a lesser offense than has been charged, say, simple assault instead of aggravated assault), the prosecutor promises to ask the judge to sentence you to time served. In other words, plead guilty and walk out of jail today (free, but with a criminal record that will make finding a job hard and ensure a stiffer sentence if you are convicted of a crime in the future), or maintain your innocence, stay in jail until trial (perhaps in a year), and then be tried for the full charge instead of the lesser offense! Not only that, the prosecutor may also threaten to press for the most severe penalty as well—for taking up the court's time. If you were the jailed defendant offered a deal like this, how would you choose? Suppose you were a poor black man not likely to be able to retain a first-rate private attorney?

An article in the *Stanford Law Review* reported that "compared to similarly situated releasees, detained defendants [those not out on bail] are 25% more likely to be convicted and 43% more likely to be sentenced to jail, and commit future crimes."[101] The future crimes were not because of the criminality of the person at the time of the bail decision, but was "consistent with other research suggesting that even short-term detention has criminogenic effects." The article concludes that "any wealth-based inequality in pretrial detention translates into wealth-based inequality in case outcomes."[102]

The advantages of access to adequate legal counsel during the adjudicative process are obvious but still worthy of mention. In 1963, the U.S. Supreme Court handed down the landmark *Gideon* v. *Wainwright* decision, holding that the states must provide legal counsel in all felony cases to those who cannot afford them to help protect individuals against the government with its enormous resources. The Court later extended this right to those accused of misdemeanors. Most criminal defendants cannot afford a private attorney so a public defender represents them.

However, rigorous studies of time use by private attorneys on criminal cases indicates that "the typical public defender had two to three times the workload they should in order to provide an adequate defense."[103] Overworked and underresourced public defender offices have been punished for refusing to take additional cases rather than providing ineffective assistance of counsel. And unfortunately, "some judges have ruled that taking illegal drugs, driving to court drunk or briefly falling asleep at the defense table—even during critical testimony—did not make a lawyer inadequate."

The problem of adequate legal representation is particularly acute in death penalty cases. According to Robert Johnson, "Most attorneys in capital cases are provided by the state. Defendants, as good capitalists, routinely assume that they will get what they pay for: next to nothing." Their perceptions, he concludes, "may not be far from right."[104] Indeed, Stephen Gettinger maintains that an inadequate defense was "the single outstanding characteristic" of the condemned persons he studied.[105] For example, Robert Wayne Holsey was an African American with a low IQ who was severely beaten as a child. He was convicted of murder and his

> trial lawyer later admitted that at the time he [the lawyer] was drinking up to a quart of vodka daily and facing theft charges that would land him in prison. He said he should not have been representing a client.[106]

Even though he was later disbarred and criminally convicted, the lawyer's defense was found to be adequate, and Holsey was executed.

A *Time* magazine article on this topic noted, "Some people go to traffic court with better prepared lawyers than many murder defendants get."[107] A 2011 study of Pennsylvania's death penalty cases found similar problems: Appointed lawyers "neglect basic steps, such as interviewing defendants, seeking out witnesses, and investigating a defendant's background." It found that court-appointed lawyers for death penalty cases "get $2,000 for trial preparation and $400 a day in court to handle cases that a veteran defense attorney said required a minimum outlay of $35,000 to $40,000."[108]

The upper-class campus drug dealers studied in *Dorm Room Dealers* had substantially better attorneys than most people facing the death penalty. While authorities generally turned a "collective blind eye" to "brazen" illegality, a few dealers did end up in the criminal justice system.[109] One dealer was caught with over 100 marijuana plants and $30,000 in growing equipment, but his parents hired a "high-profile private defense attorney" and horticultural and biological sciences experts, plus "various psychiatrists." He ended up with an 18-month "diversion program" that resulted in no jail time. And all records were expunged when he successfully completed the program, so someone running a criminal-history check would find nothing about this incident.[110]

Needless to say, the distinct legal advantages that money can buy become even more salient when we enter the realm of corporate and other white-collar crime. Indeed, it is often precisely the time and cost involved in bringing to court a large corporation with its army of legal eagles that is offered as an excuse for the genteel treatment accorded to businessman crooks. This excuse is, of course, not equitably distributed among people of all economic classes, any more than quality legal service is. This means that, regardless of actual innocence or guilt, one's chances of beating the rap increase as one's income increases.

Sentencing

The juvenile justice system has a long history of removing youth from their families and sentencing them to incarceration because of disadvantages concentrated in their neighborhoods. Research in the 1980s found that families faced with economic strain were perceived as "unstable" or "inadequate"—a pattern that continues to the present where "the economic struggles of these families often translated into negative attributions of parents (mostly mothers) and provided a basis for the removal of youth from the community."[111] Little effort has gone into fixing disadvantaged neighborhoods, so attributions based "on socioeconomic status provided the basis for removal of youth from their homes and neighborhoods, and as a result, young people were 'treated more severely merely because they face economic strain.'"[112]

Research on adult offenders consistently finds discrimination in sentencing based on offenders' economic class. Chiricos and Bales found that, for individuals guilty of similar offenses and with similar prior records, unemployed defendants were more than twice as likely as their employed counterparts to be incarcerated if found guilty.[113] McCarthy noted a similar link between unemployment and greater likelihood of incarceration.[114] In his study of 28,315 Southern felony defendants, Champion also found that offenders who could afford private counsel had a greater likelihood of probation and received shorter sentences when incarceration was imposed.[115]

Tillman and Pontell examined the sentences received by individuals convicted of Medicaid-provider fraud in California. Because such offenders normally have no prior arrests and are charged with grand theft, their sentences were compared with the sentences of other offenders convicted of grand theft who also had no prior records. While 37.7 percent of the Medicaid defrauders were sentenced to some jail or prison time, 79.2 percent of the others convicted of grand theft were sentenced to jail or prison. This was so even though the median dollar loss due to the Medicaid frauds was $13,000, more than 10 times the median loss due to the other grand thefts ($1,149). The authors point out that most of the Medicaid defrauders were health professionals, while most of the others convicted of grand theft had low-level jobs or were unemployed. They conclude that "differences in the sentences imposed on the two samples are indeed the result of the different social statuses of their members."[116]

Data on racial discrimination in sentencing tell the same story of the treatment of those who cannot afford the going price of justice. A review in 2000 by Spohn of 40 studies of both federal and state data concludes that "Black and Hispanic offenders—particularly those who are young, male, or unemployed—are more likely than their white counterparts to be sentenced to prison; they also may receive longer sentences than similarly situated white offenders."[117] A 2017 review of research leads Spohn to conclude:

> Studies of sentences imposed under federal and state guidelines reveal that blacks and Hispanics continue to receive harsher outcomes than whites, and research focusing on mandatory minimum sentences, three-strikes provisions, and habitual offender laws also find that the application of these provisions disadvantages racial minorities. These findings imply that prosecutors and judges are reluctant to base sentences on only crime seriousness and prior criminal record and that statutorily irrelevant factors such as race and ethnicity (as well as sex, age, and social class) may be factually relevant to criminal justice officials' assessments of dangerousness, threat, and culpability.[118]

The National Academy of Sciences panel on incarceration finds that the racial "disparities are enormous," not only with incarceration but also capital punishment and life sentences.[119]

Spohn's recent review and the National Academy of Sciences were evaluating research following the partial correction of the notorious "100-to-1" disparity between sentences for possession of cocaine in *powder* form (popular in the affluent suburbs) and in *crack* form (popular in poor, inner-city neighborhoods). From 1986 until 2010, federal laws required a mandatory five-year sentence for crimes involving 500 grams (a little more than a pound) of powder cocaine or 5 grams (about one-sixth of an ounce) of crack cocaine. This yielded a sentence for first-time crack offenders with no aggravating factors, such as possession of a weapon, that was longer than the sentence for kidnapping and only slightly shorter than the sentence for attempted murder![120] About 82 percent of those convicted of federal crack offenses are black; about 8 percent are white.[121]

While seen as a victory for sentencing reform, in 1995, 1997, and 2002, the U.S. Sentencing Commission recommended ending the 100-to-1 disparity between powder and crack penalties, and in an unusual display of bipartisanship, Congress rejected their recommendation and kept the law.[122] In his 2007 testimony to Congress, the Chair of the Sentencing Commission reiterated its recommendation that any ratio "be no more than 20 to 1." The Fair Sentencing Act of 2010 reduced the 100-to-1 disparity to 18-to-1. Says sociologist Nikki Jones: "What the Act suggests is that it's better for our criminal justice system to be somewhat racist rather than very racist."[123]

The effect of sentencing guidelines and mandatory minimum sentences has been not to eliminate discretion but to transfer it from those who sentence to those who decide what to charge—that is, from judges to prosecutors. Says U.S. District Judge J. Lawrence Irving of San Diego, "[T]he system is run by the U.S. attorneys. When they decide how to indict, they fix the sentence."[124] And, note, while judges need to justify their sentencing decisions, there is no review of prosecutors' discretion, so discrimination persists.

Although many mandatory sentences are still in place, the Supreme Court has ruled that the sentencing guidelines are only advisory. But, whether imposed or advisory, the National Academy of Sciences panel on incarceration noted that "racial disparities in imprisonment have worsened substantially since the early 1990s relative to racial patterns of involvement in serious crime."[125]

The research on class- and race-based discrimination notes that studies generally find some evidence of disparity, even if they cannot infer discriminatory intent. Further, studies that do not find disparity often have not accounted for the possibility of *double discrimination*—by race of victim and offender—which especially affects death penalty sentencing. Leniency for blacks who kill other blacks can erase the harshness against blacks who kill whites when all cases against black defendants are averaged together.[126]

Table 3.1 shows how justice is increasingly tempered with mercy as we deal with a better class of crime. Legislators set penalties so that the crimes of the poor lead to stiffer sentences than the crimes of the well-to-do, and the enforcement process makes sure that more of the poor are convicted. Keep in mind while looking at Table 3.1 that *each* of the "crimes of the affluent" costs the public more than *all* of the "crimes of the poor" put together.

This situation is not new. In 1990, the House Subcommittee on Financial Institutions Supervision, Regulation, and Insurance met to hold hearings on the prosecution of Savings and Loan (S&L) criminals. The chairman's opening statement noted that "crooks" were responsible for a substantial portion of losses: "The American taxpayer will be forced to pay $500 billion or more over the next 40 years, largely because of these crooks." He added:

> Frankly, I don't think the administration has the interest in pursuing Gucci-clad, white-collar criminals. These are hard and complicated cases, and the defendants often were rich, successful prominent members of their upper-class communities. It is far easier putting away a sneaker-clad high school dropout who tries to rob a bank of a thousand dollars with a stick-up note, than a smooth talking S&L executive who steals a million dollars with a fraudulent note.[127]

Later in the hearing, the Chairman questioned the administration's representative:

> You cited, Mr. Dennis, several examples in your testimony of successful convictions with stiff sentences, but the average sentence so far is actually about 2 years, compared to an average sentence of about 9 years for bank robbery. Why do we throw the book at people who rob a bank in broad daylight but we coddle people who rob the bank secretly?[128]

Twelve years later, in 2002, at a hearing of the Crime and Drugs Subcommittee of the Senate Judiciary Committee on the subject of "Penalties for White Collar Crimes: Are We Really Getting Tough on Crime?" then-Senator Joseph Biden Jr. said,

> Under federal law, if you steal a car out of my driveway and you drive it across [the state line] into Pennsylvania, ten years. Ten years, federal guideline. You take a pension by violating ERISA, the federal system to safeguard pensions, misdemeanor, maximum one year. The pension may be worth $1,800,000. My car may be worth $2,000.[129]

The simple fact is that the criminal justice system reserves its harshest penalties for its lower-class clients, and puts on kid gloves when confronted with a better class of crook. For corporate crime, penalties and enforcement are more lenient still. In his 1990 book, *Corporate Corruption: The Abuse of Power,* Marshall Clinard notes the "extensive law violations" in many industries and how "over one two-year period, the federal government charged nearly two-thirds of the *Fortune 500* corporations with law violations; half were charged with a serious violation."[130] Nevertheless, corporate executives rarely end up in handcuffs at the police station, mixing with poorer persons who had stolen much less from their fellow citizens. At subsequent stages of the criminal justice process, white-collar criminals accumulate advantages so that a "study of sanctions imposed for corporate law violations found that administrative [that is, noncriminal] penalties were employed in two-thirds of serious corporate law violations, and that slightly more than two-fifths of the sanctions... consisted simply of a warning to the corporation not to commit the offense again."[131]

TABLE 3.1   Federal Sentences Served for Different Classes of Crimes, 2014

	Percentage of Convicted Offenders Sentenced to Prison	Average Time Served in Months
Crimes of the Poor		
Robbery	97	87
Burglary	63	44
Auto theft	74	43
Crimes of the Affluent		
Fraud	67	24
Tax law violation	60	19
Embezzlement	46	18

Source: Federal Justice Statistics 2014—Statistical Tables (March 2017, NCJ 250183). Calculated from Tables 5.2 and 7.11 and rounded off.

Conduct has to be pretty shocking for an executive to be incarcerated. For example, the Sherman Antitrust Act is a criminal law. It recognizes that a free-market economy depends on real competition by businesses to drive consumer prices down, so agreements by competing firms to refrain from price competition is the equivalent of stealing money from consumers' pockets. In the historic Electrical Equipment cases in the early 1960s, executives of several major firms met secretly to fix prices on electrical equipment to a degree that is estimated to have cost the buying public well over $1 billion at that time.

The executives involved knew they were violating the law. They used plain envelopes for their communications, called their meetings "choir practice," and referred to the list of executives in attendance as the "Christmas card list." In spite of knowing originally that it was illegal, one defendant commented that the price-fixing "had become so common and gone for so many years that we lost sight of the fact that it was illegal."[132] This case is rare and famous because it was an early example in which the criminal sanction was actually imposed. Seven executives received and served jail sentences. In light of the amount of money they had stolen from the American public over many years, however, their sentences were more an indictment of the government than of the executives: *30 days in jail!*

In 2017, the government settled with Bumble Bee for conspiring with two other companies to fix the price of canned tuna between 2011 and 2013. The three companies accounted for the one billion pounds of canned tuna Americans eat each year[133], meaning the scheme picked the pockets of many people. But the government settled for a $25 million fine (substantially less than the maximum $272 million fine), payable interest-free over five years because of Bumble Bee's precarious financial position.[134] Congress requires other agencies to consider an individual's ability to pay when negotiating a fine,[135] so Trump's Consumer Financial Protection Bureau settled for a $1 fine for someone who claimed to be broke after scamming veterans out of their pensions for eight years.[136] While the policy of not wanting to bankrupt a firm (especially in an industry with little competition) can make sense, the same logic does not apply to individuals convicted of street crimes.

An earlier section started to document the wide range of fines and fees street criminals need to pay regardless of their income or family situation–criminal justice fines, court fees, public defender fees, jail fees, probation fees, drug testing fees, electronic monitoring fees, and late fees to name a few. Many end up imprisoned when they cannot pay, according to an article in the *American Conservative* entitled, "The Dickensian Return of Debtors' Prisons."[137] In spite of a Supreme Court ruling that defendants cannot be imprisoned for unpaid fines unless they are "wilfully" refusing to pay them, "modern judges routinely sentence poor Americans to jail for not paying fines or fees." In addition, 43 states suspend a person's driver's license for unpaid criminal justice debt, generally impairing their ability to work to pay back the debt—and requiring substantial fees to get the license reinstated. The article concludes: "there's no two ways about it: unpaid fines have contributed to the formation of a two-tiered society. Punishment for failure to pay fees for minor infractions should not be something that turns a person's life upside down."

Outside of anti-trust law, the situation is the same. In 2013, the global financial institution HSBC was caught helping Mexican drug traffickers, rogue regimes, and terrorist organizations launder money. Additionally, the Senate Subcommittee on Investigations found that HSBC actively worked to get around the rules regarding the provision of banking services for the Iranian government or its citizens to enable 25,000 transactions—worth about $19 billion—without disclosing that the money came from that country, a violation of the Trading with the Enemy Act. The Subcommittee also found "a failure to monitor [for money laundering] $60 trillion in wire transfer and account activity; [and] a backlog of 17,000 unreviewed account alerts regarding suspicious activity."[138] HSBC deliberately understaffed compliance and anti-money laundering positions so they could save on costs while profiting from the financial services they offered to big-time global criminals. In 2013, they received a fine of $1.9 billion, compared with 2011 profits of $22 billion. Under the Deferred Prosecution Agreement the government agreed to drop all criminal charges if certain organizational reforms were made over the next five years, so it's likely that no one at HSBC will go to jail for profiting from and helping out drug traffickers, organized crime syndicates, and terrorist organizations.[139]

More generally, Jesse Eisinger, author of *The Chickenshit Club*[140]—about how prosecutors are too scared to go after big cases—notes that the Department of Justice "occasionally brings charges against lower-level executives of major corporations, but hasn't held the chief of a Fortune 500 company accountable in more than a decade."[141] Most of that time was during the Obama presidency, and the will, policies, and resources to enforce the law have declined further under Trump.[142] By mid-2019, "in 11 of the 12 federal agencies led by a Trump-appointed official during the president's first year, penalties imposed on corporate violators dropped, in the majority of cases by more than 50 percent."[143]

FINANCIAL FRAUDS

In this section, we present several examples of major financial fraud as case studies for the economic bias discussed in previous sections. During the 1980s, the savings and loan scandal occurred, costing taxpayers $500 billion, much due to fraud at financial institutions. In December 2001, Enron filed the largest corporate bankruptcy in U.S. history to that point. This was followed by revelations of significant fraud in a large number of companies, costing shareholders hundreds of billions of dollars. Then in 2008 the financial meltdown was so severe that President George W. Bush announced that "our entire economy is in danger,"[144] and urged Congress to quickly pass a $700 billion bailout on top of *trillions* of dollars committed by the Federal Reserve, requiring ordinary people to directly and indirectly pay a substantial "Wall Street Incompetence Tax."[145]

These financial meltdowns were not natural disasters; they were caused by human beings who were responsible for the harms that resulted from their actions. All of these episodes involved control fraud, which is where executives abuse their positions of trust by working together to override financial controls and allow collective embezzlement. Rather than run the business for longer-term growth, they loot it, using fraud to take wealth from and through the institution. Firms victimized by control fraud "typically report sensational profits, followed by catastrophic failure" and bankruptcy.[146] Their efforts to lobby government for deregulation and weaken policing agencies help these efforts.

In each of the cases below, control fraud was responsible for massive financial losses and damage to the wider economy. In each case, offenders generally received minor, if any, criminal punishments for causing mass financial victimization. By briefly presenting each episode, we show how changes in laws, and limitations on policing and adjudication, led to minimal penalties for white-collar crime that led to national economic distress in a nation that otherwise is known for giving out long prison sentences.

Further, while many believe that prosecuting financial institutions and corporations destabilizes the economy, we believe that it is the crimes themselves that cause instability. Indeed, one review of the frauds leading to the economic crisis of 2008 noted that declining to prosecute fraud "creates positive incentives for more fraud."[147] Already, "our financial system teeters toward a giant racketeering enterprise," which increases the likelihood of future episodes of even worse fraud, financial instability, and redistribution of resources to the powerful.

THE SAVINGS AND LOAN SCANDAL

The federally insured system of savings and loan banks (S&Ls, also known as "thrifts") was created in the 1930s to promote the building and sale of new homes during the Great Depression. The system had built into it important restrictions on the kinds of loans that could be made and was subject to federal supervision to prevent the bank failures that came in the wake of the Depression of 1929. Starting in the 1970s and speeding up in the early 1980s, this entire system of regulation and supervision was first loosened and then largely dismantled. Although S&Ls could now make riskier investments, their deposits were still insured by the Federal Savings and Loan Insurance Corporation (FSLIC). Translation: The S&Ls could make risky investments shooting for windfall profits, with the taxpayers paying for losses. This combination proved to be financial dynamite. The thrifts made high-risk investments as well as fraudulent loans to their friends, family, and business partners that left them all substantially richer. In 1996, a Government Accountability Office report put the total cost to the American taxpayer of the S&L bailout at $480.9 billion![148]

Not all these losses are due to crime, but fraud was a central factor in 70 to 80 percent of the S&L failures.[149] Much of this fraud took the form of looting bank funds for the personal gain of bank officers at the expense of the institution. The commissioner of the California Department of Savings and Loans is quoted as saying in 1987, "The best way to rob a bank is to own one."[150] Says *Fortune* magazine, "S&L fraud dwarfs every previous carnival of white-collar crime in America."[151]

In response to the enormity of this scandal, American public opinion hardened toward white-collar crime, and federal law enforcement agencies were prosecuting, fining, and even jailing offenders at unprecedented rates. Nonetheless, considering the size of the scandal and the far-reaching damage it did to the American economy and to public trust in the banking system, the treatment was still light-handed compared with that of even nonviolent "common" crimes. According to one study, "The average prison term for savings and loan offenders sentenced between 1988 and 1992 was 36 months, compared to 56 months for burglars and 38 months for those convicted of motor vehicle theft." The study goes on to point out that S&L offenders were given lengthier sentences than first-time property crime offenders (who received an average sentence of 26 months), but the average loss in an S&L case was $500,000[152] and the average loss per property offense in 1995 was $1,251.[153] And, "the fines imposed were less than the total amount stolen."[154]

These sentenced S&L offenders represent just a small fraction of the crooks involved in the S&L looting: "from 1987 to 1992, Federal bank and thrift regulators filed a staggering 95,045 criminal referrals with the FBI. The volume was so large that more than 75 percent of these referrals have been dropped without prosecution."[155] At the same time, the Justice Department advised against funding for 425 new agents requested by the FBI, and 231 new assistant U.S. attorneys, and the administration recommended against increasing funds from $50 million to $75 million as authorized by Congress for the S&L investigations.[156] But, soon after, we find the president and the Congress ready to spend $23 billion on criminal justice and hire thousands of new police officers to keep our streets safe!

To give you a concrete idea of what some of the S&L crooks did and the treatment they received, Table 3.2 presents a roughly representative "rogues' gallery." In looking at these rogues, their acts, and their punishments, keep in mind the treatment meted out to the Typical Criminal when he steals a fraction of what they did. Also, soon after the S&L crisis, Congress went on what the authors of *Big Money Crime* describe as a wave of "cavalier" financial deregulation, creating a "paradox of increasing financial deregulation coming on the heels of the most catastrophic experiment with deregulation in history"[157] (up to that point in time).

ENRON AND A YEAR OF CORPORATE FINANCIAL SCANDALS

In 2001–2002, corporate financial shenanigans caused corporate bankruptcies, unemployment, economic turmoil, and a significant drop in stock market prices. Although the economic losses were widespread, *Fortune* magazine notes,

> The not-so-secret dirty secret of the crash is that even as investors were losing 70 percent, 90 percent, even in some cases *all* of their holdings, top officials of many of the companies that have crashed the hardest were getting immensely, extraordinarily, obscenely wealthy.[158]

At center stage was Enron, a multibillion-dollar energy-rights trading company, which declared one of the largest bankruptcies in history on December 2, 2001, with debts of over $31 billion! Enron was subsequently accused of having perpetrated massive accounting fraud, hiding the degree of its indebtedness from investors by treating loans as revenue, and camouflaging company losses by creating "special purpose vehicles"[159] with company capital and attributing losses to them rather than Enron. As Enron shares were tanking, then-CEO Ken Lay was emailing concerned employees, advising them to hold their shares and buy new ones. Meanwhile, he himself cashed in $103 million of his own shares in the company. Enron executives unloaded nearly a *billion dollars'* worth of stock. Employees, on the other hand, were locked out of selling the holdings in their pensions during much of the period in which the company's stock fell from $80 a share to $0.30. While Enron executives were making millions, Enron investors lost about $60 billion, ruining many large pension plans and the retirement savings of nearly 20,000 employees.[160]

Enron was not an isolated incident. The list of companies touched by financial scandal soon included Tyco, Global Crossing, Qwest, WorldCom, Xerox, Adelphia, AOL-Time Warner, K-Mart, and some major banks, such as Citigroup and J. P. Morgan Chase. "About one-tenth of publicly traded companies announced at least one restatement" of inaccurate financial reports.[161]

The misstatements that Enron and others made were not mere technical rule violations without real victims. One important consequence of this corporate crime and financial trickery is the elimination of many people's retirement nest eggs, forcing many older people to put off retirement and many retirees to go back to work. Other families lost college tuition money tied up in stocks, along with their dreams of a more comfortable and secure future.

The scams perpetrated by executives and companies during 2002 were a diverse collection. Some, like those of Adelphia Communications, involved relatively straightforward looting by the founding family, which used the company as its personal bank to enrich themselves. Others, like Enron's, involved

TABLE 3.2 The Savings and Loan Roster

Michael Hellerman, aka Michael Rapp	Defrauded Flushing Federal S&L (New York) of $8.4 million and Florida Center Bank of $7.5 million.	Released on parole after serving 5½ years. Fined $100,000.
Charles Bazarian Mario Renda	Convicted for "swindling $20 million from two California S&Ls and skimming at least $100,000 from a low-income H.U.D. [Housing and Urban Development] project." Also convicted with Rapp in Florida case. As partner in a brokerage business, he stole about $16 million.	Served less than two years for cooperating with authorities and has paid $18,000 of $110,000 in fines. Served 21 months after pleading guilty to two counts of wire fraud; paid a minimal amount of the ordered $9.9 million in restitution and $125,000 in criminal fines.
Herman Beebe	Involved in widespread loan fraud involving more than $30 million.	Served ten months under plea bargain and is immune from prosecution for other fraud charges.
Arthur Kick	President of North Chicago Federal S&L; stole $1.2 million by misappropriating loans.	Sentenced to three years of probation and full restitution.
Ted Musacchio	President of Columbus Marin S&L (California); stole $9.3 million and lied about it on federal disclosure forms.	Sentenced to five years of probation and required to make immediate restitution of $9.3 million but had only paid $1,000 by the time of his death three years later.

Source: Stephen Pizzo and Paul Muolo, "Take the Money and Run: A Rogues Gallery of Some Lucky S&L Thieves," *New York Times Magazine,* May 9, 1993; Alan Fomhan, "S&L Felons," *Fortune,* November 5, 1990, p. 93; "Former Columbus President Guilty of Misapplying Funds," *American Banker,* December 26, 1989; and "Why S&L Crooks Have Failed to Pay Millions of Dollars in Court-Ordered Restitution: Nineteen Case Studies," in *A Staff Report for the Subcommittee on Financial Institutions Supervision, Regulation and Insurance of the Committee on Banking, Finance and Urban Affairs, House of Representatives,* 102nd Congress, 2nd session, April (Washington, DC: U.S. Government Printing Office, 1992).

complicated financial transactions meant to inflate earnings, and thus stock prices, artificially. The SEC charged Adelphia with fraudulently excluding $2.3 billion in debt from its earnings report. AES, AOL-Time Warner, Cedent, Halliburton, K-Mart, Lucent Technologies, MicroStrategy, Rite Aid, and Waste Management are all said to have, in different ways, misstated revenues by more than $100 million in each case.

Arthur Andersen accountants served as auditors for Enron while taking in hundreds of millions of dollars from consulting deals with the company.

This dual role of auditor and consultant created an obvious conflict of interest. Andersen auditors would surely be reluctant to raise questions about work that Andersen consultants had been paid hundreds of millions of dollars for by Enron. Andersen is, of course, quite experienced at this sort of thing, having audited such other corporate suspects as Global Crossing, Halliburton Oil, Qwest, Waste Management, and WorldCom, and, before that, Charles Keating's Lincoln Savings and Loan, "which became a symbol of the nation's savings-and-loan crisis when it failed in 1989 at an eventual cost to taxpayers of $2.9 billion."[162]

Financial service firms like J. P. Morgan Chase and Citigroup earned substantial fees for loaning money to corporations and helping them hide their level of indebtedness. A *Wall Street Journal* editorial called the banks "Enron Enablers," and *Fortune* added: "They appear to have behaved in a guileful way and helped their corporate clients undertake unsavory practices."[163] In addition, brokerage firms came under fire because their high-profile analysts enthusiastically endorsed stocks publicly that they were disparaging privately, all because their firms derived fees from business with the troubled companies.[164] Merrill Lynch analyst Henry Blodgett privately described some stocks as a "piece of shit," while recommending them publicly to small investors.[165]

A summary of the most serious examples of alleged corporate wrongdoing is provided in Table 3.3, "Scoundrel Capitalism, 2005." Because of the large amount of such wrongdoing, the table focuses on the most harmful incidents and highlights the multiple dimensions of corporate misbehavior. Thus, the sentences reported here tend to be the most severe and are not necessarily representative of how the criminal justice system treats corporate criminals.

In an article on the origins of the Enron-era crisis, the *New York Times* said:

> Here we go again. In an eerie flashback to the savings and loan scandal a decade ago, it turns out that some of the lawmakers and regulators investigating some of the causes behind the Enron-Arthur Andersen scandal—Democrats and Republicans alike—may need to look no further than a mirror.

The 1995 Private Securities Litigation Reform Act—aggressively lobbied for by Arthur Andersen—helped shield companies and their accountants from liability. Five years later, a group of lawmakers

> succeeded in forcing regulators to dilute proposed restrictions on accountants. The group includes the [then] current chairman of the Securities and Exchange Commission and three House and Senate committee chairmen now involved in the cleanup who have been among the accounting industry's largest campaign [contribution] recipients.[166]

In 2002, the Sarbanes-Oxley Act became law and created a new board to oversee the accounting and auditing of publicly traded companies, limited

TABLE 3.3 Scoundrel Capitalism, 2005*	
Name/Company	**Alleged Wrongdoing**

Adelphia

The sixth-largest cable company declared bankruptcy after announcing that the founding Rigas family conspired to hide $2.3 billion in debt, some of it improperly used by the Rigas family for personal expenses. Investors lost $60 billion in value when stock fell to $0.15 from a high of $66.00; the company filed for bankruptcy and restated earnings for several years.	The founding Rigas family used the company as their personal bank, improperly took money and loans, created sham transactions and forged financial documents to cover it up, and lied to investors about the company's overall financial condition. A Securities and Exchange Commission (SEC) official describes this as "one of the most extensive financial frauds ever to take place at a public company." They found "rampant self-dealing," including the use of $252 million in Adelphia funds to repay stock market losses and purchase a $12.8 million golf club, the Buffalo Sabres hockey team ($150 million), and luxury condominiums for the Rigas family. Timothy Rigas grew concerned about his father John's "unacceptably large" spending of company money and put him on a $1 million a month allowance.
	John and Timothy were convicted on 18 felony counts each. The judge sentenced Timothy (former Chief Financial Officer) to 20 years and John (founder) to 15 years. John received a lesser sentence because of health problems, but the judge said the sentence was "substantial" and "appropriate" for the "egregious" conduct, so it would send a clear message to other corporate executives. Michael Rigas received 10 months of home confinement after pleading guilty to making a false entry in a company record.

Arthur Andersen

Andersen audited many companies that had to restate earnings. They settled with the SEC in numerous other cases: Enron, WorldCom ($8 billion restatement), Global Crossing, Qwest Communications, Baptist Foundation of Arizona ($217 million settlement), Sunbeam ($110 million settlement), and Colonial Realty ($90 million settlement). The Waste Management	Andersen officials ordered the shredding of some two tons of documents after Andersen executives acknowledged an SEC investigation into Enron's accounting practices was "highly probable" but before the SEC investigation formally started. In an argument before the Supreme Court, the Deputy Solicitor General said, "It is the equivalent of sending someone to a crime scene, and wiping up the evidence before police get there with the yellow tape." Andersen also deleted large numbers of emails relating to its internal debates on Enron's financial problems.
	Arthur Andersen's conviction for obstruction of justice ended the company as an accounting firm. The conviction was later overturned by the Supreme Court because the jury instruction about the term "corruptly

(Continued)

TABLE 3.3 (continued)	
Name/Company	**Alleged Wrongdoing**

case ($1 billion overstated earnings) led to a $229 million shareholder settlement and an SEC "cease and desist" order on misleading accounting.

persuading" the withholding of evidence "failed to convey the requisite consciousness of wrongdoing." The Court's opinion did not suggest that Andersen was innocent, and noted an incident where the head of the "engagement team" for Enron "picked up a document with the words 'smoking gun' written on it and began to destroy it, adding 'we don't need this.'"

Enron

Described by executive Jeffrey Skilling as "the world's coolest company," Enron declared the largest corporate bankruptcy in history on December 2, 2001. It restated its earnings and assets downward by $1.5 billion, wiping out 4,200 jobs and $60 billion in market value lost to shareholders.

A special committee of Enron's board (the Powers Committee) concluded that partnership arrangements allowed Enron executives to hide the company's losses and liabilities, while earning tens of millions of dollars in fees for themselves. The report was based on a three-month review without subpoena power and limited access to documents. Nevertheless, it "found a systematic and pervasive attempt by Enron's Management to misrepresent the Company's financial condition," and that Enron employees involved in the partnerships received "tens of millions of dollars they should never have received." Investigators concluded that Enron manipulated the California power crisis for financial gain, entered into transactions presenting conflicts of interest, engaged in fraudulent transactions to book revenue, and punished whistleblowers. Enron executives and directors sold $1 billion worth of shares in the three years before the company collapsed. Just before the bankruptcy announcement, employees were locked out of selling their shares because of "administrative changes" to the stock plan.

A jury found Skilling guilty on 19 counts, including conspiracy, fraud, false statements, and insider trading. Sentencing guidelines called for a 30-year sentence, although he received 24 years, which was later cut to 14 years if he waived appeals. Ken Lay was convicted of six counts of conspiracy and fraud, plus another four counts of fraud and false statements at a separate trial. He died of a heart attack before his appeal was final, so his conviction was voided and could not be used against him in civil suits to recover money from his estate. Chief Financial Officer Andrew Fastow was originally charged with 109 felonies. He pleaded guilty to two counts of conspiracy in exchange for a 10-year maximum sentence and his promise to cooperate and testify against his bosses. A judge sentenced him to six years; he was released after serving about five years.

Name/Company	Alleged Wrongdoing

Global Crossing

Optical fiber company filed the fourth-largest bankruptcy ever, with $12 billion in debt. This company is chartered in Bermuda to avoid U.S. corporate taxes, even though it is headquartered and run out of the United States and enjoys all the rights and access to government contracts that U.S. corporations enjoy.

Allegedly engaged in capacity swaps with Qwest Communications (see next company) to improperly book revenue in order to inflate stock price. In one congressional hearing, Rep. Billy Tauzin (R-LA) said executives "pursued sham transactions to put revenue on the books, to mislead investors, and to prevent further drops in their stock prices." Many of these transactions were done in the last few days, sometimes the last minutes, of the financial quarter to help meet earnings expectations. No criminal charges were filed against any Global Crossing executives. Three executives agreed to pay a civil fine of $100,000 each in an SEC settlement, but they were not required to admit any wrongdoing. The SEC enforcement division recommended a fine against Chairman Gary Winnick (who worked out of a replica of the Oval Office), but SEC commissioners rejected the idea. The expected $1 million fine was small compared to the $730 million he made in stock sales before the company filed for bankruptcy.

Qwest Communications

The dominant local telephone company in 14 states. Shares dropped to $1 each, from a high of $66.00, losing $90 billion in value for investors. Qwest restated $2.5 billion in revenue.

Alleged to have improperly engaged in hollow trades and capacity swaps with Global Crossing and other telecoms to boost revenue and meet earnings expectations. The SEC charged that CEO Joseph Nacchio and other executives knew of revenue shortfalls but "fraudulently and materially misrepresented Qwest's performance and growth to the investing public." Rep. James Greenwood (R-PA), who chaired a congressional investigating committee, said: "Investors in Global Crossing and Qwest lost billions of dollars when the truth came out about these companies' finances, while insiders walked away with billions of dollars." On several occasions, executives asked that the details of the swaps not be put in writing to avoid scrutiny. A memo by Chief Financial Officer (CFO) Robin Szeliga indicated Qwest would penalize anyone who questioned the company's handling of swaps and followed through by blocking business to Morgan Stanley, which publicly questioned Qwest's reliance on swaps. Nacchio was convicted on 19 counts of insider trading and sentenced to six years in prison in what has been called the largest insider trading case in history. CFO Robin Szeliga was sentenced to two years probation for one count of insider trading in exchange for her testimony against Nacchio. Qwest paid a $250 million penalty to the SEC.

(Continued)

TABLE 3.3 (continued)

Name/Company	Alleged Wrongdoing
Tyco This large conglomerate is chartered in Bermuda to avoid U.S. corporate taxes, even though it is headquartered and run out of the United States and enjoys all the rights and access to government contracts that U.S. corporations enjoy.	Former CEO Dennis Kozlowski and former CFO Mark Swartz looted the company and shareholders of $600 million, $150 million of which was directly stolen through improper loans and unauthorized bonuses, with the rest related to bonuses based on financial misstatements and selling stock at prices artificially inflated by their financial misstatements. The two men used the money to buy houses, art, and luxury items for themselves, including Kozlowski's infamous $6,000 shower curtain and a $2 million birthday party for Kozlowski's wife on an Italian island that included an ice sculpture of Michelangelo's David with vodka pouring from his genitals. Kozlowski also allegedly improperly bought valuable paintings by Renoir and Monet worth $13.2 million, and he evaded $1.1 million in New York State sales tax. Kozlowski and Swartz were convicted of 22 counts of grand larceny, conspiracy, securities fraud, and falsifying business records. The prosecutor described it as the largest larceny ever prosecuted in New York. They were both sentenced to between eight years and four months and 25 years in prison, less than the maximum term of 15 to 30 years. Kozlowski settled the sales tax issue relating to the art and income tax liabilities for $21.2 million.
WorldCom (now MCI) Telecommunications giant announced a series of restatements totaling about $11 billion, and its $107 billion bankruptcy displaced Enron as the largest bankruptcy filing in U.S. history. The stock price fell from $64.00 to $0.09, reducing total shareholder value by $180 billion; 17,000 employees were laid off. The New York State pension plan lost $300 million because of WorldCom investments.	The Deputy U.S. Attorney General said CFO Scott Sullivan and Controller David Myers "systematically flouted rules of accounting and lied outright to investors to perpetuate the false image that WorldCom was succeeding." With business deteriorating, executives put pressure on numerous others to, in Myers's words, engage in accounting adjustments for which "there was no justification or documentation and [that] were not in accordance with generally accepted accounting principles." WorldCom executives silenced whistleblowers, and Myers warned employees not to discuss their concerns with outside auditors. CEO Bernard Ebbers was removed from his position when WorldCom declared bankruptcy, but he negotiated a severance package worth $1.5 million a year for life. Ebbers received a 25-year sentence after being convicted of securities fraud, conspiracy, and false-statement charges. The Court of Appeals upheld the sentence

Name/Company	Alleged Wrongdoing
The large-scale fraud earned it the name "WorldCon."	as "harsh but not unreasonable," noting that the securities fraud here was "not puffery or cheerleading or even a misguided effort to protect the company" but "were specifically intended to create a false picture of profitability even for professional analysts, which, in Ebbers's case, was motivated by his personal financial circumstances." Sullivan faced 25 years because he had directed subordinates to inflate revenues but received only five years because of his cooperation in convicting Ebbers. The sentencing judge described Sullivan as the "day-to-day manager of the scheme at WorldCom." As part of plea bargains that included requirements of cooperation with the government, Myers received one year; accounting director Yates received one year; and director of management reporting Vinson received five months in jail and five months home detention.

* The title comes from a phrase used by Simon Schama in "The Dead and the Guilty," *The Guardian,* September 11, 2002, www.guardian.co.uk/septemberll/oneyearon/story/0,12361,789978,00.html.

Sources: Devin Leonard, "The Adelphia Story," *Fortune,* August 12, 2002, www.fortune.com/indexw.jhtml?channel=artcol.jhtml&doc_id=208825; *CNNMoney,* "Rigas and Sons Arrested," July 25, 2002, http://money. cnn.com/2002/07/24/news/rigas/ [currently unavailable]; George Mannes, "Adelphia Charges Up the Ante," The Street.com, July 24, 2002, www. thestreet.com/_yahoo/tech/georgemannes/10033900.html; Carrie Johnson and Christopher Stern, "Adelphia Founder, Sons Charged," *The Washington Post,* July 25, 2002, p. A1; "Swartz Got Rich Severance Deal," *Boston Globe,* September 26, 2002, www.boston.com/ dailyglobe2/269/business/Swartz_got_rich_severance_deal+.shtml; Peter Behr and Dan Eggen, "Enron is Target of Criminal Probe," *The Washington Post,* January 10, 2002, p. A1; Peter Behr and April Witt, "Visionary's Dream Led to Risky Business," *The Washington Post,* July 28, 2002, p. A1; Jonathan Krim, "Fast and Loose at WorldCom: Lack of Controls, Pressure to Grow Set Stage for Financial Deceptions," *The Washington Post,* August 29, 2002, p. A1; Jonathan Krim, "WorldCom Staff Told not to Talk to Auditor, E-Mails Show," *The Washington Post,* August 27, 2002, p. E3; David M. Ewalt and John Kreiser, "Sidgmore Steps Down as World-Com CEO; Ebbers May Lose Golden Parachute," InformationWeek.com, September 10, 2002, www.informationweek.com/story/IWK20020910S0007; Motley Fool, "The Motley Fool Take on Wednesday, Feb. 27, 2002," www.fool.com/news/take/2002/take020227. htm; Motley Fool, "The Motley Fool Take on Wednesday, June 5, 2002," www.fool.com/news/take/2002/take020605. htm; Robert O' Harrow, "Tyco Executives Free on Bond of $15 Million," *The Washington Post,* September 28, 2002, p. E1; Carrie Johnson and Ben White, "WorldCom Arrests Made," *The Washington Post,* August 2, 2002, p. A1; Ben White, "World-Com Officer Pleads Guilty to Fraud," *The Washington Post,* October 8, 2002, p. E1; and Citizen Works, "Corporate Crookbook: Corporate Scandal Sheet," http://citizenworks.org/enron/corp-scandal. php; Mark Gimein, "You Bought: They Sold," *Fortune,* September 2, 2002, pp. 64–65; "Adelphia's John Rigas and Son Report to Prison in N.C.," *USA Today,* August 13, 2007, http://www.usatod.ay. com/money/media/2007–08–13-rigas-prison-nc_N.htm; "Adelphia founder sentenced to 15 years," *CNN Money,* June 20, 2005, http://money.cnn.com/2005/06/20/news/newsmakers/rigas_sentencing/; *Arthur Andersen, LLP* v. *United States* 544 U.S. 696 (2005), note 6; Associated Press, "Former Enron Exec Gets 27

(Continued)

Month Sentence," http://www.msnbc.msn.com/id/19293341/; Kristen Hays, "Ex-Enron CFO Fastow Sentenced to 6 Years in Prison," *Houston Chronicle,* September 26, 2006, http://www.chron.com/disp/story.mpl/front/4215426.html; Carrie Johnson, "Felling 'Slap in the Face' After Fastow's Sentence," *The Washington Post,* October 3, 2006, p. D1; Stephen Taub, "No Charges for Global Crossing's Winnick," CFO.com, December 14, 2004, http://www.cfo.com/article.cfm/3493060; "3 Ex-Officials of Global Crossing Are Fined in SEC Settlement," *International Herald Tribune,* April 13, 2005, http://www.iht.com/articles/2005/04/12/business/global.php; Dan Frosch, "Court Considers New Trial for Former Chief of Quest," *New York Times,* September 25, 2008, http://www.nytimes.com/2008/09/26/technology/26qwest.html; Dan Frosch, "Ex-Quest Chief Gets 6-Year Sentence," *New York Times,* July 28, 2007; U.S. Dept of Justice, "Former Qwest Chief Financial Officer Sentenced for Insider Trading," July 28, 2006, http://www.usdoj.gov/usao/co/press_releases/archive/2006/July06/7_28_06.html; Ben White, "Ex-Tyco Executives Convicted," *The Washington Post,* June 18, 2005, p. A1; Ben White, "Ex-Tyco Executives Sentenced," *The Washington Post,* September 20, 2005, p. D1; Anthony Lin, "Former Tyco Executives Sentenced to Up to 25 Years in Prison," Law.com, September 20, 2005, http://www.law.com/jsp/article.jsp?id=1127133338866; Anemona Hartocollis, "Ex-Tyco Chief to Settle Tax Evasion Charges," *New York Times,* May 13, 2006, http://www.nytimes. com/2006/05/13/business/13tyco.html; Associated Press, "Conviction of Ex-WorldCom Chief Is Upheld," *New York Times,* July 29, 2006, http://www.nytimes.com/2006/07/29/business/29ebbers.html; Paul Leighton, "Ebbers' 25 year Sentence for WorldCom Fraud Upheld. Good," PaulsJusticeBlog.com, August 4, 2006, http://www.paulsjusticeblog.com/2006/08/ebbers_25_year_sentence_for_worldcom_fraud.php; Jennifer Bayot and Roben Farzad, "Ex-WorldCom Officer Sentenced to 5 Years in Accounting Fraud," *New York Times,* August 12, 2005, http://www.nytimes.com/2005/08/12/business/12worldcom.html; "Former Enron CEO released from prison to halfway house", *Reuters,* August 20, 2018, https://www.reuters.com/article/us-enron-sklling/former-enron-ceo-released-from-prison-to-halfway-house-idUSKCN1LG08F.

the ability of accounting firms to be both auditors and consultants of the same firms, gave shareholders five rather than three years to sue companies that mislead them, and increased possible fines and jail sentences for those who violate new and existing corporate laws. Much of the law goes in the right direction. However, political compromises in Congress led to changing the standard for holding executives liable for fraud from "reckless" to "knowing," which makes bringing such cases more difficult for prosecutors. Congress also limited *disgorgement* (restitution of money taken by fraud) only to those directly involved, not company officers and directors who only knew about misconduct but still profited from it.[167]

As soon as the ink was dry on Sarbanes-Oxley, *The Washington Post* reported, "Members of Congress from both parties accused the administration of undermining or narrowing the scope of provisions covering securities fraud, whistleblower protection and punishment for shredding documents." Critics, including the bill's authors, charged that the Justice Department drew up interpretations and prosecution guidelines that contradicted the legislative intent of the reform measure.[168]

Following up on Sarbanes-Oxley, the U.S. Sentencing Commission increased the recommended penalties for some white-collar crimes. However, "the Justice Department promptly complained that the new guidelines do not go far enough, because the panel failed to crack down harder on lower-level offenders."[169]

In March 2002, after the disclosure of Enron's bankruptcy, but before a wave of other frauds was revealed, *Fortune* magazine observed,

> The double standard in criminal justice in this country is starker and more embedded than many realize. Bob Dylan was right: Steal a little, and they put you in jail. Steal a lot, and you're likely to walk away with a lecture and a court-ordered promise not to do it again.[170]

As a case in point, Enron's Chief Financial Officer Andy Fastow was charged with 109 felony counts including conspiracy, wire fraud, securities fraud, falsifying books, obstruction of justice, money laundering, insider trading, and filing false income tax returns. He agreed to a plea bargain with a maximum of ten years in prison and was released late in 2011 after serving five years. At the same time, Leandro Andrade, a drug addicted veteran, received a sentence of 50 years for two counts of stealing videocassettes from K-Mart—a sentence upheld by the Supreme Court as not an unreasonable application of a three-strikes law.[171] A poor guy who steals less than $200 worth of goods to support his drug addiction ends up in jail for life, and a rich guy who masterminds a scam that results in billions of dollars in losses ultimately gets a much shorter sentence (and a year off for participating in the prison's substance abuse program because of his dependence on anti-anxiety medication).[172]

Some of the sentences handed down to corporate executives who went to trial have been harsher than the one Fastow received, and attention has focused disproportionately on a relatively small number of sentences that are in the range of 15 to 30 years. These harsh punishments are sometimes taken as evidence that the pendulum has swung from excessive leniency to the point of unreasonable severity. However, such a conclusion ignores the scale of these crimes. These were not run-of-the-mill white-collar crimes, but the largest frauds in U.S. history to that point; they were systematic and widespread crimes that undermined the public's faith in the financial system and caused extensive harm to employees, communities, and shareholders. The judge sentencing Enron's executive Jeffrey Skilling noted that he had "imposed on hundreds if not thousands of people a life sentence of poverty."[173] Bear in mind as well, that, while these sentences were severe, "The vast majority of those who pled received sentences of fewer than five years—the beneficiaries of sentencing guidelines that reward cooperation."[174]

So, for all the rhetoric about how tough we are on white-collar offenders, a substantial number of those involved in the biggest financial scandal ended up with sentences of less than five years, which is equivalent to what, at the time, was the mandatory sentence for possession of five grams of crack cocaine. Also, remember from Chapter 2 that willful violations of health and safety laws that result in a death are still punishable by six months in prison—half the penalty for harassing a wild burro on federal land—so there is only a limited range of crimes of the well-off on which we have genuinely gotten tougher.[175]

THE FINANCIAL MELTDOWN OF 2008

"THE BEST 18 MONTHS OF GRIFTING THIS COUNTRY HAS EVER SEEN"   Just as the final chapters of the Enron saga were being written, the United States started experiencing its worst financial crisis since the Great Depression. At its source were complex securities based on "subprime" mortgages, which lenders gave to borrowers who lacked the resources to repay them. These mortgages were in great demand by investment banks which made large profits pooling and reselling them. Credit rating agencies like Standard & Poor's and Moody's, who are paid by the investment banks, gave the securities higher credit ratings than the borrowers' underlying assets would justify. The Federal Reserve had power to regulate mortgage underwriters but failed to do so.

To make matters worse, in 2004, the SEC waived its leverage rules (ratio of debt that a bank may take on versus the capital assets it holds) for five big Wall Street firms (Goldman Sachs, Lehman Brothers, Bear Stearns, Merrill Lynch, and Morgan Stanley), allowing them to borrow larger amounts of money and take on more risk.[176] Further, many companies were involved in buying or selling "credit default swaps," which function like insurance against a company's inability to pay its debt. But unlike insurance, there is no federal or state regulation of the swaps, and thus no centralized clearinghouse to keep track of what parties have sold, how much protection they have, and whether they have the assets to cover their bets. Thus, as Wall Street firms started to run into financial trouble, no one knew which ones would have problems. This lack of transparency caused a lack of trust that helped to freeze up the credit system because no one wanted to lend money in case the borrower turned out to be in deep financial trouble.

Barry Ritholtz, CEO of a financial research firm and author of *Bailout Nation*, stated that a consistent element of the problem has been "an abdication of responsibility from the various entities assigned to supervise and regulate" our financial system.[177] He suggests that we wouldn't allow the Super Bowl to be played without referees because "we *know* that players would give in to their worst impulses,"[178] and the financial system is the same. As investigations were starting, "government officials with experience investigating corporate fraud [said] some of the patterns they [were] detecting—lying to investors, shifting debt off corporate balance sheets—are familiar." A former member of the Enron Task Force said, "The more things change, the more things stay the same."[179]

That makes the story frustratingly familiar. So does the fact that while investors have lost billions, many of those "who drove the financial ship of state aground" raked in hundreds of millions in pay, severance, and stock sales before the collapse. The CEO of Lehman Brothers, Richard Fuld Jr., sold $490 million in stocks and had a $34 million annual salary before the 158-year-old firm filed for a record bankruptcy and shares lost 94 percent of their value. During the previous year, Lehman paid out $5.7 billion in bonuses. Angelo Mozilo, CEO and founder of Countrywide Financial, cashed in over $400 million in stock before his company, which had been at the forefront of originating problematic subprime mortgages, was sued by several state attorneys general.[180] A systematic review of people employed in mortgage securities found:

> Even in the worst financial crisis in decades, the employees at the center of the crisis, including those directly tied to fraudulent deals for which their banks paid large fines, fared reasonably well. If there is no penalty for participation, employees have little incentive to identify, avoid, or correct abuses.[181]

The *New York Times* reported that "in 1995, bank regulators referred 1,837 cases to the Justice Department;" but in "a period encompassing the worst of the crisis, an average of only 72 [cases] a year have been referred for criminal prosecution."[182] Any strengthening of enforcement because of Enron has disappeared.

> Legal and financial experts say that a loosening of enforcement measures, cutbacks in staffing at the Securities and Exchange Commission, and a shift in resources toward terrorism at the FBI, have combined to make the federal government something of a paper tiger in investigating securities crimes.[183]

Although FBI officials in 2004 said that mortgage-related problems had "the potential to be an epidemic,"[184] the FBI devoted no resources to following up this concern. Then-Attorney General Michael Mukasey repeatedly rejected calls for an equivalent of the Enron Task Force that was used to prosecute earlier widespread complex financial crime.[185] As a result, the former lead prosecutor of Enron's Lay and Skilling commented that U.S. attorneys "staring at the subprime crisis find scant resources available to pursue sophisticated financial crimes."[186] William Black, a senior regulator who helped oversee savings and loan prosecutions, noted: "If you don't investigate, you don't find."[187] If you don't find evidence, you can't refer cases for prosecution and convict people. And that's just what happened.

Further, former SEC Chairman Arthur Levitt Jr., said that "the commission delayed settlements while commissioners negotiated to impose smaller penalties than the companies had agreed to pay."[188] More enforcement problems came to light when Judge Jed Rakoff rejected a proposed settlement in a case in which the SEC claimed Citicorp sold investors a product it was betting would lose value and did not disclose that information, causing investors $700 million in losses. In the settlement, Citigroup did not admit guilt but agreed to pay $285 million and said it would not violate this provision of the law again. The judge noted that the penalty was "pocket change" to Citigroup and would have no deterrent effect or make up for investor losses. Further, the promise not to violate the law in the future was the kind of relief that "Citigroup (a recidivist) knew that the S.E.C. had not sought to enforce against any financial institution for at least the last 10 years."[189] Indeed, a *New York Times* investigation found that Citigroup "agreed not to violate the very same antifraud statute in July 2010. And in May 2006. Also as far as back as March 2005 and April

2000."[190] They found 19 companies were repeat offenders who had promised not to do it again!

The cases against executives and big financial firms have been civil suits, not criminal trials. Nobel Prize winning economist Joseph Stiglitz puts these cases into the larger perspective: "Yeah, we fine them, and what is the big lesson?... you're still sitting pretty with your several hundred million dollars that you have left over after paying fines that look very large by ordinary standards but look small compared to the amount that you've been able to cash in."[191] Put another way, Phil Angelides, the former chairman of the Financial Crisis Inquiry Commission, said the fines are like someone robs a 7-Eleven of $1,000 and settles for a $25 fine with no admission of wrongdoing. "Will they do it again? Absolutely, because it pays."[192]

While not all the actions that led to the financial crisis involved a crime, Stiglitz comments that "a considerable amount of what was done should have been illegal if it wasn't."[193] But even under existing law, legal experts noted areas that should have been investigated but were not: the extent of disclosure by executives about risk due to various mortgage products, the representations they made to investors about questionable loans that were bundled and sold, excessively optimistic estimates of the value of mortgage assets that created illusory profits for which executives received bonuses, cashing in shares based on inside information about looming problems, even misleading statements to boards and regulators about such problems.[194]

Indeed, Judge Rakoff notes that the final report of the bipartisan Financial Crisis Inquiry Commission "uses variants of the word 'fraud' no fewer than 157 times in describing what led to the crisis."[195] Another careful review of public evidence of wrongdoing noted that the government has enough evidence to support tens of billions of dollars in fines, but not criminal charges: "How is it possible that you can have this much fraud and not a single person has done anything criminal?"[196]

As the crisis progressed, rampant fraud appeared in mortgage servicing and especially in the paperwork filed with courts to certify facts necessary for a bank to foreclose on people unable to pay. To deal with the rising number of foreclosures, mortgage servicers for major financial institutions hired low-paid "robosigners" who quickly signed documents to be filed with the court without checking the accuracy of any of the information. Individuals who file false statements with the court are guilty of criminal perjury, but financial institutions only had to settle civil claims.[197]

The financial crisis did produce sweeping legislation—the Dodd-Frank Wall Street Reform and Consumer Protection Act of 2010. As with the gutting of Sarbanes-Oxley soon after it became law,[198] President Trump vowed to weaken the bill after it was passed as well as financial regulation in general.[199] Congress has not increased the SEC budget by enough to allow it to fulfill all the additional responsibilities required of it by Dodd-Frank. The smaller budget does not save taxpayers anything because the SEC is funded by fees paid by the firms it regulates, so financial institutions pay less to government and have a weaker watchdog on the beat.[200] Ritholtz rightly calls this keeping the

SEC "defective by design."[201] Former SEC chairman Harvey Pitt agrees: "It's almost as if the commission is being set up to fail."[202]

Confirming Chairman Pitt's observation, in the 2008 financial crisis, there have been no criminal prosecutions of top-level executives or major financial institutions at all! Phil Angelides notes that Department of Justice vigorously prosecuted 2,700 mortgage brokers, borrowers, appraisers—"small cogs in the corrupt mortgage machine"—but none of the serious players:

> Apparently, if someone lies about 10 mortgage loans, they will face the full force of the law. If someone lies about hundreds of thousands of loans, then they can count on the shareholders of their company to pay their way to exoneration.

The firms that were "too big to fail" and too big to prosecute are now even bigger. By 2017, JPMorganChase had $2.5 trillion in assets—up 29 percent since the financial crisis.[203] And thus the enduring "core problem is that financial elites dominate the law and can subvert it for profit."[204]

More generally, we have seen in this chapter, and the previous one, that the criminal justice system is triply biased against the poor. First, there is the economic bias *among harmful acts* as to which get labeled crimes and which are treated as regulatory matters, as we saw in Chapter 2. Second, there is economic bias *among crimes* that we have seen in this chapter. The crimes that poor people are likely to commit carry harsher sentences than the "crimes in the suites" committed by well-to-do people. Third, there is economic bias *among defendants convicted of the same crimes*. Among such defendants, the poor receive less probation and more years of confinement than well-off defendants, assuring us once again that the vast majority of those put behind bars are from the lowest social and economic classes in the nation. On either side of the law, the rich get richer...

… AND THE POOR GET PRISON

We do not claim that the inmates in prison are innocent. The vast majority of them are probably guilty of the crimes for which they were sentenced. Rather, the point is that people who are equally or more dangerous, equally or more criminal, are not in prison with those inmates. The criminal justice system works systematically not to punish and confine the dangerous and the criminal, *but to punish and confine the poor who are dangerous and criminal*.

It is successful at all levels. In 1973, there were 204,211 individuals in state and federal prisons, or 96 prisoners for every 100,000 individuals (of all ages) in the general population. By year-end 2017, there were a total of 1,489,363 persons in state and federal prisons, or 440 per 100,000 Americans. Add in the 745,200 in local jails, and the result is about 2.2 million people locked up, a staggering 686 for every 100,000 in the population.[205] This enormous number of prisoners is predominantly from the bottom of society.

The criminal justice system is sometimes thought of as a kind of sieve in which the innocent are progressively sifted out from the guilty, who end up behind bars. We have tried to show that the sieve works another way as well. It sifts the affluent out from the poor, so it is not merely the guilty who end up behind bars but the *guilty poor*.

With this information, we have supported the hypotheses set forth in Chapter 2 in the section titled "The Carnival Mirror: Criminal Justice as Creative Art." The criminal justice system does not simply weed out the peace-loving from the dangerous, the law-abiding from the criminal. At every stage, starting with the very definitions of crime and progressing through the stages of investigation, arrest, charging, conviction, and sentencing, the system *weeds out the wealthy*. It refuses to define as "crimes" or as serious crimes the dangerous and predatory acts of the well-to-do—acts that, as we have seen, result in the loss of thousands of lives and billions of dollars. Instead, the system focuses its attention on crimes likely to be committed by members of the lower classes. Thus, it is no surprise to find that so many of the people behind bars are from the lower classes. The people we see in our jails and prisons are no doubt dangerous to society, but they are not *the* danger to society, not *the gravest danger* to society. Individuals who pose equal or greater threats to our well-being walk the streets with impunity.

Chapter 1 argued that the society fails to institute policies that have a good chance of reducing crime. Chapter 2 argued that the criminal justice system works to make crime appear to be the monopoly of the poor by restricting the label "crime" to the dangerous acts of the poor and rarely applying it to the dangerous acts of the well-off, Chapter 3 argued that criminal justice system continues this focus on the poor by more actively pursuing and prosecuting the poor, rather than the well-off, for the acts that are labeled crime. *The joint effect of all these phenomena is to maintain a real threat of crime that the vast majority of Americans believes is a threat from the poor.* The criminal justice system is a carnival mirror that throws back a distorted image of the dangers that lurk in our midst—and conveys the impression that those dangers are the work of the poor. Chapter 4 suggests who benefits from this illusion and how.

Summary

This chapter has mainly tried to document that, *even among those acts that our criminal justice system labels as crimes,* the system works to make it more likely that those who end up in jail or prison will be from the bottom of society. This works in two broad ways:

1. *For the same crime,* the system is more likely to investigate and detect, arrest and charge, convict and sentence, and sentence to prison (and for a longer time) a lower-class individual than a middle- or upper-class individual. To support this, we reviewed a large number of studies performed over a long period of time comparing the treatment of high- and low-socioeconomic status offenders and of white and nonwhite offenders, from arrest through sentencing for the same crimes.

2. *Between crimes that are characteristically committed by poor people (street crimes) and those characteristically committed by the well-off (white-collar and corporate crimes),* the system treats the former much more harshly than the latter, even when the crimes of the well-off take far more money from the public or cause far more death and injury than the crimes of the poor. To support this, we compared the sentences meted out for street crimes with the treatment of those responsible for death and destruction in the workplace, as well as those responsible for the S&L scandal, recent financial cheating at Enron and other major corporations, and the 2008 financial crisis.

And remember, both of these processes only affect those acts that have been labeled crimes, which, as we saw in Chapter 2, largely excludes the harmful acts of the well-off. Taken together, these facts show why it should come as no surprise that our prisons are filled with poor people.

Study Questions

1. Who is in our jails and prisons? How do the people behind bars in America compare with the general population in employment, wealth, and level of education?
2. What is meant by "white-collar crime"? How costly is it compared with the crimes on the FBI's Index?
3. What factors make it likelier that a poor person who commits a crime such as shoplifting or non-aggravated assault will be arrested than a middle-class person who commits the same crime?
4. What factors make it likelier that a middle- or upper-class person charged with a crime will be acquitted than a lower-class person charged with the same crime?
5. Are the people responsible for white-collar crime, including crimes that result in serious injury, more or less blameworthy than muggers? Do we punish white-collar criminals justly?
6. Is the criminal justice system racist? What evidence would establish or refute your view?
7. If killers of whites are more likely to be sentenced to death than killers of blacks, what should we do? Should we abolish the death penalty?
8. What do you see as the key factors behind the three large-scale outbreaks of financial fraud discussed in this chapter? What would help prevent them?

Additional Resources

Jeffrey Reiman and Paul Leighton, eds., *The Rich Get Richer and Poor Get Prison: A Reader* (Boston: Pearson, 2010). This volume is a collection of accessible articles that were either used as reference material for *The Rich Get Richer* or provide lively complementary examples or analysis. The reader is divided into sections that parallel the chapters of *The Rich Get Richer,* and each section of the reader opens with a substantial introduction, written by the editors, that provides article summaries, context, and linkages to *The Rich Get Richer.*

The authors also maintain a companion website to the text at www.paulsjusticep-age.com/reiman.htm.

Notes

1. *Challenge,* p. 44.
2. Ronald Goldfarb, "Prisons: The National Poorhouse," *New Republic,* November 1, 1969, pp. 15–17.
3. Philip A. Hart, "Swindling and Knavery, Inc.," *Playboy,* August 1972, p. 158.
4. Edwin Sutherland made the same point as far back as 1939:

   First, the administrative processes are more favorable to persons in economic comfort than to those in poverty, so that if two persons on different economic levels are equally guilty of the same offense, the one on the lower level is more likely to be arrested, convicted, and committed to an institution. Second, the laws are written, administered, and implemented primarily with reference to the types of crimes committed by people of lower economic levels (E. H. Sutherland, *Principles of Criminology* [Philadelphia, PA: Lippincott, 1939], p. 179).

5. Edwin H. Sutherland and Donald R. Cressey, *Criminology,* 9th ed. (Philadelphia, PA: Lippincott, 1974), p. 133.
6. Edwin Sutherland, Donald Cressey, and David Luckenbill, *Principles of Criminology,* 11th ed. (Dix Hills, NY: General Hall, 1992), pp. 165 and 306.
7. David Huizinga et al., *Disproportionate Minority Contact in the Juvenile Justice System: A Study of Differential Minority Arrest/Referral to Court in Three Cities,* National Institute of Justice, September 2007, document number 219743, p. 41, www.nqrs.gov/pdffiles1/ojjdp/grants/219743.pdf.
8. Cassia C. Spohn, "Thirty Years of Sentencing Reform: The Quest for a Racially Neutral Sentencing Process," in Julie Horney (ed.), *Criminal Justice 2000,* vol. 3: *Policies, Processes, and Decisions of the Criminal Justice System* (Rockville, MD: National Institute of Justice, 2000), pp. 427–428.
9. Quoted in National Research Council Committee on Causes and Consequences of High Rates of Incarceration, Jeremy Travis, Bruce Western, and Steve Redburn (eds.), *The Growth of Incarceration in the United States: Exploring Causes and Consequences.* (Washington, DC: The National Academies Press, 2014), p. 98.
10. Lauren Glaze, "Methodology: Survey of Prison Inmates, 2016," July 2019, NCJ 252210, U.S. Department of Justice, Bureau of Justice Statistics. www.bjs.gov/content/pub/pdf/mspi16.pdf, p.6; 2016 Survey of Prison Inmates (SPI) Questionnaire, November 29, 2018, OMB No. 1121-0152, Bureau of Justice Statistics, www.bjs.gov/content/pub/pdf/spi16q.pdf, pp. 126, 128, and 129.
11. Marjorie S. Zatz, "The Convergence of Ethnicity, Gender, and Class on Court Decision-Making: Looking Toward the 21st Century," in J. Horney (ed.), *Criminal Justice 2000,* vol. 3, p. 515.

12. Nathaniel Lewis, "Mass Incarceration: New Jim Crow, Class War or Both?" *People's Policy Project*, 2018, www.peoplespolicyproject.org/wp-content/uploads/2018/01/MassIncarcerationPaper.pdf, p. 22.

13. Jim Crow—named after a popular racist song of the 1800s—describes the system of laws that allowed for the discrimination and segregation of African Americans in the United States from just after the Civil War (1876) to the Civil Right Legislation of 1964.

14. See, for example, Loic Wacquant, "Deadly Symbiosis: When Ghetto and Prison Meet and Mesh," in David Garland (ed.), *Mass Imprisonment in the United States* (London: Sage, 2001), pp. 82–120.

15. William Julius Wilson, *The Declining Significance of Race*, 2nd ed. (Chicago: University of Chicago Press, 1980).

16. Gregg Barak, Paul Leighton, and Allison Cotton, *Class, Race, Gender & Crime: Social Realities of Justice in America*, 5th ed. (Lanham, MD: Rowman & Littlefield, 2018).

17. Doug Glanville, "I Was Racially Profiled in My Own Driveway," *The Atlantic*, April 14, 2014, www.theatlantic.com/national/archive/2014/04/i-was-racially-profiled-in-my-own-driveway/360615/.

18. Michelle Alexander, *The New Jim Crow* (New York: The New Press, 2011), pp. 1–2.

19. Kayla Fontenot, Jessica Semega, and Melissa Kollar for the U.S. Census Bureau, *Current Population Reports, Income and Poverty in the United States: 2017*, no. P60–263 (Washington, DC: U.S. Government Printing Office, September 2018), p. 12, Table 3.

20. Rakesh Kochhar and Anthony Cilluffo, "How Wealth Inequality has Changed in the U.S. Since the Great Recession, by Race, Ethnicity and Income," Pew Research Center, November 1, 2017, www.pewresearch.org/fact-tank/2017/11/01/how-wealth-inequality-has-changed-in-the-u-s-since-the-great-recession-by-race-ethnicity-and-income/.

21. Bureau of Labor Statistics, Current Population Survey, Annual Average Data (complete set of tables), Table 3, www.bls.gov/cps/cpsaat03.pdf. Table 5 https://www.bls.gov/cps/cpsaat05.pdf.

22. Zatz, "The Convergence of Ethnicity, Gender, and Class on Court Decision-Making," p. 511.

23. Michael Tonry, "Racial Politics, Racial Disparities, and the War on Crime," *Crime & Delinquency* 40, no. 4 (1994): pp. 483, 485–486.

24. Theodore Chiricos and William Bales, "Unemployment and Punishment: An Empirical Assessment," *Criminology* 29, no. 4 (1991): 718.

25. National Research Council Committee on Causes and Consequences of High Rates of Incarceration, Jeremy Travis, Bruce Western, and Steve Redburn (eds.), *The Growth of Incarceration in the United States: Exploring Causes and Consequences* (Washington, DC: National Academies Press, 2014), pp. 68 and 64.

26. Carrie L. Buist and Paul Leighton, "Corporate Criminals Constructing White Collar Crime—or Why There Is No Corporate Crime on USA Network's *White Collar* Series," in Gregg Barak (ed.), *Routledge Handbook of Crimes of the Powerful* (New York: Routledge, 2015), p. 80.

27. Ibid., p. 80.

28. Isidore Silver, "Introduction," in President's Crime Commission, *The Challenge of Crime in a Free Society* (New York: Avon, 1968), p. 31.

29. This is the conclusion of Austin L. Porterfield, *Youth in Trouble* (Fort Worth, TX: Leo Potishman Foundation, 1946); Fred J. Murphy, Mary M. Shirley, and Helen L. Witmer, "The Incidence of Hidden Delinquency," *American Journal of Ortho-psychiatry* 16, no. 4 (1946): pp. 686–696; James F. Short Jr., "A Report on the Incidence of Criminal Behavior, Arrests, and Convictions in Selected Groups," in *Proceedings of the Pacific Sociological Society* (1954): pp. 110–118; F. Ivan Nye, James F. Short Jr., and Virgil J. Olson, "Socioeconomic Status and Delinquent Behavior," *American Journal of Sociology* 63 (January 1958): 381–389; Maynard L. Erickson and Lamar T. Empey, "Class Position, Peers and Delinquency," *Sociology and Social Research* 49 (April 1965): 268–282; William J. Chambliss and Richard H. Nagasawa, "On the Validity of Official Statistics; A Comparative Study of White, Black, and Japanese High-School Boys," *Journal of Research in Crime and Delinquency* 6, no. 1 (1969): 71–77; Eugene Doleschal, "Hidden Crime," *Crime and Delinquency Literature* 2, no. 5 (1970): 546–572; Maynard L. Erikson, "Group Violations, Socioeconomic Status, and Official Delinquency," *Social Forces* 52, no. 1 (1973): 41–52.

30. Charles R. Tittle and Robert F. Meier, "Specifying the SES/Delinquency Relationship," *Criminology* 28, no. 2 (1990): 292. See also R. Gregory Dunaway et al., "The Myth of Social Class and Crime Revisited: An Examination of Adult and Class Criminality," *Criminology* 38, no. 2 (2002): 600.

31. Cf. Larry Karacki and Jackson Toby, "The Uncommitted Adolescent: Candidate for Gang Socialization," *Sociological Inquiry* 32 (1962): 203–215; William R. Arnold, "Continuities in Research: Scaling Delinquent Behavior," *Social Problems* 13, no. 1 (1965): 59–66; Harwin L. Voss, "Socio-Economic Status and Reported Delinquent Behavior," *Social Problems* 13, no. 3 (1966): 314–324; LaMar Empey and Maynard L. Erikson, "Hidden Delinquency and Social Status," *Social Forces* 44, no. 4 (1966): 546–554; Fred J. Shanley, "Middle-Class Delinquency as a Social Problem," *Sociology and Social Research* 51 (1967): 185–198; Jay R. Williams and Martin Gold, "From Delinquent Behavior to Official Delinquency," *Social Problems* 20, no. 2 (1972): 209–229.

32. Elliott Currie, *The Road to Whatever: Middle-Class Culture and the Crisis of Adolescence* (New York: Macmillan, 2005), p. 5.

33. William J. Chambliss, "The Saints and the Roughnecks," *Society* 11, no. 1 (1973): 24–31.

34. Ibid., p. 30.

35. Quoted in Heather Mooney and Paul Leighton, "Troubled Affluent Youth's Experiences in a Therapeutic Boarding School: The Elite Arm of the Youth Control Complex and Its Implications for Youth Justice," *Critical Criminology* 27, no. 4, doi: 10.1007/s10612-019-09466-4.

36. Ibid.

37. Currie, *The Road to Whatever: Middle-Class Culture and the Crisis of Adolescence*, p. 262.

38. Ibid., p. 47.

39. Ibid., p. 254.

40. Ibid., pp. 131 and 137.

41. Ibid., p. 12 and 97.

42. John Braithwaite. "What's Wrong with the Sociology of Punishment?" *Theoretical Criminology* 7, no. 1 (2003): 5–28.

43. Sutherland and Cressey, *Criminology*, p. 41.

44. Eugene F. Soltes, "Where is Your Company Most Prone to Lapses in Integrity?" *Harvard Business Review*, 97, no. 4 (July–August 2019): 51–54, https://hbr.org/2019/07/white-collar-crime.
45. Paul M. Healy and George Serafeim, "How to Scandal-Proof Your Company," *Harvard Business Review* 97, no. 4 (July–August 2019): 42–50, https://hbr.org/2019/07/white-collar-crime.
46. Jeffrey Reiman and Paul Leighton, *The Rich Get Richer and the Poor Get Prison: Ideology, Class, and Criminal Justice*, 10th. ed. (Abingdon, UK: Routledge, 2016), p. 132.
47. Mark A. Cohen, "The Costs of White-Collar Crime," in Shanna R. Van Slyke, Michael L. Benson, and Francis T. Cullen (eds.), *Oxford Handbook of White Collar Crime* (New York: Oxford University Press, 2016), p. 96.
48. Laureen Snider, "The Sociology of Corporate Crime: An Obituary: (Or: Whose Knowledge Claims have Legs?)", *Theoretical Criminology* 4, no. 2 (2000): 169–206.
49. Gregg Barak (ed.), *The Routledge International Handbook of the Crimes of the Powerful* (New York: Routledge, 2000).
50. Comparing socioeconomic status categories,

    "scant evidence is found that would support the contention that group delinquency is more characteristic of the lower-status levels than other socioeconomic status levels. In fact, only arrests seem to be more characteristic of the low-status category than the other categories" (Erikson, "Group Violations, Socioeconomic Status and Official Delinquency," p. 15).

51. Martin Gold, "Undetected Delinquent Behavior," *Journal of Research in Crime and Delinquency* 3, no. 1 (1966): p. 28.
52. Ibid., p. 38.
53. Terence P. Thornberry, "Race, Socioeconomic Status and Sentencing in the Juvenile Justice System," *Journal of Criminal Law and Criminology* 64, no. 1 (1973): 90–98.
54. Robert Sampson, "Effects of Socioeconomic Context on Official Reaction to Juvenile Delinquency," *American Sociological Review* 51 (December 1986): 876–885.
55. Tamar Birckhead, "Delinquent by Reason of Poverty," *Washington University Journal of Law and Policy* 38 (January 2012): 59.
56. Ibid.
57. Belinda R. McCarthy, "Social Structure, Crime, and Social Control: An Examination of Factors Influencing Rates and Probabilities of Arrest," *Journal of Criminal Justice* 19 (1991): 19–29.
58. Notes, "Developments in the Law: Race and the Criminal Process," *Harvard Law Review* 101 (1988): 1496.
59. Quoted in Jerome Miller, *Search and Destroy: African-American Males in the Criminal Justice System* (New York: Cambridge University Press, 1996), pp. 76–77.
60. David Huizinga et al., Disproportionate Minority Contact in the Juvenile Justice System:, p. 5.
61. Ibid., p. 26.
62. Birckhead, "Delinquent by Reason of Poverty," p. 58, note 9.
63. National Research Council, Travis, Western, and Redburn (eds.), *The Growth of Incarceration in the United States*, p. 96.
64. David A. Harris, "Racial Profiling," in Erik Luna (ed.), *Reforming Criminal Justice* 2 (University of Pittsburgh Legal Studies Research Paper No. 2017-30, 2017), p. 131 (emphasis in original), https://ssrn.com/abstract=3086232.

65. Emma Pierson et al., "A Large-Scale Analysis of Racial Disparities in Police Stops Across the United States," *Stanford Computational Policy Lab,* 2019: 1–10, https://5harad.com/papers/100M-stops.pdf.

66. A. Rafik Mohamed and Erik Fritsvold, *Dorm Room Dealers* (Boulder, CO: Lynne Rienner, 2010), pp. 11–12.

67. Ibid., p. 6.

68. Ibid., p. 7.

69. Victor Rios, *Punished: Policing the Lives of Black and Latino Boys* (New York: New York University Press, 2011), pp. xiv and 40.

70. Ibid., p. 44.

71. Alexandra Zayas and Kameel Stanley, "How Riding Your Bike Can Land You in Trouble with the Cops—If You're Black," *Tampa Bay Times,* April 17, 2015, www.tampabay.com/news/publicsafety/how-riding-your-bike-can-land-you-in-trouble-with-the-cops---if-youre-black/22259661/.

72. Alexandra Natapoff, "The High Stakes of Low-Level Criminal Justice," *Yale Law Journal* 128, no. 6 (2019); Matthew Shaer, "How Cities Make Money by Fining the Poor," *New York Times,* January 8, 2019, www.nytimes.com/2019/01/08/magazine/cities-fine-poor-jail.html.

73. Rios, *Punished,* pp. xiv and 158–159.

74. Devin Leonard, "The SEC: Outmanned, Outgunned, and On a Roll," *Businessweek,* April 19, 2012, www.businessweek.com/printer/articles/20972-the-sec-outmanned-outgunned-and-on-a-roll.

75. Irene Lurie, "Enforcement of State Minimum Wage and Overtime Laws: Resources, Procedures, and Outcomes," *Employee Rights and Employment Policy Journal* 15, no. 2 (2011): 422.

76. Paul Leighton, "No Criminology of Wage Theft: Revisiting 'Workplace Theft' to Expose Capitalist Exploitation," in Steve Bittle et al. (eds), *Revisiting Crimes of the Powerful* (New York: Routledge, 2018).

77. Note, "Developments in the Law," *Harvard Law Review* 101 (1988): 1520; William Bales, "Race and Class Effects on Criminal Justice Prosecution and Punishment Decisions" (Ph.D. diss., Florida State University, Tallahassee, 1987).

78. Paul Butler, "Race and Adjudication," *Reforming Criminal Justice: A Report of the Academy for Justice on Bridging the Gap between Scholarship and Reform* 3 (2017): 211–226, http://academyforjustice.org/wp-content/uploads/2017/10/10_Reforming-Criminal-Justice_Vol_3._Race-and-Adjudication.pdf.

79. Sentencing Law and Policy blog, "High-Profile Drug Arrest of Billionaire Drug Addict Spotlights Issues of What is 'Trafficking' and Who is a 'Victim' and 'Recidivist,'" August 14, 2018, https://sentencing.typepad.com/sentencing_law_and_policy/2018/08/high-profile-drug-arrest-of-billionaire-addict-spotlights-issues-of-what-is-trafficking-and-who-is-a.html.

80. Anita Raghavan, "Law Enforcement 'Not Winning' War on White-Collar Crime," New York Times, September 6, 2016, www.nytimes.com/2016/09/07/business/dealbook/law-enforcement-not-winning-war-on-white-collar-crime.html.

81. Transactional Records Access Clearinghouse (TRAC), "White Collar Prosecutions Hit All-Time Low in January 2019," March 13, 2018, https://trac.syr.edu/tracreports/crim/550/.

82. Rosa Goldensohn, "They Shared Drugs. Someone Died. Does that Make Them Killers?" New York Times, May 25, 2018, www.nytimes.com/2018/05/25/us/drug-overdose-prosecution-crime.html.

83. Barry Meier, "Origins of an Epidemic: Purdue Pharma Knew Its Opioids were Widely Abused," New York Times, May 29, 2018, www.nytimes.com/2018/05/29/health/purdue-opioids-oxycontin.html.

84. United States Government Accountability Office, Nonviolent Drug Convictions: Stakeholders' Views on Potential Actions to Address Collateral Consequences, Report, GAO-17-691, September 2017, p. 1, www.gao.gov/assets/690/687003.pdf.

85. Shaila Dewan, "The Collateral Victims of Criminal Justice," New York Times, September 5, 2015, www.nytimes.com/2015/09/06/sunday-review/the-collateral-victims-of-criminal-justice.html?_r=0.

86. Peter R. Reilly, "Justice Deferred is Justice Denied: We Must End Our Failed Experiment in Deferring Corporate Criminal Prosecutions," Brigham Young University Law Review 2015, no. 2 (2016): 307.

87. Government Accountability Office, "DOJ Has Taken Steps to Better Track Its Use of Deferred and Non-Prosecution Agreements, but Should Evaluate Effectiveness," GAO-10-110, December 18, 2009, p. 20, www.gao.gov/products/GAO-10-110.

88. Peter Reilly, "Justice Deferred is Justice Denied," p. 317 (quoting federal Judge Jed S. Rakoff).

89. See also David M. Uhlmann, "Deferred Prosecution and Non-Prosecution Agreements and the Erosion of Corporate Criminal Liability," Maryland Law Review 72, no. 4 (2013): 1295–1344.

90. Catherine Rampell, "Paul Manafort Aside, White-Collar Crimes Just Aren't Being Prosecuted Anymore," The Washington Post, August 7, 2018.

91. See, for example, Theodore G. Chiricos, Philip D. Jackson, and Gordon P. Waldo, "Inequality in the Imposition of a Criminal Label," Social Problems 19, no. 4 (1972): 553–572.

92. BJS, Jail Inmates in 2017—Statistical Tables, April 2019, NCJ251774, Tables 1 and 4; BJS, Jail Inmates at Midyear 2007, June 2008, NCJ221945, pp. 1 and 5.

93. Sentencing Law and Policy blog, "Spotlighting the Enduring Business of Jails," June 6, 2019, https://sentencing.typepad.com/sentencing_law_and_policy/2019/06/spotlighting-the-enduring-business-of-jails.html.

94. Cynthia E. Jones, "'Give Us Free': Addressing Racial Disparities in Bail Determinants," N.Y.U. Journal of Legislation & Public Policy 16, no. 4 (2013): 935.

95. Cynthia E. Jones, "'Give Us Free,'" p. 936. See also C. E. Ares, A. Rankin, and J. H. Sturz, "The Manhattan Bail Project: An Interim Report on the Use of Pre-trial Parole," NYU Law Review 38 (1963): 67; C. Foote, "Compelling Appearances in Court-Administration of Bail in Philadelphia," University of Pennsylvania Law Review 102 (1954): 1031–1079; and C. Foote, "A Study of the Administration of Bail in New York City," University of Pennsylvania Law Review 106 (1958): 693.

96. Cynthia E. Jones, "'Give Us Free,'" p. 938.

97. Partnership on AI, "Report on Algorithmic Risk Assessment Tools in the U.S. Criminal Justice System," www.partnershiponai.org/report-on-machine-learning-in-risk-assessment-tools-in-the-u-s-criminal-justice-system/.

98. Sarah Brayne, "Big Data Surveillance: The Case of Policing," American Sociological Review 82, no. 5 (2017): 977–1008.

99. Frank Pasquale, "Secret Algorithms Threaten the Rule of Law," MIT Technology Review, June 1, 2017, www.technologyreview. com/s/608011/secret-algorithms-threaten-the-rule-of-law/.

100. Abraham S. Blumberg, *Criminal Justice*, 2nd ed. (Chicago: Quadrangle Books, 1970), pp. 28–29; *Challenge*, p. 134.

101. P. Heaton, S. Mayson, and M. Stevenson, "The Downstream Consequences of Misdemeanor Pretrial Detention," *Stanford Law Review* 69, no. 711 (2017): 717–718.

102. Ibid., p. 771.

103. Richard A. Oppel, Jr. and Jugal K. Patel, "One Lawyer, 194 Felony Cases, and No Time," *New York Times*, January 31, 2019, www.nytimes.com/interactive/2019/01/31/us/public-defender-case-loads.html.

104. Robert Johnson, *Condemned to Die: Life under Sentence of Death* (New York: Elsevier, 1981), p. 138.

105. Stephen Gettinger, *Sentenced to Die: The People, the Crimes, and the Controversy* (New York: Macmillan, 1979), p. 261.

106. Erik Eckholm, "Robert Wayne Holsey Faces Lethal Injection in Georgia," *New York Times*, December 8, 2014, www.nytimes.com/2014/12/09/us/robert-wayne-holsey-faces-lethal-injection-in-georgia.html.

107. Richard Lacayo, "You Don't Always Get Perry Mason," *Time*, June 1, 1992, pp. 38–39. Perry Mason was a 1957–1966 TV series about a masterful lawyer.

108. Nancy Phillips, "In Life and Death Cases, Costly Mistakes," *Philadelphia Inquirer*, October 23, 2011, http://articles.philly.com/2011–10–23/news/30313341_1_lawyers-incapital-cases-death-penalty-appeals-death-penalty.

109. Mohamed and Fritsvold, *Dorm Room Dealers*, p. 173.

110. Ibid., pp. 161 and 167.

111. N. Rodriguez, "Concentrated Disadvantage and the Incarceration of Youth: Examining How Context Affects Juvenile Justice," *Journal of Research in Crime and Delinquency* 50, no. 2 (2013): 195 and 207.

112. Tamar Birckhead, "Closing the Widening Net: The Rights of Juveniles at Intake," *Texas Tech Law Review* 46, no. 1 (2013): 178.

113. Chiricos and Bales, "Unemployment and Punishment," pp. 701–724.

114. Belinda R. McCarthy, "A Micro-Level Analysis of Social Control: Intrastate Use of Jail and Prison Confinement," *Justice Quarterly* 7, no. 2 (1990): 334–335.

115. Dean J. Champion, "Private Counsels and Public Defenders: A Look at Weak Cases, Prior Records, and Leniency in Plea Bargaining," *Journal of Criminal Justice* 17, no. 4 (1989): 143.

116. Robert Tillman and Henry Pontell, "Is Justice 'Collar-Blind'? Punishing Medicaid Provider Fraud," *Criminology* 30, no. 4 (1992): 560.

117. Cassia C. Spohn, "Thirty Years of Sentencing Reform," pp. 455 and 481.

118. Cassia Spohn, "Race and Sentencing Disparity," *Reforming Criminal Justice: A Report of the Academy for Justice on Bridging the Gap Between Scholarship and Reform* 4 (2017): 182, http://academyforjustice.org/wp-content/uploads/2017/10/9_Criminal_Justice_Reform_Vol_4_Race-and-Sentencing-Disparity.pdf.

119. National Research Council, Travis, Western and Reburn (eds.), *The Growth of Incarceration in the United States*, p. 91.

120. *Criminal Justice Newsletter*, March 1, 1995, p. 3; *Criminal Justice Newsletter*, April 17, 1995, p. 5.

121. BJS, *Federal Drug Offenders, 1999, with Trends 1984–1999*, November 2001, NCJ 187285, Table 8, p. 11.

122. Statement of Ricardo Hinjosa, Chair United States Sentencing Commission, before the Senate Judiciary Committee, February 12, 2008, www.ussc. gov/testimony/Hinososa_Testimony_021208.pdf.

123. Nikki Jones, "Something Smells Like Pig, You Say?" *The Public Intellectual*, May 2, 2011, http://thepublicintellectual.org/2011/05/02/if-it-smells-like-a-pig/. She puts the sentencing of crack cocaine in the context of post-Civil War "pig laws," which "took a crime more likely to be committed by black people and made the penalty for that infraction harsher" (p. 1).

124. Mary Pat Flaherty and Joan Biskupic, "Rules Often Impose Toughest Penalties on Poor, Minorities," *The Washington Post*, October 9, 1996, p. A26.

125. National Research Council, Travis, Western and Reburn (eds.), *The Growth of Incarceration in the United States*, p. 94.

126. David Baldus, Charles Pulaski, and George Woodworth, "Comparative Review of Death Sentences: An Empirical Study of the Georgia Experience," *Journal of Criminal Law and Criminology* 74, no. 3 (1983): 661–725. See also Raymond Paternoster, "Prosecutorial Discretion in Requesting the Death Penalty: A Case of Victim-Based Racial Discrimination," *Law and Society Review* 18, no. 3 (1984): 437–478; Samuel R. Gross and Robert Mauro, "Patterns of Death: An Analysis of Racial Disparities in Capital Sentencing and Homicide Victimization," *Stanford Law Review* 37, no. 1 (1984): 27–153; Michael L. Radelet and Glenn L. Pierce, "Race and Prosecutorial Discretion in Homicide Cases," *Law and Society Review* 19 (1985): 587 and 615–619; Anthony G. Amsterdam, "Race and the Death Penalty," in Steven Jay Gold (ed.), *Moral Controversies: Race, Class, and Gender in Applied Ethics* (Belmont, CA: Wadsworth, 1993), pp. 268–269; Susan Levine and Lori Montgomery, "Large Racial Disparity Found by Study of Md. Death Penalty," *The Washington Post*, January 8, 2003, pp. A1 and A8; Although focused on the presentence stage, Free gives a good overview of methodological problems in racial discrimination research: Marvin D. Free, Jr., "Racial Bias and the American Criminal Justice System: Race and Presentencing Revisited," *Critical Criminology* 10, no. 3 (2001).

127. "When Are the Savings and Loan Crooks Going to Jail?" Hearing before the Subcommittee on Financial Institutions Supervision, Regulation and Insurance of the Committee on Banking, Finance, and Urban Affairs, House of Representatives, 101st Congress, 2nd Session, June 28, 1990 (Washington, DC: U.S. Government Printing Office, 1990), p. 1.

128. Ibid., p. 21.

129. "Penalties for White Collar Offenses: Are We Really Getting Tough on Crime?" Hearing of the Crime and Drugs Subcommittee of the Judiciary Committee, U.S. Senate, 107th Congress, 2nd session, July 11, 2002 (Washington, DC: U.S. Government Printing Office, 2002).

130. Marshall Clinard, *Corporate Corruption: The Abuse of Power* (New York: Praeger, 1990), p. 15.

131. Ibid.

132. Quoted in G. Barak, G. P. Leighton, and A. Cotton, *Class, Race, Gender & Crime*, 5th ed. (Lanham, MD: Rowman & Littlefield, 2018) p. 179.

133. Mark Huffman, "CEO of Bumble Bee Foods Indicted on Price-Fixing Charge," *Consumer Affairs*, May 17, 2018, www.consumeraffairs.com/news/ceo-of-bumble-bee-foods-indicted-on-price-fixing-charge-051718.html.

134. Cliff White. "DOJ Grants Reduced Fine Bumble Bee to Protect It from Insolvency," *Seafood Source*, July 25, 2017, www.seafoodsource.com/news/business-finance/doj-grants-reduced-fine-bumble-bee-to-protect-it-from-insolvency.

135. Sarah Krouse, "The FCC has Fined Robocallers $208 Million. It's Collected $6,790. U.S. Telecom Regulators Impose Penalties and Seek to Recoup

Ill-Gotten Gains from Robocallers, but have Struggled to Collect," *The Wall Street Journal* (Online), March 28, 2019, www.wsj.com/articles/the-fcc-has-fined-robocallers-208-million-its-collected-6-790-11553770803.

136. David Dayen, "Trump's CFPB Fines a Man $1 for Swindling Veterans, Orders Him not to Do It Again," *The Intercept*, January 26, 2019, https://theintercept.com/2019/01/26/cfpb-mulvaney-discount/.

137. Dan King, "The Dickensian Return of Debtors' Prisons," *The American Conservative*, July 19, 2018, www.theamericanconservative.com/articles/the-dickensian-return-of-debtors-prisons/.

138. Senate Permanent Subcommittee on Investigations, "HSBC Exposed U.S. Financial System to Money Laundering, Drug, Terrorist Financing Risks," July 16, 2012, www.hsgac.senate.gov/subcommittees/investigations/media/hsbc-exposed-us-finacial-system-to-money-laundering-drug-terrorist-financing-risks.

139. Christie Smythe, "HSBC Judge Approves $1.9B Drug-Money Laundering Accord," *BloombergBusiness*, July 3, 2013, www.bloomberg.com/news/articles/2013–07–02/hsbc-judge-approves-1–9b-drug-money-laundering-accord.

140. Jesse Eisinger, The *Chickenshit Club*: Why the Justice Department *Fails to Prosecute Executives* (New York: Simon & Schuster, 2017).

141. Yves Smith, "White-Collar Criminals Got Off Scot-Free After the 2008 Financial Crisis – and that Helped Fuel President Trump's Rise," Naked Capitalism, August 28, 2018, www.nakedcapitalism.com/2018/08/white-collar-criminals-got-off-scot-free-2008-financial-crisis-helped-fuel-president-trumps-rise.html; see also Jesse Eisinger. "Why Manafort and Cohen Thought They'd Get Away with It," ProPublica, August 24, 2018, www.propublica.org/article/why-manafort-and-cohen-thought-theyd-get-away-with-it.

142. Brandon L. Garrett, "Declining Corporate Prosecutions," American Criminal Law Review V57#1 2020, www.law.georgetown.edu/american-criminal-law-review/sample-page/declining-corporate-prosecutions/.

143. Tami Abdollah, "Trump Goes Easy on Corporate Criminals Despite Pushing Tougher Punishments for Common Crimes," *Business Insider*, July 25, 2018, www.businessinsider.com/trump-goes-easy-on-corporate-criminals-despite-pushing-tough-on-crime-2018-7.

144. Sheryl Stolberg and David Herszenhorn, "Bush and Candidates to Meet on Bailout," *New York Times*, September 24, 2008, www.nytimes.com/2008/09/25/business/economy/25bush.html?_r=1.

145. The phrase "Wall St Incompetence Tax" is from financial blogger Barry Ritholtz, who in September 2008 estimated it to be $5,000 to $10,000 for every man, woman, and child in the United States, http://bigpicture.typepad.com/comments/2008/09/ceo-clawbackpr.html.

146. Gregg Barak, *Theft of a Nation: Wall Street Looting and Federal Regulatory Colluding* (Lanham, MD: Rowman & Littlefield, 2012), p. 73 (quoting William Black).

147. Mary K. Ramirez and Steven Ramirez, *The Case for the Corporate Death Penalty: Restoring Law and Order on Wall Street* (New York: New York University Press, 2017), p. 2.

148. "Indirect Costs Raise Total for S&L Bailout to $480.9 Billion," *The Wall Street Journal*, July 15, 1996, p. B8A.

149. Henry N. Pontell and Kitty Calavita, "White-Collar Crime in the Savings and Loan Scandal," *The Annals of the American Academy of Political and Social Science*

525 (January 1993): 32, citing U.S. Government Accountability Office, "Failed Thrifts: Internal Control Weaknesses Create an Environment Conducive to Fraud, Insider Abuse and Related Unsafe Practices," Statement of Frederick D. Wolf, Assistant Comptroller General, before the Subcommittee on Criminal Justice, Committee on the Judiciary, House of Representatives, March 22, 1989; and U.S. Congress, House, Committee on Government Operations, "Combating Fraud, Abuse and Misconduct in the Nation's Financial Institutions," 72nd report by the Committee on Government Operations, October 13, 1989.

150. Pontell and Calavita, "White-Collar Crime in the Savings and Loan Scandal," p. 37.

151. Alan Fornham, "S&L Felons," *Fortune,* November 5, 1990, p. 92.

152. *Criminal Justice Newsletter,* December 15, 1994, p. 5.

153. *UCR-1995,* p. 36.

154. David Friedrichs, *Trusted Criminals: White Collar Crime in Contemporary Society,* 4th ed. (Belmont, CA: Wadsworth/Cengage, 2010), p. 177.

155. Stephen Pizzo and Paul Muolo, "Take the Money and Run: A Rogues' Gallery of Some Lucky S&L Thieves," *New York Times Magazine,* May 9, 1993, p. 26.

156. "When Are the Savings and Loans Crooks Going to Jail?" p. 2.

157. Kitty Calavita, Henry Pontell, and Robert Tillman, *Big Money Crime: Fraud and Politics in the Savings and Loan Crisis* (Berkeley: University of California Press, 1997), p. 131.

158. Mark Gimein, "You Bought: They Sold," *Fortune,* September 2, 2002, pp. 64–65.

159. Under the rules of special purpose vehicles (SPVs) ("independent" off-balance sheet entities), if 3 percent of the money comes from outside and is "at risk" then it is considered independent. Because the Enron deals were so large, they had a difficult time finding people to put up the other 3 percent. Enron ended up guaranteeing people substantial returns for being part of the deal, meaning the money of the outside individual was not truly at risk.

160. Allan Sloan, "Free Lessons on Corporate Hubris, Courtesy of Enron," *The Washington Post,* December 4, 2001, p. E3; see also Gimein, "You Bought: They Sold."

161. Daniel Gross, "The Crime: Slow Job Growth. A Suspect: Enron," *New York Times,* September 11, 2005, www.nytimes.com/2005/09/11/business/11view.html?_r=2.

162. David Hilzenrath, "Two Failures with a Familiar Ring: Arthur Andersen Audited Foundation, S&L that Collapsed," *The Washington Post,* December 6, 2001, p. A21.

163. Julie Creswell, "Banks on the Hot Seat," *Fortune,* September 2, 2002, p. 80.

164. In one case, the National Association of Securities Dealers fined the Salomon Smith Barney Unit of Citigroup $5 million for "materially misleading research reports" on Winstar Communications. Analysts kept a $50 target price and a "buy" rating on the company until the price of a share hit $0.14. An article for TheStreet.com notes that Salomon made $24 million in fees from Winstar. "[T]he NASD trumpets that this settlement is the third largest in NASD's history. Well, if we were the NASD and we wanted to strike fear in the hearts of brokerage firms, we would keep that little statistic a secret," George Mannes, "The Five Dumbest Things on Wall Street This Week," TheStreet.com, September 27, 2002, www.thestreet.com/story/10065679/the-five-dumbest-things-on-wall-street-this-week.html.

165. David Teather, "The Whores of Wall Street," *The Guardian*, October 2, 2002, www.guardian.co.uk/usa/story/0,12271,802926,00.html.

166. Stephen Labaton, "Now Who, Exactly, Got Us into This?" *New York Times*, February 3, 2002, www.nytimes.com/2002/02/03/business/now-who-exactly-got-us-into-this.html?pagewanted=1.

167. The particulars of the legislation and some of its limitations are from Citizen Works, http://citizenworks.org/enron/accountinglaw.php.

168. Jonathan Weisman, "Some See Cracks in Reform Law," *The Washington Post*, August 7, 2002, p. E1.

169. Carrie Johnson, "Panel Boosts Penalties for White-Collar Offenses," *The Washington Post*, January 9, 2003, p. E1.

170. Clifton Leaf, "Enough Is Enough," *Fortune*, March 18, 2002, p. 63, https://fortune.com/2002/03/18/white-collar-crime/.

171. "Three strikes" is one form of the "tough on crime" movement. Borrowing from baseball games, the law imposes mandatory sentences of 25 years to life in prison for a third felony conviction (anything with a sentence greater than one year). Its original intention was to lock up repeat violent offenders, but the popularity of "tough on crime" lead politicians to expand its application to "repeat and violent offender," which included many nonviolent offenders who filled the prisons.

172. Jeffrey Reiman and Paul Leighton, *A Tale of Two Criminals: We're Tougher on Corporate Criminals, but They Still Don't Get What They Deserve* (Boston: Allyn & Bacon, 2005), www.paulsjusticepage.com/RichGetRicher/fraud2004.htm. See also www.paulsjusticeblog.com/2008/02/getting_tough_on_corporate_crime.php.

173. Carrie Johnson, "Skilling Gets 24 Years for Fraud at Enron," *The Washington Post*, October 24, 2006, p. A1.

174. Emily Barker et al., "Progress Report," *Federal Sentencing Reporter* 20, no. 3 (February 2008): 206–210.

175. Matt Taibbi, "Wall Street's Bailout Hustle," *Rolling Stone*, February 17, 2010, www.rollingstone.com/politics/news/wall-streets-bailout-hustle-20100217.

176. Barry Ritholtz, "A Memo Found in the Street," *Barrons*, September 29, 2008, http://online.barrons.com/article/SB122246742997580395.html.

177. Ritholtz, "Nonfeasance in Financial Oversight."

178. Barry Ritholtz, "Where's the Ref?" *Forbes*, September 12, 2008, www. forbes.com/home/2008/09/12/lehman-greenspan-regulation-opinions-cx_br_0912ritholtz.html.

179. Carrie Johnson, "Prosecutors Expected to Spare Wall St. Firms," *The Washington Post*, October 3, 2008, p. D1.

180. Barry Ritholtz, "CEO Clawback Provisions in Bailout?" *The Big Picture*, September 24, 2008, www.ritholtz.com/blog/2008/09/ceo-clawback-provisions-in-the-bailout/1; Yalman Onaran and Christopher Scinta, "Lehman Files Biggest Bankruptcy After Suitors Balk (Update 1)," *Bloomberg*, September 15, 2008, http://noir.bloomberg.com/apps/news?pid=newsarchives&sid=a6cDDYU5QYyw.

181. John M. Griffin, Samuel Kruger, and Gonzalo Maturana, "Do Labor Markets Discipline? Evidence from RMBS Bankers," *Journal of Financial Economics*, 133, no. 3 (2018): 726–750, https://ssrn.com/abstract=2977741 or http://dx.doi.org/10.2139/ssrn.2977741.

182. Gretchen Morgenson and Louise Story, "In Financial Crisis, No Prosecutions of Top Figures," *New York Times,* April 14, 2011, www.nytimes.com/2011/04/14/business/14prosecute.html.
183. Eric Lichtblau, "Federal Cases of Stock Fraud Drop Sharply," *New York Times,* December 24, 2008, www.nytimes.com/2008/12/25/business/25fraud.html?r=1.
184. Richard Schmitt, "FBI Saw Threat of Loan Crisis," *Los Angeles Times,* August 25, 2008, p. A1.
185. Eric Lichtblau, David Johnson, and Ron Nixon, "FBI Struggles to Handle Financial Fraud Cases," *New York Times,* October 18, 2008, www.nytimes.com/2008/10/19/washington/19fbi.html.
186. Schmitt, "FBI Saw Threat of Loan Crisis."
187. Yves Smith, "Bill Black: The High Price of Ignorance," November 7, 2011, www.nakedcapitalism.com/2011/11/bill-black-the-high-price-of-ignorance.html.
188. Floyd Norris, "Can Mary Schapiro Save the SEC?" *New York Times,* December 17, 2008, http://norris.blogs.nytimes.com/2008/12/17/can-she-save-the-sec/.
189. *U.S. Securities and Exchange Commission v Citigroup Global Markets,* 11-cv-07387 JSR (28 November 2011), p. 11.
190. Edward Wyatt, "Promises Made, and Remade, by Firms in S.E.C. Fraud Cases," *New York Times,* November 7, 2011, www.nytimes.com/2011/11/08/business/in-sec-fraud-cases-banks-make-and-break-promises.html.
191. Sam Gustin, "Joseph Stiglitz Interview Transcript," *AOL Daily Finance,* October 20, 2010, www.dailyfinance.com/2010/10/22/joseph-stiglitz-interview-transcript/.
192. Robert H. Tilman and Henry N. Pontell, "Corporate Fraud Demands Criminal Time," *New York Times,* June 29, 2019, www.nytimes.com/2016/06/29/opinion/corporate-fraud-demands-criminal-time.html.
193. Gustin, "Joseph Stiglitz Interview Transcript."
194. Morgenson and Story, "In Financial Crisis, No Prosecutions of Top Figures."
195. Jed S. Rakoff, "Why Have No High Level Executives been Prosecuted in Connection with the Financial Crisis?" *The Big Picture,* November 12, 2013, http://ritholtz.com/2013/11/judge-rakoff-why-have-no-high-level-executives-been-prosecuted-in-connection-with-the-financial-crisis/.
196. Ramirez and Ramirez, *The Case for the Corporate Death Penalty,* p. 207.
197. See Congressman Alan Greyson's letter to FBI Director Mueller, www.ritholtz.com/blog/2010/10/grayson-to-fbi-prosecute-the-frauds/. See also Barry Ritholtz, "Why Foreclosure Fraud Is so Dangerous to Property Rights," *The Big Picture,* October 12, 2010, www.ritholtz.com/blog/2010/10/why-foreclosure-fraud-is-so-dangerous-to-property-rights/.
198. Gary Rivlin, "The Billion-Dollar Bank Heist: How the Financial Industry is Buying Off Washington—and Killing Reform," *Newsweek,* July 11, 2011, www.thedailybeast.com/newsweek/2011/07/10/the-billion-dollar-bank-heist.html.
199. Lydia Wheeler and Lisa Hagen. "Trump Signs '2-for-1' Order to Reduce Regulations," *The Hill,* January 30, 2017, https://thehill.com/homenews/administration/316839-trump-to-sign-order-reducing-regulations.
200. James Stewart, "As a Watchdog Starves, Wall Street is Tossed a Bone," *New York Times,* July 15, 2011, www.nytimes.com/2011/07/16/business/budget-cuts-tosec-reduce-its-effectiveness.html?_r=3&ref=business.

201. Barry Ritholtz, 2010, "SEC: Defective by Design?" *The Big Picture,* March 18, 2010, www.ritholtz.com/blog/2010/03/sec-defective-by-design/.
202. Edward Wyatt, SEC, "Hurt by Disarray in Its Books," *New York Times,* February 2, 2011, www.nytimes.com/2011/02/03/business/03sec.html?_r=1&hpw.
203. Ramirez and Ramirez, *The Case for the Corporate Death Penalty,* p. 218.
204. Ibid., p. 204.
205. U.S. resident population in 2017 was 325,719,000, *Stat-Abs-2018,* Table 2.

CHAPTER 4

To the Vanquished Belong the Spoils

Who Is Winning the Losing War Against Crime?

*In every case the laws are made by the ruling party in its own interest;
a democracy makes democratic laws, a despot autocratic ones, and
so on. By making these laws they define as "just" for their subjects
whatever is for their own interest, and they call anyone who breaks
them a "wrongdoer" and punish him accordingly.*

—Thrasymachus, Plato's *Republic*

*When plunder becomes a way of life for a group of men living together
in society, they create for themselves in the course of time a legal
system that authorizes it and a moral code that glorifies it.*

—Frederic Bastiat, *The Law*

Chapter 4 of *The Rich Get Richer* examines why a failing criminal justice system that neither protects society nor achieves justice is allowed to continue. The criminal justice system actually fails in three ways: It fails (1) to substantially reduce crime; (2) to treat as crimes harmful acts of the well-off; and (3) to eliminate bias against the poor in arrest, conviction, and sentencing. This chapter argues that this happens because the current system's failure produces benefits for the wealthy in America. This is due not to a conspiracy but to historical inertia—the persistence of a criminal justice system dating from preindustrial times, which does not recognize many of the harmful acts of the well-off. A key idea here is that the criminal justice system contributes to an *ideology,* a widely held set of false or misleading beliefs that justify the status quo and its inequalities. The criminal justice system does this by conveying the message that the poor are the worst threat to society and that their criminality is the result of individual failings rather than social inequities.

WHY IS THE CRIMINAL JUSTICE SYSTEM FAILING?

The streams of our argument flow together at this point in a question: *Why is it happening?* We have shown how it is no accident that "the offender at the end of the road in prison is likely to be a member of the lowest social and economic groups in the country."[1] We have shown that this is not an accurate group portrait of who threatens society—it is a picture of whom the criminal justice system *selects* for arrest and imprisonment from among those who threaten society—an image distorted by the shape of the criminal justice carnival mirror. This much we have seen, and now we want to know: *Why is the criminal justice system allowed to function in a fashion that neither protects society nor achieves justice? Why is the criminal justice system failing?*

Answering these questions will require looking at who benefits from this failure and who suffers from it. We will argue that the rich and powerful in the United States—those who derive the greatest advantage from the persistence of the social and economic system as it is currently organized—reap benefits from the failure of the criminal justice system. However, this analysis is not a "conspiracy theory."

A conspiracy theory would argue that the rich and the powerful, seeing the benefits to be derived from the failure of criminal justice, consciously set out to use their wealth and power to make it fail. There are many problems with such a theory. First, it is virtually impossible to prove. A conspiracy is only successful if it is kept secret. Thus, evidence for a conspiracy would be as difficult to obtain as the conspiracy were successful. Second, conspiracy theories strain credibility precisely because the degree of secrecy they would require seems virtually impossible in a society as open and fractious as our own. If there is a "ruling elite" in the United States that comprises a group as small as the richest *one-thousandth of 1 percent* of the population, it would still be made up of more than 3,000 people. To think that a conspiracy to make the criminal justice system fail in the way it does could be kept secret among this number of people in a country like ours is unbelievable. Third, conspiracy theories are not plausible because they do not correspond to the way most people act most of the time. Although there are plenty of conscious misstatements and manipulation by interest groups and politicians, most people most of the time sincerely believe that what they are doing is right. Whether this is a tribute to human beings' creative capacities to rationalize what they do or merely a matter of their shortsightedness, it seems a fact. Fourth, a conspiracy is something that works in secret while the decisions we have talked about are largely public: the laws establishing penalties for crimes in the streets and crimes in the suites; the laws, budgets, and strategies aimed at solving "the crime problem"; and the stances of politicians about regulating and policing business misconduct.

For all these reasons, it is not plausible that so fateful and harmful a policy as the failure of criminal justice could be intentionally maintained by the rich and powerful. Rather, we need an explanation that is compatible with believing that policy makers, on the whole, are doing what they sincerely believe is right.

To understand how the Pyrrhic defeat theory explains the current shape of our failing criminal justice policy, note that this failure is really *three* failures that work together. First, there is the failure to implement policies that stand a good chance of reducing crime and the harm it causes. (This was argued in Chapter 1.) Second, there is the failure to treat as crimes the harmful acts of the rich and powerful. (This is the first of the hypotheses listed in Chapter 2, and confirmed by the evidence presented there.) Third, there is the failure to eliminate economic bias in the criminal justice system so that the poor continue to have a substantially greater chance than better-off people of being arrested, charged, convicted, and penalized for committing the acts that are treated as crimes. (This corresponds to the second through fourth hypotheses listed in Chapter 2, and is confirmed by the evidence presented in Chapter 3.)

The effect of the first failure is that there remains a large amount of crime—even if crime rates dip largely as a result of factors outside the control of the criminal justice system, such as the declining use of crack cocaine and the reduction of lead in the environment. The effect of the second failure is that the acts treated as crimes are those done predominantly by the poor. The effect of the third failure is that the individuals who are arrested and convicted for crimes are predominantly poor people. The effect of the three failures working together is that we are largely unprotected against the harmful acts of the well-off, while at the same time we are confronted on the streets and in our homes with a real and large threat of crime, and in the courts and prisons with a large and visible population of poor criminals. And lest it be thought that the public does not feel threatened by crime, consider that polls shows that, though crime has generally declined since the early 1990s, for most of those years Americans were more likely to believe that crime was increasing rather than decreasing. During more than 20 years of substantially declining crime rates, in only one year (2001) did a higher percentage say crime was decreasing (43%) rather than increasing (41%).[2]

The Pyrrhic defeat theory aims to explain the *persistence* of this failing criminal justice policy rather than its origins. It is not the origin of criminal justice policy and practices that is puzzling. The focus on one-on-one harm reflects the main ways in which people harmed each other in the days before large-scale industrialization; the refusal to implement policies that might reduce crime (such as legalization of drugs or amelioration of poverty) reflects a defensive and punitive response to crime that is natural and understandable, even if neither noble nor farsighted. The existence of economic bias in the criminal justice system reflects the real economic and political inequalities that characterize American society. What is puzzling, then, is not why these policies came to be, but why they persist in the face of their continued failure to achieve either security or justice. The explanation we offer for this persistence is called "historical inertia."

The historical inertia explanation argues that current criminal justice policy persists because it fails in two ways that do not give rise to an effective demand for change. First, this failing system provides benefits for those with the power to make changes, while it imposes costs on those without such power. Second, because the criminal justice system shapes the public's conception of what is dangerous, it creates the impression that the harms it is fighting are *the real threats* to society—thus, even when people see that the system is less than a roaring success, they only demand more of the same: police cracking down on crime and sending criminals to prison.

Consider first the benefits that the system provides for those with wealth and power. We have argued that the triple failure of criminal justice policy diverts attention from the harmful noncriminal acts of the well-off, and confronts us in our homes and on our streets with a real, substantial threat of crime, and in the courts and prisons with a large and visible population of poor criminals. This conveys a vivid image to the American people, namely, that *there is a real threat to our lives and limbs, and it is a threat from the poor*. This image deflects the public's attention away from the harmful things done by rich people, and it carries an *ideological message* that serves to protect their wealth and privilege.

Ideology involves ideas that distort reality in ways that hide society's injustices and thus secure uncritical allegiance to the existing social order. The people who have little far outnumber those who have plenty, so the wealthy need the rest of society to believe that they are not being exploited or treated unfairly, and that the existing distribution of wealth is about the best that human beings can create. The criminal justice system plays a role in promoting these beliefs. Put simply, its message is this:

- The threat to law-abiding Middle America comes from below them on the economic ladder, not above them.
- The poor are morally defective, and thus their poverty is their own fault, not a symptom of social or economic injustice.

The effect of this message is to create (or reinforce) in Americans fear of, and hostility toward, the poor. It leads Americans to ignore the ways in which they are injured and robbed by the acts of the affluent, and leads them to demand tough doses of "law and order" aimed mainly at the lower classes. Most important, it nudges Americans toward a *conservative* defense of American society with its large disparities of wealth, power, and opportunity—and nudges them away from a *progressive* demand for equality and a more equitable distribution of wealth and power.

On the other hand, but equally important, is that those who are mainly victimized by the failure to reduce our high rates of street crime are the poor themselves. The people who are hurt the most by the failure of the criminal justice system are those with the least power to change it. As Table 4.1 shows, rates of victimization for violent and serious violent crime are substantially

TABLE 4.1   Rate of Violent Victimization and Serious Violent Victimizations, by Demographic Characteristics of Victims, 2017

	Family Income			
	Less than $10,000	$10,000 to $14,999	$35,000 to $49,999	$75,000 or More
Violent victimization	49.8	21.9	18.8	14.6
Serious violent victimization	22	8.3	7.6	4.5

Source: BJS, *Criminal Victimization, 2017*, December 2018, NCJ 252472, Table 8

higher for the poorest segment of the population and drop dramatically as we ascend the economic ladder.

That pattern is not new and applies to property crime as well. The Brookings Institution notes,

> In 2008, the latest year for which data are available, the victimization rate for all personal crimes among individuals with family incomes of less than $15,000 was over three times the rate of those with family incomes of $75,000 or more.[3]

The difference in the rates of property-crime victimization between rich and poor understates the difference in the harms that result. The poor are far less likely than the affluent to have insurance against theft, and because they have little to start with, what they lose to theft takes a much deeper bite out of their ability to meet their basic needs. Also, the various noncriminal harms documented in Chapter 2 (occupational hazards, pollution, poverty, and so on) fall more harshly on workers and those at the bottom of society than on those at the top.

Those who suffer most from the failure to reduce street crime (and the failure to treat noncriminal harms as crimes) are not in a position to change criminal justice policy. Those who are in a position to change the policy are not seriously harmed by its failure—indeed, they actually benefit from that failure because of the ideological messages. Note that we have not said that criminal justice policy is created in order to achieve this distribution of benefits and burdens. Instead, the claim is that the criminal justice policy that has emerged piecemeal over time and usually with the best of intentions happens to produce this distribution of benefits and burdens—with the result that there is no inclination to change the criminal justice system among people with the power to do so. Moreover, because the criminal justice system shapes the public's conception of what is dangerous, it effectively limits the public's conception of how to protect itself to demanding more of the same. Thus, though it fails, it persists.

Before proceeding, it is worth noting that private prisons and elements of the larger "criminal justice-industrial complex" make money from the system as it is, so they consciously lobby to protect and improve their profits. The National Academy of Sciences panel on incarceration noted that

> by the mid-1990s, the new economic interests—including private prison companies, prison guards' unions, and the suppliers of everything from bonds for new prison construction to Taser stun guns—were playing an important role in maintaining and sustaining the incarceration increase.[4]

The nature of these vested interests can most clearly be seen with private prisons that are for-profit businesses in which commercial firms are contracted to build and/or manage government prisons. "Get tough" policy initiatives such as mandatory minimum sentences and the "three-strikes-and-you're-out" statutes led to the rapid and enormous increase in the U.S. prison population over the past 40 years at the same time as politicians promised tax cuts. That growth placed strains on government budgets that gave governments an incentive to hire out their prison facilities to private contractors, even though cost savings were exaggerated or non-existant.[5] The American Legislative Exchange Council, an organization that lobbies state legislators and that received contributions from Corrections Corporation of America (now CoreCivic), said proudly that lawmakers on its crime task force have been actively leading in the drive for more incarceration in the states and paving the way for privatization.[6] The result is 121,420 inmates in private prisons in 2017, and although that number has been declining slightly, private prison contractors are expanding their operations into immigration detention centers and various aspects of community corrections.[7]

Private prisons are a multi-billion-dollar-a-year business, and the two largest private prison firms are traded on the stock exchange. As such, they are required to discuss "risk factors" in their business in their Securities and Exchange Commission filings, and the GEO Group's annual report notes:

> The demand for our correctional and detention facilities and services could be adversely affected by changes in existing criminal or immigration laws, crime rates in jurisdictions in which we operate, the relaxation of criminal or immigration enforcement efforts, leniency in conviction, sentencing..., and the decriminalization of... drugs.[8]

CCA's annual report includes similar language and adds as factors that may limit growth: "Legislation that could lower minimum sentences for some non-violent crimes and make more inmates eligible for early release based on good behavior."[9]

In short, a multi-billion-dollar industry has a powerful economic interest in maintaining existing harsh policies. In *Punishment for Sale*, Donna Selman and Paul Leighton critique the growth of incarceration and note that private prisons were born from an incarceration binge "that has fostered injustice—and that these entities, pursuing their own economic interests rather than the public good, perpetuate policies causing injustice because they profit from them."[10] Beyond private prisons, the prison-industrial complex includes companies that regard the $80 billion in corrections expenditures each year "not as a burden on American taxpayers but as a lucrative market."[11]

The term prison-industrial complex is a nod to the "military-industrial complex," of which President Eisenhower warned in his farewell address. Eisenhower's concern was that a large and permanent defense industry would have a negative effect on public policy.[12] Likewise, the expansion of the criminal justice system, combined with the involvement of Wall Street investment banks, created a similar critical mass that can distort policy in its own interests. Adding to the prison- and larger criminal justice-industrial complex are politicians who fan the public fear of crime to collect votes, as well as media that have dramatically expanded sensational crime coverage for advertising revenue, and economically devastated regions that saw prison construction as economic development.

Thus far in this book we have been pointing out how *the rich get richer WHILE the poor get prison,* but the privatization movement and analysis of the criminal justice-industrial complex point to how *the rich get richer BECAUSE the poor get prison!*

Our argument in the remainder of this chapter turns from considering the direct influence of big business to examining ideology. The following section, titled "The Poverty of Criminals and the Crime of Poverty," spells out in detail the content of the ideological message broadcast by the failure of the criminal justice system. The section titled "Ideology, or How to Fool Enough of the People Enough of the Time" discusses the *nature* of ideology in general and the *need* for it in America. For those who doubt that our legal system could function in such questionable ways, we present here evidence on how the criminal justice system has been used in the past to protect the rich and powerful against those who would challenge their privileges or their policies. These sections, then, flesh out the historical inertia explanation of the failure of criminal justice by showing the ideological benefits that the failure yields and to whom.

Ultimately, the test of the argument in this chapter is whether it provides a plausible explanation for the failure of criminal justice and draws the arguments of the previous chapters together into a coherent theory of contemporary criminal justice policy and practice.

THE POVERTY OF CRIMINALS AND THE CRIME OF POVERTY

Criminal justice is a very visible part of the American scene. As fact and fiction, countless images of crime and the struggle against it assail our senses daily, even hourly. Newspapers, TV, radio, blogs, and social media are filled with criminal justice stories. It is as if we live in an embattled city, besieged by the forces of crime and bravely defended by the forces of the law, and as we go about our daily tasks, we are always conscious of the war raging not very far away. News brings us frequent reports from the "front." Between reports, we are vividly reminded of the stakes and the desperateness of the battle by fictionalized portrayals of the struggle between the enforcers of the law and the breakers of the law. Media paint offenders as "animalistic, irrational and innate predators," and swell their numbers "from a rare offender in the real world to a common, ever-present image."[13]

If we take detective, police, and other criminal justice-related programs and add to this the news accounts, the panel discussions, the movies, the novels, the video games, the comic books, and the TV cartoon shows, as well as the political speeches about crime, there can be no doubt that, as fact or fantasy, criminal justice is vividly present in the imaginations of most Americans.

This is no accident. Everyone can relate to criminal justice in personal and emotional terms. Everyone has some fear of crime, and as we saw in Chapter 3, just about everyone has committed some crime. Everyone knows the primitive satisfaction of seeing justice done and the evildoers served up their just deserts. Furthermore, in reality or in fiction, criminal justice is naturally dramatic. To identify with the struggle against crime is to expand one's experience vicariously to include the danger, the suspense, the triumphs, and the meaningfulness—in a word, the drama—often missing in ordinary life. Unsurprisingly, Americans have a seemingly bottomless appetite for the endless repetition, in only slightly altered form, of the same theme: the struggle of the forces of law against the forces of crime. Criminal justice has a firm grip on the imaginations of Americans and is thus in a unique position to convey a message to Americans with drama and conviction.

Let us now look at this message in detail. Our task falls naturally into two parts. There is an ideological message supportive of the status quo built into *any* criminal justice system by its very nature. Even if the criminal justice system were not failing, even if it were not biased against the poor, it would still—by its very nature—broadcast a message supportive of established institutions. This is the *implicit ideology of criminal justice.* Beyond this, there is an additional ideological message conveyed by the *failure* of the system and by its *biased* concentration on the poor. This is the *bonus of bias.*

The Implicit Ideology of Criminal Justice

Any criminal justice system like ours conveys a subtle yet powerful message in support of established institutions. It does this for two interconnected reasons. First, it concentrates on *individual* wrongdoers. This means that *it diverts our attention away from our institutions, away from consideration of whether our institutions themselves are wrong or unjust or indeed "criminal."*

Second, the criminal law is put forth as the *minimum neutral ground rules* for any social living. We are taught that no society can exist without rules against theft and violence, and thus the criminal law seems to be politically neutral: the minimum requirements for *any* society, the minimum obligations that every individual owes his or her fellows to make social life of any decent sort possible. Because the criminal law protects the established institutions (the prevailing economic arrangements are protected by laws against theft, and so on), attacks on those established institutions become equivalent to violations of the minimum requirements for any social life at all. In effect, the criminal law enshrines the established institutions as equivalent to the minimum requirements for *any* decent social existence—and it brands the individual who attacks those institutions as one who has declared war on *all* organized society and who must, therefore, be met with the weapons of war. Let us look more closely at this process.

What is the effect of focusing on individual guilt? Not only does this divert our attention from the possible evils in our institutions, but it also puts forth half the problem of justice as if it were the *whole* problem. To focus on individual guilt is to ask whether the individual citizen has fulfilled his or her obligations to his or her fellow citizens. *It is to look away from the issue of whether the fellow citizens have fulfilled their obligations to him or her.* To look only at individual responsibility is to look away from social responsibility. Writing about her stint as a "story analyst" for a prime-time TV "real crime" show based on videotapes of actual police busts, Debra Seagal describes the way focus on individual criminals deflects attention away from the social context of crime and how television reproduces this effect in millions of homes daily:

> By the time our 9 million viewers flip on their tubes, we've reduced fifty or sixty hours of mundane and compromising video into short, action-packed segments of tantalizing, crack-filled, dope-dealing, junkie-busting cop culture. How easily we downplay the pathos of the suspect; how cleverly we breeze past the complexities that cast doubt on the very system that has produced the criminal activity in the first place.[14]

Seagal's description illustrates as well how a television program that shows nothing but videos of actual events can distort reality by selecting and recombining pieces of real events.

A study of 69 TV crime dramas finds that fictional presentations of homicide focus on individual motivations and ignore social conditions: "Television crime dramas portray these events as specific psychological episodes in the characters' lives and little, if any, effort is made to connect them to basic social institutions or the nature of society within which they occur."[15] Criminology, too, generally focuses on individual- and micro-level explanations of crime, while structural and macro-level theories are "the road not taken."[16]

To look only at individual criminality is to close one's eyes to social injustice and to close one's ears to the question of whether our social institutions have exploited or violated the individual. Criminologists James Unnever and Shaun Gabbidon in their important book *A Theory of African American Offending* link black criminality with a "long history of public dishonor and ritualized humiliation"—including by the criminal justice system—due to racism.[17] As a result, African Americans are less likely to have respect for the law and weaker bonds with conventional institutions. Focusing only on individual responsibility obscures the contribution of racism to African American criminality.

Justice is a two-way street—but criminal justice is a one-way street. Individuals owe obligations to their fellow citizens because their fellow citizens owe obligations to them. Criminal justice focuses on the first and looks away from the second. *Thus, by focusing on individual responsibility for crime, the criminal justice system effectively acquits the existing social order of any charge of injustice!*

This is an extremely important bit of ideological alchemy. It stems from the fact that the same act can be criminal or not, unjust or just, depending on the circumstances in which it takes place. Killing someone is ordinarily a crime, but if it is in self-defense or to stop a deadly crime, it is not. Taking property by force is usually a crime, but if the taking is retrieving what has been stolen, then no crime has been committed. Robin Hood's thefts from the rich to give to the poor are seen as heroic and just even though the legal system run by the rich declared him a criminal. Acts of violence are ordinarily crimes, but if the violence is provoked by the threat of violence or by oppressive conditions, then, like the Boston Tea Party,[18] what is ordinarily called criminal (even terrorist) is celebrated as just.

This means that when we call an act a crime, *we are also making an implicit judgment about the conditions in response to which it takes place.* When we call an act a crime, we are saying that the conditions in which it occurs are not themselves criminal or deadly or oppressive or so unjust as to make an extreme response reasonable or justified or noncriminal. This means that when the system holds an individual responsible for a crime, *it implicitly conveys the message that the social conditions in which the crime occurred are not responsible for the crime,* that they are not so unjust as to make a violent response to them excusable.

Judges are prone to hold that an individual's responsibility for a violent crime is diminished if it was provoked by something that might lead a "reasonable person" to respond violently, and that criminal responsibility is eliminated if the act was in response to conditions so intolerable that any "reasonable person" would have been likely to respond in the same way. In this vein, the law acquits those who kill or injure in self-defense and treats leniently those who commit a crime when confronted with extreme provocation. By this same logic, when we hold an individual completely responsible for a crime, we are saying that the conditions in which it occurred are such that a "reasonable person" should find them tolerable. Thus, by focusing on individual responsibility for crimes, *the criminal justice system broadcasts the message that the social order itself is reasonable and not intolerably unjust* due to inequality of opportunity, racism, or other forms of discrimination, or the widespread poverty that our rich nation tolerates. By focusing moral condemnation on individuals, the criminal justice system deflects it away from the social order that may have either violated the individual's rights or dignity or pushed him or her to the brink of crime. This sends the message that the justice of our institutions is obvious, not to be doubted.

The second way in which a criminal justice system always conveys an implicit ideology arises from the presumption that the criminal law is nothing but the politically neutral minimum requirements of any decent social life. As already suggested, this presumption transforms the prevailing social order into justice incarnate and all violations of the prevailing order into injustice incarnate. This process is so obvious that it may be easily missed. Consider, for example, the law against theft. It does seem to be one of the minimum requirements of social living. As long as there is scarcity, any society—capitalist or socialist—will need rules to deter individuals from taking what does not belong to them. However, the law against theft is not simply against theft, it is *a law against stealing what individuals presently own*. Such a law has the effect of making the present distribution of property part of the criminal law.

Because stealing is a violation of the law, this means that the present distribution of property becomes the implicit standard of justice against which criminal deviations are measured. Because criminal law is thought of as the minimum requirements of any social life, the result is that the present distribution of property is treated as the equivalent of the minimum requirements of *any* social life. The criminal who would alter the present distribution of property becomes someone who is declaring war on all organized society.

This suggests yet another way in which the criminal justice system conveys an ideological message in support of the established society. By blaming the individual for a crime, society is acquitted of the charge of *complicity* in that crime. This is a point worth developing because many observers have maintained that modern competitive societies, such as our own, have structural features that tend to generate crime. Thus, holding the individual responsible for his or her crime serves the function of taking the rest of society off the hook for their role in sustaining and benefiting from social arrangements that produce crime. Let us take a brief detour to look more closely at this process.

Cloward and Ohlin argued in their book, *Delinquency and Opportunity*,[19] that many crimes are the result of the discrepancy between social goals and the legitimate opportunities available for achieving them. The same point is basic to "strain theory," including variations like Messner and Rosenfeld's *Crime and the American Dream*.[20] Simply put, in our society everyone is encouraged to be a success—usually defined in terms of possessing wealth—but the legitimate avenues to success are open only to some. The conventional wisdom of our free-enterprise democracy is that anyone can be a success if he or she works hard. Thus, if one is not a success, it is because of one's own shortcomings, like laziness. On the other hand, opportunities to achieve success are not equally open to all. Access to the best schools and the best jobs is effectively closed to all but a few of the poor, and becomes more available only as one goes up the economic ladder. The result is that many are called, but few are chosen. Many who have accepted the belief in the importance of success, and the belief that achieving success is a result of individual ability, must cope with feelings of frustration and failure that result when they find the avenues to success closed. Cloward and Ohlin argue that one method of coping with these stresses is to develop alternative avenues to success. Crime is such an alternative avenue.

Crime is a means by which people who believe in the American dream pursue it when they find the traditional routes barred. It is plain to see that the goals pursued by most criminals are as American as apple pie. One of the reasons that American moviegoers enjoy gangster films—movies in which outlaws like Al Capone, Bonnie and Clyde, or Butch Cassidy and the Sundance Kid[21] are the heroes (as distinct from police and detective films, whose heroes are defenders of the law)—is that even when we deplore the hero's methods, we identify with his or her notion of success because it is ours as well, and we admire the courage and cunning displayed in achieving that success.

It is important to note that the discrepancy between success goals and legitimate opportunities in America is not an aberration. It is a structural feature of modern, competitive, industrialized society, a feature from which many benefits flow. Cloward and Ohlin write that

> a crucial problem in the industrial world is to locate and train the most talented persons in every generation, irrespective of the vicissitudes of birth, to occupy technical work roles. Since we cannot know in advance who can best fulfill the requirements of the various occupational roles, the matter is presumably settled through the process of competition. But how can men throughout the social order be motivated to participate in this competition?

One of the ways in which the industrial society attempts to solve this problem is by defining success goals as potentially accessible to all, regardless of race, creed, or socioeconomic position.[22]

Because these universal goals encourage a competition to select the best, there are necessarily fewer openings than seekers. Because those who achieve success are in a particularly good position to exploit their success to make access for their own children easier, the competition is rigged to work in favor of the middle and upper classes. As a result, "many lower-class persons are the victims of a contradiction between the goals toward which they have been led to orient themselves and socially structured means of striving for these goals."[23] "[The poor] experience... a desperation made all the more poignant by their exposure to a cultural ideology in which failure to orient oneself upward is a moral defect."[24] The outcome is predictable: "Under these conditions, there is an acute pressure to depart from institutional norms and to adopt illegitimate alternatives."[25]

This means that the very way in which our society is structured to draw out the talents and energies that go into producing our high standard of living has a costly side effect: *It produces crime.* By holding individuals responsible for this crime, those who enjoy that high standard of living can have their cake and eat it too. They can reap the benefits of the competition for success and escape the responsibility of paying for the costs of the competition.

William Bonger, the Dutch Marxist criminologist, maintained that competitive capitalism produces egotistic motives and undermines compassion for the misfortunes of others and thus makes human beings literally *more capable of crime*—more capable of preying on their fellows without moral inhibition or remorse—than earlier cultures that emphasized cooperation rather than competition.[26] Here again, the criminal justice system relieves those who benefit from the American economic system of the costs of that system. By holding criminals morally and individually responsible for their crimes, we can forget that the motives that lead to crime—the drive for success, linked with the beliefs that success means outdoing others and that violence is an acceptable way of achieving one's goals—are the *same motives* that powered the drive across the American continent and that continue to fuel the engine of America's prosperity. (Appendix I presents the Marxian critique of criminal justice and spells out the Marxian understanding of the motives and moral status of criminals.)

Political economist David Gordon maintains "that nearly all crimes in capitalist societies represent perfectly *rational* responses to the structure of institutions upon which capitalist societies are based."[27] Like Bonger, Gordon believes that capitalism tends to provoke crime in all economic strata. This is so because most crime is motivated by a desire for property or money and is an understandable way of coping with the pressures of inequality, competition, and insecurity, all of which are essential ingredients of capitalism. In capitalism, Gordon writes,

> Individuals must fend for themselves, finding the best available opportunities to provide for themselves and their families. Driven by the fear of economic insecurity and by a competitive desire to gain some of the goods unequally distributed throughout the society, many individuals will eventually become "criminals."[28]

To the extent that a society makes crime a reasonable alternative for a large number of its members from all classes, that society is itself not very reasonably or humanely organized and bears some degree of responsibility for the crime it encourages. Because the criminal law is put forth as the minimum requirements that can be expected of any "reasonable person," its enforcement amounts to a denial of the real nature of the social order to which Gordon and the others point. Here again, by blaming the individual criminal, the criminal justice system serves implicitly but dramatically to acquit the society of its criminality.

The Bonus of Bias

We now consider the additional ideological bonus derived from the criminal justice system's bias against the poor. This bonus is a product of the association of crime and poverty in the popular mind. This association, the merging of the "criminal classes" and the "lower classes" into the "dangerous classes," was not invented in America. The word *villain* is derived from the Latin *villanus*, which means a farm servant.[29] In this respect, our present criminal justice system is heir to a long tradition of associating crime with the lower classes.

The value of this association was already seen when we explored the average citizen's concept of the Typical Criminal and the Typical Crime. It is quite obvious that throughout the great mass of Middle America, far more fear and hostility are directed toward the predatory acts of the poor than toward the predatory acts of the rich. Compare the fate of politicians in recent history who call for income redistribution, and any sort of regulation of business that would make it better to serve American social goals with that of politicians who erect their platform on a call for a smarter and tougher criminal justice system—and consider this in light of the real dangers posed by corporate crime and "business as usual."

It seems clear that Americans have been effectively deceived as to what are the greatest dangers to their lives, limbs, and possessions. That Americans continue to tolerate the comparatively gentle treatment meted out to white-collar criminals, corporate price fixers, industrial polluters, and political-influence peddlers[30] while being willing to support policies that lock up more poor people indicates the degree to which they harbor illusions as to who most threatens them. The vivid portrayal of the poor—and, of course, blacks—as hovering birds of prey waiting for the opportunity to snatch away the workers' meager gains serves also to deflect opposition away from the upper classes. A politician who promises (through racially coded language) to keep communities free of minorities and prisons and detention centers full of them can get votes, even if these policies amount to continuation of the favored treatment of the rich at that community's expense.[31]

The most important "bonus" derived from the identification of crime and poverty is that it paints the picture that the threat to decent Middle Americans comes from those below them on the economic ladder not from those above. For this to happen, the system must not only identify crime and poverty *but also fail enough in the fight to reduce crime so that crime remains a real threat.* Doing this deflects the fear and discontent of Middle Americans away from the wealthy.

There are other bonuses as well. For instance, if the criminal justice system sends out a message that bestows legitimacy on the present distribution of property, its dramatic impact is greatly enhanced if the violator of the present arrangements is without property. The crimes of the well-to-do "redistribute" property among the wealthy, and–in the cases of financial crisis–to the wealthy. They do not pose a symbolic challenge to the larger system in which some have much and many have little or nothing. If the criminal threat can be portrayed as coming from the poor, then the punishment of the poor criminal becomes a morality play which dramatically affirms the sanctity and legitimacy of the system in which some have plenty and most have little or nothing.

There is yet another bonus for the powerful in America produced by the identification of crime and poverty. It might be thought that the identification of crime and poverty would produce sympathy for the criminals. But, in fact, it produces or at least reinforces the reverse: *hostility toward the poor.* There is little evidence that Americans are very sympathetic to poor criminals. Very few Americans believe poverty to be a cause of crime (6 percent of those questioned in a 1981 survey, although 21 percent thought unemployment was a cause—in keeping with our general blindness to class, these questions are not even found in recent surveys). Other surveys find that most Americans believe that courts do not deal harshly enough with criminals (58 percent of those questioned in 2014), and that the death penalty should be used for convicted murderers, most of whom are poor (56 percent of those questioned in 2018).[32]

Our view is that, because the criminal justice system, in fact and fiction, deals with *individual legal and moral guilt,* the association of crime with poverty does not mitigate the belief in individual moral responsibility for crime. It does the reverse: It generates the association of poverty and individual moral failing and, thus, *the belief that poverty itself is a sign of poor or weak character.* The clearest evidence that Americans hold this belief is to be found in the fact that attempts to aid the poor are regarded as acts of charity rather than as acts of justice. Our welfare system has all the demeaning attributes of an institution designed to give handouts to the undeserving and none of the dignity of an institution designed to make good on our responsibilities to our fellow human beings. If we acknowledged the degree to which our economic and social institutions themselves breed poverty and maintain economic inequality, we would have to recognize our own responsibilities toward the poor. If we can convince ourselves that the poor are poor because of their own shortcomings, particularly moral shortcomings and bad choices, then we need acknowledge no such responsibility to the poor. Indeed, we can go further and pat ourselves on the back for our generosity in handing out the little that we do, and, of course, we can make our recipients go through all the indignities that mark them as the undeserving objects of our benevolence. By and large, this has been the way in which Americans have dealt with their poor.[33]

Obviously, no ideological message could be more supportive of the present social and economic order than the association of crime and poverty. It suggests that poverty is a sign of individual failing, not a symptom of social or economic injustice. It tells us loud and clear that massive poverty in the midst of abundance is not a sign pointing toward the need for fundamental changes in our social and economic institutions. It suggests that the poor are poor because they deserve to be poor, or at least because they lack the strength of character to overcome poverty. When the poor are seen to be poor in character, then economic poverty coincides with moral poverty and the economic order coincides with the moral order. As if a divine hand guided its workings, capitalism leads to everyone getting what he or she morally deserves!

If this association takes root, then when the poor individual is found guilty of a crime, the criminal justice system acquits the society of its responsibility not only for the crime *but for poverty as well.*

With this, the ideological message of criminal justice is complete. The poor rather than the rich are seen as the enemies of the majority of decent Americans. Our social and economic institutions are held to be responsible for neither crime nor poverty and thus in need of no fundamental questioning or reform. The poor are poor because they are poor of character. The economic order and the moral order are one. To the extent that this message sinks in, the wealthy can rest easily—even if they cannot sleep the sleep of the just.

We can now understand why the criminal justice system is allowed to create the image of crime as the work of the poor and to fail to reduce it, so that the threat of crime remains real and credible. The result is ideological alchemy of the highest order. The poor are seen as the real threat to decent society. The ultimate sanctions of criminal justice dramatically sanctify the present social and economic order, and *the poverty of criminals makes poverty itself an individual moral crime!*

Such are the ideological fruits of a losing war against crime whose distorted image is reflected in the criminal justice carnival mirror and widely broadcast to reach the minds and imaginations of America.

IDEOLOGY, OR HOW TO FOOL ENOUGH OF THE PEOPLE ENOUGH OF THE TIME

What Is Ideology?

The view that the laws of a state or nation are made to serve the interests of those with power, rather than to promote the well-being of the whole society, is not a new discovery. It is a doctrine with a pedigree even older than Christianity. Writing during the fourth century BCE, virtually at the dawn of Western thought, Plato expressed this view through the words of Thrasymachus.[34] A more contemporary and more systematic formulation of the idea is found in the works of Karl Marx, written during the nineteenth century, not long after the dawn of Western industrialism. Marx (and Engels) observed that the bourgeoisie—the class of owners of businesses and factories, the class of capitalists—has "conquered for itself, in the modern representative State, exclusive political sway. The executive of the modern State is but a committee for managing the common affairs of the whole bourgeoisie."[35]

Anyone who thinks this is a ridiculous idea ought to look at the backgrounds of our political leaders. The vast majority of the president's cabinet, the administrators of the federal regulatory agencies, and the members of the two houses of Congress come from the ranks of business or are lawyers who serve business. Many still maintain their business ties or law practices, with no sense of a conflict of interest with their political role.[36] Even those who start from humble beginnings are usually quite rich by the time they finally make it into office. If either Thrasymachus or Marx is right, there *is* no conflict with their political role because that role is to protect and promote the interests of business.

It is clear that the most powerful criminal justice policy makers come from the have-plenties not from the have-littles. It is no surprise that legislators and judges—those who make the laws that define criminality and those who interpret those laws—are predominantly members of the upper classes, if not at birth then surely by the time they take office.

Further, there is considerable evidence that the American criminal justice system has been used throughout its history in rather unsubtle ways to protect the interests of the powerful against those of the lower classes and political dissenters. The use of the FBI and local police forces to repress dissent by discrediting, harassing, and undermining dissident individuals and groups has been abundantly revealed. The FBI, often with active cooperation or tacit consent of local police, has engaged in literally hundreds of illegal burglaries of the offices of law-abiding, left-wing political parties,[37] and in political sabotage against the Black Panthers (e.g., "a Catholic priest, the Rev. Frank Curran, became the target of FBI operations because he permitted the Black Panthers to use his church for serving breakfasts to ghetto children").[38] It conducted a campaign to discredit the late Martin Luther King Jr. ("the FBI secretly categorized King as a 'Communist' months before it ever started investigating him").[39] Directors of the FBI have said that the bureau is "truly sorry" for these past abuses and that they are over. Later reports indicate that abuses have continued.[40] Police arrested and discharged pepper spray in the faces of nonviolent Occupy Wall Street protesters.[41] They have done aerial and other types of surveillance against the Black Lives Matter movement at least since 2014,[42] and increased surveillance of Native American activists because of the Standing Rock protests of the Dakota Access Pipeline.[43]

These acts of repression are part of a long tradition. The first organized uniformed police force in the English-speaking world was established in London in 1829. They came to be called "bobbies" because of the role played by Sir Robert Peel in securing passage of the London Metropolitan Police Act, which established the force. The first full-time uniformed police force in the United States was set up in New York City in 1845.[44] It was also in the period from the 1820s to the 1840s that the movement to build penitentiaries to house and reform criminals began in New York and Pennsylvania and spread rapidly through the states of the young nation.[45] That these are also the years that saw the beginnings of a large industrial working class in the cities of England and America is a coincidence too striking to ignore.

The police were repeatedly used to break strikes and harass strikers.[46] The penitentiaries were used mainly to house the laborers and foreigners (often one and the same) whom the middle and upper classes perceived as a threat.[47] Throughout the formative years of the American labor movement, public police forces, private police like the Pinkertons, regular army troops, and the National Guard were used repeatedly to protect the interests of capital against the attempts of labor to organize in defense of its interests. The result was that "the United States has had the bloodiest and most violent labor history of any industrialized nation in the world"—with most of the casualties on the side of labor.[48]

Marx, of course, went further. Not only are the laws of a society made to protect the interests of the most powerful economic class, but also, Marx argued, the prevailing ways of thinking about the world—from economic theory to religion to conventional moral ideas about good and evil, guilt and responsibility—are shaped in ways that promote the belief that the existing society is the best of all possible worlds. Marx wrote that "the ideas of the ruling class are in every epoch the ruling ideas.... The class which has the means of material production at its disposal, has control at the same time over the means of mental production."[49]

Because those who have economic power own the newspapers, endow the universities and think tanks, finance the publication of books and journals, and (in our own time) control television, radio, and other electronic media, they have a prevailing say in what is heard, thought, and believed by the millions who get their ideas—their picture of reality—from these sources. This does not mean that the controllers of the "means of mental production" consciously deceive or manipulate those who receive their message. What it means is that the picture of reality held by these controllers—believed by them, no doubt sincerely, to be an accurate representation of reality—will be largely the picture of reality that fills the heads of the readers and viewers of the mass media.

For example, the story of an eight-year-old chess champion who has been homeless for a year "will make you smile," says the headline. He has talent, yes, but the story never asks "how it was possible for a child in one of the richest cities in the world to be homeless?[50] Stories of kids recycling to pay for college or selling lemonade to pay for a parent's chemotherapy are "uplifting," rather than asking "why children have to literally wade through garbage to get a decent education in the richest country in world history," or point out that in no other developed country would it be necessary for child labor to pay for medical bills like that. These stories paint the world as the wealthy want to see it–where "every problem is understood through an individualist lens, and not as a result of systemic forces that dominate society."

The average man or woman is almost wholly occupied with the personal tasks of earning a living, piloting a family, and the like. He or she lacks the time (and usually the training) necessary to seek out and evaluate alternative sources of information. Most people are lucky when they have the time to catch a bit of news on television, in the papers, or on the Internet. Moreover, except when there is division of opinion among those who control the media, the average person is so surrounded by unbroken "consensus" that he or she takes it simply as the way things are.

Consequently, the vast majority of people will accept, as a true picture of reality, the picture held by those who control the media. This is likely to be a distorted picture, even if those who create it act with the best of intentions and sincerity. The point is that, for a wide variety of reasons, people tend to view the world in ways that make their own role in it (particularly the advantages and privileges they have) seem morally just, indeed part of the best of all possible worlds. Thus, without any intention to deceive at all, without any "conspiracy," those who control the content of the mass media are virtually certain to convey a picture of reality that supports the existing social order.

As a result, even in a society such as ours, where freedom of expression has reached a level unparalleled in history, there is almost never any fundamental questioning of our political or economic institutions on television and radio, in the major newspapers, or the news weeklies such as *Time* or *Newsweek*. There is much criticism of individuals and of individual policies. How often, though, does one find the mass media questioning whether the free-enterprise system is really the best choice for America, or whether our political and legal arrangements systematically promote the domination of society by the owners of big business? These issues are rarely, if ever, raised. Instead, it is taken for granted that, though they need some reform from time to time, our economic institutions are the most productive, our political institutions the freest, and our legal institutions the most just that there can be.

We are told that the interests of the powerful coincide with the common interests of us all,[51] "what's good for General Motors is good for the country." (This old slogan echoes eerily now after GM has teetered on the brink of bankruptcy, and the government must cope with firms that are "too big to be allowed to fail.") Where this picture of reality shows up some blemishes, they will always be portrayed as localized problems that can be remedied without fundamental overhaul of the entire social order, aberrations in an otherwise well-functioning social system. Indeed, the very willingness to publicize these blemishes "proves" that there is nothing fundamentally wrong with the social system because if the media are free, willing, and able to portray the blemishes, they would surely portray fundamental problems with the social system if there were any—and because they do not, there must not be any! *When ideas, however unintentionally, distort reality in a way that justifies the prevailing distribution of power and wealth, hides society's injustices, and thus secures uncritical allegiance to the existing social order, we have what Marx called ideology.*[52] (Appendix I discusses in greater detail the Marxian theory of ideology and of the role of criminal justice in capitalist society.)

Ideology is not conscious deception. People may spout ideology because it is all they know or all they have been taught or because they do not see beyond the "conventional wisdom" that surrounds them. This can be just as true of scholars who fail to see beyond the conventional assumptions of their disciplines as it is of laypersons who fail to see beyond the oversimplifications of what is commonly called "common sense." Such individuals do not mouth ideology out of a willful desire to deceive and manipulate their fellows but rather because their own view of reality is distorted by untruths and half-truths—and criminal justice is one source of such distortion. One way in which this works without conscious deception is that we have become so used to the criminal justice carnival mirror (described in Chapter 2) that we don't notice its curves. It looks flat, and thus we take it as an accurate picture of who threatens us in society.

Not everyone uses the term "ideology" as Marx did and as we have, namely to point to beliefs that are deceptive. Some writers speak of ideology as if it meant any individual or group's "belief system" or "value system" or *Weltanschauung,* that is, "worldview."[53] This moral neutralization of the concept of "ideology" is itself a good example of the work of ideology! It dulls a conceptual instrument that thinkers such as Marx and others had sharpened into an effective tool for cutting through the illusions that dog our political life. Such tools are few and hard to come by. Once we have them, they should be carefully preserved, especially when concepts such as "belief system" and "worldview" are available to perform the more neutral function.

The Need for Ideology

A simple and persuasive argument can be made for the claim that the rich and powerful in America have an interest in conveying an ideological message to the rest of the nation. The have-nots and have-littles far outnumber the have-plenties. This means, to put it rather crudely, that the have-nots and the have-littles could have more if they decided to take it from the have-plenties. This, in turn, means that the have-plenties need the cooperation of the have-nots and the have-littles. Because the have-plenties are such a small minority that they could never *force* this cooperation on the have-nots and have-littles; this cooperation must be voluntary. For the cooperation to be voluntary, the have-nots and the have-littles must believe it would not be right or reasonable to take away what the have-plenties have. In other words, they must believe that for all its problems, the present social, political, and economic order, with its disparities of wealth and power and privilege, is about the best that human beings can create. More specifically, the have-nots and have-littles must believe that they are not being exploited or being treated unfairly by the have-plenties, and these beliefs must be in some considerable degree false, because the distribution of wealth and power in the United States is so evidently arbitrary and unjust, ergo the need for ideology.

A disquisition on the inequitable distribution of wealth and income in the United States is beyond the scope and purpose of this book. This subject, as well as the existence of a "dominant" or "ruling" class in America, has been documented extensively by others. We will make only two points here. First, there are indeed wide disparities in the distribution of wealth and income in the United States. Second, these disparities are so obviously unjust that it is reasonable to assume that the vast majority of people who must struggle to make ends meet put up with them only because they have been sold a bill of goods, that is, an ideology.

In 2017, the richest 20 percent of American households received 51.5 percent of the income received by all families, whereas the poorest 60 percent of American households received 25.6 percent of the total income. In crude terms, this means that while the wealthiest 25 million American households have more than half the money pie to themselves, the least wealthy 75 million American households share about a quarter of that pie among them. At the outer edges the figures are more extreme: For 2017, the richest five percent of households received 22.3 percent of total income, substantially more than the poorest 40 percent of households, who received 11.3 percent. This means that the richest six million households have nearly twice as much money to divide among themselves as the 48 million households who make up the bottom 40 percent.[54] It happens in an economy in which more than 40 percent of workers earn less than $15 an hour.[55]

The distribution of *wealth* (property such as homes and stocks, as well as ownership of businesses and land that generate income and tend to give one a say in major economic decisions) is even more unequal than the distribution of income.[56] In 2018, the poorest 50 percent collectively owned 1 percent of all the wealth, and the top 1 percent owned 32 percent; the richest 1 percent own more wealth than the bottom 90 percent.[57] To be on the *Forbes* 400—the 400 wealthiest individuals in the United States–requires a minimum of $2.1 billion. The 400, together, own $2.9 *trillion,* a record high,[58] and more than twice what the bottom 50 percent own. And in contrast to the trillions owned by a few, the Federal Reserve reports that "four in 10 adults, if faced with an unexpected expense of $400, would either not be able to cover it or would cover it by selling something or borrowing money."[59]

Americans generally underestimate the amount of inequality in the country, and when asked to construct their ideal distribution of wealth, it is more equal still. Some of the results of Michael Norton and Dan Ariely's survey of 5,522 Americans are shown in Table 4.2. They note that analysis of responses by sex, political party, and current income showed "much more consensus than disagreement among these different demographic groups."[60] Ideology is at work in making people perceive a lower level of inequality than actually exists, and in accepting the vast difference between what exists and what they believe is fair.

We offer no complicated philosophical argument to prove that these disparities are unjust, although such arguments abound for those who are interested.[61] It is a scandal that, in a nation as rich as ours, some 39.7 million people (somewhat less when reckoned with the most generous valuation of in-kind benefits, such as food stamps) live below what the government conservatively defines as the poverty level, and that many millions more must scramble to make ends meet.[62] It is tragic that in our wealthy nation so many millions cannot afford a proper diet, a college education, a safe place to live, and decent health care. Because we are nowhere near offering all Americans a good education and an equal opportunity to get ahead, we have no right to think that the distribution of income reflects what people have truly earned. The distribution of income in America is so fundamentally shaped by factors such as race, educational opportunity, and the economic class of one's parents that few people who are well-off can honestly claim they deserve *all* that they have. Those who think they do should ask themselves where they would be today if they had been born to migrant laborers in California or to a poor black family in a ghetto.

TABLE 4.2 Actual, Perceived, and Ideal Distributions of Wealth in the United States

Wealth of poorest 60%		Wealth of richest 20%
5%	Actual amount of wealth	84%
20%	Perceived amount of wealth	59%
45%	Ideal amount of wealth	32%

Source: Michael Norton and Dan Ariely, "Building a Better America—One Wealth Quintile at a Time," *Perspectives on Psychological Science 6(1),* p. 10, (2011).

Enough said. We take it, then, as established that the disparities of wealth and income in America are wide and unjustified. For the vast majority, the many millions struggling hard to satisfy basic needs, to acquiesce to the vast wealth of a small minority, it is necessary that the majority come to believe that these disparities are justified, that the present order is the best that human beings can accomplish, and that they are not being exploited by the have-plenties. In other words, the system requires an effective ideology to fool enough of the people enough of the time.

This account of the nature and need for ideology, coupled with the historical inertia explanation of the persistence of criminal justice in its current form and the analysis of the ideological benefits produced by the criminal justice system, add up to an explanation of the continued failure of criminal justice in the United States and its persistent bias against the poor. We believe that we have proven the Pyrrhic defeat theory of American criminal justice.

Summary

This chapter has presented the Pyrrhic defeat theory's explanation of the triple failure of criminal justice in the United States (1) to institute policies likely to reduce substantially the high incidence of crime, (2) to treat as crimes the dangerous acts of the well-off, and (3) to eliminate the bias against the poor in the treatment of those acts labeled "crimes." The persistence of this triple failure was explained by appeal to the notion of "historical inertia": The current shape of criminal justice policy emerged at an earlier time when it corresponded to the real threats to people's bodies and possessions, and it has persisted, in spite of its failures, because its failures mainly harm the poor while they benefit the well-off; thus criminal justice policy does not generate incentives to change the system for those with the power to do so. The failing criminal justice system benefits those with the power to change things by broadcasting the message that the threat to Americans' well-being comes from below them on the economic ladder, not from above them, and that poverty results not from social causes but from the moral failings of the poor. It was also argued that, aside from these "bonuses of bias," there is an implicit ideological message of any criminal justice system, insofar as such systems, by focusing on individual guilt, implicitly broadcast the message that the social system itself is a just one.

Study Questions

1. What is a conspiracy theory? What are the shortcomings of such a theory? Is the Pyrrhic defeat theory a conspiracy theory?
2. What is meant by "ideology"? What is the difference between ideology and propaganda? Why is ideology needed in the United States?
3. How does any criminal justice system broadcast an ideological message supportive of the prevailing social and economic arrangements?
4. What additional ideological benefits result from the bias against the poor in the definition and treatment of crime?

5. Why are poor people in the United States poor?
6. Now that you have reviewed the historical inertia explanation of criminal justice in the United States, has the Pyrrhic defeat theory been proven?
7. What problems are posed by the privatization of prisons and the criminal justice-industrial complex?

Additional Resources

Jeffrey Reiman and Paul Leighton, *The Rich Get Richer and Poor Get Prison: A Reader* (Boston: Pearson, 2010). This volume is a collection of accessible articles that were either used as reference material for *The Rich Get Richer* or provide lively complementary examples or analysis. The reader is divided into sections that parallel the chapters of *The Rich Get Richer,* and each section of the reader opens with a substantial introduction, written by the editors, that provides article summaries, context, and linkages to *The Rich Get Richer.*
The authors also maintain a companion website to the text at www.paulsjusticep-age.com/reiman.htm.

Notes

1. *Challenge,* p. 44.
2. Jim Norman, "Americans' Concerns About National Crime Abating," *Gallup,* November 7, 2018, https://news.gallup.com/poll/244394/americans-concerns-national-crime-abating.aspx
3. Melissa S. Kearney et al., "Ten Economic Facts about Crime and Incarceration in the United States," The Hamilton Project Report, *Brookings,* May 1, 2014, www.brookings.edu/research/ten-economic-facts-about-crime-and-incarceration-in-the-united-states/.
4. National Research Council Committee on Causes and Consequences of High Rates of Incarceration, Jeremy Travis, Bruce Western, and Steve Redburn (eds.), *The Growth of Incarceration in the United States: Exploring Causes and Consequences* (Washington, DC: The National Academies Press, 2014), p. 126.
5. "For example, it was discovered that, rather than the projected 20 percent savings, the average saving from privatization was only about 1 percent, and most of that was achieved through lower labor costs." James Austin and Garry Coventry, *Emerging Issues on Privatized Prisons,* U.S. Department of Justice, Office of Justice Programs, Bureau of Justice Assistance, NCJ 181249, February 2001, p. iii.
6. John Biewen, "Corrections, Inc: Corporate-Sponsored Crime Laws," American RadioWorks, April 2002, http://americanradioworks.publicradio.org/features/corrections/.
7. BJS, *Prisoners in 2017,* NCJ 252156, April 2019, Table 17; Ava Kofman, "Digital Jail: How Electronic Monitoring Drives Defendants into Debt," *New York Times Magazine,* July 3, 2019, www.nytimes.com/2019/07/03/magazine/digital-jail-surveillance.html.
8. Quoted in Leighton and Selman, "Private Prisons, the Criminal Justice-Industrial Complex and Bodies Destined for Profitable Punishment," in Walter DeKeserdy and Molly Dragiewicz (eds.), *Routledge Handbook of Critical Criminology* (New York: Routledge, 2012), p. 270.

9. Ibid.

10. Donna Selman and Paul Leighton, *Punishment for Sale* (Lanham, MD: Rowman & Littlefield, 2010), p. 21.

11. BJS, *Justice Expenditure and Employment Extracts, 2009—Preliminary,* NCJ 237913, May 2012, Table 1; Eric Schlosser, "The Prison-Industrial Complex," *Atlantic Monthly,* December 1998, p. 54.

12. Paul Leighton and Donna Selman, "Private Prisons, the Criminal Justice-Industrial Complex and Bodies Destined for Profitable Punishment," p. 270.

13. Ray Surette and Rebecca Gardiner-Bass, "Media Entertainment and Crime," in Bruce Arrigo and Heather Bersot (eds), *The Routledge Handbook of International Crime and Justice Studies* (New York: Routledge, 2014), p. 374.

14. Debra Seagal, "Tales from the Cutting-Room Floor: The Reality of 'Reality-Based' Television," *Harper's Magazine,* November 1993, p. 52; "junkie-busting cop culture" refers to the raids, arrests, and roundups of drug addicts. "Junkie" is a pejorative for a drug abuser, usually of heroin. It is less formal English that is used here to emphasize deep addiction and all the bad that happens to people with that condition.

15. David Fabianic, "Television Dramas and Homicide Causation," *Journal of Criminal Justice* 25, no. 3 (1997): 201.

16. Quoted in Travis C. Pratt and Francis T. Cullen, "Assessing Macro-Level Predictors and Theories of Crime: A Meta-Analysis," *Crime and Justice* 32 (2005): 374.

17. James Unnever and Shaun Gabbidon, *A Theory of African American Offending* (New York: Routledge, 2011), p. 168.

18. On December 16, 1773, a group of Massachusetts colonists raging against British governmental policies boarded British ships and destroyed tea belonging to the East India Company, valued then at about $1 million, by throwing it into Boston Harbor. The incident, an early skirmish of the American War of Independence, was in protest of a tea tax imposed by the British and grew out of the colonists' beliefs that they should only be taxed by their own elected representatives ("no taxation without representation!").

19. Richard A. Cloward and Lloyd E. Ohlin, *Delinquency and Opportunity: A Theory of Delinquent Gangs* (New York: Free Press, 1960), esp. pp. 77–107.

20. Steven Messner and Richard Rosenfeld, *Crime and the American Dream,* 3rd ed. (Belmont, CA: Wadsworth, 2000).

21. All of these were mafia gangsters or cowboy outlaws who committed felonies from the end of the nineteenth to the early twentieth century in the U.S. See Paul Kooistra, *Criminals as Heroes* (Bowling Green, OH: Bowling Green State University Popular Press, 1989).

22. Cloward and Ohlin, *Delinquency and Opportunity,* p. 81.

23. Ibid., p. 10.

24. Ibid., p. 107.

25. Ibid., p. 10.

26. Willem Bonger, *Criminality and Economic Conditions,* abridged and with an introduction, by Austin T. Turk (Bloomington: Indiana University Press, 1969), pp. 7–12 and 40–47. Willem Adriaan Bonger was born in Holland in 1876 and died by his own hand in 1940 rather than submit to the Nazis.

27. David M. Gordon, "Capitalism, Class and Crime in America," *Crime and Delinquency* 19, no. 2 (1973): 174 (emphasis in original).

28. Ibid.

29. William and Mary Morris, *Dictionary of Word and Phrase Origins,* vol. 2 (New York: Harper & Row, 1967), p. 282.

30. The full phrase "political-influence peddler" is meant to refer to political corruption and those in government who use their public authority to illegally benefit those who pay the politicians. Bribery is the most obvious form, and political lobbying/campaign donations are the legal aspect of this.

31. See, for example, Jon Hurwitz and Mark Peffley, "Playing the Race Card in the Post-Willie Horton Era: The Impact of Racialized Code Words on Support for Punitive Crime Policy," *Public Opinion Quarterly* 69, no. 1 (2005): 99–113.

32. The Associated Press-NORC Center for Public Affairs Research, "Crime and Law Enforcement in America: Racial and Ethnic Differences in Attitudes Toward the Criminal Justice System," issue brief, 2014; Justin McCathy, "New Low of 49% in U.S. Say Death Penalty Applied Fairly," *Gallup*, October 22, 2018, https://news.gallup.com/poll/243794/new-low-say-death-penalty-applied-fairly.aspx.

33. Historical documentation of this can be found in David J. Rothman, *The Discovery of the Asylum: Social Order and Disorder in the New Republic* (Boston: Little, Brown, 1971) and in Frances Fox Piven and Richard A. Cloward, *Regulating the Poor: The Functions of Public Welfare* (New York: Pantheon, 1971); Tim Wise. *Under the Affluence: Shaming the Poor, Praising the Rich and Sacrificing the Future of America* (San Francisco: City Lights Publishers, 2015).

34. *The Republic of Plato,* trans., F. M. Cornford (New York: Oxford University Press, 1945), p. 18 [I. 338]. Plato was born in Athens in the year 428 BCE (or 427, depending on the reckoning) and died there in 348 BCE (or 347). See S. J. Frederick Copleston, *A History of Philosophy,* vol. 1: *Greece and Rome* (Westminster, MD: Newman Press, 1946), pp. 127–141.

35. Karl Marx and Friedrich Engels, *Manifesto of the Communist Party,* in Robert C. Tucker (ed.), *The Marx-Engels Reader* (New York: Norton, 1972), p. 337.

36. An article on congressional ethics in *Newsweek* (June 14, 1976) makes the point so graphically that it is worth quoting at length:

> *Some of the Hill's most powerful veterans have long earned part of their income from outside business interests—and may be tempted to vote with their own bank accounts in mind when legislation affecting those interests has come before Congress. House Whip Thomas P. (Tip) O'Neill is active in real estate and insurance in Massachusetts, Minority Leader John Rhodes of Arizona is a director and vice-president of a life insurance company and scores of other senior members are involved with the banking industry, oil and gas companies and farming operations. Do these connections destroy their judgment? Not necessarily, argues Russell Long of Louisiana, chairman of the powerful Senate Finance Committee and a reliable defender of oil interests—who nevertheless refuses to disclose the size of his personal oil and gas holdings, most of them inherited from his father, former Gov. Huey Long. "A long time ago I became convinced that if you have financial interests completely parallel to your state, then you have no problem," says Long. "If I didn't represent the oil and gas industry, I wouldn't represent the state of Louisiana." Even more difficult to trace is the influence of representatives who keep their law practices—and their clients, many of whom do business with the Federal government—when they become members of Congress (p. 25).*

For other analyses of the marriage of economic and political power, see William Greider, *Who Will Tell the People? The Betrayal of American Democracy*

(New York: Touchstone/Simon & Schuster, 1993); Phillip Stern, *Still the Best Congress Money Can Buy*, rev. and expanded ed. (Washington, DC: Regnery Gateway, 1992); John Jackley, *Hill Rat: Blowing the Lid Off Congress* (Washington, DC: Regnery Gateway, 1992); Donald Axelrod, *Shadow Government: The Hidden World of Public Authorities—and How They Control over $1 Trillion of Your Money* (New York: Wiley, 1992); Michael Useem, *The Inner Circle: Large Corporations and the Rise of Business Political Activity in the US and UK* (New York: Oxford University Press, 1984); Kim McQuaid, *Big Business and Presidential Power: From FDR to Reagan* (New York: Morrow, 1982).

37. See Ross Gelbspan, *Break-Ins, Death Threats and the FBI: The Covert War Against the Central American Movement* (Boston: South End Press, 1991); Margaret Jayko, *FBI on Trial: The Victory in the Socialist Workers Party Suit Against Government Spying* (New York: Pathfinder Press, 1988); "F.B.I. Burglarized Leftist Offices Here 92 Times in 1960–66, Official Files Show," *New York Times*, March 29, 1976, p. A1; and "Burglaries by FBI Listed in Hundreds," *The Washington Post*, July 16, 1975, p. A1. See also Cathy Perkus, ed., *Cointelpro: The FBI's Secret War on Political Freedom*, intro. Noam Chomsky (New York: Monad Press, 1975).

38. "Hill Panel Raps FBI's Anti-Panthers Tactics," *The Washington Post*, May 7, 1976, pp. A1 and A22.

39. George Lardner, Jr., "FBI Labeled King 'Communist' in '62," *The Washington Post*, May 6, 1976, pp. A1 and A26; Michael Friedly and David Gallen, *Martin Luther King, Jr: The FBI File* (New York: Carroll & Graf, 1993). See also Carson Clayborne and David Gallen, *Malcolm X: The FBI File* (New York: Carroll & Graf, 1991) and Kenneth O'Reilly, *"Racial Matters": The FBI's Secret File on Black America, 1960–1972* (New York: Free Press, 1989).

40. John M. Goshko, "Kelley Says FBI Is 'Truly Sorry' for Past Abuses," *The Washington Post*, May 9, 1976, pp. A1 and A14; George Lardner, Jr., "FBI Break-Ins Still Go On, Panel Says," *The Washington Post*, May 11, 1976. For more recent accounts, see Terry Atlas, "FBI Tactics Questioned in Probe of Activists," *The Chicago Tribune*, March 2, 1990, p. 1 and 5; Robert A. Jones, "Here Come the '60s, with FBI in Tow," *Los Angeles Times*, June 26, 1990, p. A3; Peter Matthiessen, *In the Spirit of Crazy Horse* (New York: Viking, 1983), which discusses the FBI's conflicts with the American Indian Movement (AIM), regarding which the FBI sued the author and delayed publication for several years; and Rex Weyler, *Blood of the Land: The Government and Corporate War Against First Nations* (Philadelphia: New Society Publishers, 1992), which also covers the FBI and AIM. For other agencies of the government, see for example, "Military Spied on King, Other Blacks, Paper Says: Army Reportedly Targeted Southern Churches," *The Washington Post*, March 21, 1993, p. A16.

41. Note that JPMorgan Chase & Co. gave the New York police a $4.6 million gift: Yves Smith, "Is JP Morgan Getting a Good Return on $4.6 Million 'Gift' to NYC Police? (Like Special Protection from OccupyWallStreet?)" *Naked Capitalism*, October 2, 2012, www.nakedcapitalism.com/2011/10/is-jp-morgan-getting-a-good-return-on-4-6-million-gift-to-nyc-police-like-special-protection-from-occupywallstreet.html; Beau Hodai, "Dissent or Terror: How the Nation's Counter Terrorism Apparatus, in Partnership with Corporate America, Turned on Occupy Wall Street," Center for Media and Democracy, DBA Press, May 2013, www.prwatch.org/files/Dissent%20or%20Terror%20FINAL_0.pdf.

42. David Grinberg, "Tracking Movements: Black Activism, Aerial Surveillance, and Transparency Optics," *Media, Culture & Society*, 41, no. 3 (2019): 294–316, https://doi.org/10.1177/0163443718810921.

Amna Toor, "'Our Identity Is Often What's Triggering Surveillance': How Government Surveillance of #blacklivesmatter Violates the First Amendment Freedom of Association," *Rutgers Computer & Technology Law Journal*, 44, no. 2 (2018): 286.

43. J. Harb and K. Henne, "Disinformation and Resistance in the Surveillance of Indigenous Protesters," in B. Haggart, K. Henne, and N. Tusikov (eds), *Information, Technology and Control in a Changing World*, International Political Economy Series (Basingstoke: Palgrave Macmillan, 2019); see generally Eveline Lubbers, "Undercover Research: Corporate and Police Spying on Activists. An Introduction to Activist Intelligence as a New Field of Study," *Surveillance & Society* 13, nos. 3/4 (2015): 338–353.

44. James F. Richardson, *Urban Police in the United States* (Port Washington, NY: Kennikat Press, 1974), pp. 8–13 and 22. See also Richardson's *The New York Police: Colonial Times to 1901* (New York: Oxford University Press, 1970).

45. Rothman, *The Discovery of the Asylum*, pp. 57–108, especially pp. 79–81. Cf. Michel Foucault, *Discipline and Punish: The Birth of the Prison*, trans. Alan Sheridan (London: Allen Lane, 1977).

46. Richardson, *Urban Police in the United States*, pp. 158–161. See also R. Boyer and H. Morais, *Labor's Untold Story* (New York: United Electrical, Radio & Machine Workers of America, 1976).

47. Rothman, *The Discovery of the Asylum*, pp. 253–254.

48. Philip Taft and Philip Ross, "American Labor Violence: Its Causes, Character, and Outcome," in H. D. Graham and T. R. Gurr (ed.), *The History of Violence in America* (New York: Bantam, 1969), pp. 281–395, especially pp. 281 and 380; and Richard E. Rubenstein, *Rebels in Eden: Mass Political Violence in the United States* (Boston: Little, Brown, 1970), p. 81 inter alia. See also Center for Research in Criminal Justice, *The Iron Fist and the Velvet Glove* (Berkeley: University of California Press, 1975), pp. 16–19.

49. Karl Marx, *The German Ideology* in *The Marx-Engels Reader*, p. 136.

50. Alan Macleod, "The Homeless 8-Year-Old Chess Champion and Other Horrific 'Uplifting' Stories," Fairness & Accuracy In Reporting (FAIR), March 25, 2019, https://fair.org/home/the-homeless-8-year-old-chess-champion-and-other-horrific-uplifting-stories/.

51. Each new ruling class "is compelled, merely in order to carry through its aim, to represent its interest as the common interest of all the members of society," Marx, *The German Ideology*, p. 138.

52. Marx was not the first to use the term "ideology." The term was coined by a Frenchman, Antoine Destutt de Tracy, who was among the intellectuals named in 1795 to direct the researches of the newly founded Institut de France. The *idéologues* of the Institut generally believed that existing ideas were prejudices rooted in individual psychology or in political conditions and that the path to liberation from these prejudices and thus toward a rational society lay in a science of ideas (literally, an "idea-ology"), which made human beings aware of the sources of their ideas. Thomas Jefferson tried (albeit unsuccessfully) to have Destutt de Tracy's theory made part of the original curriculum of the University of Virginia. See George Lichtheim, "The Concept of Ideology," *History and Theory* 4, no. 2 (1965): 164–195; and Richard H. Cox (ed.), *Ideology, Politics, and Political Theory* (Belmont, CA: Wadsworth, 1969), pp. 7–8. Needless to say, Marx used the term "ideology" in ways that neither Destutt de Tracy nor Jefferson anticipated.

53. Lichtheim's essay provides a good discussion of the philosophical antecedents of the gradual separation of the notion of ideology from that of false consciousness. Undoubtedly, this separation is of a piece with the current wisdom that insists that all views of the world are conditioned and rendered partial by the limits of the viewer's historical and social vantage point and thus shrinks from trying to say anything true about the human condition. An illuminating example of this "current wisdom" applied to the criminal justice system is Walter B. Miller, "Ideology and Criminal Justice Policy: Some Current Issues," *Journal of Criminal Law and Criminology* 64, no. 2 (1973): 141–162. We shall use the concept of ideology in the Marxian sense, that is, to include that of false consciousness.

54. U.S. Bureau of the Census, *Income and Poverty in the U.S.: 2017*, Table 2.

55. Claire Zillman, "Who Makes Less than $15 per Hour? An Explainer in 3 Charts," *Fortune*, April 13, 2015, https://fortune.com/2015/04/13/who-makes-15-per-hour/.

56. Alan S. Blinder, "The Level and Distribution of Economic Well-Being," in Martin Feldstein (ed.), *The American Economy in Transition* (Chicago: University of Chicago Press, 1980), p. 466.

57. Board of Governors of the Federal Reserve System, "Distribution of Household Wealth in the U.S. Since 1989," Table: 2019 Q1 for top 1 percent and bottom 90 percent.

58. Kerry A. Dolan, "Forbes 400 2018: A New Number One and a Record-Breaking Year for America's Richest People," *Forbes*, October 3, 2018, www.forbes.com/sites/kerryadolan/2018/10/03/forbes-400-2018-a-new-number-one-and-a-record-breaking-year-for-americas-richest-people/.

59. Board of Governors of the Federal Reserve System, *Report on the Economic Well-Being of U.S. Households in 2017* (Washington, DC: Federal Reserve Board, May 2018), www.federalreserve.gov/publications/files/2017-report-economic-well-being-us-households-201805.pdf.

60. Michael Norton and Dan Ariely, "Building a Better America—One Wealth Quintile at a Time," *Perspectives on Psychological Science* 6, no. 1 (2011): 10.

61. Undoubtedly, the most interesting work on this topic is John Rawls's *A Theory of Justice* (Cambridge, MA: Harvard University Press, 1971; revised ed., 1999). The noted British philosopher Stuart Hampshire has called it the most important work in moral philosophy since World War II. It has largely dominated theoretical discussions of political, legal, and economic justice. Rawls's approach is essentially "naturalistic"; that is, he takes the "good" to be that which people rationally desire and the "moral good" to be that which would best serve all people's rational desires. From this, he takes justice to be those social (legal, political, and economic) arrangements that best serve the interests of all. To reach specific principles of justice, he asks which principles would be rational for all people to agree to if each person was not able to use force or influence to tailor these principles to his or her own interests. On the question of the distribution of income or wealth, this way of questioning leads to the principle that economic inequalities are just only if they work to everyone's advantage, for instance, as incentives that work to raise the level of productivity and thus the level of well-being for all. It would be the task of government to rectify inequalities that exceed this point by means of taxes and transfers. We cannot, of course, do justice here to what Rawls takes 600 pages to explain and defend. However, we offer this short summary to suggest that the disparities of income in the United States are far from just in the light of contemporary moral philosophy. Clearly, those disparities are far greater

than anything that could be claimed to be necessary to increase the well-being of all. Indeed, one would have to be blind not to see that they are not increasing the well-being of all. Robert Nozick has replied to Rawls in *Anarchy, State and Utopia* (New York: Basic Books, 1974), which no doubt represents the free-enterprise system's theory of justice. Nozick holds that no theory (such as Rawls's) that calls for government intervention to rectify income distribution can be just. His argument is that if people acquire their property (including money) legitimately, then they have the right to sell or spend it as they wish. If this leads to disparities in wealth, one cannot alter this outcome without denying that those sellers or spenders had the right to dispose of their property or money as they saw fit. We shall not try to answer Nozick here. It should be noted, however, that his view starts from the assumption that the property or money that is sold or spent was acquired legitimately. In light of the fact that so much U.S. property was stolen at gunpoint from Indians or Mexicans and so much wealth was taken from the labor of and trade in black slaves, applying Nozick's theory in the U.S. context would require a massive redistribution of wealth to reach the starting point at which we could say that individuals own what they own legitimately. For an extended discussion of these theories of justice, see Jeffrey Reiman, *Justice and Modern Moral Philosophy* (New Haven, CT: Yale University Press, 1990).

62. U.S. Bureau of the Census, *Income and Poverty in the U.S.: 2017*, Figure 4, www. census.gov/content/dam/Census/library/publications/2018/demo/p60-263. pdf.

Conclusion
Criminal *Justice* or *Criminal* Justice

*Justice being taken away, then, what are
kingdoms but great robberies?*

—St. Augustine, *The City of God*

*... unjust social arrangements are themselves
a kind of extortion, even violence.*

—John Rawls, *A Theory of Justice*

*... the policeman moves through Harlem, therefore,
like an occupying soldier in a bitterly hostile country;
which is precisely what, and where he is, and the
reason he walks in twos and threes.*

—James Baldwin, *Nobody Knows My Name*

A criminal justice system is a system of *justice* only if it protects equally the rights and interests of all members of society. For that it must punish even-handedly the rich as well as the poor who violate these rights or endanger these interests. When it does not do this, the system is *criminal*. The biased use of the system's coercive power—police, courts, prisons—is force used against some members of society to promote the interests of others. This is to say, it does precisely what crime does, and thus its force is morally equivalent to criminal violence. Later in this conclusion, we point out several policies that must be put in place if our system is to be a system of *justice*.

THE CRIME OF JUSTICE

Robbers, extortionists, and *occupying soldiers* are terms used to characterize those who enforce an unjust law and an unjust order. This is not merely rhetoric. There is a very real and very important sense in which those who use force unjustly or who use force to protect an unjust social order are no different from a band of criminals or an occupying army. If this isn't understood, you are likely to think that what has been described in the first three chapters, and accounted for in the fourth, amounts to only another call for reform of the criminal justice system to make it more effective and fairer, when in fact it is much more. A criminal justice system that functions like ours—that imposes its penalties primarily on the poor and not equally on all who threaten society, that does not protect us against threats to our lives and possessions equal to or graver than those presently defined as "crimes," and that fails even to do those things that could better protect us against the crimes of the poor—*is morally no better than the criminality it claims to fight.*

In the next section, "Rehabilitating Criminal Justice in America," we propose some reforms. These should not be taken as proposals aimed merely at improving the effectiveness or fairness of American criminal justice. In our view, these proposals represent the necessary conditions for establishing the moral superiority of criminal justice to criminality—thus they are a matter of rehabilitating the system not merely reforming it. They are the conditions that must be fulfilled if the criminal justice system is to be acquitted of the indictment implicit in the statements above from St. Augustine, Rawls, and Baldwin. Bear in mind that the "criminal justice system" does not mean only police, courts, and prisons; it includes the entire legal system, from lawmakers to law enforcers to judges and prison guards and parole boards.

What is common to the charge in the statements of St. Augustine, Rawls, and Baldwin is the idea that *injustice transforms a legal system into its opposite.* What is common to the robber, the extortionist, and the occupying soldier is that each uses force (or the threat of force) to coerce people to serve the interests of others at their own expense. The occupying soldier uses force to subject one people to domination by another. The robber and the extortionist use force to make other people hand over things of value. The injustice that characterizes criminal acts is the forcing of people to serve the interests of others.

A legal system, of course, also uses force. Its defenders, however, maintain that it uses force to protect all people's bodies and their property. They claim that the legal system protects all people's possessions against robbers and extortionists and protects their autonomy against those who would try to impose their will on them by force. In short, although both a legal system and its opposite, either criminality or military domination, use force, the moral superiority claimed for the legal system lies in the fact that it uses force to protect the interests of *all* people equally, whereas criminals and occupying troops use force to subject some people to the interests of others. *The moral legitimacy of a legal system and the lack of legitimacy of crime and military domination hinge, then, on the question of whether coercion is being used in the interests of all equally or to promote some people's interests at the expense of others.*

This adds up to something that should be obvious but is not: *A criminal justice system is criminal to the extent that it is not truly a system of justice.* A criminal justice system is a system of justice to the extent that it protects equally the interests and rights of all and to the extent that it punishes equally all who endanger these interests or who violate these rights. When it veers from these goals, the criminal justice system is guilty of the same sacrificing of the interests of some for the benefit of others that it exists to combat. It is, therefore, morally speaking, guilty of crime. Which is it then? Criminal justice or just criminal?

The experience of the twentieth century has taught us not to take for granted that every legal system is a system of justice. Hitler's Germany and Stalin's Soviet Union, as well as South Africa under apartheid, are testimony to the fact that what is put forth as law may well be outrageously unjust. An example closer to home would be the U.S. legal system that, under the Supreme Court's *Dred Scott* decision of 1857, defined black slaves as property even after they had lived in a "free" state that prohibited slavery. Slaves who escaped plantations and made it to northern states were still the legal property of their masters; they were subject to arrest and forced to return to slavery.

In such instances, we easily recognize the truth implicit in the statements of St. Augustine, Rawls, and Baldwin that open this chapter: What is put forth under the authority of law may be morally no better than crime or tyranny. Therefore, we cannot take for granted that our own legal order is just merely because it is legal. We must subject it to the moral test of whether it serves and protects the interests of all to make sure it is not injustice disguised as justice or criminality wearing the mask of law. (Appendix II, "Between Philosophy and Criminology," argues that criminology requires a moral evaluation of crime as part of its identification of its object of study.) We do not, of course, equate the U.S. legal system with that of Hitler's Germany or Stalin's Soviet Union. There is much in the system that is legitimate, and many are caught by the system who should be. Stated precisely, our claim is this:

> *To the extent that* the American criminal justice system fails to implement policies that could significantly reduce crime and the suffering it produces (as argued in Chapter 1),
>
> *To the extent that* the American criminal justice system fails avoidably to protect Americans against the gravest dangers to their lives and property (as argued in Chapter 2),
>
> *To the extent that* the American criminal justice system apprehends and punishes individuals not because they are dangerous but because they are *dangerous and poor* (as argued in Chapter 3),
>
> *Then, to that same extent*, the American criminal justice system fails to give all Americans either protection or justice, aids and abets those who pose the greatest dangers to Americans, and uses force in ways that do not serve equally the interests of all who are subject to that force, and *thus its use of force is morally no better than crime itself.*

REHABILITATING CRIMINAL JUSTICE IN AMERICA

The criminal justice system in America is morally indistinguishable from criminality insofar as it *violates its own morally justifying ideals: Protection and justice*. Once this is understood, the requirements for rehabilitating the system follow rather directly. The system must institute policies that make good on its claim to protect society and to do justice. The remainder of this chapter briefly sketches the outlines of a "treatment strategy" for *helping the system go straight*. It cannot be reiterated too frequently that these proposals are not offered merely as a means of *improving* the system. Nor are we under any illusion that these proposals will be easily adopted or implemented. They are presented as the necessary requirements for establishing the criminal justice system's moral difference from, and moral superiority to, *crime;* and even if not implemented, they stand as a measure against which this moral difference and superiority can be judged. The proposals fall under the headings of the two ideals that justify the existence of a criminal justice system: protecting society and promoting justice.

Protecting Society

Every day that we refuse to implement those strategies that have a good chance of cutting down on the predatory and violent street crimes people fear, the system is an accomplice to those crimes and bears responsibility for the suffering they impose. Thus,

> *We must put an end to the crime-producing poverty and inequality in our midst.*

Throughout this book we have documented the striking persistence of large-scale poverty in the United States, which is a source of much of the crime people fear the most. In Chapter 1, we reviewed how poverty and inequality were sources of crime, and that inequality breeds crimes of greed by the wealthy. Although these predatory and exploitative acts are not as feared as street violence, they can be more destructive. Reducing inequality lessens the crimes of need by the poor and crimes of greed by the rich.

The elimination of poverty is the most promising crime-fighting strategy there is and, in the long run, the most cost-effective. It is sometimes observed that poverty itself doesn't cause crime, because, for example, there was more poverty in earlier times than now and yet less crime. There is an important truth here, but it is easy to miss it. The truth is that it is not poverty as such that breeds crime, but the things that poverty brings with it in a modern, free, and free-enterprise society like ours: lack of good education (because public schools are financed primarily out of local property taxes and the best schools are expensive private ones), disruption of families, lack of cohesive local community (because those who can will escape the poor inner cities as quickly as possible), lack of allegiance to social institutions (due to feeling left out), and so on. It is these things, rather than lack of money itself, that lead to crime. Investing in our inner cities and providing high-quality public education, job training, and jobs for the unemployed will give us more productive citizens with a stake in playing by the rules. And it will be cheaper than paying for police and prisons to house those who break the rules.

Eliminating the debilitating and crime-producing poverty around us is essential to any serious, long-term effort to protect society from crime. But along with it, we must

> *Let the crime fit the harm and the punishment fit the crime: treat the harmful acts of the well-off as crimes, and decriminalize "victimless crimes."*

For the criminal justice system to justify its methods, it must make good on its claim to protect society. This requires that the criminal law be redrawn so that the list of crimes reflects the real dangers that individuals pose to society. As we explained in Chapter 2, we must make new and clear laws against imposing certain dangers on workers and citizens generally, and then hold people to those laws no matter what their economic class is and no matter how big their corporation is. Crime in the suites should be prosecuted and punished as vigorously as crime in the streets, and in proportion to the harm it does.

The law must be drawn carefully so that individuals are not punished for harm they could not foresee or could not have avoided or that others have freely consented to risking. Moreover, this is not a matter of punishing people for anything and everything they do that might lead to harm. The pursuit of security must not swamp the legitimate claims of liberty and progress. Some risks are the inevitable companions of freedom, and some are part of modern life. For every mile of highway we build, we can predict the number of people who will be killed in accidents on it. This does not justify treating the highway engineer as a murderer. Rather, we must have an open and ongoing discussion about risk, especially where some profit by imposing risks on workers, consumers, and citizens generally. This discussion is especially important where corporations can create structured unaccountability or "organized irresponsibility"[1] so that those who profit from putting others at risk are shielded from responsibility for their decisions.

Within this framework, we must stop treating *indirect* harm as merely a regulatory matter and start *treating all intentional harm-producing acts in proportion to the actual harm they produce. We must enact and implement punishments that fit the harmfulness of the crime without respect to the class of the criminal.* Because responsibility for corporate actions tends to be spread or even blurred in large organizations, we need to implement a standard of "reckless supervision" in sentencing guidelines for corporate offenses so that individuals with supervisory authority can be held responsible for failure to exercise that authority when there is substantial risk of harm.[2] The Sarbanes-Oxley financial reform legislation took a step in this direction by requiring executives to certify the accuracy of financial statements, so that they cannot get paid big money to run a company and then claim they had no idea about massive frauds. The principle is sound and should be applied more widely in the business world.

But this is only the beginning. There is much more that can and should be done. In his book, *Corporate Crime and Violence,* Russell Mokhiber sets out a "50-Point Law-and-Order Program to Curb Corporate Crime."[3] Mokhiber's suggestions are quite realistic, and many fit well within the framework just outlined. A current list of recommendations for new laws would require corporate executives to report activities that might cause death or injury; make it a criminal offense to willfully, recklessly, or negligently fail to oversee an assigned activity that results in criminal conduct; enable federal prosecutors to bring federal homicide charges against companies that have caused death on a national scale; facilitate class action suits against corporations; require convicted companies to make their misdeeds public by advertising them; better protect whistleblowers from reprisal; increase the penalties for convicted corporate executives; use fines to support independent watchdog organizations; track and regularly report the extent and cost of white-collar crime; and establish a specialized corporate crime task force within the Department of Justice.[4] For serious and repeat offenses, the government should force a corporate restructuring. While sometimes called a corporate death penalty, the idea is that corporations could be broken up, criminal managers could be fired and/or indicted, but employees would have jobs at the restructured company—and honest employees would have opportunities to advance.[5] Such laws, duly applied, would begin to make the criminal justice system's response proportionate to the real dangers in our society.

The other side of the coin is the decriminalization of "victimless crimes," acts such as prostitution, gambling, vagrancy, and recreational drug use—acts that produce no harm to individuals who have not freely chosen to risk it. As long as these acts involve only adults who have freely chosen to participate, they are no threat to the liberty of any citizen. This also means that there is generally no person who is harmed by these acts and who is ready and able to press charges and testify against the wrongdoers. Therefore, police have to use a variety of shady tactics involving deception and actions bordering on entrapment, which undermine the public's respect for the police and the police officers' respect for themselves. The use of such low-visibility tactics increases the likelihood of corruption, arbitrariness, and discrimination in the enforcement of the law. Beyond this, because these acts produce no tangible harm to others, laws against them make criminals out of people who have no intention of injuring or taking advantage of others. In short, such laws fill our prisons with people who aren't dangerous, while we leave truly dangerous people on the streets and in the suites. To make good on its claim to protect society, the criminal justice system must not only treat the dangerous acts of business executives as crimes but also decriminalize those acts that are not clearly dangerous.[6]

More than 150 years ago, John Stuart Mill formulated a guiding principle, still relevant to our time, for the design of legislation in a society committed to personal liberty:

> That principle is, that the sole end for which mankind are warranted, individually or collectively, in interfering with the liberty of action of any of their number, is self-protection. That the only purpose for which power can be rightfully exercised over any [sane adult] member of a civilized community, against his will, is to prevent harm to others.[7]

Although this principle needs to be modified in recognition of some of the ways in which individuals can cause future harm to themselves in modern society where people must deal with machines and chemicals beyond their understanding,[8] the core of the principle is still widely accepted. This is the notion that a necessary condition of any justifiable legal prohibition is that it forbids an act that does foreseeable harm to someone other than the actor himself. Because priority should be given to freedom of action, this harm should be *demonstrable* (i.e., verifiable by some widely agreed-upon means, say, those used by science), and it should be of sufficient gravity to outweigh the value of the freedom that is to be legally prohibited.[9]

This principle should not only guide legislators and those engaged in revising and codifying criminal law but should also be raised to the level of an implicit constitutional principle. The U.S. Supreme Court recognizes certain traditional principles of legality as constitutional requirements even though they are not explicitly written into the Constitution. For instance, some laws have been held unconstitutional because of their vagueness[10] and others because they penalized a condition (such as being a drunk or an addict) rather than an action (such as drinking or using drugs).[11] The tenor of the Bill of Rights is to enshrine and protect individual liberty from the encroachment of the state, and thus Mill's principle is arguably already implicitly there.

Whether as a legislative or a judicial criterion, however, applying Mill's principle would undoubtedly rid our law of the residues of our puritanical moralism. And it would eliminate the forced induction into criminality of the individuals, mainly from the lower class, who are arrested for "victimless crimes." It would eliminate the pressure toward secondary crime (the need of the prostitute for a pimp to provide protection, theft by drug addicts to support their habits, violent turf wars between drug gangs, and so on). And it would free up resources for the fight against the really dangerous crimes. Thus,

> We must legalize the production and sale of "illicit drugs" and treat addiction as a public health problem.

In Chapter 1 we reviewed why current drug policy was a source of crime. When drug addicts cannot obtain their fix legally, they will obtain it illegally.

Because those who sell it illegally have a captive market, they will charge high prices to make their own risks worthwhile. To pay the high prices, addicts must, will, and do resort to crime. Thus, every day in which we keep the acquisition of drugs a crime, we are using the law to protect the high profits of black marketeers in the drug trade, *and* we are creating a situation in which large numbers of individuals are virtually physically compelled to commit theft. There can be little doubt that our present "cure" (arrests and incarceration) for narcotics use is more criminal (and crime-producing) than the narcotics themselves. Ethan Nadelmann, of the Woodrow Wilson School of Public and International Affairs, points out that

> there is no single legalization option. Legalization can mean a free market, or one closely regulated by the government, or even a government monopoly.... Legalization under almost any regime, however, does promise many advantages over the current approach. Government expenditures on drug-law enforcement would drop dramatically. So would organized crime revenues.[12]

Many observers seem to agree that the British system in which doctors may prescribe heroin for addicts is superior to our own punitive system. For example, an editorial in the *Montreal Gazette* states,

> A Dutch study found prescribing heroin to abusers is not only cost-effective, but provided better quality of life to addicts. Savings to society were estimated at more than $20,000 a year per addict in reduced policing costs and property crime. Without this program, addicts on average were spending $1,500 a month on heroin, and were involved in a crime every three days to get extra money for drugs.[13]

A number of experts have gone even further. Norval Morris and Gordon Hawkins urge that narcotics use be decriminalized and the drugs be sold in pharmacies by prescription. Kurt Schmoke (who, prior to being president of the University of Baltimore was the mayor of Baltimore, and Maryland's state attorney) has called for permitting health professionals to give drugs to addicts as part of a treatment and detoxification plan. Jerry Wilson, former Washington, DC, police chief, has suggested the possibility of treating opiates and cocaine derivatives the way alcohol currently is treated, while keeping some psychoactive drugs available only at pharmacies with a doctor's prescription.[14]

Because marijuana is arguably the least harmful drug, any reasonable plan of legalization will start by decriminalizing pot, not just allowing it for "medical" use by those who can afford an exam and license. On the other hand, there may be some drugs that are so addictive or so likely to stimulate people to violence that we must keep them illegal. If this turns out to be true (and the government has so exaggerated the dangers of illicit drugs over the years that healthy skepticism is warranted about these claims), it may be necessary to exclude these from the general program of decriminalization.

With less dangerous drugs decriminalized, however, many users of crack might switch to the less dangerous ones, and, in any event, already over-stretched law enforcement resources would be freed up to concentrate on the really dangerous drugs and on the crucial problem of keeping drugs away from youngsters.

Ending poverty, criminalizing the really dangerous acts of the well-off, and decriminalizing victimless crimes will protect society, reduce crime over-all, and free up our police and prisons for the fight against the criminals who really threaten our lives and limbs. For these, however,

> *We must develop correctional programs that promote rather than undermine personal responsibility, and we must offer ex-offenders real preparation and a real opportunity to succeed as law-abiding citizens.*

Chapter 1 explained why prisons were a source of crime. Prison reform is necessary because the scandal of our prisons has been amply documented for decades.[15] Like our drug policy, our prisons seem more calculated to pro-duce than to reduce crime. The enforced child-like dependency of imprison-ment may be the painful penalty that offenders deserve, but if it undermines their capacity to go straight after release, we are cutting off our noses to spite our faces. Philosopher Richard Lippke contends that, if we punish people be-cause they have failed to act morally, we must respect and preserve their ca-pacity to act morally.[16] But, people cannot learn responsible self-control if they have spent years living in a violent environment having every aspect of their lives—the hour they wake, the number of minutes they spend washing up, the time and content of eating and working and exercising, and the hour at which lights go out—regulated by someone else.

Add to this the fact that convicts usually emerge with no marketable skill and little chance of getting a decent job with the stigma of a criminal re-cord excluding them from much in the society they are reentering. The result is a system in which we never let criminals finish paying their debt to society and instead give them every incentive to return to crime. What's needed is the encouragement of restorative justice, the adoption of proven rehabilita-tive programs, and a transformation of prisons to infuse hope, personal re-sponsibility, and respect for human dignity into our correctional practices.[17]

Lippke contends that the harsh conditions that generally characterize American prisons should be replaced with what he calls the minimum con-ditions of confinement. These minimum conditions are already enough to de-prive offenders of freedom of movement and association, attenuate their ties with loved ones and friends, curtail their privacy, subject them to low levels of amenities, limit their work options and access to forms of entertainment, make them subservient to extensive bureaucratic control, and impose upon them a lasting stigma. Greater deprivations than these cause "near-extinction of the agency [the capacity to form responsible judgments and act on them] of inmates," and thus run afoul of the requirement that offenders be respected and preserved as autonomous moral agents.[18]

The National Academy of Sciences panel on incarceration suggests that policy makers take steps to "provide better conditions for those in prison" and "improve the experience of incarcerated men and women and reduce the unnecessary harm to their families and communities."[19] Francis Cullen goes further: "the rehabilitative ideal draws its power from its nobility and its rationality—from the promise that compassionate science, rather than vengeful punishment, is the road to reducing crime. Rehabilitation allows us to be a better and safer people."[20]

Former National Institute of Justice Director, Jeremy Travis, points out that 630,000 people leave prison each year and reenter society: "Reentry reflects the iron law of imprisonment: they all come back."[21] Yet, as criminologist Joan Petersilia poignantly notes:

> The average inmate coming home will have served a longer prison sentence than in the past, be more disconnected from family and friends, have a higher prevalence of substance abuse and mental illness, and be less educated and less employable than those in prior prison release cohorts. Each of these factors is known to predict recidivism, yet few of these needs are addressed while the inmate is in prison or on parole.[22]

If we are going to continue to punish people by depriving them of their liberty, we must do it in a way that prepares them for the life they will lead when their liberty is returned. Anything less than this is a violation of the Constitution's Eighth Amendment guarantee against "cruel and unusual punishment." Depriving a person of his or her liberty may be an acceptable punishment, but *depriving people of their dignity and a chance to live a law-abiding life when their punishment is supposed to be over is cruel and* (should be but sadly is not) *unusual!*

To be clear, we do not want a better system of mass incarceration. Other proposals would result in a smaller prison population, and also we believe that prisons are in need of a fundamental transformation.

To release offenders back into a safer and more peaceful society in the meantime, however,

We must enact and vigorously enforce stringent gun controls.

As Chapter 1 explained, guns are a source of crime and responsible for America's high rate of lethal violence. Americans are armed to the teeth. The handgun is the most easily concealed, the most effective, and the deadliest weapon there is. Its ubiquity is a constant temptation to would-be crooks who lack the courage or skill to commit crime without weapons or to chance hand-to-hand combat. Its ubiquity also means that any dispute may be transformed into a fatal conflict beyond the desires or expectations of the disputants.

A large number of accidental injuries and deaths are also linked to the prevalence of guns. And the problem is not limited to handguns. In recent years, it has become relatively easy to obtain rapid-firing assault rifles as well as other guns that house more bullets and fire them faster. Trying to fight crime while allowing such easy access to guns is like trying to teach a child to walk and tripping him each time he stands up. In its most charitable light, it is hypocrisy. Less charitably, it is complicity in murder.[23]

If, because of the Second Amendment, we continue to allow private individuals to own guns, we can at least require that gun owners be registered and perhaps certified after completing a course on the safe use of guns (safety classes are already commonly required as part of qualifying for gun permits). All gun sales should be accompanied by a background check. We can surely ban assault rifles and require all guns to have trigger locks that children and gun thieves cannot open.[24] We can make gun tracing easier for police to do, and we can allow the CDC and other public health authorities to research the prevention of gun violence.

These changes proposed here, taken together, would be likely to reduce dangerous crime and to bring us a legal order that actually punished (and, it is hoped, deterred) all and only those acts that really threaten our lives, limbs, and possessions, and punished them in proportion to the harm they really produce. Such a legal system could be truly said to protect society.

Promoting Justice

The changes recommended above would, in part, make the criminal justice system more just because people would be punished in proportion to the seriousness of their harmful acts, and the number of innocent persons victimized by those acts would be reduced. At the same time, however, we have seen that the criminal justice system is biased against the poor, and until poverty is eliminated, much must be done to assure justice for the poor people who get caught up in the criminal justice system. Thus, to begin with,

> *The criminal justice system should arrest, charge, convict, and sentence individuals with an eye only to their crime not to their economic class.*

Chapter 3 documented the rampant problem of economic class bias in criminal justice. More frequent arrests or harsher penalties for poor persons than for others accused of the same crime constitute a grave injustice that undermines the legitimacy of the criminal justice system. Unfortunately, the criminal justice system is fraught with class bias, but it collects almost no statistics on income, wealth, or occupation of arrestees or offenders, so the bias remains under-scrutinized. Further, many of the decisions that work to the disadvantage of the poor—police decisions to arrest, prosecutors' decisions to charge, and judges' decisions on how long to sentence—are exercises of discretion often out of public view. So,

> *We must narrow the range in which police officers, prosecutors, and judges exercise discretion, and we must develop procedures to hold them accountable to the public for the fairness and reasonableness of their decisions.*

Unlike prosecutors' or judges' decisions, the police officer's decision *not* to arrest is *not* a matter of record, thus it is the least visible exercise of discretion and the most difficult to control. Our best hope to make arrests by police more just lies in increased citizen awareness and educating police officers so that they become aware of the operation and impact of their own biases. As for prosecutorial and judicial discretion, two approaches seem potentially fruitful. First, lawmakers ought to spell out the acceptable criteria that prosecutors may use in deciding whether or what to charge. The practice of multiple charging (charging an accused burglar with "the lesser included crimes" of breaking and entering, possession of burglar's tools, and so on) should be eliminated. It is used by prosecutors to "coax" accused persons into pleading guilty to one charge by threatening to press *all* charges. Of all the dubious features of our system of bargain justice, this seems most clearly without justification because it works to *coerce* a plea of guilty that should be *voluntary* if it is to be legally valid.[25]

Federal sentencing guidelines (followed by the adoption of sentencing guidelines by many states) are an important step toward reducing discretion, and thus discrimination, in the criminal justice system. But they are only a step. They have not eliminated discrimination. As pointed out in Chapter 3, there are still disparities by race and class in sentencing. What's more, sentencing guidelines have not so much eliminated discretion as shifted it from judges to prosecutors (who decide what to charge). Because prosecutors are less insulated from political pressures than judges, that makes prosecutorial discretion more worrisome and harder to control. Thus, sentencing guidelines for judges must be matched with charging guidelines for prosecutors.[26]

Neither sentencing nor charging guidelines should be so rigid as to leave no room for the expert judgment of judges or prosecutors. (In 2005, the Supreme Court decided that sentencing guidelines are only advisory and not legally binding on judges, but research by the U.S. Sentencing Commission indicates that sentencing practices in the year following the Court's decision are consistent with earlier sentencing under the guidelines so all the problems with them remain.)[27] Rather than rigid rules, we need public accountability, timely release of data about the status of cases, and explanations for decisions about cases that are dropped.

Moreover, the sentencing guidelines that we have arose during the Reagan era, with its emphasis on extreme punitiveness. They often call for draconian mandatory minimum sentences for small crimes, particularly drug crimes, or life sentences for a third offense no matter how minor. In response to this, an advocacy group called "Families Against Mandatory Minimums" was formed. Their "files bulge with cases of citizens serving drug sentences of 5, 10 and 20 years without parole chances for first and often minor offenses."[28] Because this very punitive approach has dramatically expanded our prison populations with only small gains in crime reduction, it is time to separate the task of assuring evenhanded sentencing from that of hard-fisted sentencing. Whichever way we achieve it, it is clear that to make the criminal justice system function justly,

> *The criminal justice system must be used for public safety and community justice not for raising revenue.*

In response to the police shooting of an unarmed black teenager in Ferguson, Missouri, in 2014 a Department of Justice (DOJ) investigation found that the City Finance Director and City Manager asked the Police Chief to aggressively issue citations so that revenue from court fees could be increased because of other budget shortfalls. Management carefully monitored police "productivity" (number of citations issued), so DOJ found that "many officers appear to see some residents, especially those who live in Ferguson's predominantly African American neighborhoods, less as constituents to be protected than as potential offenders and sources of revenue."[29] They found further that "this emphasis on revenue has compromised the institutional character of Ferguson's police department"[30] and of its municipal court, which "does not act as a neutral arbiter of the law or a check on unlawful police conduct."[31] These practices especially harm the poorer residents because "minor offenses can generate crippling debts, [and] result in jail time because of an inability to pay."[32] As noted in the *Harvard Law Review*,

> assessing and collecting such debt may not be justifiable on penal grounds. Instead, it seems to be driven primarily by the need to raise revenue, an illegitimate state interest for punishment, and one that, in practice, functions as a regressive tax[33] [on the poor].

"That these taxes fall most heavily on poor, non-White people is a significant feature of the New Policing."[34]

The problem is not confined to Ferguson. The Justice Department's top civil rights prosecutor noted, "The Ferguson report really does highlight some issues that jurisdictions around the country are plagued with."[35] Indeed, a year after the Ferguson report, DOJ sent out a letter to courts around the country expressing concern over the "illegal enforcement of fines and fees"; it reminded them that "in *Bearden v. [Georgia* (1983)], the Court prohibited the incarceration of indigent probationers for failing to pay a fine because '[t]o do otherwise would deprive the probationer of his conditional freedom simply because, through no fault of his own, he cannot pay the fine'."[36] However, this guidance was revoked by President Trump's then-Attorney General Jefferson Sessions.[37]

Also, at a time when governments increasingly use private, for-profit businesses to provide services, some of those businesses share revenue with the government in ways that take advantage of people caught up in the criminal justice system. The "vast network of private companies profiteering from the criminalization of poverty and communities of color"[38] can use the threat of incarceration to coerce money from people and leads to consumer abuses by private companies supporting the criminal justice system.

Because even a criminal justice system genuinely working for public safety and community justice will still process people accused of crimes,

> *We must transform the equal right to counsel into the right to equal counsel.*

All the changes proposed here still leave standing what is probably the largest source of injustice to the poor in the system: *unequal access to quality legal counsel.* We know that privately retained counsel will have more incentive to put in time and effort to get their clients off the hook. The result is that, *for similar crimes,* those who can retain their own counsel are more likely to be acquitted than those who cannot. The present system of allocating assigned counsel or public defenders to the poor and privately retained lawyers to the affluent is little more than a parody of the constitutional guarantee of *equal protection under the law.*

In our system, even though lawyers are assigned to the poor, justice has a price. Little over a century ago, before there was a public police force in every town and city, people got "police protection" by hiring private police officers or bodyguards if they could afford it. Protection was available for a price, and so those who had more money were better protected under the law. Today, we regard it as every citizen's right to have police protection, and we would find it outrageous if police protection were allocated to citizens on a fee-for-service basis. *But this is precisely what we do with respect to the legal protection provided by lawyers!* As long as this continues, we cannot claim that there is equal treatment before the law in the criminal justice system.

Although this would appear to be a clear requirement of the equal protection and due process clauses of the Constitution, the Supreme Court has avoided it, perhaps because it surely poses great practical problems. However, the creation of public police forces to protect everyone posed great practical problems in its time as well.

It would not be appropriate, however, to use the police as a model for resolving the problem of equal counsel. To establish a government legal service for all—in effect, to nationalize the legal profession—might make equal legal representation available to all. It would, however, undermine the adversary system by undercutting the independence of defense attorneys from the state. Some form of national legal insurance to enable all individuals to hire private attorneys of their own choice, however, could bring us closer to equal legal protection without compromising the adversarial relationship.

Such insurance would undoubtedly have to be subsidized by the government, as are the police, courts, and prisons, but it would not necessarily have to be totally paid for out of taxes. People can rightly be expected to pay their legal bills up to some fraction of their income, if they have one. The rest would be paid for by a government subsidy that would make up the difference between what the accused could afford and the going rate for high-quality legal counsel. Nothing in the system need interfere with the freedom of the accused to select the lawyer of his or her choice, or interfere with the independence of the lawyer.

Undoubtedly, such a system would be costly. Our commitment to equal justice, however, remains a sham until we are willing to pay this price. Americans have paid dearly to protect the value of liberty enshrined in the Constitution. Is it too much to ask that they pay to realize the ideal of justice enshrined there too?

One final recommendation remains to be made.

> *We must establish a more just distribution of wealth and income, and make equal opportunity a reality for all Americans.*

We have already argued that any criminal justice system, by its very nature, protects the prevailing economic distribution. Therefore, it is an error to think of the criminal justice system as an entity that can be reformed in isolation from the larger social order. A criminal justice system protects that social order, and it can be no fairer than the order it protects. A law against theft may be enforced with an even and just hand, but if it protects an unjust distribution of wealth and property, the result is *injustice evenly enforced.*

Without economic and social justice, the police officer in the ghetto is indeed an occupying soldier with no more legitimacy than his or her gun provides. When the criminal justice system protects an unjust distribution of property, it uses coercion to force some to serve the interests of others at the expense of their own, and is thus morally indistinguishable from the criminal. *A criminal justice system can be no more just than the society its laws protect.* The achievement of economic and social justice is a necessary condition for establishing the criminal justice system's moral superiority to crime.

The National Academy of Sciences panel on incarceration noted that sentencing reform will not "relieve the underlying problems of economic insecurity, low education, and poor health that are associated with incarceration in the nation's poorest communities."[39] This is not merely about throwing money in the direction of poor people. It is a call for investment in our most important resource: human beings—and for targeting that investment where it is most urgently needed and morally required. The report suggests that solutions require changes in policies that "address school dropout, drug addiction, mental illness, and neighborhood poverty."[40] It also requires a real opportunity for poor people to lift themselves out of poverty without lowering themselves into dependency. This would amount to a redistribution of wealth and income in the direction of greater social and economic justice. Because it would also reduce the temptations to crime produced by poverty, as well as the alienation from social institutions that it gives rise to, it brings us full circle to the first recommendation that we made for protecting society. *Here the requirements of safety and justice converge.*

Summary

Every step toward reducing poverty and its debilitating effects, toward criminalization of the dangerous acts of the affluent and vigorous prosecution of white-collar crime, toward decriminalization of recreational drug use and other "victimless crimes," and toward domestic disarmament; every step toward creating a correctional system that promotes human dignity, toward giving ex-offenders a real opportunity to go straight, toward giving all individuals accused of crime equal access to high-quality legal expertise in their defense, toward making the exercise of power by police officers, prosecutors, and judges more accountable and more just; and every step toward establishing economic and social justice are steps that move us from a system of *criminal* justice to a system of criminal *justice*. The refusal to take those steps is a move in the opposite direction.

Study Questions

1. What do the three quotations at the beginning of this chapter mean? How do they apply to the American criminal justice system?
2. What are the necessary conditions for establishing the moral superiority of criminal justice to criminality?
3. What is meant by "victimless crimes"? Why do the authors believe they should not be kept criminal?
4. Would you be willing to pay more taxes to provide equal-quality legal counsel for the poor?
5. Is the distribution of wealth and income in America just? How is this related to the justice of the criminal justice system?
6. Are the recommendations made in this chapter likely to be instituted? What does your answer imply about your view of the American legal system?

Additional Resources

Jeffrey Reiman and Paul Leighton, *The Rich Get Richer and Poor Get Prison: A Reader* (Boston: Pearson, 2010). This volume is a collection of accessible articles that were either used as reference material for *The Rich Get Richer* or provide lively complementary examples or analysis. The reader is divided into sections that parallel the chapters of *The Rich Get Richer*, and each section of the reader opens with a substantial introduction, written by the editors, that provides article summaries, context, and linkages to *The Rich Get Richer*.
The authors also maintain a companion website to the text at www.paulsjusticepage.com/reiman.htm.

Notes

1. Dean Curran, "The Organized Irresponsibility Principle and Risk Arbitrage," *Critical Criminology*, 26, no. 4 (2018): 595–610, https://doi.org/10.1007/s10612-018-9415-x.
2. Kip Schlegel, *Just Deserts for Corporate Criminals* (Boston: Northeastern University Press, 1990), p. 137.
3. Russell Mokhiber, *Corporate Crime and Violence: Big Business Power and the Abuse of Public Trust* (San Francisco: Sierra Club, 1988), pp. 38–65.
4. Ibid.; David Friedrichs, *Trusted Criminals* (Belmont, CA: Wadsworth/Cengage, 2010), pp. 364–366; Mary Ramirez Kreiner, "Prioritizing Justice: Combating Corporate Crime from Task Force to Top Priority," *Marquette Law Review* 93, no. 3 (2010): 971–1018; Brandon L. Garrett, "Declining Corporate Prosecutions," *American Criminal Law Review,* v 57 #1 (2020).
5. Mary Kreiner Ramirez and Steven Ramirez, *The Case for the Corporate Death Penalty: Restoring Law and Order on Wall Street* (New York: New York University Press, 2017).
6. See Norval Morris and Gordon Hawkins, *The Honest Politician's Guide to Crime Control* (Chicago: University of Chicago Press, 1970), Ch. 1, "The Overreach of the Criminal Law," pp. 1–28; Herbert Packer, *The Limits of the Criminal Sanction* (Stanford, CA: Stanford University Press, 1968); Jeffrey H. Reiman, "Can We Avoid the Legislation of Morality?" in Nicholas N. Kittrie and Jackwell Susman (eds.), *Legality, Morality and Ethics in Criminal Justice* (New York: Praeger, 1979), pp. 130–141.
7. John Stuart Mill, *On Liberty* (1859; reprint, New York: Appleton-Century-Crofts, 1973), p. 9.
8. See, for example, Gerald Dworkin, "Paternalism," in Richard Wasserstrom (ed.), *Morality and the Law* (Belmont, CA: Wadsworth, 1971), pp. 107–126; and Joel Feinberg, "Legal Paternalism," in Richard Wasserstrom (ed.), *Today's Moral Problems* (New York: Macmillan, 1975), pp. 33–50.
9. See Peter T. Manicas, *The Death of the State* (New York: Putnam, 1974), Ch. 5, "The Liberal Moral Ideal," pp. 194–241; and H. L. A. Hart, *Law, Liberty and Morality* (New York: Vintage, 1963).
10. Jerome Hall, *General Principles of Criminal Law,* 2nd ed. (New York: Bobbs-Merrill, 1960), pp. 36–48. For a constitutional and philosophical argument for treating Mill's harm principle as an implied constitutional principle, see David

A. J. Richards, *Sex, Drugs, Death, and the Law: An Essay on Human Rights and Over-criminalization* (Totowa, NJ: Rowman & Littlefield, 1982), pp. 1–34, inter alia.

11. See *Robinson* v. *California*, 370 U.S. 66 (1962), in which the court held that a state law penalizing a person for the "status" of addiction constitutes "cruel and unusual punishment" in violation of the Eighth Amendment to the Constitution. Discussed in Nicholas N. Kittrie, *The Right to Be Different: Deviance and Enforced Therapy* (Baltimore, MD: Johns Hopkins University Press, 1971), pp. 35–36, inter alia.

12. Ethan Nadelmann, "U.S. Drug Policy: A Bad Export," in Robert Lang (ed.), *Drugs in America* (New York: Wilson, 1993), p. 232.

13. "Prescription Heroin? It Just Might Work," *Montreal Gazette,* June 8, 2005, p. A24.

14. Jerry V. Wilson, "Our Wasteful War on Drugs," *The Washington Post,* January 18, 1994, p. A20.

15. National Research Council Committee on Causes and Consequences of High Rates of Incarceration, Jeremy Travis, Bruce Western, and Steve Redburn (eds.), *The Growth of Incarceration in the United States: Exploring Causes and Consequences* (Washington, DC: The National Academies Press, 2014).

16. Richard L. Lippke, *Rethinking Imprisonment* (New York: Oxford University Press, 2007), pp. 111–112.

17. Francis Cullen and Karen Gilbert, *Reaffirming Rehabilitation* (Cincinnati, OH: Anderson, 1982); Francis Cullen, "Make Rehabilitation Corrections' Guiding Paradigm," in Jeffery Reiman and Paul Leighton (eds.), *The Rich Get Richer: A Reader* (Boston, MA: Allyn & Bacon, 2010) pp. 180–189; John Braithwaite, "Encourage Restorative Justice," in *The Rich Get Richer: A Reader*, pp. 174–180; Lynn Branham "The Mess We're In: Five Steps Towards The Transformation of Prison Cultures," *Indiana Law Review* 44 (2011): 703–733.

18. Lippke, *Rethinking Imprisonment*, pp. 105–108, 111–113, 150, 241.

19. National Research Council, *The Growth of Incarceration in the United States*, p. 9.

20. Quoted in Paul Leighton, "A Model Prison for the Next 50 Years: The High-Tech, Public-Private Shimane Asahi Rehabilitation Center," *Justice Policy Journal* 11, no. 1 (Spring 2014).

21. Jeremy Travis, *And They All Come Back* (Washington, DC: Urban Institute Press, 2005), p. xxi.

22. Quoted in National Research Council, *The Growth of Incarceration in the United States*, p. 193.

23. See the thoughtful recommendations for gun control and their rationale in Morris and Hawkins, *The Honest Politician's Guide to Crime Control*, pp. 63–71.

24. Joseph Blocher, "The Right Not to Keep or Bear Arms," *Stanford Law Review* 64, no. 1 (2012): p. 104. The author argues that people who believe they are safer without guns are attempting to protect themselves from a risk of future violence, just like those who choose to keep a gun. The author then asks, "If self-defense is the 'core' of the Amendment, why should only one of these decisions be constitutionally protected?"

25. We have already pointed out (Chapter 3) that the vast majority of persons convicted of crimes in the United States are not convicted by juries. They plead guilty as the result of a "bargain" with the prosecutor (underwritten by the judge) in which the prosecutor agrees to drop other charges in return for the guilty plea. Kenneth Kipnis argues that the entire system of bargain justice is a violation of the ideal of justice because it amounts to coercing a guilty plea and often to

punishing an offender for a crime other than the one he or she has committed. See Kenneth Kipnis, "Criminal Justice and the Negotiated Plea," *Ethics* 86, no. 2 (1976): 93–106.

26. This proposal is also made in a Note, "Developments in the Law: Race and the Criminal Process," *Harvard Law Review* 101 (1988): 1550–1551. The authors recommend that charging guidelines be supplemented with an "impact-inference standard." Under this standard, a defendant who believes that he or she has been discriminatorily charged would have to show that (1) he or she is the member of an identifiable class, (2) there is statistical evidence of discriminatory impact of prosecutorial decisions in the jurisdiction, and (3) the prosecutor's office lacked internal guidelines and procedures adequate to prevent abuse. If a defendant succeeded in showing these three elements, the burden of proof would shift to the government to explain its actions. Ibid., pp. 1552–1553.

27. See John Council, "Survey Reveals Little Change in Sentencing Habits after 'Booker,'" law.com, www.law.com/jsp/article.jsp?id=1123684510748. The U.S. Sentencing Commission regularly monitors sentencing practices, and the latest reports are available at U.S. Sentencing Commission, www.ussc.gov/bf.HTM.

28. Colman McCarthy, "Justice Mocked: The Farce of Mandatory Minimum Sentences," *The Washington Post,* February 27, 1993, p. A23.

29. U.S. Department of Justice, Civil Rights Division, *Investigation of the Ferguson Police Department,* March 4, 2015, p. 2, www.justice.gov/sites/default/files/opa/press-releases/attachments/2015/03/04/ferguson_police_department_report.pdf.

30. Ibid.

31. Ibid., p. 3.

32. Ibid., p. 4.

33. Christopher Hampson, "State Bans on Debtors' Prisons and Criminal Justice Debt," *Harvard Law Review* 129 (2016): 1025, https://ssrn.com/abstract=2827221.

34. Jeffrey Fagan, *Race and the New Policing, Reforming Criminal Justice, Vol. 2: Policing,* Erik Luna (ed.), (Phoenix: Arizona State University, 2017); Columbia Public Law Research Paper No. 14-561(2017), https://scholarship.law.columbia.edu/faculty_scholarship/2058.

35. Campbell Robertson, Shaila Dewan, and Matt Apuzzo, "Ferguson Became Symbol, but Bias Knows No Border," *New York Times,* March 7, 2015, www.nytimes.com/2015/03/08/us/ferguson-became-symbol-but-bias-knows-no-border.html. See also Douglas Evans, *The Debt Penalty—Exposing the Financial Barriers to Offender Reintegration* (New York, NY: Research & Evaluation Center, John Jay College of Criminal Justice, City University of New York, 2014); Tamar Birckhead, "The New Peonage," *Washington & Lee Law Review* 72, no. 4 (2015): 1595–1678.

36. U.S. Department of Justice, Civil Rights Division letter, March 14, 2016, pp. 1 and 3, www.justice.gov/crt/file/832461/download.

37. Charlie Savage, "Justice Dept. Revokes 25 Legal Guidance Documents Dating to 1975," *New York Times,* December 21, 2017, www.nytimes.com/2017/12/21/us/politics/justice-dept-guidance-documents.html.

38. Alex Kornya et al., "Crimsumerism: Combating Consumer Abuses in the Criminal Legal System," *Harvard Civil Rights-Civil Liberties Law Review* (CR-CL) 54 o. 3 (2019): 111, https://ssrn.com/abstract=3354644.

39. National Research Council, *The Growth of Incarceration in the United States,* p. 10.

40. Ibid.

The Marxian Critique of Criminal Justice*

— Jeffrey Reiman

In the first appendix,[1] I shall try to present the reader with an overview of Marxian theory that goes from Marxism's theory of capitalism to its theory of law and from there to criminal justice. This addresses some of the same aspects of criminal justice discussed in the main text of this book, but it sets them in a theoretical framework different from (although not incompatible with) the Pyrrhic defeat theory, with its historical inertia explanation of the peculiar failure of criminal justice. I shall close with comments on the ethical implications of the Marxian analysis.

Criminal justice has a concrete reality comprising police, prisons, courts, guns, and the rest. What is most important for our purposes, however, is the particular shape that this concrete reality takes in capitalism. This shape is governed according to certain principles that spell out what shall count as violations, what shall be done to violators, and so on. (For simplicity's sake, I shall use the term *criminal justice* as shorthand for the principles that normally govern criminal justice practices and practitioners in capitalism, and use the term *criminal justice system* as shorthand for the concrete reality of the practices and practitioners so governed.) Marxian analysis is in the first instance directed toward these governing principles. It aims to show that these principles are "economic reflexes," that is, they reflect and thus support the existing economic arrangements—in our case, the capitalist mode of production.

Criminal justice plays an ideological role in support of capitalism because people do not recognize that the principles governing criminal justice practices are reflections of capitalism. The principles of criminal justice appear instead to be the result of pure reason, and thus a system that supports capitalism is (mistakenly) seen as an expression of rationality itself! Engels—Marx's longtime collaborator—writes that "the jurist imagines he is operating with *a priori* [i.e., purely rational] principles, whereas they are really only economic

*Copyrighted material is reprinted by permission of The Institute for Criminal Justice Ethics, 524 West 59th Street, Rm. 08.70.00, New York, NY, 10019–1029.

reflexes; so everything is upside-down. And it seems to me obvious that this inversion... so long as it remains unrecognized, forms what we call *ideological conception*."[2] As a consequence of this "inversion," criminal justice embodies and conveys a misleading and partisan view of the reality of the whole capitalist system. Because capitalism requires laws that give individual capitalists the right to own factories and resources, a view of these laws that makes them appear to be purely rational makes capitalism appear purely rational as well.

Before proceeding, a few words about the nature of Marxian theory are in order. First of all, Marx's theory of capitalism is separate from his advocacy of socialism and communism. Marx might be right about how capitalism works or about capitalism's unjust nature, even if socialism or communism would in fact be worse or even if they are merely utopian dreams that cannot be made real. This is important because of the tendency to think that the collapse of communism in Eastern Europe and the former Soviet Union (as well as the unpalatable features of that communism before it collapsed) refutes Marxian theory generally. This is quite untrue. What the collapse of Eastern European and Soviet communism refutes is, if anything, the theories of Lenin and Stalin about how to establish communism. Marx himself said very little about such things, and what he does say generally favors a much more democratic kind of socialism and communism than what Lenin and Stalin managed to bring about. Accordingly, it is still useful to look at what Marx thought about capitalism, even if one is convinced by recent events of the undesirability of actual communism or the impossibility of ideal communism.

Second, when we turn to Marx's theory of capitalism, we see that Marx portrays capitalism in pure form. He does so not to claim that that is how it actually exists anywhere, but rather to show the shape to which it tends everywhere. Actual systems will be a product of the force of that tendency versus the force of local factors, traditions, talent, innovation, luck, resources, the success or failure of particular human actions, and so on. Likewise, a Marxian analysis of criminal justice will indicate the pure form toward which criminal justice systems tend insofar as they support the functioning of capitalism. Actual criminal justice systems will be approximations of this tendency. Actual criminal justice systems will also clearly be shaped by human actions—often substantially so. No Marxist needs to deny that the criminal justice system in the capitalist United States is much different from the criminal justice system in, say, capitalist Chile. What he or she must claim, rather, is that as capitalism develops in both countries, their criminal justice systems will increasingly tend to take on the shape that the theory implies.

I shall try to show how Marxism leads to a theory of the structure that criminal justice systems tend to have under capitalism, while at the same time recognizing that any existing criminal justice system is only an approximation of this structure. To give the reader as complete a picture as possible (in this short space) of the whole of Marxian theory—from general theory of capitalism to particular theory of criminal justice, and from there to ethical evaluation—I will have to sacrifice a lot of detail. I shall largely ignore the differences that individual actions may make in determining the shape of actual systems. I hope I have said enough to suggest that this in no way implies that human actions are irrelevant to actual historical outcomes.

I proceed in the following way. In the first section, "Marxism and Capitalism," I sketch out enough of Marx's theory of the capitalist mode of production as is necessary to lay the foundation for a Marxian theory of law. Because law is, for Marxism, a form of ideology, we shall have to see how ideology works in capitalism. I take this up in the next section, "Capitalism and Ideology." In "Ideology and Law," I develop the Marxian theory of law and from it the Marxian theory of criminal justice. Then, in the final section, "Law and Ethics," I consider the characteristic Marxian moral judgments about criminal justice—particularly about guilt and punishment—that are appropriate in light of the Marxian account.

MARXISM AND CAPITALISM

Marx says that capitalism is a system of "forced labour—no matter how much it may seem to result from free contractual agreement."[3] Here is both the truth that Marx asserts about capitalism and the legal ideology that shrouds that truth. To understand precisely how this works, we must consider the nature of the coercion that Marx discovered in capitalism.

For Marx, the value of any commodity is equivalent to the average amount of labor-time necessary to produce it.[4] Under capitalism, the worker's ability to labor—Marx calls this *labor-power*—is sold to the capitalist in return for a wage. Because labor-power is also a commodity, its value is equivalent to the average amount of labor-time necessary to produce it. *Producing labor-power* means producing the goods needed to maintain a functioning worker. The value of labor-power then is equivalent to the labor-time that on the average goes into producing the goods (food, clothing, shelter, and so on) necessary to maintain a functioning worker at the prevailing standard of living, which Marx understood to differ among countries depending on their respective histories (*Capital*, vol. 1, p. 171). The worker receives this in the form of a wage, that is, in the form of the money necessary to purchase these goods.

The capitalist obtains the money she pays as a wage by selling what the worker produces during the time for which he is employed. If the worker produced an amount of value equivalent only to his wage, there would be nothing left over for the capitalist and no reason for her to hire the worker in the first place. Labor-power, however, has the unique capacity to produce more value than its own value (*Capital*, vol. 1, pp. 193–194). The worker can work longer than the labor-time equivalent of the value of the wage he receives. Marx calls the amount of labor-time that the worker works to produce value equivalent to his wage *necessary labor.* The additional labor-time that the worker works beyond this is called *surplus labor,* and the value it produces, *surplus value.* The surplus value, of course, belongs to the capitalist and is the source of her profit (*Capital*, vol. 1, pp. 184–186); that is, when the capitalist sells the product made by the worker, the capitalist gives some of the money she gets back to the worker as wage (this corresponds to the value that the worker put into the product during his necessary labor-time), and the capitalist keeps the rest as profit (this corresponds to the surplus labor-time that the worker puts in after his necessary labor-time).

Profit, then, rests on the extraction of unpaid surplus labor from the worker. To see this, one needs to only recall that although all products in the economy are produced by labor, only a portion of those products are wage-goods that the workers get paid with (wages only have value because they can be traded for wage-goods). The remainder belongs to their bosses and is effectively uncompensated. The wage-goods only compensate necessary labor-time to which they are equivalent in value. What workers produce beyond this goes to the capitalist gratis. Thus, writes Marx, "The secret of the self-expansion of capital [that is, the secret of profit] resolves itself into having the disposal of a definite quantity of other people's unpaid labour" (*Capital*, vol. 1, p. 534).

For Marx, however, capitalism is not only a system in which unpaid labor is extracted from workers, it is also a system in which workers are *forced* to provide this unpaid labor. Workers are not merely shortchanged; they are enslaved. Capitalism is "a coercive relation" (*Capital*, vol. 1, p. 309). The coercion, however, is not of the direct sort that characterized slavery or feudal serfdom. It is, rather, an indirect force built into the very fact that capitalists own the means of production and laborers do not. Means of production are things, such as factories, machines, land, and resources that are necessary for productive labor. Lacking ownership of means of production, workers lack their own access to the means of producing a livelihood. *By this very fact,* workers are compelled to sell their labor to capitalists for a wage because the alternative is (depending on conditions) either painful or fatal: relative pauperization or absolute starvation.

This compulsion is not in conflict with the fact that the terms upon which the worker works for the capitalist are the result of free contractual agreements. Indeed, the compulsion works *through* free agreements. Because the agreements are free, each side must offer the other a reason for agreeing. If workers offered capitalists only as much labor as went into the wage-goods they will get back in return from the capitalists, the capitalists would have no reason to purchase their labor. It follows that, no matter how free the wage contract is, as long as it occurs in a context in which a few own all the means of production, those who do not own means of production will be compelled to give up some of their labor without compensation to those who do. Thus, Marx describes the wage-worker as a "man who is compelled to sell himself of his own free will" (*Capital*, vol. 1, p. 766). The compulsion of the worker operates through the structure of property relations: "The dull compulsion of economic relations completes the subjection of the labourer to the capitalist. Direct force, outside economic conditions, is of course still used, but only exceptionally" (*Capital*, vol. 1, p. 737).

The very existence of the social roles of capitalist and worker—defined by ownership and nonownership of means of production, respectively—is what coerces the worker to work without compensation. It coerces in the same way that a social structure that allotted to one group ownership and thus control of all the available oxygen, would coerce. Beyond what was necessary to defend this group against challenges to its ownership of the oxygen, no additional force would be necessary for the coercion to operate. Indeed, it would operate quite effectively by means of bargains freely struck in which the nonoxygen-owners had to offer something to the owners to get the chance to breathe. They, too, would be compelled to sell themselves of their own free will. The same can be said of capitalism. Once its structure of social roles is in place, all that is necessary is that individuals choose, from among the alternatives available to them in their roles, the course of action that best serves their self-interest, and the extraction of unpaid surplus labor is enforced without further need for overt force.

As with the oxygen-owning society, so too with capitalism: Overt force is used or threatened to defend owners against challenges to their ownership. That is just another way of saying that, in capitalism, the state uses overt force to protect private property. And this force is used to protect both the property of the capitalist (her factories and resources) and the property of the worker (his labor-power). This differs crucially from the way in which overt force is exercised in social relations like slavery. In slavery, the use of overt force is part of the normal exercise of the master's power. In capitalism, overt force is used to defend all against forceful interference with their right to dispose of whatever property they happen to own, be it means of production or labor-power. Accordingly, such force is not part of the capitalist's power, but is left to a third party that, in this respect, functions neutrally toward all owners—the state.

With both capitalists and workers protected in their capacity to dispose of what they own, the process by which workers are forced to work gratis can proceed apace. This effect can be achieved with the state functioning neutrally. Although the state normally favors the interests of capitalists over workers,[5] it can serve the process of forced extraction of unpaid labor by protecting both capitalists and workers alike in their freedom to dispose of what they happen to own. Thus, the state can treat capitalists and workers as having the same or "equal" property rights over what they own. It just turns out that what capitalists happen to own is means of production, and what workers happen to own is the muscles in their arms. Capitalism, then, naturally appears as a system of free exchanges between people with equal rights (over unequal amounts of property). This brings us to the phenomenon of ideology.

CAPITALISM AND IDEOLOGY

Of the study of social revolutions, Marx writes,

> In considering such transformations a distinction should always be made between the material transformation of the economic conditions of production, which can be determined with the precision of natural science, and the legal, political, religious, aesthetic or philosophic—in short, ideological forms in which men become conscious of this conflict and fight it out.[6]

The legal, then, is an ideological form. This is not to say that it is merely mental. It has a material reality in the form of police and prisons and guns and courts and legislators and law books, and the rest. What is crucial is how this material reality is shaped, and for that we must understand how ideology is shaped.

As its etymology suggests, *ideology* means the science of ideas, where science can be taken in the ordinary sense as the study of causal connections. (Recall the discussion of ideology in Chapter 4.) In the context of Marxian theory, ideology comes to mean the ideas caused by the mode of production (in our case, the capitalist mode of production), and, equally important for Marxism, the caused ideas are in some important way false. Thus understood, for Marxism, the study of ideology denotes the study of how the mode of production gives rise to people's false beliefs about society. In *The German Ideology*, Marx writes,

> If in all ideology men and their circumstances appear upside down as in a camera obscura, this phenomenon arises just as much from their historical life-process as the inversion of objects on the retina does from their physical life-process.
>
> The phantoms formed in the human brain are also, necessarily, sublimates of their material life-process, which is empirically verifiable and bound to material premises.[7]

As this statement makes clear, the study of ideology requires that both the existence and the falsity of ideological beliefs be given a *materialist* explanation.

To understand this requirement, consider that Marxian materialism is the conjunction of two distinct claims, an ontological claim and a social scientific one. The *ontological* claim is that what exists is material, that is, physical objects in space. Mind and spirit, in any immaterial sense, are chimera. ("From the start the 'spirit' is afflicted with the curse of being 'burdened' with matter, which here makes its appearance in the form of agitated layers of air, sounds, in short, of language" [*German Ideology*, p. 19].) The *social scientific* claim is that the way in which a society is organized for the production of the material conditions of its existence and reproduction ("the mode of production") plays the chief (though by no means the only) causal role in determining the nature and occurrence of social events. ("The mode of production of material life conditions the social, political and intellectual life process in general.")[8] According to this social scientific claim, the belief that societies are shaped primarily by their members' attitudes, or that history is shaped by the progressive development of knowledge or ideals, is false. Rather, it is primarily the organization of production that shapes people's attitudes, and the progressive development of modes of production that shapes history. ("That is to say, we do not set out from what men say, imagine, conceive, nor from men as narrated, thought of, conceived, in order to arrive at men in the flesh. We set out from real, active men, and on the basis of their real life-process we demonstrate the development of the ideological reflexes and echoes of this life-process" [*German Ideology*, p. 14]; "it is not the consciousness of men that determines their being, but, on the contrary, their social being that determines their consciousness.")[9]

Of these two claims, the social scientific is more restrictive than the ontological. The ontological claim requires only that we attribute ideology to material realities, be they brains or agitated layers of air or modes of production. The social scientific claim requires that among these material realities, priority be given to the mode of production as the primary cause of ideological beliefs. This means that the *main* source of false ideology is to be found not in the perceiving subject but in the perceived objects. It is not a "subjective illusion," the result of faulty perception by individuals of their material conditions, but an "objective illusion," the result of more or less accurate perception of those conditions.[10] Viewing ideology this way has the added benefit of leaving the door open just wide enough so that the theory of ideology does not exclude the possibility of all true beliefs—and thus of the very science upon which it is based. A materialist theory of ideology, then, must show that false ideology is an *objective illusion* arising primarily from a more or less accurate perception of the organization of material production, rather than from some subjective error.[11] Bear in mind that this is a matter of placing primary emphasis on objective factors, not of absolutely excluding subjective ones.

We can fix the idea of an "objective illusion" by considering a very common example of one, namely, the illusion that the sun goes around the earth. Any illusion, any erroneous belief that an individual holds, can be *stated* as a subjective error—but not every erroneous belief arises primarily *because* of a subjective error. A person who believes that the sun rises above a stationary horizon in the morning makes a mistake. However, this sort of mistake differs crucially from, say, the mistake that a color-blind person might make of believing that the light is green when it is red, or the mistake a person balancing her checkbook might make of believing that a number is 4 when it is 2. In these latter cases, the mistaken beliefs are not merely held by the individuals; they arise in the individuals primarily as the result of a defective perceptual faculty or misuse of a sound one. These are subjective illusions. In these cases, correcting the defect in the perceptual faculty (or in its use) should undo the mistake. The mistaken belief that the sun goes around the earth, by contrast, arises as a result of a sound perceptual faculty properly exercised. This is an objective illusion. Neither healthier vision nor looking more carefully will enable an individual to correct this mistake and see that what occurs at dawn is not the sun rising above the horizon, but the horizon tipping down below the sun.

The ideology of capitalism is the illusion that capitalism is noncoercive. This illusion is a mistake of the same type as the illusion that the sun goes around the earth. What corresponds in capitalism to the movement of the sun seen from the earth is the free exchange of wages and labor-power between capitalists and workers. That the sphere of exchange is the objective basis of ideology is recognized in effect by Marx, when he writes that this sphere,

> within whose boundaries the sale and purchase of labour-power
> goes on, is in fact a very Eden of the innate rights of man. There alone

rule Freedom, Equality, Property. Freedom, because both buyer and
seller of a commodity, say of labourpower, are constrained only by
their free will.

(Capital, vol. 1, p. 176)

The normal perception of what goes on in exchange gives rise to the
ideological illusion that capitalism is uncoercive. This is not because the freedom in exchange is an illusion. The fact is that, for Marx, capitalism works
only because the moment of exchange, through which the circuit of capital
continually passes, is truly free.

> For the conversion of his money into capital, therefore, the owner
> of money must meet in the market with the free labourer, free in the
> double sense, that as a free man he can dispose of his labour-power
> as his own commodity, and that on the other hand, he has no other
> commodity for sale, is short of everything necessary for the realiza-
> tion of his labour-power.

(Capital, vol. 1, p. 169)

That the second of these senses of freedom is the worker's "freedom from"
ownership of means of production does not deny the reality of the first sense,
without which we would have slavery or serfdom rather than capitalism.

In exchange, the power that capitalists have over workers recedes from
view. If we distinguish two sorts of power—the power to withhold one's commodity until offered something preferable, and the power to command obedience and back this up with violent force—then it is clear that, in the sphere
of exchange, the latter power is suspended and all that remains is the former
power. This former power is a power that all parties to the exchange have
equally. Thus, the unequal power of capitalist and worker appears as their
equal power to withhold from exchange what they happen to own, and their
social inequality appears as the difference between the things that they happen to own. To use the famous words of Marx's analysis of the fetishism of
commodities, a "social relation between men assumes, in their eyes, the fan-
tastic form of a relation between things" (*Capital*, vol. 1, p. 72).

If this accurate perception of what goes on in exchange is to explain
how capitalism appears uncoercive, we need to understand how the sphere
of exchange—which is only part of capitalism—should be the source of beliefs about the whole of capitalism. Why should the experience of freedom in
exchange, rather than, say, the experience of taking orders on the production
line, determine the beliefs that members of capitalist societies come naturally
to have? How is the representation of exchange *generalized* into a view of capitalism as a whole?

Marx offers a clue to the answer to this question when he says that the
fetishism of commodities results because "the producers do not come into
contact with each other until they exchange" (*Capital*, vol. 1, p. 73). Exchange
transactions are the salient points of social contact for economic actors in capitalism. They punctuate capitalist social relations. Every social interaction

between individuals playing roles in the capitalist mode of production begins with such a transaction (say, the signing of a wage contract exchanging labor-power for money) and can be ended with such a transaction (say, the dissolution of the wage contract). Each of these beginnings and endings is characterized by the absence of either party having the power to command the other's obedience and use violence to get it. Each party knows that he can enter or withdraw from any capitalist social interaction without being subject to the command or the overt force of the other. What constraint either feels seems to be only a matter of what they happen to own, which naturally appears as a feature of their own good or bad fortune rather than a condition coercively imposed by the other. Thus, *all* capitalist social interactions, *not just the exchanges themselves*, appear as voluntary undertakings between equal people who happen to own different things.

Exchange accurately perceived and then generalized is what leads workers in capitalist societies to believe that they are free, although they take orders most of their waking lives. Thus, ideologically false beliefs about capitalism result from an accurate perception of exchange, when the rest of capitalism is, by default, assumed to be more of the same. The law follows suit.

IDEOLOGY AND LAW

"Law," wrote Marx in *The Poverty of Philosophy*, "is only the official recognition of fact."[12] For capitalist law, the fact is exchange. Law in capitalism is the official recognition of the fact of the economic relations in which the exchangers stand to one another. This insight—which will guide the materialist explanation of criminal law that I shall develop in this section—must be credited to the work of the Soviet legal theorist Evgeny Pashukanis, whose *General Theory of Law and Marxism* was published in Russian in 1924.[13] Among the things for which Pashukanis argued was that law was a product of capitalism and consequently had no legitimate place in socialism. As Stalin took firm control of the Soviet Union and saw fit to use the law to shore up that control, Pashukanis came eventually into disfavor. He recanted his views to some extent, but it was too late. By 1937 he had been declared an enemy of the people, and he "disappeared" shortly thereafter. Recently rediscovered by Western Marxists, Pashukanis's work was first the object of lavish praise and subsequently the target of harsh criticism. I do not intend to endorse or defend the whole of Pashukanis's theory. He aimed at a general theory of law and made only a few observations about criminal law, which is my main concern here. I shall try to show that his basic insight about the relation between law and exchange can be developed into an explanation of the content of the criminal law and of the constitutional protections relevant to criminal justice.

Marx writes that parties to an exchange

must behave in such a way that each does not appropriate the commodity of the other, and part with his own, except by means of an act done by mutual consent. They must, therefore, mutually

recognize in each other the rights of private proprietors. This jurid-
ical relation, which thus expresses itself in a contract, whether such
contract be part of a developed legal system or not, is a relation between two wills, and is but the reflex of the real economic relation
between the two.

(Capital, vol. 1, pp. 88–89)

Exchangers must in fact refrain from forcing those with whom they
would trade to part with their goods or services or money. Official recognition of this fact takes the form of granting to exchangers "the rights of private
proprietors." Because this recognition is related to the ideological failure to
perceive the coerciveness reproduced in exchanges between proprietors of
capital and proprietors of labor, exchanges are understood legally as acts of
the free will of the parties as long as no overt violence is used or threatened.
Consequently, exchangers treat one another as *free subjects* whose freedom is
expressed in their *right to dispose of their property without interference from others.*

It is the difference between what capitalists own and what workers own
that, for Marx, makes it possible to reproduce a coercive relation through free
exchange. If the law follows ideology in representing the relation between exchangers as noncoercive, then the law must abstract from this difference in
what is owned and treat each party as having the same right to dispose of his
property regardless of what that property is. The law reflects this in its formal-
ity. The legal right of property is an empty form to be filled in with different
content, depending on what an individual owns. Capitalists and workers have
the same right of property; they just happen to own different things. It just happens that what some people own are factories and what others own are their
bodies, but their property rights in these things are the same. Their freedom to
dispose of their property also is the same.[14] Thus, exchangers treat each other as
equal free subjects with equal property rights—that is to say, as legal *persons.*[15]

We saw in the previous section that ideology is not to be understood as
merely a subjective illusion. Ideology reflects the real way in which capitalism
appears to its participants. By the same token, the ideological nature of law
reflects the real relations in which exchangers stand to one another. The written law, even the institutions of law (from lawmakers to law enforcers) are not
the source of law. They reflect real, objective relations between members of a
capitalist society, relations that exist, so to speak, on the ground first and only
later on the page or in the courts for that matter. It is here that the "inversion"
of which Engels wrote does its ideological work. Although the law is a reflection of the relations of exchangers on the ground, it appears that the law is an
expression of rationality itself, with the consequence that the relations among
exchangers seem so as well.

Here, however, a problem arises for the Marxian materialist: If law is the
reflection of the actual practice of economic exchange, how does law come to
function as a norm? A simple reflection would represent whatever occurs and
thus could not identify some actions as infractions. How can the materialist

account for the normative dimension of law that arises as a reflection of economic relations?

The answer to this is that law is not a simple reflection of economic relations, but an *idealized* reflection. Actual exchanges will be characterized by the full range of violations and deviations, from failure to meet agreed-upon deadlines to gross expropriation with the threat or use of violence. Such violations tend to undermine the likelihood of the same parties exchanging again. Because it is generally in people's long-term interest that stable trading relationships be maintained, it will generally be in people's interest to eliminate such violations. Accordingly, over time the vast majority of exchanges, particularly those between people in continuing exchange relationships, will tend to be free of violations. Thus, an average core of exchange, characterized by absence of violence and fraud as well as by dependable fulfillment of agreements, will emerge as the norm. The law in general will represent this norm.

This tendency to go from what happens "on average" to what is normative is a common feature of human social existence. People tend to take what usually happens as what should happen. This tendency of the statistical norm (what people can generally be expected to do) to become the moral norm (what is expected of people) is visible in early civilization (where, for example, natural and moral law are not distinguished from each other) and in advanced civilization (where, for example, existing business practice is often taken by courts as creating legally enforceable obligations).

This brings us to a second question. It would seem that law that reflects (even the idealized "average" core of) exchanges would include not only the criminal law but also what we currently understand as contract or civil law. How can the theory that traces law to exchange account for the nature of the criminal law per se, with its special content and its unique remedies?

To answer this, note first that there is considerable overlap in the content of criminal and civil law; criminal acts, such as theft or battery, also can be causes of civil action. This overlap, however, is largely asymmetrical: Virtually any criminal act can be a cause of civil action, but only some civil causes are subject to criminal prosecution. This suggests that the criminal law is more distinctive in its remedies than in its content. In general, criminal prosecution seeks punishment of the guilty, and civil action seeks recovery of damages from the one responsible for a loss. Now, on the materialist theory, both sorts of law—criminal and civil—represent the "essential core" of normal exchange and aim to rectify violations of or deviations from that core. Thus, to explain the nature of the criminal law per se, we must show why some class of deviations from normal exchange is singled out for the distinctive "criminal" remedy, namely, punishment. Because punishment is generally a graver matter than recovery of damages, we should expect the criminal law to be addressed to the most serious violations of normal exchange, whereas the civil law can be addressed to all violations.

Violations of normal exchange can be distinguished in the following way: Some threaten the very possibility of free exchange by depriving people of the ability to dispose of their property. Other violations threaten not the possibility of free exchange but its success in meeting the wishes of the exchangers. What threatens the very possibility of exchange are acts of violence that overtly block the capacity of individuals to exercise their wills, acts of theft that overtly bypass the capacity of individuals to choose how their property is disposed of, and acts of deception that have the same effect, so to speak, behind the backs of their victims. These are so serious that they must be prevented in advance—and that requires a standing threat of punishment. Accordingly, the criminal law is primarily aimed at acts of violence, theft, and fraud.[16]

Less serious violations are compatible with the existence of exchange, but cause exchanges in some way to fall short of the legitimate expectations of the exchangers. These violations are mainly failures to live up to the terms of explicit or implied contracts. They can be remedied by requiring performance or payment from the one responsible. These are suitable targets for the civil law, although nothing is lost by allowing the civil law to apply to recovery of losses due to the more serious violations as well.

On the whole, then, although the entire law in capitalism reflects the conditions of normal exchange, the content of the criminal law is composed of those acts that threaten the very possibility of normal exchange. These are the acts that are identified as "crimes." Moreover, because the normal relations of exchange are not only idealized but also (as we saw in the previous section) generalized to the whole of capitalism, they will shape people's normative expectations beyond exchange. Thus, they determine the limits that will be imposed on officials taxed with the job of finding and prosecuting criminals, the shape of court proceedings, the relation of punishment to offense, and the emphasis on the free will of the offender. Accordingly, by tracing law to its source in exchange, we can account for at least the general content of criminal law and the general shape of the criminal justice system and of the constitutional limits within which that system operates. Here, briefly sketched and numbered for ease of identification, are the main ways in which this works.

1. Normal exchange presupposes that people are treated as having property rights in whatever they are to trade, and that must mean not only goods but their bodies as well, because bodily actions are what workers trade with capitalists for their wage. Crime, then, is any violation by one individual of the property rights of another in whatever he owns, including his body. This explains why the criminal law is directed primarily against acts of violence, theft, and fraud. Moreover, because criminal law protects an individual's body because he owns it (and not, say, because it is the earthly vessel of his immortal soul), the law will be concerned primarily with injuries done to people's bodies against their will—otherwise, such injuries do not violate the individual's ownership of his body. This accounts for the liberal principle *volenti non fit injuria* (no injustice is done to one who consents) and thus, via generalization, for the tendency in capitalism to decriminalize (or reduce in importance) "victim-less crimes" or "morals offenses."

2. This account also tells us what we are not likely to see as crime in capitalist society, namely, exercises of the power inherent in the ownership of property itself. Thus, we will not generally find that death due to preventable dangers in the workplace will be taken as murder because that would assume that the worker was somehow forced into the workplace by the power inherent in his boss's private ownership of the means of production. Because that is just the power that is invisible in capitalism, the worker is taken as freely consenting to his job and thus freely accepting its risks. Accordingly, when the criminal law is used against employers to get them to eliminate occupational hazards, it is never with the understanding that employers who do not eliminate such hazards are violent criminals. If the criminal law is used in these cases at all, it is as a regulatory mechanism applied to employers because this is the most efficient way to reduce the social costs of occupational injury and disease. The treatment of guilty employers is generally light-handed, even though far more people lose their lives due to preventable occupational hazards than as a result of what the law currently treats as murder. In capitalism, subjection to one person is seen as arbitrary and thus unlawful coercion, but subjection to the capitalist class is not seen at all. (Here is how the Marxian theory understands the phenomena discussed in the main text of this book and accounted for with the historical inertia explanation.)

3. The other side of criminal law—the limits placed on legal officials in their pursuit of suspected criminals (for example, in the Bill of Rights)—likewise reflects the generalized conception of people as owners of their bodies and other property. Accordingly, we find protections against official invasions of suspects' property (for example, the Fourth Amendment protections against unreasonable search and seizure) and against penetration of suspects' bodies or minds (for example, the Fifth Amendment protection against self-incrimination). Moreover, this explains why corporal punishment, which was the norm in feudalism and slavery, tends to be eliminated in capitalism. The bodies of slaves are literally owned by their masters, and lords have natural (that is, parent-like) authority over their serfs. In those cases, corporal punishment fits the existing social relations. In capitalism, employer and employee meet as owners of their respective bodies, and thus corporal punishment looks increasingly out of place.

The existence of these various limitations on what can be done to enforce the law is evidence that the Marxian view of law includes recognition of the way law functions not only to control the working class but also as a limit on the behavior of the ruling class. Indeed, the Marxian view can be taken as claiming that it is precisely as a system that protects everyone alike in their property (including their body), by limiting both what citizens and law enforcers can do to the bodies (and other property) of other citizens, that the law most effectively serves the purpose of keeping the working class selling its labor-power to the owners of means of production—both classes safe in the knowledge that no one can interfere with their right to dispose of what they happen to own.

4. As crime is a violation of normal exchange, punishment is thought of on the same model of equivalence as exists in exchange. "Punishment emerges as an equivalent which compensates the damage sustained by the injured party."[17] The commercial model doesn't end here. The adversary system reproduces it in court. "The public prosecutor demands a 'high' price, that is to say a severe sentence. The offender pleads for leniency, a 'discount,' and the court passes sentence in equity."[18] Crime deforms exchange by taking with force rather than payment. Punishment restores exchange by using force to pay back the criminal for his force. This is the *tribute* in retribution. The court is the extraordinary market where this extraordinary exchange is negotiated. The scales in Justice's hands are the same as those used by the merchant.

5. Because exchange normally brings payment to an individual only when she freely chooses to offer up her goods or services for it, the payment of punishment comes due only when the offender has freely chosen to commit the offense for which the punishment is payment. Accordingly, liability for punishment is subject to conditions of the same sort as apply to liability to contractual obligations. One is not bound by a contract that she has not signed freely, or that she signed while insane or in ignorance of its contents, and so on. Likewise, the offender is liable to punishment, and thus is truly a criminal, only if he has committed his violation freely, sanely, and with knowledge of what he was doing. By the same logic, the law generally prohibits ex post facto attribution of criminal liability because a person cannot choose freely to violate a law before it has been passed.

Here, then, we read off the face of exchange, albeit idealized and generalized, the main contours of criminal justice as it develops in capitalism. As I suggested at the outset, this is no more than a skeleton. It does not aim to account for the full, rich detail of any particular criminal justice system. Actual criminal justice systems exist in societies with other modes of production present alongside capitalism and are affected by the complex interplay of human actions, and so on, so that each actual system—like each actual face—will have a distinct physiognomy while sharing in the basic structure. Some criminal justice systems will be slower in eliminating "morals offenses," some will be stricter on occupational hazards, some will abolish the death penalty while others will retain it, and so on.[19] These specific outcomes will be a function of the strength that various social groupings (such as religious organizations, labor unions, academia, the press, and the like) come to have in the specific history of specific countries, and of all the largely unpredictable features that determine the outcome of particular battles over the content of the law and the funding of the legal apparatus. This notwithstanding, the Marxian claim is that criminal justice (principles and systems) in capitalist countries will tend toward the shape sketched out above.

LAW AND ETHICS

We now reach the question of the moral stance toward capitalist criminal justice that is appropriate if the Marxian account is correct. Marxism describes capitalism as an exploitative system, meaning one in which workers are forced to work for capitalists without compensation. Marxists characteristically regard exploitation, and consequently capitalism, as unjust or immoral. Broadly speaking, they reach this condemnation by one of three routes. One is to view capitalist exploitation as wrong because it promotes antagonistic or alienated relations between human beings.[20] The second way is to view capitalist exploitation as wrong because it is a form of forced servitude or slavery.[21] The third way is to view capitalist exploitation as wrong because it is based on an unjust distribution of wealth, namely, the unjustifiable exclusive ownership by a few of the means of production.[22] I shall call these three views, respectively, the *alienation charge,* the *slavery charge,* and the *maldistribution charge.* Each of these has moral implications for capitalist criminal justice. The task of identifying these implications is simplified by the fact that the second and third charges incorporate each other. The slavery charge accepts that private ownership of means of production is a case of unjust maldistribution (because it is a means of forcing servitude), and the maldistribution charge accepts that private ownership of means of production is a means of enslavement (because it is a power wrongly monopolized by a few). For our purposes, then, the charges against capitalism can be reduced to two: the alienation charge and the slavery-maldistribution charge.

Those who raise the alienation charge point out that capitalism is a system in which each person's well-being is in conflict with that of others. Capitalism pits class against class (competing over the division of the economic product into wages versus profit), worker against worker (competing for jobs), and capitalist against capitalist (competing for market shares). Moreover, proponents of this charge hold that antagonism of interests is neither a necessary feature of human life nor a desirable condition. It is caused by capitalism. It was less marked in feudalism and might be eliminated in the future if a more cooperative arrangement, such as socialism, could be established. Criminal justice as it emerges in capitalism is understood as a means to regulate this antagonism of interests. Because it assumes that this antagonism is inevitable, criminal justice serves to confer permanent validity on capitalism. Moreover, criminal justice promotes this antagonism by teaching people that the rights of each are in conflict with the rights of others rather than mutually supportive, that freedom is *freedom from* invasion by others rather than freedom to develop with others, that what people owe each other is noninterference rather than a helping hand.

Also important is the fact that a society based on antagonism of interests is one in which people earn their daily bread only as long as someone else can profit as a result. When that changes, workers may find themselves in need and with little in the way of help from the rest of society. On this view, then, the high crime rates characteristic of capitalism are due to the fact that people in capitalism are taught to see their interests as in conflict with others' and thus they are trained to have limited altruism and fellow feeling, and to the fact that a society based on antagonism of interests is one in which economic need and insecurity are endemic. When limited fellow feeling meets economic need and insecurity, the result is crime. (Recall the views of Bonger and Gordon, discussed in Chapter 4.) The same system that calls criminals individually guilty, then, is responsible for the antagonism of interests that breeds crime in the first place. The upshot of this charge is that criminals are not—or at least not wholly—guilty of the crimes they commit. On this charge, criminals are in large measure unjustly punished for actions caused by the very system that punishes them.

On the slavery-maldistribution charge, the emphasis is on the wrongness and coerciveness of private ownership of means of production. Capitalism promotes a system of criminal justice based on protecting the freedom of individuals to dispose of what they rightly own; but the system itself is based on the wrongful appropriation of means of production, and with it the power to coerce others to labor without compensation. On this view, socialism would cure capitalism not so much by replacing antagonism of interests with harmony, but by replacing private ownership of means of production by a few with social ownership by everyone.

To understand the moral implications for criminal justice of this charge, imagine for a moment that we see someone take a sheep from a field owned by another. In response, suppose that we make the normal judgment that a theft, an unjust expropriation, has occurred. Now suppose further that we learn that the field owner had himself stolen the sheep from the sheep taker some time before. According to these new facts, we shall change our views about the moral status of the sheep taking. Now we are likely to say that the one we saw take the sheep was not, morally speaking, a criminal but the opposite, a victim responding justifiably to an earlier crime. Likewise, if we come to see ownership of means of production as itself a violation of justice (because it is unjustly maldistributive or unjustifiably coercive), we will see the "crimes" that people do in response to it are more just than they appeared when we didn't question the justice of ownership of means of production. Recall the discussion in Chapter 4 of how a judgment that an individual is guilty of a crime presupposes that the social context in which his act occurred was just. By the same logic, judgment that the social context is unjust, weakens the judgment that the individual is guilty of a crime.

On the slavery-maldistribution view, then, the individuals normally labeled "criminal" are seen as the victims of a prior "crime" to which they are responding. That criminals may not (and usually do not) see themselves as doing this only reflects the fact that they are taken in by capitalist ideology no less than law-abiding folks are. The "criminal," then, is not a doer of injustice, but the reverse. He is a victim of injustice trying to improve his situation by means that have been made necessary by the fact that capitalism leaves him few alternatives. The upshot of this charge is that criminals are not really morally guilty. They are in large measure unjustly punished for *re*acting against crimes perpetrated by the very system that punishes them.

In sum, the Marxist critique of criminal justice does lead to a moral condemnation of criminal justice under capitalism. This moral condemnation comes in two forms, both of which share the claim that capitalist criminal justice wrongly punishes people who do not deserve to be punished. In the first form, the alienation charge, criminals are thought not to deserve punishment because their acts are caused by socially conditioned antagonism to their fellows in conjunction with limited and unstable opportunities to satisfy their needs and desires. In the second form, the slavery-maldistribution charge, criminals are thought not to deserve punishment because their apparent crimes are legitimate reactions against conditions that are themselves, morally speaking, criminal. Needless to say, it is possible for the same person to endorse both forms of condemnation.

Several things that apply to both charges are worth noting. First of all, in both cases, the features of capitalist criminal justice that come in for ethical condemnation reflect the failure to see the way criminal justice reflects the mode of production—mentioned at the outset. In the case of the alienation charge, the failure is that of not seeing that capitalist criminal justice emerges to regulate the antagonistic relations between human beings that capitalism produces. Seeing capitalist criminal justice as the product of independent reason, it sees those antagonistic relations as a natural feature of human life that always must be so regulated. Then, capitalist criminal justice rather than protecting the interests of capitalists appears merely to be the necessary condition of any peaceful social coexistence.

In the case of the slavery-maldistribution charge, the failure is of not seeing how property in capitalism is an expression of a particular and morally questionable constellation of social forces. Seeing capitalist criminal justice as the product of independent reason, it sees the property that criminal justice protects as a natural feature of human life that is always in need of such protection. Then, capitalist criminal justice, rather than protecting the interests of capitalists, appears merely to be protecting everyone's interest.

What's more, it follows that the continued and heavily publicized activities of criminal justice serve to reinforce ideological blindness: on the first view, blindness to capitalism's role in causing the alienated and antisocial attitudes and conditions that lead to crime; and, on the second view, blindness to the moral dubiousness of capitalist property relations.

It also must be borne in mind that the ethical implications of both charges are general propositions that will fit actual criminals in varying degrees. For example, while the alienation charge suggests that criminals are not culpable because they are shaped by an antagonistic society, in actual cases the degree to which individual lawbreakers have been so shaped will vary. There may be some who have largely escaped the deleterious influences and yet, out of selfishness or greed, commit crimes. Marxism naturally claims that the number of criminals of this sort is small compared with the number of criminals all told. Marxism, however, need not deny that there are some criminals like this and that they deserve punishment. Likewise, on the slavery-maldistribution charge, whereas criminals are generally taken to be victims of the prior injustice of private ownership of means of production, actual criminals differ in the degree to which they are so victimized and in the degree to which their actual crimes can be thought of as reactions thereto. Relatively privileged persons, or others whose crimes bear little relation to their class position (some rapists, for example), may well be more culpable than the general run of criminals. It seems to me appropriate for Marxists to view responsibility—and thus guilt—as existing in varying degrees, relative to the actual impact of the social structure on a given individual's criminal act.

Finally, note that on neither of the two views we have discussed does the criminal emerge as any kind of "proto-revolutionary," as is sometimes asserted of Marxism. On the alienation charge, the criminal is at best relieved of responsibility because he has been shaped by the social system to have antisocial attitudes and fated by that system to experience need and insecurity that, together with those attitudes, lead to crime. On the slavery-maldistribution charge, the criminal is at best a victim because he is the object of the unjust coercion or expropriation characteristic of private ownership of means of production. His crime, rather than being a kind of rebellion against what victimizes him, is most often a narrowly self-interested striking out against whatever he can get his hands on. On both charges, Marxism does imply reduced or no blame for (most) criminals; but it does not imply any celebration of their acts. This is particularly so in light of the fact that most victims of crime are other exploited people, members or would-be members of the working class. Crime and criminality must on the whole be placed by Marxism among the costs of capitalism, lined up alongside poverty, unemployment, pollution, and the rest.

Notes

1. This appendix is a revised and shortened version of an article that appeared in *Criminal Justice Ethics* 6, no. 1 (Winter–Spring 1987): 30–50. Peter Darvas assisted me with the research for that article.
2. Frederick Engels, "Letter to Conrad Schmidt (October 27, 1890)," in Karl Marx, *Selected Works,* ed. V. Adoratsky (Moscow: Cooperative Publishing Society of Foreign Workers in the USSR, 1935), vol. 1, p. 386.
3. Karl Marx, *Capital* (New York: International Publishers, 1967), vol. 3, p. 819.
4. Note that Marx does not hold that the value of a commodity is equivalent to the actual amount of labor-time that goes into producing it. On that view, commodities would increase in value the more inefficiently they were produced. Instead, recognizing that a commodity will command a price no higher than that for which commodities like it are selling, Marx takes the commodity's value to be determined by the average or socially necessary labor-time it takes to produce commodities of its kind. See *Capital,* vol. 1, p. 189. Furthermore, although Marx claims that value is equivalent to average labor-time, he assumes that values and market prices coincide only for the purposes of the argument of volume 1 of *Capital* about the fundamental nature of capitalism. In the subsequent volumes, Marx

shows at length the mechanisms in capitalism that lead prices to diverge from values. Even after these common misinterpretations of the theory are eliminated, it must be admitted that Marx's labor theory of value has come in for so much criticism in recent years that many, even many Marxists, have given it up for dead.

5. See, for example, G. William Domhoff, *Who Rules America?* 4th ed. (New York: McGraw-Hill, 2001); M. Green, J. Fallows, and D. Zwick, The Ralph Nader Congress Project, *Who Runs Congress?* (New York: Grossman, 1972); Edward S. Greenberg, *Serving the Few: Corporate Capitalism and the Bias of Government Policy* (New York: Wiley, 1974); and Ralph Miliband, *The State in Capitalist Society* (New York: Basic Books, 1969).

6. Karl Marx, "Preface to *A Contribution to a Critique of Political Economy,*" in Robert Tucker (ed.), *The Marx-Engels Reader,* 2nd ed. (New York: Norton, 1978), p. 5.

7. Karl Marx and Friedrich Engels, *The German Ideology,* pts. 1 and 3 (New York: International Publishers, 1947), p. 14.

8. Marx, "Preface to *A Contribution to a Critique of Political Economy,*" p. 4.

9. Ibid.

10. "It is not the subject who deceives himself, but reality which deceives him"; Maurice Godelier, "Structure and Contradiction in Capital," in Robin Blackburn (ed.), *Ideology in Social Science* (Glasgow: Fontana/Collins, 1977), p. 337.

11. Examples of theories of ideology that trace its distortions to subjective illusions are the attempt by some members of the Frankfurt School to explain the affection of German laborers for fascism by means of a Freudian account of the persistence of irrational authoritarian attitudes and the attempt of some sociologists to trace ideology to an existential need to reify a mythic worldview as protection against the terrors of meaninglessness. For the former, see Martin Jay, *The Dialectical Imagination: A History of the Frankfurt School and the Institute for Social Research, 1923–1950* (Boston: Little, Brown, 1973). For the latter, see Peter Berger and Thomas Luckmann, *The Social Construction of Reality* (New York: Doubleday, 1966).

12. Karl Marx, *The Poverty of Philosophy* (Moscow: Progress Publishers, 1955), p. 75.

13. Evgeny B. Pashukanis, *Law and Marxism: A General Theory,* trans. B. Einhom, ed. C. Arthur (London: Ink Links, 1978).

14. As Frederick Engels wrote,

   The labor contract is to be freely entered into by both parties. But it is considered to have been freely entered into as soon as the law makes both parties equal on paper. The power conferred on the one party by the difference of class position, the pressure thereby brought to bear on the other party—the real economic position of both—that is not the law's business. (Frederick Engels, *The Origin of the Family, Private Property, and the State* [New York: International Publishers, 1942], p. 64)

15. Pashukanis, *Law and Marxism,* pp. 112–113, inter alia.

16. Pashukanis approvingly attributes to Aristotle "the definition of crime as an involuntarily concluded contract" (ibid., p. 169).

17. Ibid., p. 169; see also Alan Norrie, "Pashukanis and 'the Commodity Form Theory': A Reply to Warrington," *International Journal of the Sociology of Law* 10 (1982): 431–434.

18. Pashukanis, *Law and Marxism,* p. 177.

19. See Georg Rusch and Otto Kirchheimer, *Punishment and Social Structure* (New York: Russell & Russell, 1968), for a classic Marxian-inspired historical study of the relationship between penal policy and the supply and demand for labor.

20. This is the view of, for example, Allen Buchanan in *Marx and Justice* (Totowa, NJ: Rowman & Littlefield, 1982).
21. This is essentially the view argued for by, for example, Allen Wood in "The Marxian Critique of Justice," *Philosophy & Public Affairs* 1, no. 3 (Spring 1972): 244–282.
22. This is the view of, for example, G. A. Cohen in "Freedom, Justice and Capitalism," *New Left Review* 126 (March–April 1981): 3–16. There is, by the way, a substantial literature on the question of whether Marxism holds that capitalism is wrong because it is unjust or that justice is part of what's wrong with capitalism. See articles in M. Cohen, T. Nagel, and T. Scanlon (eds.), *Marx, Justice, and History* (Princeton, NJ: Princeton University Press, 1980); K. Nielsen and S. Patten (eds.), *Marx and Morality, Canadian Journal of Philosophy* 7 (suppl., 1981); and J. Pennock and J. Chapman (eds.), *Nomos XXVI: Marxism* (New York: New York University Press, 1983); as well as Norman Geras's review of the whole discussion, "The Controversy about Marx and Justice," *New Left Review* 150 (March–April 1985): 47–85. My own views are presented in "The Possibility of a Marxian Theory of Justice," in Nielsen and Patten, *Marx and Morality,* pp. 307–322.

Between Philosophy and Criminology

—Jeffrey Reiman

Though *The Rich Get Richer and the Poor Get Prison* is more frequently assigned in criminology courses than in philosophy courses,[1] it raises a philosophical question, perhaps *the* central philosophical question of criminology, namely, "What should be a crime?"; and it aims to use that question to shed a special kind of light on the criminal justice establishment in the United States, but I suspect as well on just about any criminal justice system anywhere.[2]

I say this by way of introduction because my aim here is to explore the relationship between philosophy and criminology. In light of criminology's multidisciplinary nature, however, criminology might be thought already to include philosophy. Thus, to be precise, I should say that I want to explore the relationship between philosophy and the nonphilosophical aspects of criminology, that is, between philosophy and criminology considered as a social science. In general, this is what I shall mean when I speak of *criminology*.

To give you a hint about where I am headed, I shall argue that criminology needs philosophy, and not only in the way that, as I also believe, everything and everyone needs philosophy, but also in very special ways. For example, I shall argue that criminology has a special need for philosophy because criminology is in the unusual position of being a mode of social inquiry whose central concept—*crime*—is defined officially, by governments. We hear a lot these days about the politics of knowledge and of research, but this is politics with a vengeance. Politics openly, necessarily, insinuates itself into the heart of criminology. Political systems hand criminology a ready-made research agenda. And so I shall argue that criminology needs philosophical reflection on the concept of crime in order to establish its intellectual independence of the state, which to my mind is equivalent to declaring its status as a social science rather than an agency of social control, as critical rather than servile, as illumination rather than propaganda.

This is not, however, where I shall start. Rather, I will start, so to speak, at the outer ring of a series of concentric circles, by indicating the philosophical assumptions that I think are necessary to all forms of social science. I shall proceed from there to talk about the philosophical assumptions that I think are special to criminology, the ones it especially needs. And then, arriving at the smallest inner circle, I shall say something about my own particular philosophical commitments, the ones that underlie *The Rich Get Richer and the Poor Get Prison*. I hope that somewhere along the line, readers will recognize some of their own philosophical assumptions, and thus be in a better position to reflect on them, to consider what else they entail, and to decide whether in the end they are ready to endorse them explicitly, or want to consider others.

Before starting this, I want to make one thing clear. I shall be talking about "what criminology needs," but this is shorthand for what I think people who practice criminology need in order to do criminology in a coherent and plausible way. Moreover, when I say, for example, that criminology needs a theory of crime, I do not mean that it needs one particular theory. This too is shorthand, in this case for the idea that everyone who practices criminology needs *some* theory of crime, not that all need the same one. I put these all as claims about "what criminology needs" rather than as about what criminologists need, to emphasize that the needs are disciplinary and conceptual, not personal or psychological.

PHILOSOPHICAL ASSUMPTIONS OF SOCIAL SCIENCE GENERALLY

First of all, to engage in social science, you must believe that there is such a thing as society, and that it can become an object of knowledge. That there is such a thing as society means that there are real human beings, in real social relations, in a real world, manipulating real objects, and so on. That there can be knowledge of society means that knowledge is possible, and that we can know when we have got some. In short, a social scientist cannot be a thoroughgoing *ontological* skeptic or agnostic.[3] He or she cannot suppose that society is only an idea or a construct, and all the more so, he or she cannot suppose society to be an illusion. Nor can a social scientist be a thoroughgoing *epistemological* skeptic or agnostic.[4] To seek knowledge of society is to assume that such knowledge is possible for us.

Along the same lines, I believe that social scientists must believe it is important to aim at *scientific objectivity,* and that this aim can be adequately achieved. Some authors writing about the development of modern science in the time of Bacon and Galileo speak of the attempt at scientific objectivity as nothing but following certain conventions aimed at giving science a higher status than, say, religious inspiration.[5] My claim is that, even if the attempt at scientific objectivity is this, it cannot be *only* this.

No one could use conventions of objectivity without believing that they were effective ways of getting at the way things are, anymore than one can use language without believing that one is speaking about things beyond the words one uses. Even those who think of objectivity as just so many conventions, think that *that* is the objective truth! They think that they are telling us the way things are, not the way they would like them to be. Notice here that

I am not claiming that we always succeed in freeing ourselves of our biases. What a social scientist must believe is that the attempt to represent the world as it is, as opposed to how we wish it were, can succeed generally and does succeed in many particular cases.

In affirming that, as social science, criminology must presuppose that there are real people performing real actions in a real world and that we can have knowledge of them, I do not mean to resurrect some hoary positivistic model of science. I grant that the facts we study may be the product of the interaction of beliefs and language and objects. However, for the study of those facts to be fruitful, the process by which beliefs and language and objects interact must itself be knowable as an objective reality. It is a general philosophical requirement of social theorizing that one's theory leave open the possibility of its own status as knowledge—this is a test that many statements of postmodernist theory, and of relativism generally, seem to me to fail, even as their practitioners produce valuable *objective* knowledge in spite of what they say they are doing.

Before leaving the discussion of the general philosophical requirements of social science, I want to say a word about *value-neutrality*. Value-neutrality is related to objectivity, but it's not the same thing. Later I shall suggest that criminology needs some value commitments, at least to some conception of justice. Thus, I do not think that criminology should be value-neutral all the way down, even though I think it should aim at objective knowledge. There is no contradiction here.

The point is this. I believe that the proper study of crime requires taking some position on the justice of the social system in which certain acts are treated as criminal. Suppose that I make explicit the ideal of justice that I endorse. This doesn't mean I am no longer objective. First of all, I believe, and I may try to show, that my ideal of justice is appropriate, not merely what I want or what serves my interests. Second and equally important is that, once I have stated my ideal of justice, I want to know objectively whether or to what extent that ideal is realized. If I misperceive or bend the facts because I want to show that the criminal justice system is unjust, I fool myself as much as anyone else. I am not honestly committed to my ideal of justice unless I am willing to apply it as objectively as I can.

I turn now to consider the special philosophical needs of criminology.

SPECIAL PHILOSOPHICAL NEEDS OF CRIMINOLOGY

I shall make three arguments aimed at showing that criminology has a special need for philosophical reflection. First, I will contend that criminology has such a need because it is a multidisciplinary study and thus requires an explanation for why crime is worthy of its own organized inquiry. Second, I will make the political argument for criminology's need for philosophy, at which I hinted in my opening remarks. And, third, I will argue that the need for philosophy arises from the topic itself, that crime cannot be studied without coming to some judgment about its moral status, which requires philosophical reflection.

Consider first the fact that criminology is a multidisciplinary mode of inquiry. The traditional disciplines, history or sociology or philosophy, are not defined by their topics. Rather than study *something* in the world, some problem or problem area, they study *everything,* but from a particular angle. Criminology is the reverse. It studies the problem area of crime and criminal justice, from a wide variety of angles. But, then, why *this* problem area?

What makes crime an interesting focus of study? That it is crime, or a violation of a rule, is not enough of an answer. Why not study people who cheat at solitaire, or those who arrive late for dates with friends, or drivers who fail to put on their turn signal before turning left, or folks who have bad manners, or speakers who say *ain't?* They are all rule violators. And these rule violations are all subject to penalties of some sort, but hardly worth devoting a special discipline to their study. What makes crime worthy of its own study?

Since the mere fact that crime is a rule violation does not earn it special treatment, the mere fact that it is a law violation will not do so either. Responding to this need for explanation requires you to say what you think crime is, such that it is an important occurrence in a society. Is crime a breakdown in social order, an alternative career route, a way of coping with acute need or insecurity, a rebellion against injustice, a cry for help, a form of play, a form of self-defense, an exciting walk on the wild side, a symptom of individual or social pathology, a label—and accompanying treatment—applied for political purposes? Choosing among alternatives like these requires you to say what you think a society is, such that crime is important to it. Is society a rational association among individuals, a site of conflict or consensus or of continual negotiation between the two; is it a mechanism of control of labor and resources, a struggle among classes, a pluralistic ragbag of interest groups?

I do not mean to suggest that these ways of thinking about crime and about society exhaust the possibilities. My point is that unless you have some thought like this about crime and society, you don't really have an answer to why crime is worth studying. And, then, you do not have an answer to why there should be a field of social inquiry devoted specially to the study of crime. A thought like this about crime is a theory of crime, and a theory of crime is a part of a theory of society. And a theory of society is a work of philosophizing.

To move now to the political dimension of the issue, consider this question: What's the difference between what criminologists do and what the FBI does in compiling the annual *Uniform Crime Report (UCR)?* Both seek to amass and disseminate knowledge about crime; both chart trends and correlations. There are numerous differences, but one is, to my mind, of chief importance. The *UCR* simply accepts the legal system's definitions of crimes as well as the legal system's grading of their gravity. It needs no more; in fact, it would exceed its mandate if it varied from this. But criminology cannot simply accept the legal definition of crimes and the legal system's determination of their gravity, because criminology is not a branch of law or of the legal system.

Unless criminologists have their own view of what crime is and what makes it especially important, if they simply study what the legal system calls crimes in the order of gravity the legal system assigns them, then criminology accepts the research agenda handed to it by the government. Criminology is then an arm of the state. Even if it comes up with some news that the state would rather not hear, it is doing the state's work, which is to amass and disseminate knowledge about law violations.

To affirm its intellectual independence from the state as a social science, criminology must look at crime while staying open to the idea that the legal definitions and, just as crucially, all the righteous beliefs that normally surround the legal enterprise are less than the whole truth, and perhaps even misleading or ideological. This means that criminology must keep its distance from the legal system as such, and this in turn requires that criminology seek its own understanding of what crime is. And I contend again that this requires a theory of crime, and a theory of crime is part of a theory of society, and a theory of society is a work of philosophizing.

You may think that this argument only amounts to showing that criminologists need a bit of social theory, which may be an interesting fact, but not very startling. You may think that social theory is a thing different from social philosophy, something that sociologists do rather than philosophers. I disagree. I think that social theorizing is philosophizing, but that doesn't mean that it can or should only be done by philosophers.

Every discipline has a place where it overlaps with philosophy, where its questions become philosophical questions. When art historians ask what art or beauty is, when psychologists ask what a mind is, when political scientists ask what a state is, and when sociologists or criminologists or anyone else asks what crime or society is, the questions they ask are philosophical ones. One clear reason that they are philosophical questions is that they are distinctively about the *validity* of norms or criteria—what makes the *Mona Lisa* beautiful, what makes a property mental rather than physical, when is a group a state, what should be prohibited by criminal law? To be sure, sociologists and others also study norms and criteria. Their focus is on the existence and consequences of norms and criteria. The questions that are distinctive to philosophy are those about the *justification* of norms and criteria. Philosophy aims to evaluate their credentials and, where those credentials pass muster, to defend the norms and criteria as valid ones.

That said, be clear that I do not think that philosophical questions can *only* be asked or competently answered by people with PhDs in philosophy. I think rather that whoever answers them should recognize that he or she is no longer in the realm of empirical scientific endeavor, but is engaged in the conceptual and normative reflection that is properly philosophy's domain.

I do not want to leave the issue here. There is a dimension to the theorizing needed about crime that I think is uncontroversially philosophical. We reach this dimension by recognizing that crime is a *violation,* and not just any old violation. It is not just the sort of rule violation that is involved in saying *ain't*. It's not the sort of violation that occurs when someone cheats at solitaire.

Because crime affects other people and often in very serious ways, it is a morally consequential act. And, as a result, you cannot say *what crime is* without taking a position on its moral status. That in turn will require a position on the moral obligation to obey the law. I am not saying that you must believe that the criminal does a moral wrong or violates a moral obligation. My point rather is that you must have *some* position on this. You cannot be neutral. If you are neutral, you treat crime as no different from any old rule violation, which is less than what crime is, and thus a distortion of your object of study.

This, then, is my third argument. Crime itself requires moral assessment. To be studied, it must be identified for what it is, and that includes its moral nature. Even if you do not think that criminals violate a moral obligation in committing crimes, you probably do think that many, if not most, crimes would, under normal circumstances, constitute immoral actions. After all, all crimes with victims violate the Golden Rule. The criminal does things to people that he wouldn't want done to him. And this is important. It constitutes, so to speak, the default position on the moral status of crimes. Suppose you think that violating laws against illicit drug use or prostitution involves no violation of a moral obligation. Then, you probably think that those acts should not be crimes. This implies that you assume that the sorts of things that should be crimes are the sorts of things the doing of which do violate moral obligations.

Or, suppose you think something rather radical, say, that inner-city violence against the police is not immoral because it is a kind of legitimate self-defense or even retribution. Even here, you are taking a position on the moral status of criminal acts. Most importantly, calling an act *self-defense* or *retribution* is a way of saying that an act that is normally immoral is morally permissible in light of what it is a response to. You are assuming that the same acts, if not done in self-defense or as retribution, would be immoral.

That is what I mean by saying that the view that crime is a moral violation is the default position. Crime is prima facie a moral violation; that is, it is a moral violation, unless reasons to the contrary can be given. To hold that crime is a moral violation is to affirm part, not just of a social theory of crime, but of a moral theory about what human beings owe to their fellows in the way of conduct. And, insofar as you affirm such a moral theory, not blindly, but after reflecting on its validity, you are squarely in philosophy's jurisdiction.

There's another way to make this argument. Many criminologists believe—as I do—that the legal catalogue of crimes is biased in certain ways; for example, it focuses on the acts of poor people and ignores much of the antisocial behavior of the well-off. Those criminologists may also believe—as I do—that this bias weakens in some measure the obligations of the poor to obey the law. Other criminologists disagree on both the claim of bias and on the weakening of obligation, or they might accept one of these and not the other. What is this disagreement about?

Well, certainly, it is a disagreement about what should be crime. This is clearly a normative disagreement. In disagreeing about what should be crime, we are disagreeing more generally about what kind of conduct individual human beings owe to each other. This is a disagreement about the requirements of *interpersonal justice*. In disagreeing about how bias in the legal determination of crime affects the moral obligations of the victims of that bias, we are disagreeing about what society as a whole owes its members. This is a disagreement about the requirements of *social justice*. Both are philosophical disagreements that arise from trying to say what crime really is in the society that we are studying. And since all criminologists must believe either that the definitions of crime are biased or that they aren't or that some are and some aren't, and they must believe as well that this does or does not weaken obligation, it follows that all criminologists must hold philosophical views that fill out their notions of what crime is. And the reflection that leads them to believe that these philosophical views are valid is philosophical reflection.

I now turn to the specific philosophic commitments that underlie *The Rich Get Richer and the Poor Get Prison*.

THE RICH GET RICHER AND THE POOR GET PHILOSOPHY

I got the idea for *The Rich Get Richer* while reading Richard Quinney's seminal work, *The Social Reality of Crime*.[6] That provocative book contended that crime was not some real, objective event in the world, but the creation of a labeling process, the crucial step in which was the definition of crimes by lawmakers. In short, crime has a social rather than a physical reality. What's more, Quinney held that this social reality was created in a politically biased way. Quinney contended that the labeling of some acts as crimes by lawmakers reflected the interests of the wealthy and powerful in the society at the expense of the rest. I found this conclusion very believable, but I was dissatisfied with the argument by which Quinney arrived at it. In effect, he contended that lawmakers were from the wealthy and powerful groups in society; that they tended to act in their own self-interest; and consequently, that the criminal laws they wrote must reflect their interests, which is to say, the interests of the wealthy and powerful and not the interests of the rest of society.[7]

This argument has the advantage of being neat and economical, but the disadvantage of being inconclusive. It assumes that, because people *tend* to act in their self-interest, then we can conclude of anything they do that it is in their self-interest. But, sometimes people act contrary to their self-interest. They may occasionally act to do their duty, or to do what they think is right. Think, for example, of people who risked their own lives and the lives of their families to hide Jews from the Nazis during the Second World War—it can happen that people are motivated to do the morally right thing! And it's just possible that lawmakers were doing this at the moment that they were writing criminal laws, even if in general they tend to act in their own interest.

Moreover, that something is in the interest of the wealthy and powerful doesn't entail that it is *not* in the interests of others. It might be that what is in one person's interest is also in that of others, such that when the person acts in his own self-interest, he serves the interests of the others in spite of himself. And this is arguably the case regarding the criminal law, since both wealthy people and poor ones have an interest in, say, not being robbed or murdered. Then, even if the wealthy and powerful draw up laws against robbery and murder to serve their own interests, they would be serving the interests of the rest of society at the same time.

To get to the politically critical conclusion that Quinney wanted to reach, a different sort of argument was needed. What sort? First of all, as I have been suggesting all along in this appendix, it was necessary to take some distance from the legal system's list of crimes. That required establishing some normative standard of what *should* be crime, against which the actual legal definitions could be assessed as fair or biased. The normative standard that I stated in *The Rich Get Richer* was simple and uncontroversial. I contended that a criminal justice system ought to be protecting the lives and limbs and possessions of the citizenry, and thus the legal list of crimes ought to follow this imperative. The most serious crimes should be the gravest threats to life, limb, or property; and the gravest threats to life, limb, or property should be the most serious crimes.

With this notion in mind, I looked at the most serious threats to life, limb, and property in society and compared them to the law's list of crimes. What I found was that, while the criminal law did treat some acts that posed great threats as crimes, many equally or even more dangerous acts were not treated as crimes: Either they were not labeled crimes, or they were not labeled serious crimes in proportion to the danger they threatened, or, if they were labeled serious crimes, they were rarely treated as such in practice. I noted as well that some acts labeled crimes did not seem to be threatening or dangerous to society at all—here I have in mind the so-called "victimless crimes" of voluntary recreational drug use by adults, consensual commercial sex, and so on.

This, in turn, led me to ask what the acts labeled crimes had in common and what the dangerous acts not labeled crimes had in common. And my conclusion was that the acts labeled crimes, instead of being all dangerous acts, were predominantly acts of the poor in society. And the dangerous acts not labeled crime were predominantly acts of the well-off. With these conclusions, I could show that Quinney's conclusion was indeed largely correct: The law's definitions of crimes serve the interests of the wealthy and powerful at the expense of the rest of society. I say *largely correct* because there are crimes in the law's list that are acts that threaten the poor (many of the crimes tracked in the FBI's *UCRs* certainly do), and there are dangerous acts of the well-off that are occasionally treated as serious crimes (as Enron's Andrew Fastow and WorldCom's Bernard Ebbers have recently learned). But *largely correct* is correct enough to support the critical conclusion.

My point here is that reaching this conclusion required a reflection on what crime is that could not rest satisfied with legal or conventional understandings. It had to be a normative, and thus philosophical, reflection on what crime should be in order to compare reality to this and find it lacking. The route from which acts are and are not crimes to the conclusion that the legal definitions of crime serve the interests of the wealthy and powerful had to pass through a theory of what *should* be crime. In sum, the social inquiry that leads to the view defended in *The Rich Get Richer,* namely, that the criminal justice system is biased against the poor, relies on an irreducibly normative and thus philosophical conception of crime.

Moreover, this conception of crime was not simply pulled out of a hat. It was the product of philosophical reflection. This philosophical conception of crime is based on an equally philosophical conception of social and political justice. I contend that the ways in which the coercive apparatus of the law is used must be justified in principle to all citizens. This is so for three reasons.

First, both our tradition and our social order take freedom—the right of sane adults to do what they want—as a paramount value. Freedom is important because people tend to enjoy acting as they wish, and because it is the necessary condition of having a life that can be seen as one's own accomplishment, a life of which one can be proud. Without freedom, we are playing out a script of which we are not the author. Freedom is also important as a source of new ideas and creativity and thus of social progress. For these reasons and others, I start with the idea that freedom is a great value and thus that those who would limit it owe a satisfactory justification to those whose freedom is to be limited.

Second, on the social contract tradition in political and moral philosophy (which is enshrined in the *Declaration of Independence)* and, indeed, on any democratic view, the coercive power of the state—police, prisons, and so on—represents the people's own power, and thus can only legitimately be used for the people's own purposes. Consequently, the exercise of that power must be justifiable to the people in terms of their own purposes.

Third, the legal system appeals to the citizens morally, that is, it implicitly and explicitly asserts that the citizens are morally obligated to comply with it. But, on the contract model, obligation is a matter of owing fair compensation for benefits one receives. And, thus, only laws that benefit people can obligate people. Ultimately, this has to be cashed out individually, because it is as individuals that we are obligated or not. The law must benefit me, protect me against something that really threatens me, for me to be morally obligated to obey it. The law must serve people's interests to be morally binding on them. And thus the claim of the law to morally obligate citizens requires that it be justifiable to them in light of their interests.

This is not the whole story. I am, for example, also benefited by the fact that the law is the product of a democratic process, whose benefits are only available on the assumption that laws will be binding even on those who do not approve of them or find them in their interest. And, I am benefited by order itself, by the predictability and regularity of my fellow citizens' conduct that come of their obeying the law even if they are unhappy with it. Consequently, the argument as to whether I am or am not obligated to a particular law starts with consideration of whether it serves an interest I have, but it doesn't end there. Even if a particular law doesn't benefit me, some weight must be given to the fact that democratic lawmaking systems are beneficial generally, and order is as well, and that both democracy and order require people to accept laws which they don't think serve their interests. Nonetheless, if a law or a whole legal system significantly veers from serving all citizens' interests and toward serving the interests of some segment of society at the expense of the rest, the weight of democracy and order will not be enough to preserve the obligatory nature of the law. Such veering away from serving all citizens' interests will weaken, if not eliminate, the obligations of those whose interests are served less or not at all.

This is the philosophical reflection that underlies the simpler claim that the criminal law should be protecting citizens' life and limb and possessions generally. Because it must serve all citizens' interests, a just legal order must criminalize behavior that threatens the interests of all citizens, and it must do so in proportion to the gravity of the threat posed. It must not be protecting citizens only or even mainly against threats posed by the poor, while leaving the threats posed by the wealthy either untouched or only lightly grazed. This philosophical argument also creates a presumption against the legitimacy of laws against victimless crimes because laws that criminalize actions that do not clearly have victims—actions that some people detest but others accept—will surely appear to many in society as nothing more than the majority building its moral preferences into the law with no more justification than that they are the majority. Large numbers of citizens will tend not to view themselves as obligated by such laws and, in my view, they will often be correct. Thus, not only does my argument pass through a normative theory of crime but also that theory is itself based on a theory of social justice.

Moreover, since a theory of crime is part of a theory of society, this conception of crime reflects a conception of how society works that is, to my mind, equally a matter of philosophical reflection. Basically, my view of U.S. society is that it works roughly the way Marx supposed it would. It is dominated by the capitalist mode of production, which brings with it a crucial class divide between those who own means of production and those who don't. This has the consequence that, in a certain significant sense, the nonowners are forced to work for the owners. The divide between owners and nonowners amounts to an inequality in power between the two classes, which goes far toward explaining what is and what is not treated as crime in capitalist societies.

However, the Marxian view has even richer resources for explaining this bias. It holds that the capitalist mode of production is accompanied by an ideology, the core of which is blindness to the coerciveness of ownership of means of production vis-à-vis nonowners.[8] I believe, by the way, that, within these coercive relations, a capitalist economy works pretty much the way neoclassical economists—such as Milton Friedman—think it does (and Marx generally believed this as well). This accounts for the general success of neoclassical economics, while its blindness to the coerciveness explains how neoclassical economics can be ideological even as it accurately describes market tendencies.

Blindness to the coerciveness of private ownership of means of production is not primarily due to active deception by those in power. It is rather the way in which capitalism normally looks to its participants who view it, so to speak, up close. The illusion that capitalist transactions are fully free is similar to the illusion that the sun goes around the earth—it's just what you would expect people to see from where they are standing. Up close, the fact that capitalists, unlike feudal lords or slave owners, cannot use violence to get people to work for them makes the transactions between owners and nonowners of means of production appear free. They are, of course, free in important ways, but not as free as they seem. Workers are free to choose among capitalists, but not free to avoid working for one of them after all (leaving aside the marginal alternatives, working for the church or the government, stealing, or begging—and, for the few who have the initiative and willingness to sacrifice as well as plenty of luck, the possibility of going into business on one's own).

Since most of the ways that the wealthy pose dangers to the rest of society are as threats either to employees (subjecting them to preventable occupational hazards) or to consumers (subjecting them to shoddy products or to higher prices due to corporate skullduggery), blindness to the coerciveness of capitalism makes it appear as if employees and consumers—who are, of course, the same people—have signed on freely to the risks involved. Consequently, those responsible for these threats don't seem like criminals, because criminals characteristically force dangers on their victims. In light of the coerciveness of capitalism, however, this difference is largely illusory. For all intents and purposes, occupational harms are forced on workers (they must choose among the jobs that are available), and product risks as well as corporate financial shenanigans are forced on consumers (they must choose among the products that are available, and they must pay for the losses due to corporate misdeeds when they are passed on in the form of higher prices). Nonetheless, the law in capitalism continues the illusion that these dangers are voluntarily accepted, by focusing mainly on one-on-one theft and violence, while treating deadlier preventable occupational hazards as well as consumer risks and costlier financial misdeeds as merely regulatory matters. Consequently, the Marxian view will lead us to expect just the bias in the legal definition of crimes that *The Rich Get Richer* documents.

I should add that my Marxism is tempered by recognition of two interconnected failings in Marxian analysis. One is the failure to see how dangerous to human freedom socialism could be, even though there is a good Marxian reason for expecting socialism to be dangerous. If ownership of the means of production is the main instrument of coercion in a society, one must have a very idealistic view of human beings to be willing to place that instrument of coercion, whole and entire, into the hands of a single institution, the government. Socialism only has a chance of being a truly liberating social form for a society in which democracy is already very well developed, and in which citizens are already extremely sophisticated about the exercise of their democratic power. This leads me to believe that the likelihood of a truly liberating socialism is way off in the future. For the foreseeable future, the future in which we are all likely to live and die, I can see no truly liberating alternative to capitalism. And, sad to say, the current and recent examples of socialism—China, North Korea, and the former Soviet Union—confirm this bleak conclusion.

On the other hand, there is a good Marxian reason to expect capitalism to maintain individual freedom. As a system of multiple competing owners of means of production, capitalism distributes the main instrument of social coercion among a multiplicity of separate agents. Thus, capitalism maintains a space for individual freedom that results, not from an enlightened citizenry or officialdom, but rather from the material conditions of capitalist production itself. In a kind of Madisonian fashion, the multiple competing owners each have an interest in resisting the control of the economy by other firms and thus in keeping the market generally open and the government in a wide variety of hands. Moreover, capitalism does, as Marx very explicitly noted, create enormous technological progress that reduces unwanted toil and increases the material income of the workers. The impoverishment to which Marx thought capitalism led is a matter of workers' decreasing relative share of the product of their labor—but, since this is caused by the fact that labor under capitalism becomes increasingly productive, this share buys more and more goods.

To be sure, capitalism is also a system that generates large (and, recently, growing) inequalities, which in turn give some people great power to determine the way others live. That is, capitalism not only makes some people richer than others, but also makes some people freer than others. Moreover, capitalism subjects all of us, but the poor most of all, to forces and developments beyond our control, making life uncertain for most and painful for many. These facts, taken together with the dangerousness of socialism and the freedom-maintaining tendency of capitalism, mean that Marxism implies of capitalism roughly what Winston Churchill said of democracy, namely, that it is the worst form of economic system, except for all the others.

The second failing in Marxian analysis offers some compensation for this conclusion, which some readers may find too dismal. The second failing is that of not seeing how progressive capitalism is culturally, that is, in the dimension that Marx called the *relations of production*. Marx and Marxists saw clearly that capitalism is progressive with respect to the *means of production*, that is, the development and implementation of laborsaving technology. But, Marx and Marxists did not (though Marx did more so than Marxists) see that capitalism is also progressive with respect to the relations of production, that is, *the growth and spread of liberal values and institutions*.

Under these, I include the preference for greater personal freedom (tending toward the requirement of harm as a justification for restricting freedom, and against victimless crimes or other restraints based on faith or tradition or custom), the inclination toward using rational criteria for evaluating people (tending toward use of merit and conduct to judge people rather than race or gender or creed or age), and the insistence on more effective and responsive government (demanding freedom to vote and the progressive extension of eligibility to vote, freedom to assemble, and the rest). These progressive tendencies are, of course, very imperfectly realized. Nonetheless, that does not mean that they are unimportant or without effect. I think that Jürgen Habermas has gone some distance toward integrating this progressive dimension of capitalism's liberal culture into Marxian theory.[9]

The second failing is connected to the first in several ways. One way of explaining why existing or recent socialist societies have been as unattractive as they have is that they embraced capitalist technology without embracing capitalist liberalism. Socialists failed to realize that socialism itself is sure to be oppressive unless it is staffed by officials who are deeply imbued with liberal values, and held democratically accountable by a populace that is equally so imbued.

But the second failing has a bright side as well. In recognizing the progressiveness of capitalism with regard to the relations of production, we can see a way in which the fact that we are probably stuck with capitalism for our lives and beyond presents a special opportunity. Capitalism produces the cultural tools needed to push it to become fairer. The struggle to make people freer and more equal is a struggle to make capitalism live up to its own liberal ideals. And, there is reason to hope that this struggle can succeed, since the values that guide it are the very ones affirmed by cultural institutions within capitalism.

This, to my mind, locates *The Rich Get Richer and the Poor Get Prison* in philosophical space. *It is a radical critique of criminal justice in capitalism that works by confronting capitalist criminal justice with capitalism's own liberal moral philosophy.*

Notes

1. This appendix is a revised version of my article of the same title that appeared in the *Journal of Law* 1 (2004): 42–58, which in turn was a revised version of my keynote address to the second annual conference of the Canadian Society of Criminology, Toronto, April 1, 2004.

2. For its relevance to Canadian criminal justice, see, for example, Stuart Henry, "Law Commission of Canada's Discussion Paper 'What Is a Crime?' A Commentary on the Issue of Power," a paper presented at the annual meeting of the American Society of Criminology, Denver, November, 19–22, 2003.

3. *Ontology* is the philosophical study of what is real. An ontological skeptic about society doubts that society exists, and an ontological agnostic about society believes we cannot know if society exists.

4. *Epistemology* is the philosophical study of what knowledge is and how or if it is possible. An epistemological skeptic about social science doubts that social science provides knowledge; an epistemological agnostic about social science believes that we cannot know whether social science provides knowledge.

5. See, for example, Julie R. Solomon, *Objectivity in the Making: Francis Bacon and the Politics of Inquiry* (Baltimore, MD: Johns Hopkins University Press, 1998).

6. Richard Quinney, *The Social Reality of Crime* (Boston: Little, Brown, 1970).

7. Quinney, *Social Reality*, p. 15 inter alia; and see the section titled "Criminal Justice as Creative Art" in Chapter 2 of the present book.

8. This analysis of Marxian theory and its relationship to the issue of what is and what is not treated as crime in capitalist societies is developed in Appendix I of this book, "The Marxian Critique of Criminal Justice." That appendix is a shorter version of an article that was originally published in *Criminal Justice Ethics* 6, no. 1 (Winter–Spring 1987): 30–50.

9. See, for example, Jürgen Habermas, *Communication and the Evolution of Society* (Boston: Beacon Press, 1979), esp. Chapters 4 and 5.

INDEX

Note: **Bold** page numbers refer to figures and tables.

Adelphia Communications 136–137, **139**
addiction: crime 38–42, 145, 201–202; treatment 19–20, 81, 202; prevention 40–41; public health 19–20, 38–39, 81, 201; *see also* drugs
adjudication 125–128, 134
African Americans *see* blacks
aggravated assault 22, 69, 82, 85, 98
Agnew, Robert 68
A. H. Robbins Company 79
air pollution 64–65, 92–95
alcohol 39–42, 77–78, 202
Alexander, Michelle 114
American Academy of Pediatrics (AAP) 93, 95
American Bar Association 124
American Cancer Society (ACS) 90–91
American Conservative 133
American Journal of Preventive Medicine 98
American Journal of Public Health 78
American Legislative Exchange Council (ALEC) 170
American Medical Association (AMA) 84, 88–89
antitrust 116, 132–133
AOL-Time Warner 136–137
apartheid 197
Ariely, Dan 185
arrests: blacks and 66, 113–115, 121–122; discretion and 2–4, 205–206; for drugs 17–18, 115, 201–202; socioeconomic class and 5, 112–113, 116–118, 120–122, 129, 150–151, 205; statistics on 17, 23, 31, 35, 39, 66; Typical Criminal and 66–70
Arthur Andersen 137–138, **139**–140
asbestos 78, 86
Ashford, Nicholas 92
assault 3, 41, 79–80, 82–85; *see also* aggravated assault
assault weapons 24, 64, 205
attorneys *see* legal counsel
auditing 137–138, **139**–**140**, 144; safety audits 64
Australia 37, 76, 96
auto theft **132**, 135

bail 113, 123–127
Bailout Nation (Ritholtz) 146, 148
Baldwin, James 195–197
Bales, William 128

bankruptcy: of Adelphia **139**; of Enron 134, **140**, 145; fraud 134–149; of Global Crossing **141**; of GM 183; Lehman Brothers 146; of WorldCom **142**
Barr, William P. 12, 15
Barrett, Kimberly 25
Bastiat, Frederic 165
BAT Industries *see* British American Tobacco Company (BAT Industries)
Bear Stearns 146
Bearden v. Georgia 207
belief system *see* ideology
bias: bonus of 172, 177–180, 186; criminal justice system and 4–7, 72–73, 98, 121, 126, 165–167, 172, 177, 195, 205–206; economic 4–5, 72–73, 113–115, 118, 121–122, 134, 149, 167, 205; racial 113–115, 118–126, 178
Biden Jr, Joseph 131
Big Money Crime (Calavita et al) 135
Bill of Rights 201
BJS *see* Bureau of Justice Statistics (BJS)
Black Lives Matter 181
Black Panthers 181
Black, William 147
blacks: arrests and 112–115, 121–122; bail for 126–127; biking-while- 122; cancer and 97–98; capital punishment and 129–130; economic class and 33–34, 113–114, 121; employment of 34, 80, 115; health care and 96–98; incarceration and 36, 113–115; juvenile crime by 24, 34, 121–122; media and 67, 122; policing and 41, 114, 121–122, 207; poverty and 34, 36, 66, 96–98, 114–115, 121–122; racial discrimination and 34, 36, 41, 66, 112–115, 121–122, 126–130, 174, 206; sentencing and 113, 129–130; toxic waste dumps and 80–81, 97; Typical Criminal 66–68; wrongful convictions and 113, 126–129
Blodgett, Henry 138
Blumstein, Alfred 23–24, 39–40, 42
Bonger, William 176–177
Bonnie and Clyde 176
Boston Tea Party 174
bourgeoisie 180
Brady Law 38
Braithwaite, John 33–34
Brennan Center for Justice 21–22
British American Tobacco Company (BAT Industries) 94

British Journal of Criminology 20
British Petroleum (BP) 64–65
broken windows theory 23
Brookings Institution 66, 169
Brown & Williamson Tobacco Corporation
(B&W) 94
brown lung *see* byssinosis
Bumble Bee 132
Bureau of Alcohol, Tobacco and Firearms
(ATF) 37–38
Bureau of Justice Statistics (BJS) 9, 17, 35,
41, 126
Bureau of Labor Statistics (BLS) 83–85
Bureau of Prisons (BOP) 14–15
burglary 8, 22, 40, **132**
Bush, George H. W. 12
Bush, George W. 13, 20, 134
Butch Cassidy and the Sundance Kid 176
byssinosis 86

California: Department of Savings and Loans
135, **137**; drug sales in 122; homicide rates
22; inmate release 16, 22; power crisis **140**;
prisons 16, 22; sentencing in 129
campaign contributions 138
Canada: C-45 bill 76; Insite 28;
decriminalization of marijuana in 28; safe
injection centers 28
cancer: chemicals and (*see* hazardous
material/waste) 84–85, 91–92; chemical
warfare and 90–95; in children 84, 93;
environmental 91–93; from food additives
92, 95; health care and 92; occupational
exposure and 78, 84–85, 91; pesticides
93; pollution and 92, 93; racial difference
in 97–98; socioeconomic status and
97–98; survival rates 97; from tobacco or
smoking 40, 92, 94–95
capital punishment 12–13, 28, 127–130, 179
capitalism 47, 176–180; *see also* Marx, Karl
Capone, Al 176
carnival mirror: criminal justice system and 63,
65–72, 98, 111–113, 150, 166, 180, 182–183;
dangerous poor and 63–64, 71, 112,
149–150, 177, 197; media and 71–72, 180
carpal tunnel syndrome 86
Carter, James (Jimmy) 12, 123
The Case for More Incarceration (DOJ) 12
CCA *see* Corrections Corporation of America
(CCA)
Cedent 137
Centers for Disease Control and Prevention
(CDC) 19, 88, 94, 205
The Challenge of Crime in a Free Society 9, 27,
66, 81

Chambliss, William 118
Champion, Dean 129
charging 120–125, 150, 206
cheap on crime 15
chemical warfare 90–95
The Chickenshit Club 133
Chief Financial Officer (CFO) **139–141**, 145
child labor 80, 182
children: delinquency and 21–25, 43; guns and
37, 205; health and 25, 84–85, 90, 92–95;
of inmates 21; poverty and 32–35, 96, 198;
media and 182; reducing crime and 25,
42–43, 48
Christianity 180
cigarette smoking *see* Tobacco
Citicorp 147
Citigroup 136–138, 147
The City of God (Augustine) 195–197
civil penalties 28, 124
Civil Rights Act 12
class *see* socioeconomic class
Clean Air Act 65, 93
Clear, Todd 35
Clinard, Marshall 131
Clinton, Bill 14, 19; Community Oriented
Policing Services (COPS) and 22;
The Violent Crime Control and Law
Enforcement Act of 1994 and 13
Cloward, Richard A. 131
coal dust 78, 86
cocaine 18–19; crack 14, 23–24, 41–42, 129–130,
202; death from 39; disparity 129–130;
drug war 18–19, 23–24
The Color of Crime (Russell) 66
Commission for the Dissuasion of Drug
Addiction 19
Commission on Safety and Abuse in
America's Prisons 35
community: incarceration and 12, 17, 21–22,
36, 115, 128–131; policing and 12–14,
21–24, 118; prevention with 21, 23–25,
42–44, 198–199; solidarity of 24, 32–33,
44–45
Community Oriented Policing Services
(COPS) *see* Clinton, Bill
concentrated disadvantage 32–33, 128
Congress (U.S. House and Senate): chemical
food additives and 92–93; disgorgement
and 144; financial deregulation and 148;
financial frauds and 132–135, 144; gun
policy 37–38; "100-to-1" disparity and
130; mandatory minimums 13; members
of 144, 180; OSHA and 84–87; tobacco
control bills and 94; TSCA and 92;
unemployment benefits and 24

Congressional Quarterly Almanac 27
conspiracy theory 5–6, 165–166
constitution 23, 42, 201–204, 208–209
consumer deception 69
Consumer Financial Protection Bureau 132
conviction: Brady Law and 38; criminal 71,
    124–126; plea bargaining and 126, 127
CoreCivic *see* Corrections Corporation of
    America (CCA)
*Corporate Corruption: The Abuse of Corporate
    Power* (Clinard) 131
corporate crime: arrests and charging of 73,
    124, 131, 133; bonus of bias 151; cases
    of 73, 124, 133–149; chemical warfare
    and 90–95; conviction of 135; Financial
    Meltdown of 2008 134, 146–149;
    incarceration for 135, 145; law violations
    76, 119, 131–133, **137**, **139–140**, 144, 200;
    sentencing and 131–133, 144–145, 199;
    violence and 73–78, 199–200; *see also*
    socioeconomic; white collar crime
Corporate Crime and Violence (Mokhiber) 200
Corporate Manslaughter Act 76
corrections 2–4, 15–16, 28, 170–171, 203
Corrections Corporation of America
    (CCA) 170
corruption 41–42, 131, 149
Countrywide Financial 146
credit default swaps 146
Cressey, Donald 113
crime: abortion and 25; American dream
    and 33, 175; carnival mirror and 63–71,
    98–99, 150, 166; cost of 42, 93–94, 119–120,
    130, 134–135, 200–202; decline in rates 2,
    13–16, 20–26, **31**, 48, 167; definitions of
    4, 7–8, 68–69, 71, 78, 82, 98–99, 112, 119,
    150, 180, 186; drugs and 3, 14–20, 27–28,
    38–42, 115–118, 201–203; Durkheim and
    7–8, 44–46, 48–49; economic 7, 14–15, 24,
    32–35, 39–40, 124, 128, 177; FBI index 82,
    69–71, 117; fear (threat) of 1–5, 37, 46–48,
    66–74, 85–89, 98, 112, 166–168, 177–178;
    Foucault and 44–49; guns and 23–24,
    37–38, 204–205; immigration and 14, 25,
    170; incarceration (*see* incarceration);
    juveniles and 23–25, 28–35, 42–43,
    115–122, 128–129; labels and 65, 67–68,
    71, 149–150; media and 30, 67, 71–74, 116,
    171–172; of the powerful 33, 120, 167, 178;
    one-on-one model 72–74, 79, 81–82, 87,
    167; police and 2–3, 11–14, 19–21, 41–42,
    71–72, 114, 117–124, 180–181, 206–208;
    poverty and 7–8, 12, 32–35, 98, 168–171,
    177–180, 198–199, 205, 208–210; property
    (*see* property crimes); prevention of

15–25, 32, 42–43, 86, 88–94; race and
    (*see* race); rate 1–2, 11–32, 37–38, 48–49,
    113, 119–121, 124, 167–170; reality of
    4–5, 7, 63–72, 172–173; recidivism and
    3, 37, 41, 204; secondary 3, 201; social
    construction (image) of 4–5, 7–8, 64–73,
    112–113; socioeconomic class and (*see*
    socioeconomic class); sources of 7, 11–12,
    21–26, 32, 35–37, 40–42, 198, 201–206;
    statistics of 17–**18**, **30–31**, 35, 41, 66, 69–70,
    82–83, 85, 89, 113, 117–120, 126, **132**; street
    20–27, 32–33, 38, 66–71, 87, 116, 120–124,
    133, 151, 166–169, 198; Typical Crime
    65–67, 69–75, 80, 112, 177–178; Typical
    Criminal and 65–80, 112, 135, 177–178;
    victimization and 6, 116–120, 134,
    168–**169**; violent (*see* violent crime); war
    on 5, 12, 20–23, 26–27, 48, 66, 112, 165, 180;
    white-collar (*see* white collar crime); *see
    also* Uniform Crime Reports; victimization
Crime and Drugs Subcommittee of the Senate
    Judiciary Committee 131
Crime and the American Dream (Messner and
    Rosenfeld) 175
crime control/prevention *see* crime
Crime in the United States see Uniform Crime
    Reports (UCR)
criminal justice system: carnival mirror
    and 63, 65–72, 98–99, 111–113, 150, 166,
    183; class biases in 4–5, 72–73, 113–116,
    121–123, 126, 149, 177–180, 205–206; costs
    of 28, 168, 176, 209; crime definitions and
    4, 71, 82, 98–99, 150, 180, 196; crime rates
    and (*see* crime); crime reduction and 1–2,
    20–23, 207; criminal focused 8, 173–174,
    177, 179; Defenders and 63, 74–75, 79, 81;
    drugs and (*see* drugs); expansion of 125,
    171; failures of 2, 4–8, 11–14, 26–27, 44–49,
    65, 70–71, 165–171, 186, 197; fines and
    court fees 122, 124, 133, 135, 207; Foucault
    on 46–49; harmful actions of 70, 169, 186;
    homicides and (*see* homicide); ideological
    function of 7, 46, 168–169, 171–175, 177,
    179–180, 183, 186; justice focused 195–199,
    209–210; media and 67, 71–74, 171–172;
    plea bargaining and 125, 145, 206; poverty
    and 8, 113–114, 179–180, 205; promoting
    justice and 198, 205–210; protecting
    society and 70–71, 81–82, 98, 165–168,
    172–173, 195–205, 209–210; punishment
    and 2–3, 23–27, 199; pyrrhic defeat theory
    and 5–7, 44–49, 65, 71, 167; race and (*see*
    race); reforms of 15, 74, 130, 196, 209;
    regulation and 124, 178; rehabilitation
    of 198–210; repressive function of the 7;

social order and 5–8, 47, 168, 174–175, 179–180, 209; white-collar crime and (*see* white collar crime)
criminal justice-industrial complex 169–171
criminal law: antitrust 116, 132; carnival mirror 63–68, 71; creation of 71–72; economic bias 115, 118, 121, 134, 149, 177; ideology 171–172, 174, 180; morality and 75–76, 81, 181, 196–197, 201; origins of (*see* historical inertia); protection 65, 81, 148
"Criminalblackman" 66
Criminology 29, 36, 67–68, 71–72, 118–120, 173, 197
Criminology (Sutherland and Cressey) 113
Criminology & Public Policy 43
Cullen, Francis 204
culpability 63–78
cumulative disadvantage and advantage 113–117, 123
Currie, Elliott 16, 29, 32, 42, 117–118

Dakota Access Pipeline 181
Dalkon Shield 79
dangerous classes 177
death penalty *see* capital punishment
deaths: chemical warfare and 90–95; firearm related 37, 205; from medical treatment 88–90; occupational 64–65, 73–88, 151, 200; from poverty 95–98; from tobacco and other drugs 19–20, 39, 94–95
Debs, Eugene V. 111
decline in crime rates *see* crime
The Declining Significance of Race (Wilson) 114
decriminalization *see* drugs
Deepwater Horizon 65
Deferred Prosecution Agreements (DPAs) 125, 133
delinquency 21–25, 47–48, 117–121, 175
Delinquency and Opportunity (Cloward and Ohlin) 175
Department of Health and Human Services (HHS) 97
Department of Justice (DOJ) 9, 12, 93, 85, 113, 124–125, 133, 144, 147, 149, 200, 207
Department of Labor (DOL) 83
depression (economic) 134, 146
deregulation 134–136, 176
deviance 30, 44–46, 119
differential treatment 113–114, 121–122; *see also* discrimination
DiIulio, John 20
Discipline and Punish (Foucault) 46–49
discretion 4, 130, 206

discrimination: criminal justice system and 81, 117, 174, 200, 206; double 130; economic 34, 114, 128–130; gender 114; legal 114–115, 129–130; racial 80, 114–115, 129–130
disgorgement 144
disorganization 21, 33, 115
Disproportionate Minority Contact (DMC) 113, 121
Diverting *Children from a Life of Crime* (Rand Corporation) 43
Division *of Labor in Society* (Durkheim) 44
Dodd-Frank Wall Street Reform and Consumer Protection Act of 2010 148
Dorm *Room Dealers* (Mohamed and Fritsvold) 122, 128
Dred Scott decision 197
drug czar 14, 20
drugs: addiction (*see* addiction); corruption and 41–42, 133; cost of 18–19, 38, 40; class and 127–128, 145; criminalization of 19–20, 38–40; Foucault and 46–48; global war on 18–20; homicide and 23–24, 27, 42, 77–78; legalization of 14, 19–20, 28, 170, 199–203, 210; pharmacological consequences of 39, 88–89; policy 11–12, 15, 17–20, 124, 131, 203; prescription 39–41, 89, 118–119; race 66, 115, 122–123; sentencing and 12, 14–15, 17, 20, 170, 207; trade 24, 39, 41, 202; treatment 19–20, 40–41, 43, 202; use and addiction of 38–41, 118–119, 122–124; war on 15–20, 24, 27–29, 95
due process 208
Durkheim, Emile 7, 26, 44–46, 48–49
Dylan, Bob 145

Ebbers, Bernard **142–143**
economic bias 7, 115, 121–122, 134, 149, 166–169, 177–186, 205–210; *see also* socioeconomic class
economics 7–8, 12, 14–15, 24, 32–33, 87, 96–97, 115, 124, 128, 134–136, 170–173
eighth amendment 204
Eisenhower, Dwight 171
Eisinger, Jesse 133
Elders, Joycelyn 19
Electrical Equipment cases 132
embezzlement 116, 132, 134
Engels, Frederick 63, 180, 215
Enron: Arthur Andersen and 137–138, **139–140**; auditing for 138, **139–140**; bankruptcy of 134, **140**, 145; enablers 134, 138, **139–140**; financial scandal of 33, 79, 134, 136–147, 151; task force 146–147
Environmental Protection Agency (EPA) 25, 65, 84, 92–93

Epstein, Samuel 84
equal protection 70, 197–198, 201, 208
Erikson, Kai 7, 26, 44–49
Europe 28–29, 91, 95, 216
European Union 27, 29, 95

Fair Sentencing Act of 2010 130
Fairness *and Effectiveness in Policing:*
    The Evidence (National Academy of
    Sciences) 13
Families Against Mandatory Minimums 207
Farrington, David 49
Fastow, Andrew **140**, 145
Federal Bureau of Investigation (FBI): crime
    rates and 16–17, 29, 39, 41, 69–71, 82,
    88–89, 98, 113, 117, 119; repressive
    function and 180–181; savings and loans
    scandals and 135; terrorism and 147;
    on white-collar crime 119–120; *see also*
    Uniform Crime Reports (UCR)
Federal Reserve 20, 134, 146, 185
Federal Savings and Loan Insurance Corp
    (FSLIC) 135
felony 35, 38, 65, 73, 127–129
Ferguson, MO 207
financial crisis of 2008 14–15, 33, 79, 124, 134,
    146–149, 151
Financial Crisis Inquiry Commission 148
financial deregulation 134–136
financial fraud *see* fraud
First Step Act 2018 15
food additives 92, 95
Food and Drug Administration (FDA) 95
Forbes 96, 185
Fortune (companies) 119, 131, 133
Fortune (magazine) 135–136, 138, 145
Foucault, Michel 26, 44–49
Frank R. Lautenberg Chemical
    Safety 92
fraud: with bankruptcy 134, 136, 139–142,
    145–146; consumer 69, 72, 148; control
    134; corporate 134, 136, **139–143**, 144–146;
    of Enron 33, 79, 134, 136–147; financial
    33, 79, 116, 119, 134–148, 200; insurance
    120, 135, 146; liable for **140**, **142**, 144; with
    Medicaid 129; securities **142–143**, 144–145,
    147; tax 69, 116, **132**, **141–142**, 145
"free consent" 80–81, 199
freedom 48, 182, 201–203, 209
free-enterprise system 175, 182, 198
Fuld, Richard Jr 146

Gabbidon, Shaun 173
gangs 24, 36, 38, 42, 73
General Motors 183

GEO Group 170
Germany 28, 29–**30**, 37, 197
"getting tough on crime" 11–15, 131
Gideon v. Wainwright 127
Glanville, Doug 114
Global Commission on Drug Policy 20
Global Crossing 136, 138–**139**, **141**
Goldman Sachs & Co. 146
Goldstein, Paul 39
Gordon, David 177
Government Accountability Office (GAO) 22,
    42, 83, 125, 135
Great Britain 76
Great Depression 134, 146
Green, William 41
Greenwood, Peter 43
Gross, Hyman 75–77
guns 23–24, 37–38, 204–205; *see also* assault
    weapons

Habitual criminal laws 119–129
Halliburton 137–138
handguns *see* Guns
harm: actions 33, 65, 68, 74–82, 199–201;
    corporate 33, 69–70, 75–76, 119–120,
    134, 138, 145, 199–200; criminal 8–9, 19,
    39–40, 63, 65, 68–82, 85, 98, 165–169,
    199–202; drugs 14, 19, 39–42, **89**, 201–202;
    economic bias 116, 134, 149, 167, 186, 205;
    by guns (*see* guns); by incarceration 124,
    204; indirect 74–75, 78–81, 87, 199; by
    medical care 81; morality 9, 74–77, 81, 201;
    occupational 69, 75–80, 84–89; one-on-one
    72–74, 81–82, 87, 167; physical 39, 68, 72,
    76–77, 84–89; preventable 68–69, 89–99;
    reduce 19, 26, 167–169, 204–205
harm-reduction *see* harm
Hart, Philip 112
Harvard Business Review 119
Harvard Law Review 121, 123, 207
Harvard Medical Practice Study 88
Harvard School of Public Health 97
Hawkins, Gordon 81, 202
Hawkins, Robert 64
hazardous material/waste 79, 84, 93
Health and Human Services, Department of
    see Department of Health and Human
    Services (HHS)
health care 35–36, 88–90, 96–97, 185
health insurance 83–85
Hemenway, David 37
heroin 18, 39–40, 202
higher education 16, 97, 185
*Hidden Tragedy: Underreporting of Workplace
    Injuries and Illnesses* 83

Hispanics: differential treatment and 41, 114–115, 122, 129; police corruption and 41, 122; poverty and 34, 96, 114–115
historical inertia 6, 71–72, 165–168, 186–187
Hitler, Adolf 197
Holder, Eric 14
Holden, Mark 22
Holsey, Robert Wayne 127–128
homelessness 182
homicide: arrests and 22–24, 69; blacks and 130; declining rates of 22–25, 27, 29; drug trade and 24, 38, 41, 77; epidemic 23; FBI Index and 29, 69, 88–89; guns and 23–24, 37–38; health care and 88–89; media and 72–74; occupational 64–65, 73–79, 83–87, 89; poverty and 8, 42, 95–96, 179; statistics on **30**, 82, 89; Typical Criminal and 65, 69, 72–74
House Committee on Education and Labor 83
House Subcommittee on Financial Institutions, Supervision, Regulation and Insurance 130
Houston Chronicle 65
HSBC 133
Human Rights Watch 36
Hunter, Beatrice 95
hypercriminalization 122
hyperincarceration *see* incarceration

ideology: about 180; criminal justice system and (*see* criminal justice system); Marxian theory of 176, 183; nature of 171–172; need for 184–186
immigration 14, 25, 170
Immigration and Customs Enforcement (ICE) 14
incapacitation 21
incarceration: binge 11–12, 15, 21–22, 24, 114, 170, 204; crime rates and 2–3, 12–13, 15–18, 21–22, 28; crime reduction and 12–13, 21–22, 25–26, 43, 45, 203; for drugs 18–20, 27–28, 40, 131, 145, 170, 203; international comparison of 28; race and 36, 41, 66, 112–115, 121–122, 124, 129–130; rates of 12, 15–**18**, 27–28, 149, 170; socioeconomic status and 113–115, 122, 128–132; unemployment and 24, 124; *see also* prison
income *see* socioeconomic class
individual responsibility 173, 174, 176–177, 179, 199
industrialization 84, 167
inequality: capitalism and 177; crime and 11–12, 35, 42; criminal justice system and 127–129, 166, 174; economic 12, 32–35,

128–129, 166, 179, 185; poverty and 32–35, 97–98, 127–129, 198–199; racial 12, 32–35; social 12, 174; *see also* bias; discrimination
insider trading **140–141**, 145
Institute of Medicine (IOM) 89–90
insurance *see* health insurance
Investing in Our Children (Rand Corporation) 43
Irving, J. Lawrence 130

Japan 29–**30**
Jim Crow 114
jobs: economic bias 129, 175; lost 3, 24, 83, **140**; reduce crime 24, 34–35, 199–200; reentry 2–4, 18, 21, 36, 203; worker risks 75–80, 83–86; *see also* occupational
Johnson, Lyndon B. 12, 26
Johnson, Robert 11, 127
Jones, Nikki 130
Journal of the American Medical Association (JAMA) 88, 94, 97
J.P. Morgan Chase 136, 138, 149
juvenile crime 23–24, 28–32, 35, 42–43, 117–122
juvenile justice 28, 35, 120–122, 128; *see also* youth control complex

Keating, Charles 138
Kellogg 77
Kerner Commission 17
King, Martin Luther Jr. 181
Kleiman, Mark 25, 43
K-Mart 136–137, 145
knives 24, 37–38, **89**
Koch brothers 22
Kozlowski, Dennis **142**

Labels *see* crime
Labor movement 181
The Lancet 92–93
larceny **142**
Latinx *see* Hispanics
The Law 165
Law & Order (TV show) 72–73
"Law and order" 12, 168, 200
law enforcement: community policing 14, 22–24, 44–45, 207–208; crime reduction and 2, 13–14; drugs 202–203, 207; efforts 13, 40, 87, 118, 170; officers 2, 13, 41–42, 207; officials 41–42, 147; *see also* police
lawmaking 12–13, 48, 67–68, 71, 138, 170, 199–200
laws: crime reduction and 21–22, 26–27, 38, 42; cynicism and 21; definitions and 4, 7–8, 38, 68, 71, 82, 112, 180, 196–197; gun

38, 204–205; habitual criminal 119, 129; immigration 170; incarceration and 12–16, 22, 27, 124, 129–130, 132, 170; life-without-possibility-of-parole 16, 28; OSHA and 76, 83, 87; poverty and 7–8, 12, 111–116, 145, 208; self-defense 174; sentencing 12–16, 22, 27, 71, 128–130, 144, 170; society and 67–68, 82, 165–166, 172–173, 175–177, 181, 199–201; three strikes 12, 16, 129, 145, 170, 199, 206–207; traffic 122; truth-in-sentencing 16; violations 41, 87, 119, 131–133, 175; wage 123; white collar crime 131–133, 149; *see also* criminal law
Lay, Ken 136, **140**, 147
lead 24–25, 96, 167
legal counsel 115, 125–127, 208–209
Lehman Brothers 146
Levitt, Arthur Jr. 147
life expectancy 96–97
Lippke, Richard 203
Lincoln Savings and Loans 138
London 181
London Metropolitan Police Act 181
London School of Economics 19
Lord, Miles 79
Lucent Technologies 137

mandatory minimum sentences 12–16, 22, 129–130, 170, 207
manslaughter 63, 76, 82
Manville, John 78
marijuana: class and 123; decriminalization 12, 14, 19–20, 39, 202–203; medical 202–203; war on 19, 39, 94; *see also* drugs
Marx, Karl 7, 176, 180–183
mass incarceration *see* incarceration
mass murders 73
MCI *see* WorldCom
means of production 181–182
media 67, 71–74, 81, 116, 122, 171–172, 182–183
Medicaid 129
medical treatment: cost of 8, 88, 97, 202; deaths from 84–85, 88–90, 97–98; negligence and 36, 89–90; occupation related 69, 84; poverty and 96–97; race and 97–98
men: crime and 66, 129; Typical Criminal and 30, 66, 72
Menninger, Karl 1
mental health: chemicals and 92–93; drugs and 39; Foucault and 47; lead and 24–25; poverty and 96; prisons and 21, 28, 35–36; white-collar crime and 116
Merrill Lynch & Company Inc 138, 146
Messner, Steven 175
methamphetamines 39

Mexico 20
MicroStrategy 137
military-industrial complex 171
Mill, John Stewart 201
Miller, Jerome 121
Milton S. Eisenhower Foundation 17
mines 78–79
The Mirage of Safety (Hunter) 95
misdemeanor 23, 35, 87, 122, 124, 131
Mokhiber, Russell 200
Mollen Commission 41
Moody's 146
moral beliefs 6, 74–75, 81, 165
Morgan Stanley **141**, 146
mortgage fraud *see* subprime mortgages
Morris, Norval 43, 81, 202
motor vehicle theft *see* auto theft
Mozilo, Angelo 146
Mukasey, Michael 147
murder *see* homicide

Nacchio, Joseph **141**
Nadelmann, Ethan 202
National Academy of Sciences 13, 19, 22–23, 25, 86, 89, 91, 96, 113, 115, 122, 129–130, 170, 204, 209
National Advisory Commission on Civil Disorders (Kerner Commission) 17
National Advisory Commission on Criminal Justice Standards and Goals 35
National Cancer Institute (NCI) 91
National Census of Fatal Occupational Injuries 84
National Center on Addiction and Substance Abuse (NCASA) 36
National Commission on the Causes and Prevention of Violence 16–17
National Crime Victimization Survey (NCVS) 31, 85
National Guard 181
National Institute of Justice (NIJ) 35, 204
Native Americans 181
negligence 68, 75–77, 90
Netherlands 27, 29–**30**
The New England Journal of Medicine 91, 97
The New Jim Crow (Alexander) 114
New York **137**, **142**, 181
New York City 23–24, 41, 122, 124, 181
New York Police Department (NYPD) 41
New York Times: occupational 64; health care 90; inequality 87; police corruption 4; white collar crime 124, 138, 147
New Zealand **30**, 37
Newsweek 182
Nicholas, Henry 123
nicotine 40, 94; *see also* smoking; tobacco

Nixon, Richard 12, 17
Nobody Knows My Name (Baldwin) 195
nonnegligent manslaughter 82
Non-Prosecution Agreements (NPAs) 125
nonviolent crime 124, 135, 170
nonviolent offenders 14–15, 17
Norton, Michael 185

Obama, Barack 14, 20, 124, 133
occupational: disease 69, 76–79, 83–**89**, 91;
    fatalities 64, 78–79, 83–87; hazards 64,
    75–80, 83–86, **89**, 91
Occupational Safety and Health
    Administration (OSHA) 64, 76, 83–84,
    86–87
Occupy Wall Street 181
Office of National Drug Control Policy
    (ONDCP) 19
Office of Technology Assessment 92
Ohlin, Lloyd E. 175–176
ONDCP *see* Office of National Drug Control
    Policy (ONDCP)
one-on-one harm (interpersonal harm) 72–74,
    81–82, 87, 167
opium 18
OSHA *see* Occupational Safety and Health
    Administration (OSHA)
*Oxford Handbook of Criminological
    Theory* 32
Oxford Handbook of White Collar Crime 119
OxyContin 39, 124

panopticon 47
parole 2–4, 16, 27–28, 113, **137**, 196, 204, 207
Paulson, John 34
The Peanut Corporation of America 73, 77, 80
Peel, Robert 181
Penalties for White Collar Crimes (Congressional
    Hearing) 131
Petersilia, Joan 204
Pew Environmental Health Commission 97
Pinkertons 181
Pitt, Harvey 149
Plague of Prisons (Drucker) 12
Plato 180
Plato's *Republic* 165
plea bargaining 123, 125, 126, 127, **137, 143**,
    145, 206
police: acts of repression 14, 29, 41, 48, 118,
    180–181, 209; arrests and charging 3, 23,
    27, 71, 117, 120–124, 206; broken windows
    23; brutality 2–3, 23, 181, 207–208;
    corruption of 41–42, 200; communities
    and 12, 14, 22–24, 44–45, 118, 122, 207–208;
    crime reduction and 2, 13–14, 20–23;

criminal justice-industrial complex and
    170–171; discretion 2–4, 66–67, 71, 115,
    117, 119, 206; drug dealers and 18, 23–24,
    41–42, 122; firearms and 23–24, 37; hiring
    of 12–13, 124, 135, 208; media and 67,
    71–72, 122, 172–173, 176; politicians and
    12–13, 26–27, 71; private 27, 181, 208;
    proactive 23; race and 114, 121–123, 144;
    reactive 22; socioeconomic status and 47,
    67, 71–73, 114, 117–119, 120–123, 168–169,
    181, 199–203, 205; statistics and 22, 85,
    113, 117; *see also* law enforcement
Police Foundation 39
policy: American criminal justice 1, 4–7, 11–12,
    26–27, 43–44, 71, 167–171, 180, 186; drug
    12, 15, 17–20, 27–28, 42–43, 167, 170, 201–
    203; evidence-based 19–20, 35, 42; federal
    crime 19–20; financial deregulation
    134–136; firearm 37–38; incarceration
    and 11–12, 15, 17, 27, 35, 170, 204; life
    without the possibility of parole 16, 28;
    military-industrial complex 171; president
    administrations and 12, 15, 17, 20, 91, 171,
    180; social 27, 32; sources of crime 11–12,
    32; "tough on crime" 11–15, 20, 27–28, 87,
    131, 170; zero-tolerance 14, 23
politicians 12–15, 25–26, 71, 74, 166, 170,
    177–178
Pontell, Henry 129
Portugal 19–20, 28, **30**
poverty: adjudication and 125; arrests and 8,
    115, 205; bias against the poor 98, 114–115,
    172, 177–180, 186, 205; children and
    32–35, 96, 198; character 169, 179; crime
    and 7–8, 12, 32–35, 98, 168–171, 177–180,
    198–199, 205, 208–210; death from 95–98;
    fear of crime and the poor 168, 177–178;
    Foucault and 48; health 96–98; inequality
    and 32–35, 174, 179, 185, 198; media and
    73; prison and 47, 66, 111–112, 114–117,
    121–123, 130, 133, 150–151, 207–209;
    probation and 121–123, 149, 207; race and
    34, 97–98, 114–115, 129–130; sentencing
    and 111–113, 117, 128–131, 205–206; toxic
    wastes and 96; Typical Criminal 66, 73–74,
    112, 116; unemployment and 32–34, 178;
    victimization of 168–169; war on 12; white
    collar crime and 8, 33, 210
power 4–7, 44–48, 120, 181–183, 186, 195, 201
Powers Committee (Enron) **140**
President's Cancer Panel 90–91
President's Commission on Law Enforcement
    & Administration of Justice 26, 66, 81, 112
President's Crime Commission 37, 117
price-fixing 132

prison construction 21, 170–171
prison guards 170, 196
prison-industrial complex 170–171
prisons: costs of 2, 16, 22, 170, 209; crime
  rates and 12–13, 15–18, 21–22, 28; crime
  reduction and 12–13, 21–22, 25–26, 43,
  45, 203; drug offenses and 14, 18–20,
  27–28, 40, 131, 145, 170, 203; education
  and 16, 115, 199; expansion of 12–13, 16,
  170–171; Foucault on 46–49; gangs and
  36; incarceration rates and 12, 15–18,
  27–28, 149, 170; increasing population
  in 2, 14–17, 22, 25–26, 28, 149, 170;
  international comparisons and 27–28;
  job training in 4, 36; media and 67, 171;
  overcrowding in 36; poverty and 4–5,
  35, 47, 66, 98, 111–113, 115–117, 166–168,
  171, 208; privatization of 13, 169–170;
  public opinion and 27, 67; race and 36,
  66, 112–115, 122, 129–130, 150–151, 178;
  rape in 36; recidivism and 3, 37, 46,
  204; rehabilitation programs and 15, 43,
  203–204; socioeconomic status and 67,
  112–118, 122–123, 129, 132–133, 149–151,
  170–171, 209; source of crime 2, 11, 21,
  32, 35–37; "tough on crime" and 12–15,
  145, 170–171; unemployment and 36, 115,
  129; white-collar crime and 67, 116, 123,
  125–128, 134–135, 144–145, 149, 200; *see
  also* incarceration
private prisons *see* prisons
Private Securities Litigation Reform Act 138
probation 27–28, 66, 113, 121–123, 129, 149, 207
prohibition 19, 38–42, 201
property crimes: juveniles and 31; narcotic
  addiction and 40–41, 202; rates 22,
  31; statistics on 31, 72, 119, 126, 169;
  victimization of 169; white-collar crime
  and 116, 119, 135
prosecutors: charges by 87, 124, 126–127, 206;
  discretion and 3, 71, 79, 123, 130, 205–206;
  narcotics and 14; racial discrimination
  123, 129–130; sentencing and 130; white
  collar crime 124, 133, 144, 200
prostitution 3, 27, 41, 200–201
public safety 15, 21–22, 69, 207–208
Punishment for Sale (Leighton and Selman) 170
Pyrrhic Defeat Theory: criminal justice system
  and 5, 46, 65, 71, 167, 186; defined 5–7, 11,
  167; Durkheim, Erickson, and 26, 44–46,
  48; hypotheses 71; Marxian theory and 7;
  television crime and 71–73

Quinney, Richard 7
Qwest 136, 138–**139**, **141**

race/ethnicity: arrests and 66, 113, 115,
  121–122; criminal justice system and 12,
  112–113, 115; employment and 34–36, 80;
  health and 96–98; industrial society and
  176; police and 114, 121–122; sentencing
  and 113, 126, 129–130, 206; socioeconomic
  status and 33–36, 96–98, 113–116, 121–123,
  130, 185; toxic wastes and 80, 96; victim-
  offender relationship 113, 130; *see also*
  blacks; Hispanics; whites
Rakoff, Jed 147–148
Rand Corporation 43
rape 3–4, 22, 36, 68–69, 85
Rawls, John 195–197
Reagan, Ronald 15
Reason 14
"reasonable person" 174–177
recidivism 3, 35, 37, 41, 46, 204
reentry 3, 25, 35–36, 203–204
rehabilitation 15, 21, 35, 43, 198, 203–204
Reiman, Jeffrey 2, 99
repeat offenders 23, 148, 200
repetitive motion injuries 86
*Report of the President's Commission on Law
  Enforcement and Administration of Justice* 9,
  66, 81, 112
restorative justice 203
Reyes, Jessica 25
right to vote 3, 36, 124
Rios, Victor 122
risk assessment 15, 92, 126
Rite Aid 137
Ritholtz, Barry 146, 148
The Road to Whatever (Currie) 117
Robin Hood 174
robbery: complex social practices and 4;
  international comparisons of 37; narcotics
  and 40; sentencing bias 115–116, 131;
  socioeconomic status and 115–116, **132**
"robosigners" 148
Rosenfeld, Richard 24, 175
ruling elite (ruling class) 166, 181, 184
Russell, Kathryn 66
Russia 29

Safe Streets Act 27
safety hazards 64, 74–76, 78–80, 83, 91–93
The Saints and the Roughnecks (Chambliss) 118
Sampson, Robert 121
Sarbanes-Oxley Act (2002) 138, 144, 148, 200
Saving Children from a Life of Crime (Farrington
  and Welsh) 43
Savings and Loan scandals (S&L): about 33,
  134–136; cases of 137; Lincoln Savings and
  Loan 138; prosecutions of 124, 130–131,

134–135; roster of **137**; sentencing and 130–131, 134–135; *see also* white collar crime

Schmoke, Kurt 202

schools for crime 21

Schwarzenegger, Arnold 16

Science magazine 97–98

Science and Secrets of Ending Violent Crime (Waller) 43

The Science of Marijuana (Iverson) 39

Scoundrel Capitalism 138–**143**

second amendment 205

secondary crime *see* crime

"secondhand" smoke 94–95

Securities and Exchange Commission (SEC) 123, 137–**141**, 146–149, 170

segregation 35, 80

Selman, Donna 170

Senate Subcommittee on Investigations 133

sentencing: of blacks 36, 113, 115, 129–130; crime rates and 12–13, 16, 20–21, 71, 207; discretion and 4, 130, 205–206; discrimination in 113, 115, 117, 128–130, 206; disparity in 14, 129–130; guidelines for 129–130, **140**, 144, 199–200, 206–207; of Hispanics 115, 129–130; by judges 3, 71, 113, 129–130, 205–206; mandatory minimums and 12, 13–14, 16, 22, 129–130, 170, 207; private prisons and 13, 170; reform 14–16, 22, 42, 130, 206; socioeconomic class and 112–113, 123, 128–130, **132**, 145, 150–151, 205; for white-collar crime 124, 128, 131, 135, 145

Sentencing Project 36

Sessions, Jefferson 15, 208

Sherman Antitrust Act 132

Skilling, Jeffrey **140**, 145, 147

Smart on Crime program 14

smoking 39–40, 92, 94–95; *see also* tobacco

Snider, Laureen 120

social class *see* socioeconomic class

Social Cost of Drug Abuse 42

social order 5, 7–8, 46–47, 168, 174, 176–177, 179–180, 182–184, 186, 196, 209

social responsibility 173

socioeconomic class: bias and 4–5, 73, 113–116, 118, 121–122, 126, 149, 177, 205–206; capitalism and 47, 176–177; crime and 4–5, 7, 33–34, 46–49, 72–73, 111–112, 116–118, 130–132, 149–151, 176–178, 199, 205; criminal justice system and 4, 7, 87–88, 111–112, 120–126, 128, 130–132, 149–151, 178, 205–206; delinquency and 47–48, 117–121; Foucault and 46–49; health and 96–98; income mobility and

33–34, 96; industrialized society and 176, 181–182; legal advantages and 115, 120, 125–126, 128, 205–206; "law and order" and 168, 200; police and 46–47, 114–115, 118–122, 180–181, 206; policies and 4–5, 7, 44, 114–115, 168, 178, 180; prisons and 5, 46–47, 111–112, 115–117, 126, 129, **132**, 149–150; race and 96–98, 113–115, 121, 126, 130, 185, 206; sentencing and 112–113, 128–131, 199, 206; Typical Criminal and 72–73, 177; *see also* poor; poverty; white collar crime

soft on crime excuse 27

Solis, Hilda 86

Sourcebook of Criminal Justice Statistics 9, 113

South Africa 197

Soviet Union 197

Spohn, Cassia 113, 129

St. Augustine 195–197

Stalin, Joseph 197

Standard & Poor's 146

Stanford Law Review 127

Standing Rock 181

Stephens, James Fitzjames 81

Stiglitz, Joseph 33, 148

stigma 2–3, 36, 121, 203

Stop, Question, and Frisk programs (stop-and-frisk) 22–23, 122

strain theory 32–33, 176

subprime mortgages 146–147

substance abuse *see* addiction; alcohol; drugs; marijuana

Sullivan, Scott **142–143**

Sunbeam **139**

Surgeon General 19, 94

surveillance 47–49, 181

Sutherland, Edwin 113, 116, 119–120

Swartz, Mark **142**

Sweden 30, 37

Switzerland 20, 27, **30**

Szeliga, Robin **141**

tax cheating/fraud 69, 116, 131–**132**, **141–142**, 145

tax evasion 116, 131–**132**, **141–142**

television crime/violence 67, 72–73, 171–173, 181–182

terrorist 91, 147, 133

Texas 64–65, 123

Texas City explosion 64–65

Texas Department of Health 80

theft: auto **132**, 135; criminal law and 172–175, 202, 209; drug addicts and 41–42, 201–202; economic arrangements and 169, 172; employer/wage 69, 120, 123; grand 129;

Medicaid 129; race 127; reports of 42, 69, 120; socioeconomic status and 98, 118, 129, **132**, 169; statistics on 41, 129, **132**; *see also* larceny

A Theory of African American Offending (Unnever and Gabbidon) 173

A Theory of Justice (Rawls) 195

Thornberry, Terence 120–121

Thrasymachus 165, 180

"three-strikes" law 12, 16, 129, 145, 170

thrifts 134–135

Tillman, Robert 129

Time Magazine 128

tobacco 39–40, 42, 94–95; *see also* nicotine; smoking

Tokyo, Japan 29

Tonry, Michael 15, 25, 36

"too big to fail" 33, 149

tough on Crime 11–15, 27–28, 131, 170

Toxic Substances Control Act of 1976 (TSCA) 91

toxic waste *see* hazardous material/waste

Trading with the Enemy Act 133

traffic laws *see* law

Travis, Jeremy 204

Trump Administration 92–93

Trump, Donald 14–15, 91, 124, 132–133, 148, 208

Turner, Maurice 40

21st Century Crime Bill 13

Tyco 69, 136, **142**

Typical Crime 72–74, 80, 112, 177

Typical Criminal 66, 69–70, 72, 74–75, 77, 112, 135, 177

UCR *see* Uniform Crime Reports (UCR)

unemployment: crime decline and 24; as a crime source 32, 178; financial scandals and 136; incarceration and 124; race and 34, 114–115; rate 34; socioeconomic status and 178

Uniform Crime Reports (UCR): arrest rates **18**, **31**; criminal justice system failure and 71; definition 9; homicide and 82, **89**; Typical Criminal and 69

United Kingdom *see* Great Britain

United Nations 20, 29

United States: child poverty in 34, 96; crime in 11, 15–16, 19, 25, 27–29, 32, 44, 121, 197; drugs in 18–20, 27–28, 38, 40–42; financial meltdown in 33, 146–149; guns and 37; health in 91, 94–97; homicide and 27, 29; incarceration and 11–12, 15–16, 21, 28, 35, 149–150, 170; occupational disease and fatalities in 84, 91–93; sentencing in 12–16,

28, 65, 130, 144, 206; violence in 29; wealth distribution in 33–34, 96; white-collar crime in 65, 119, 123, 134, 144–145, 147

unnecessary surgery 69, 88

Unnever, James 173

urbanization 29–30, 48

U.S. Chemical Safety and Hazard Investigation Board 64

U.S. Court of Appeals **142**

U.S. Customs Service 41

U.S. Fish and Wildlife Service 123

U.S. Homeland Security 19

U.S. Senate *see* Congress

U.S. Sentencing Commission 14, 130, 144, 206

U.S. Supreme Court 16, 127, 130, 133, **139**, 145, 197, 201, 208

value system 183

Van den Haag, Ernest 8

Vera Institute of Justice 36

Vicodin 39

victimization: from aggravated assault 85; crime decline and 31; fears of 2; guns and 37–38; income and 168–169; from nonviolent crime 135, 136; occupational hazards and 75–76, 78–79, 80, 85; oppression and 9; race and 80, 113, 130; from rape 36; socioeconomic class and 47, 113, 116, 168–169; Typical Criminal and 73, 75, 77; from violent crime 31, 38, 79, 85, 168–169; white-collar crime and 116, 119–120, 134, 136

victimless crimes 199–203

violent crime: arrests for 66–67; drugs and 24, 39, 41–42; fear of 12–13, 30; guns and 23–24, 38, 204–205; incarceration for 17–18, 21–22; media and 67, 72, 172; metropolitan areas and 16–18, 29–30; policy and 14–16, 38, 43, 169; race and 66; rates of 13, 16–17, 22, 27, **30**–32; "reasonable person" and 174; sources of 25, 32–33; *see also* assault; guns; homicide

Violent Crime Control and Law Enforcement Act of 1994 13

vocational training 43

Wackenhut Corrections *see* GEO Group

Wage and Hour Division 123

wage theft *see* theft

Wales 27

Wall Street 123, 134, 146, 171

Wall Street Journal 138

Waller, Irvin 43

war against crime 5, 26, 165, 180

war on Drugs/drug war 14, 17, 18–20, 24, 28, 38, 41, 95, 122
Washington, DC 9, 40, 202
Washington Post 16, 73, 97
Waste Management 137–**139**
Wayward Puritans (Erikson) 44
wealth: crime and 33–34, 47–48, 125, 134, 136, 178; criminal justice system 5–6, 115–117, 125, 126, 128, 150–151, 168, 178, 205; disparities 4–5, 46, 98, 115, 184–186; distribution of 33–34, 168, 184–186, 209–210; police discretion and 118, 120–121; race and 97–98, 114–115; social 74; success and 145, 166, 175; *see also* socioeconomic
"weeding out the wealthy" 114–116, 150
welfare 16, 179
Welsh, Brandon 43
Weltanschauung 183
whistleblower **140**, **142**, 144, 200
White Collar 116
white collar crime: arrests for 8, 124–125, 131; bonus of bias 177; costs of 119, 130–132, 134–135, 144–145; incarceration and 145, 128, 131–132; legal advantages for 123–125, 128, 133; media and 67; offenders and 125, 134–135; penalties for 124, 131, 133–134, 144–145, 200; prosecutions for 124–125, 134–135, 144; public opinion of 135; sentencing for 131–132, 135, 144–145; source of crime and 8, 33; *see also* Savings and Loan scandals

White House 1
White House Office of Faith-Based and Community Initiatives 20
whites: arrests of 113, 115, 121–122; bail and 126; drugs and 115, 118, 122; health and 97–98; homicides of 130; incarceration of 113–115, 129–130; juvenile justice and 121–122; in poverty 96–97; sentencing for 113, 129–130; socioeconomic status and 33, 113–115; traffic laws and 122; unemployment and 34, 114–115
Wilson, James Q. 39
Wilson, Jerry 202
Wilson, William Julius 114
Winnick, Gary **141**
women 25, 79–80, 97–98, 204
workplace injury 83–84
workplace safety *see* jobs; occupational
World Bank 27
World Health Organization (WHO) 92
WorldCom 136, 138–**139**, **142–143**
Worldview *see* Weltanschauung

Xerox 136

Yale Law School 65
youth control complex 122
youth population 31–32

Zatz, Marjorie 113, 115